Céline

Céline: Man of Hate

by
BETTINA L. KNAPP

with a preface by
Senator Jacob K. Javits

THE UNIVERSITY OF ALABAMA PRESS
University, Alabama

The University of Alabama Press
Standard Book Number: 0-8173-7606-2
Library of Congress Catalog Card Number: 73-13432

Manufactured in the United States of America

CONTENTS

ACKNOWLEDGMENTS

My deepest thanks go to Hunter College and the City University of New York, for the Faculty Research Grant awarded me for this project; to Mr. Vernon Brooks and Professor Alba Amoia for their editorial help; to Professors Salo W. Baron, Sidney B. Hoenig, and Jeanine-Parisier Plottel, for their kind suggestions; and to Mr. and Mrs. John Trubin and my husband Russell S. Knapp for their encouragement.

PREFACE

HATE IS A DESTRUCTIVE FORCE—A FACT OF LIVING THAT WE must confront and overcome. Whether activated in politics, on college campuses, or in personal relations, it aborts the best in each of us and erodes the motivation to build harmony within our nation. Yet the current popularity of authors who pander to the most unhealthy aspects of aggressiveness, alienation, and hostility, who use their works to spread these contagions, tends to certify to their readers, so many of whom are young, that hostility is acceptable behavior. This is all the more true the more admirable an author's work is thought to be from a purely literary standpoint.

I am *not* suggesting, certainly, that the works of authors who suborn hatred should be subject to censorship or control of any kind, even when, in a particular case, the work is of little or no literary merit! I do feel, however, that there is a need for a counterliterature exposing the negativism of such works for what it is, without denying their authors their just due as literary artists. This is the task to which Bettina Knapp has here devoted her talent and erudition.

In her study of Louis-Ferdinand Céline, Professor Knapp shows how this very significant twentieth-century author of *Journey to the End of the Night, Death on the Installment Plan,* and other creative works, and a doctor of medicine as well, was agitated to the very foundations of his being—was in a very real sense crippled—by hatred. In the hate-filled, artistically questionable polemical tracts that he published just before World War II and during the German Occupation of France, the Black, the Jew, the Oriental, the Communist—to mention but a few of his targets—were all singled out for invective.

As Professor Knapp points out, hatred, whether covert or overt, must be examined lucidly and objectively, if the destructive forces that it encourages are to be transmuted into positive and viable elements in human relations. Hatred is found to be both an individual and a collective problem. Only by discovering its motivations and analyzing the climate that encourages it can hatred as an evil be disarmed. This Professor Knapp has understood in her fine work.

To study hatred from a philosophical, literary, and psychological point of view, as Professor Knapp has done in this volume, offers a positive approach to the whole subject. It gives the reader a method, a frame of reference, a basis from which to study man's hostility as a personal problem and as a collective one. To face the disease of hatred through self-probing, to transform its negative aspects into a positive force, must benefit not only the individual but the nation.

JACOB K. JAVITS
United States Senate

Céline

INTRODUCTION

WHAT IS HATE? WHAT FOSTERS IT? WHAT DOES IT MEAN FOR society, for the individual? What kinds of people are prone to it? What is their "way" in life, their outlook, their desires, their dreams, their personality, their means of giving artistic expression to their virulent emotions?

So dynamic a force has hate-power become today that it has virtually flooded all the artistic media: fiction, theater, poetry, film, music . . . The horrors and cruelties depicted, projected, or sounded forth are, irrespective of the artistic merits of the works in question, manifestations of sickness corroding man's soul.

The work of painters, composers, writers, must be taken seriously even when the products of such endeavors may not always be considered enjoyable or aesthetically appealing. The creative individual enjoys a very special talent. He is a kind of forerunner of what is to be: a prototype of many people, a prophet, a "retort in which [the] poisons and antidotes of the collective are distilled."[1] How many times has it been said of a painter—a Cézanne or a Van Gogh, for example—that "he saw into the future . . . he lived before his time . . . etc." Such statements are not lacking in meaning.

All the great movements, whether artistic, religious, or philosophical, have had their founding prophets.[2] The creative genius is able to perform his miracles because he senses the unknown and transmutes the impalpable into the palpable, the evanescent into the eternal. The artist responds more powerfully to the deepest layers within himself—to that transpersonal realm known, since Jung, as the collective unconscious. The contents and sensations that spring forth from this region of infinite riches, from the unconscious to the conscious, in the form of archetypal motifs, are the substance, the *prima materia*, with which the artist molds and shapes his forms, colors, and tones, and which the public will experience in poems, novels, paintings, musical compositions. Nations, peoples, societies are "conditioned by the power of inner psychic realities which often enough appear in the first place as fantasies in the mind of an individual."[3]

Great creative endeavors must be looked upon, therefore, not merely as personal expressions but as revelations, not simply as individual offerings extracted for their authors' depths but as an indication of what lies hidden "behind the scenes" for the collective and of what is likely to come to pass in the world of "reality." For this reason the artist's audience must be doubly aware of his message and function and conscious at all times of what he is producing.

It is at our peril that we dismiss the artist as the Trojans did their prophetess Cassandra! Troy was destroyed!

I

In this volume we will be concerned with hate as a destructive and constructive force in the fictional and polemical works of Louis-Ferdinand Céline, one of the great literary artists of this century.

Philosophically, it must be said at the outset, hate is not a totally negative force. On the contrary, hate implies opposition, or duality, between two forces in nature, opposition that gives rise to activity in much the same way that friction generates a form of energy. Without opposition there can be no activity. Motion, looked upon as perpetual combat or destruction, is a process implicit in the cosmic flow, in life. From antagonism between opposing entities, there arises, on the other hand, an equally strong drive for unity, or synthesis. Unity predominates in the phase of pre-existence known as the void, before creation and differentiation have come into being. Such oneness is incompatible with life as we live it nowadays, with all its differentiation and activity. Hate, therefore, is an important force in life. Used positively, conflicting forces make for fruitfulness and growth. Their negative manifestations, however, can tear a person asunder, can stifle, overwhelm, and blind him, can bring destruction and death.

Hatred in its various manifestations is abundantly present in Céline's philosophical outlook and in his images, symbols, archetypal motifs, characters, and style. These are the aspects of Céline's literary works that I propose to explicate and evaluate in terms of the author and his time, in terms of our own time.

Each of Céline's fictive and nonfictive works will be considered individually in chronological sequence. Each chapter will contain a plot summary of the particular volume under discussion and an analysis of the themes involved, whatever these may be, but always in relation to the main topic, that of hatred as a fact of life—everyone's life.

Céline, perhaps more than any other writer in the twentieth century, expresses hatred for man as an individual and for society as a whole. His heroes (or anti-heroes) are, for the most part, Janus-faced, peering outward in the external world of reality, and inward to the equally immense and fascinating subliminal realm. They see no answer to man's problems, no redemption, in either realm.

In Céline's first novel, *Journey to the End of the Night,* the protagonist's feelings of anger and hatred are mitigated by a still powerful need for love, for relatedness, for the fluidity of communication with his fellow man. In his second novel, *Death on the Installment Plan,* images of tenderness and the warmth of friendship are almost entirely lacking. His anti-hero was rejected as a child by both family and society, causing a withering of burgeoning forces within his personality. He was stunted, stifled, muzzled. Psychologically, he could be described as maimed, as lame—Hephaestus-like. A medley of forces came into play: hate, violence, fear, anger, each grating on the other, creating rhythmic patterns, affecting the anti-hero's rational outlook, actions, gestures, speech. A progressive disintegration of personality and stylistic coherence occurs in each succeeding novel: *Guignol's Band, Fairy-play for Another Time, From Castle to Castle, North, Rigodon.*

Symbols and archetypal imagery, already present in the first two novels, appear and reappear with increasing virulence and antagonistic force in succeeding ones. Huge verbal frescoes loom forth, horrendous-looking giants trample about, paraplegics, paralytics, gnomes, bloodied remnants hover over the narrations: scenes of dismemberment, insanity, murder, disease parade before the readers' eyes in all of their sublime and hideous grandeur. The figures and images that Céline created issue forth from both the realm of the spirit and the unvitiated material world, daemonic forces ravaging and insinuating their way, transcendental and timeless, in Céline's unconscious world—uncontrolled in their fury, spasmodic in their cruelties, unrestrained in their ability to create fantasies.

Céline's hideous, scurrilous, chthonic hallucinations have been compared to the nightmarish configurations with which Ensor, Breughel, Hogarth, Dürer, Goya, and Cranach splattered their canvases. These artists, and Céline likewise, expressed what was running rampant within them, invading every phase of their existence. They all glimpsed a primal world in which death, decay, and rot are the supreme actors and activators; they all churned, dredged up the sludge from within their cesspool souls.

Images and symbols are not alone in expressing the depth of the protagonist's hatred in Céline's works: style also enters the picture. The extreme dynamism, the extraordinary virility of Céline's word power; the fullness of his labile prose, the inventiveness of his sentence structures; the large place accorded to the irrational; the ambiguous and complex cacaphonies, the strident, jarring, even deafening sounds, the tremulous notes, the juxtaposition of rhythms, all served not merely to expel Céline's personal rage but also to disorient the reader, to provoke him, to unnerve and antagonize him. In this manner Céline carries his hatred to the reader and urges him to retaliate.

It is in Céline's three polemical and supposedly rational works that one finds perhaps the most insane forces at work. In these volumes, *Bagatelles for a Massacre* (1937), *School for Cadavers* (1939), and *Some State of Affairs* (1941), Céline's hatred reaches its zenith and flows forth with such violence that it submerges all logical arguments and obliterates all clarity. Lies, exaggerations, plagiarisms, and deceits are replete in the outbursts that make up these three works. The man who wrote them was a man possessed. They were published just before and during World War II, at a time when mass killings were *de rigueur,* when torture and murder in Nazi concentration camps were stylish, the radical chic of the day. They acted as catalyzing agents, stirring and prodding man's lust for blood. They provided the irrational, frenzied, and raging people at this juncture in man's history with "rational" justifications for torture and murder and hatred. Yet these works could not have won the admiration of so many had minds not already been trampled upon by the beast within, had not the collective already been salivating with wild fury for what Céline had to offer. Céline's readers were gourmands gorging themselves on blood! Blood had become their new myth. The multitudes had become their own shadows—had yielded to their negative selves. Instinctuality had erupted with torrential force.

Yet catastrophes, in certain instances, may pave the way for self-knowledge and in so doing transform what is destructive into something constructive. As we read in Goethe's *Faust*,

> Part of that power which would
> Ever work evil, but engenders good.[4]

Can hate indeed be transformed from a negative to a positive force? If it can be, a mere analysis of it, a mere exposition of its manifestations in Céline's works, will not suffice. One needs to go beyond this initial stage and use hate in a practical way to help solve the problems that plague the individual and, by extension, the collective.

To this end, let the reader of this work enter into complicity with its author, acknowledging Céline as a great literary artist and innovator, but also as a tortured man who encouraged extreme hatred, viciousness, and rage through his writings. Our purpose will be defeated, however, if we look upon Céline as the essence of all that is pernicious and vicious in the world and imagine ourselves as being without sin or shame. Céline is an extreme case, but his hatred and rage differs from yours and mine largely in degree. He is a distorting mirror in which, if we observe ourselves honestly, we may see something of our own shadow—something of our own negative, unacceptable, and unadaptive traits.

Céline was never able to "encounter" his own shadow—to accept the figures peopling the *mysterium magnum* that was his unconscious world. His problems, society's problems, were always the fault of that "other" person or group. But to reject one's own errors and to see them only in others is to be oblivious to, or to repress, what one considers the less "admirable" characteristics of one's own subliminal realm, to stifle, to imprison these characteristics within one's depths. Nature, however, has a way of playing tricks on her offspring. Frequently, and especially during moments of crisis, the repressed or imprisoned forces within the self-styled "perfect" individual erupt with tidal force, crushing every rational, coherent, logical attitude he might have had. Céline's novels and polemics were, in part, the results of such onslaughts; his fantasizing was a release for his rage and a manifestation of an organism shaken into a state of frenzy.

But let us be wary. In following Céline's meanderings, let us come to recognize our own hates and animosities and allow them to come into the cleansing light of consciousness. Let us peer into our own murky depths, those dismal regions where repressed feelings take on the stench of decay. Once we see ourselves *plain*, once we accept and assimilate our own failings, the things in our make-up that we have always tried to bury or ignore, the negative or "shadow" side, may not only be rendered harmless but may even be transformed into a positive attribute within the framework of our life and society's life.

To become aware of our own negative characteristics and to accept and assimilate them can be an excruciatingly painful experience. How much personal distress can be involved is well illustrated by a case (admittedly extreme) reported by Anneliese Aumüller, who practised psychiatry in Hitler's Germany. The patient was a fighter pilot in his early twenties whose life had been devoid of any kind of inner conflict. Hitler had always been his god, and anything that helped him was good, anything that hindered him, evil. The pilot sought psychiatric treatment because something very peculiar was happening to him: he could no longer distinguish black from white. There was nothing wrong with him physically, but in both his dream world and the workaday world everything that had been white had become black and vice versa—causing him serious difficulties in his work as a pilot. During the first six weeks of analysis he could report only part of a single dream, one in which he saw his brother, a member of the SS, wearing a white uniform and having a black face. His sister figured in a later dream. She, it seems, had joined forces with an anti-Hitler underground movement, and the pilot and his family had severed all relations with her. In his dream, however, he saw her wearing a black prison dress and having a brilliantly white face. He realized at this point that, in his dreams, what he had considered good appeared black and what he looked upon as evil had been transformed into white. Everything seemed to be the opposite of what it was in real life. Aumüller asked him whether a prison outfit was bad and an SS uniform good. "Oh, the outside appearance does not matter," he replied. "It's the face that's important." After making this statement the patient began to show signs of progress, for he was now capable of differentiating between externals (the *persona,* or mask) and the face that expressed the inner man. Soon other dreams emerged, all of them disruptive to his simplistic Hitler-is-God philosophy. In one of them he saw "a long column of concentration camp inmates with radiantly white faces march past Hitler. Hitler's face was black and the hand he raised was a deep red color, that of blood." The patient now decided to visit the concentration camp in question. After doing so, he wrote Aumüller: "I believed [for] too long that black was white. Now the many colors of the world won't help me any more" [5]—and committed suicide. The scope and meaning of this man's acts, hitherto unconscious, had emerged into consciousness. He could not face the role he had played in furthering and perpetrating mass destruction and killing. Unable to accept himself whole, he destroyed himself.

This case, this all-too-human situation, illustrates the difficulties that can develop when one confronts one's own shadow. One who seeks to bring what was unconscious to the light of consciousness does well to proceed with caution. Yet if the feat can be accomplished, the rewards can be manifold, for only the individual who is fully conscious of himself can hope to cope positively with the vast, unlimited world of the unconscious. The person's motivations, his acts and their effects, will take on the gleam of beauty—that of glass-blown crystal—the repository of the sun's blaze and the moon's more muted rays.

Hate is a contagious disease. The cure for it, or its possible transmutation into something positive, can only come from within each of us. We can no longer look upward, we can no longer believe in the myth of the Paraclete, as formerly conceived; we must look inside ourselves and there discover the seeds for our self-transformation.

II

Louis-Ferdinand-Auguste Destouches was born on May 27, 1894, at Courbevoie (Seine), not far from Paris. His paternal grandfather was a teacher of literature at the *lycée* at Le Havre. His father, Ferdinand-Auguste Destouches, who had earned the *licence ès lettres* degree, worked for an insurance company, Le Phénix, and retired as vice-president of the firm.

It was from his mother, Marguerite-Louise-Céline Guilloux, that Louis-Ferdinand would adopt the name under which he became famous as a writer. Madame Destouches was a businesswoman specializing in expensive antique lace. She was not only cautious but discerning in her business activities, and she earned quite a bit of money. She even bought diamonds, which her granddaughter still wears to this day.

Shortly after their marriage, Ferdinand and Marguerite moved to Courbevoie, where Madame Destouches continued her business activities. It was here that her son Louis-Ferdinand was born. The Destouches bought a small villa on the Seine at Ablon. There, Monsieur Destouches used to go fishing and sailing, indulging in the two sports he loved so much.

When finally the couple retired, Madame Destouches gave up her store on Passage Choiseul and moved into an apartment on the Rue Marsellier. At this period she became a sales representative for a "fine lace" company whose customers included such stores as the Grande Maison de Blanc and the Cour Batave. It was in this capacity that she visited many stores, carrying under her arm a large box of samples of Alençon and Bruges lace.

According to all reports, including those of Céline himself, Louis-Ferdinand was a "devilish" child, undisciplined and always desirous of unlimited freedom. His parents first sent him to a neighborhood school in Paris on Louvois Square, then to another on Rue Argenteuil. Céline was a good student and his parents decided to send him to Germany so that he might become fluent in the language of that country. In 1908, at the age of fourteen, he left for Diepholz in Lower Saxony. The following year he was sent to University College in Rochester (England). Both times, amorous escapades led to his being returned to his parents.

Back in Paris again, Céline worked at several jobs, including one as a ribbon salesman and another as aide to a diamond merchant, from both of which he was fired, and continued studying for his baccalaureate examination. He passed the first part on September 28, 1912. Then, still undisciplined and willful, he enlisted, perhaps on the spur of the moment, in the army for three years. He was attached to the 12th Cavalry Division, stationed at Rambouillet, and was wounded in one of the earliest battles of World War I, on October 25 at Poelkapelle in Flanders. On October 29, he was awarded a citation of the day from his regiment (No. 114), and on November 24 he was awarded a military medal by Joffre.

Céline always fictionalized reality in his novels and was what one might call the mythomanic type. In *Death on the Installment Plan,* for example, he describes his childhood as having been horrendous, ignominious, spent in utter filth, poverty, degradation. His father is depicted as cruel, vulgar, coarse, a brute; his mother, as pathetic, vicious, crippled, a mender of old and ragged lace. Certainly there is nothing unethical in creating a fictional world; on the contrary, the novel can be an ideal medium in which to do so. But when the fiction is passed off as fact, when the myth is fed to interviewers, journalists, and scholars as reality, then the validity of the story related becomes questionable. Céline chose to fantasize about his war wounds as well. For years his reading public and acquaintances alike thought he had been trepanned, that he had suffered severe head wounds in World War I. So Céline wanted everyone to believe. What was the actual story? He had suffered a severe fracture of the shoulder bone, the result of a burst of shell fire. It was a serious enough wound and he had to spend several months in a military hospital because of it; he never regained the full use of his right arm. But the wound was no trepanation.

In 1915, Céline was sent to London to work in the passport division of the army. On September 2, however, he was declared to be "disabled" and given a military discharge.

At this juncture, in 1916, he decided to take a job with the Sangha-Oubangui forestry company and go to what had formerly been German Cameroon. It was here that he contracted both malaria and amoebic dysentery, diseases that would afflict him off and on for the rest of his life. After spending March and April of 1917 in the hospital, Céline returned to France for reasons of health. Seemingly always interested in medicine, he was engaged during this period, in 1918, by the Rockefeller Foundation to give a series of lectures on ways and means of diagnosing and curing tuberculosis.

Self-taught in many ways, the young Céline decided to take the second part of his baccalaureate examination at Bordeaux. He passed it on July 2, 1919, with *mention bien.* On August 11 he married Edith Follet, a daughter of the director of the medical school at Rennes, where he enrolled as a student in the spring of 1920. A child, Colette, was born to the couple on June 17, 1920.

Céline passed his medical examinations in 1923 and wrote his doctoral dissertation, *The Life and Work of Philippe Ignace Semmelweis,* shortly thereafter. He defended the thesis on May 1, 1924, and was awarded his medical degree forthwith. In 1925, he opened an office at the Place des Lices, in Rennes, and he published an article on the *Therapeutic Use of Quinine.* After just a few months, however, he grew weary of the routine with which he was faced and simply abandoned his wife, child, and home forever. He obtained a medical job with the League of Nations, working first in Geneva, then in Liverpool, and finally in Cameroon, where yellow fever and sleeping sickness were endemic. A few months later, still restless, Céline went to the United States. The year was 1926.

Our analysis of Céline's literary life begins with the year 1923 and his doctoral dissertation on the Hungarian physician Semmelweis. This work in no way resembles the rather pedantic and dull volumes that students are wont to write. Céline's dissertation lives; it breathes fire. Far from being the objective and scientific treatise of the sort usually composed to fill the requirements of a medical degree in France, his work was a subjective and highly emotional biography. The themes that emerge are those with which Céline himself will be preoccupied throughout his life: heroism, martyrdom, persecution, evil, death, and the emotions concomitant with these states: hate, fear, revenge, rage, etc. They are all to be found, strange to say, in this doctoral dissertation.

Observe one man's evolution through his works, and perhaps our own evolution, too, as we wander through the corridors of a soul.

Mephistopheles: . . . before you part from me!
You know the devil, that is plain to see.
Here, take the key.
Faust: That little thing! But why?
Mephistopheles: First grasp it; it is nothing to decry.
Faust: It glows, it shines, increases in my hand!
Mephistopheles: How great its worth, you soon shall understand.
The key will smell the right place from all others:
Follow it down. . . .[6]

Part One

ARTIST

. . . I hate all men,
Some because they are wicked and harmful,
Others for being obliging to the wicked,
And for not having that vigorous hatred
That vice ought to arouse in virtuous souls.

MOLIÈRE, *The Misanthrope*

1

THE LIFE AND WORK OF PHILIPPE IGNACE SEMMELWEIS

Show me a hero and I will write you a tragedy.
F. SCOTT FITZGERALD, *The Crack-up*

THE HUNGARIAN PHYSICIAN IGNAZ PHILIPP SEMMELWEIS (1818–1865), it will be remembered, was the man who discovered the contagious nature of puerperal fever fifty years before Louis Pasteur proved the existence of bacteria. Why, one may wonder, did Céline choose him as the subject of his dissertation. A precursor of antiseptic medicine, Semmelweis had devoted all of his days, his sanity, and his life to scientific investigation with the purpose of reducing suffering and death in the hospitals of his day. Céline must have felt some kind of affinity for this man, whose integrity, idealism, and genius placed him so far above the ordinary medical men of his period.

Because Céline's dissertation was deeply subjective and creative, a work fired with idealism, energy, torment, fear, anger, and hatred, it may be looked upon as an expression of the passions living within him at this time, as a document touching upon themes that preoccupied him at this point in his life and would become obsessions in later years: time, death, the hero figure, the martyr, hate, insanity.

I

The opening paragraphs of the dissertation are devoted to a historical picture of the period preceding Semmelweis' birth. A panoramic view is drawn of the French Revolution, of Mirabeau's thundering voice, of Versailles, of death all about: passions, enthusiasms, heroism, chaos, murder, blood—all, Céline intimates, in the name of "progress" and "reason." "Homicide was a daily occurrence among the people; regicide, however, was something new for the French."[1] To Céline, the revolutionaries were butchers, mass murderers intent upon destroying all vestiges of civilization preceding their advent. With the coming of Napoleon, more conquest was in store, more blood, more rage. But this gave way to a period of relative quiescence—a period of romanticism. Society went to the opposite extreme: people wept over the death of a turtle-dove, saccharine relationships permeated literature, tenderness and ultrasensitive and high-strung personalities seemed to people the earth. Such was the state of the world when Semmelweis was born. As Céline put it: "The soul of a man is going to flourish, with such great pity, flower with such magnificence that man's fate will be, because of it, sweetened forever." [2]

Semmelweis was born in Budapest, one of eight children. His mother, Céline informs us, was an industrious and beautiful woman who died early in life, much to the sorrow of her husband and children. Semmelweis' father, a grocer, was well-meaning and hard-working, quite able to support his family rather comfortably.

The young Semmelweis hated school. He preferred to roam the streets of his native city, dreaming and indulging in fantasies. His inner world, Céline explains, was rich and productive. He rejected restrictions, the "ordered" in life, and was attracted rather to chance, to experience in all domains. Yet destiny has a way of curtailing a man's freedom, of inflicting pain and sorrow on innocent beings. "It was probably written that he would be unhappy with men." [3]

As Céline's hero emerges in the dissertation, parallel evil forces also make their presences known: Destiny and Death. "In the History of time, life is nothing but a type of drunkenness, Truth is Death." [4]

Semmelweis went to Vienna with the intention of studying law but enrolled in medical school instead. He spent long hours observing the great doctors at work—Doctor Skoda, for example, whose diagnostic techniques were notable for their finesse. Semmelweis was particularly fascinated with the dissecting procedures, and it was at this period of his training that he first came into contact with death in a concrete form—as the cadaver with which he had to work and not merely as a figment of his fantasy, as some remote emanation.

All was not joyful in "gay" Vienna for the young Semmelweis. A sensitive lad, he was deeply hurt when his fellow medical students mocked his foreign accent and "strange" ways. Quite often, he was consumed by anger. He felt that he was being persecuted, that he was the object of xenophobia. And yet he toiled. As his medical knowledge deepened he came to have less and less faith in the abilities of the "great" doctors, the internationally "famous" surgeons. Why? Because the mortality rate in the hospitals, and in the obstetric wards in particular, was very high. An unexplored area opened up for Semmelweis in terms of medicine and research. He began to probe.

Semmelweis' professor, Skoda, with whom he had worked during his five years in medical school, understood his complex personality. Skoda recognized his rebellious spirit and, to a great extent, feared it. He realized only too well that the most brilliant students are the ones most likely to destroy or overthrow their masters. Skoda evidently was not prepared to accept the new and to suffer dethronement from his powerful position in the hospital. Rather than hire Semmelweis as an assistant upon his graduation (1844), as he had promised to do, Skoda chose another doctor, justifying his bad faith on the grounds of the other man's "seniority." Though patience was not Semmelweis' forte—his personality was made up of "fire," according to Céline [5]—he waited for another opening.

Despite this setback, Semmelweis continued his work in surgery and, later, in obstetrics with a Doctor Klin. The death rate was constantly on the increase and finally reached the point when surgery was virtually useless since the patients died anyway. No doctor had ever really tried to discover the reasons for such a high mortality rate; why some patients recovered and others did not was simply not known.

According to Céline, Doctor Klin was an utterly mediocre man but one who had great influence at court. When Semmelweis entered his service, the death rate from puerperal fever was extraordinarily high. Almost all pregnant women succumbed to it. Tragedy upon tragedy unfolded before his eyes, bruising him emotionally. A woman had a better chance of surviving if she gave birth in the street than if she did so in a hospital. Semmelweis' mind began questioning once again. Was puerperal fever contagious? How was it contracted? Spread? The answer given by the doctors—it was all a matter of "destiny"—failed to satisfy him.

Semmelweis was fired by a messianic spirit, Céline observed, quoting the Hungarian doctor as follows:

> Destiny has chosen me . . . to be the missionary of truth with respect to the measures to be taken to avoid and combat the puerperal scourge. I stopped long ago responding to the attacks forever being launched at me. The order of things will prove to my adversaries that I was entirely correct, without its being necessary for me to participate in polemics that would in no way serve to further the progress of truth.[6]

After months of private research and deductive reasoning, Semmelweis discovered that when the medical students left the dissecting rooms, where they had spent time with infected cadavers, they would go to the obstetric ward and examine pregnant women, who were more susceptible to disease at this time than under normal circumstances. As chief of a particular division in obstetrics, Semmelweis required the students under him to wash their hands with lime chloride. When this practice was enforced the death rate decreased noticeably, and Semmelweis informed Doctor Klin of the fact. The head of obstetrics refused to believe him. In fact, he was hostile toward Semmelweis from that time on: he would not even speak to him. Moreover, Doctor Klin pointedly refused to wash his own hands; the request was ridiculous, he declared, unheard of, unscientific. As for the students, they were annoyed at the extra work involved and considered the entire idea to be nonsense. When Doctor Klin refused to wash his hands, Semmelweis, forgetting the deference due so eminent a physician, lost his temper. As a result, he was summarily dismissed from Doctor Klin's service.

After a brief sojourn in Venice, Semmelweis returned to work in a Viennese hospital (thanks to Doctor Skoda's good offices), still obsessed with his discovery. He realized, however, that his contention was greeted with disbelief and mockery because proof was lacking. Once again, using the process of deduction and availing himself of scientific methods, he proved to his own satisfaction that puerperal fever was indeed being spread by medical students and doctors alike, from one individual to another, and that it was not a matter of chance or of destiny. The medical authorities still refused to believe him. They greeted him with "hatred."[7]

Semmelweis suffered deeply from their enmity. In time, he no longer had the courage to show his face in the hospital. He was not strong enough to endure the ridicule, the insults, the derision. "Never had a human conscience been so covered with shame . . . as [Semmelweis'] during the months of 1849,"[8] wrote Céline. Finally, Semmelweis was ordered by the Viennese hospital authorities to leave not only the hospital but the city of Vienna. Too many misunderstandings had arisen; too much ill will had been activated.

Upon his return to Budapest, Semmelweis found a rebellion raging: Hungary was trying to free herself from Austrian domination. He also found that he could barely earn a living practicing medicine. Becoming more and more withdrawn, remaining alone in his room for days on end, he wrote nothing and sought the company of no one. Thanks to the intervention of a friend, however, Semmelweis was finally hired by a maternity hospital in Budapest. It was during this period that he started work on his study of the *Etiology of Puerperal Fever.* Once again Semmelweis preached cleanliness in the hospitals, once again he was vilified, and once again he was unable to withstand the attacks, the unflagging hatred, leveled at him. His mind gave way. He was in the grip of irrational, incoherent forces; he was obsessed by the feeling that he was a victim of terrorizing attacks. He suffered, in modern parlance, from paranoia.[9]

Semmelweis became dangerous. Convinced that he was being pursued by enemies, he ranted and raved, he screamed, he fought. Then, one day he rushed into an anatomy class in the medical school in Budapest, grabbed a scalpel, and made an incision in a cadaver, touching some putrefied tumorous areas with his knife. Inadvertently, he cut himself slightly with the scalpel. His wound bled. Finally, he was disarmed. It was too late, however; infection was already setting in. When Doctor Skoda heard of the incident he went to Budapest and took Semmelweis back to Vienna with him. On June 22, 1865, Semmelweis was placed in a mental institution. He died there on August 16, 1865, at the age of forty-seven. Ironically, he had proved his own theory—he had been his own guinea pig.

II

Considering the extensive thrust of Céline's imagination and the passion and fervor that he brought to this dissertation, we may forgive its many inaccuracies, exaggerations, and omissions. It is more an expression of Céline, the man, than it is an analysis of Semmelweis, the doctor. It introduces us to themes that will be important in the works to come—time and death, the hero, the martyr (hate), insanity.

Time and death are of extreme importance to Céline. He even begins his dissertation with a historical picture and so indicates a concern with the fluidity of time, its fleeting and temporal nature. There is a close correlation in the dissertation between historical time (the French Revolution or any of the historical episodes narrated by Céline and considered therefore as an event having a beginning and an end) and death.

Céline was torn by a conflict between two types of time: historical time, commonly termed eschatological time, which arose with consciousness and with civilization, and primitive, or primordial, time, as measured in terms of cyclical events.

The primitive sees each day as a victory over night, as a new beginning in an eternal process, as a cycle or circle to be understood and experienced by him. There is no beginning and no end. The concept of past, present, and future is nonexistent. Living close to nature, the primitive feels himself to be at one with the cosmos and thus "within" an endless series of cycles.[10] There being no split between himself and nature, he has no consciousness of himself as an entity separate from the forces surrounding him, separate from the world of phenomena. Death, for the primitive, is part of organic phenomena, of personal changes. It is not looked upon as a separation or as an end. Fear, therefore, does not enter into the picture in the way that it does for "civilized" man.

The advent of Judaism and Christianity brought a new "eschatological" consciousness. Past, present, and future became distinct phases of existence, and the belief in a "temporal consciousness" altered man's status in relation to the cosmos and so with himself. He emerged as an entity separate from nature. With this cleavage, death loomed as a fearful experience, as a problem, as something painful, as a separation or end.

This "temporal consciousness" arose when the concept of creation *ex nihilo* was adopted by the Hebrews in the Old Testament. In Genesis, for example, it is stated that the world was created in seven days out of chaos or nothingness. The world, therefore, had a beginning and will have an end. The notion of *aeternitas,* or of the *aeion,* gave way to the belief in *sempiternitas.*[11] The more conscious man became of his identity and individuality, the more fragmented his existence seemed to him—hence such concepts as the century, the decade, the year, the day, the hour, the minute, the second. Time became linear, or eschatological. The belief in an end after death was inherent in early Judaism. With the passage of years, man increasingly severed himself from nature. But without nature's strength and support and her eternal qualities, man found himself increasingly alone. He could no longer face the idea of death as a void, as an end in itself, as a severance from life. He could not face the idea of an eternal god and a mortal man born from dust and returning to it.

> Man that is born of woman is of few days, and full of trouble. He cometh forth like a flower, and is cut down: he fleeth also as a shadow, and continueth not.

The more intolerable the belief in death as an end to life became, the greater was man's longing for another world after death. Thus was another realm imagined by the Hebrews, by Plato (the realm of essences and perfection), and by Christians (heaven, hell, limbo, resurrection).

With the advent of science and technology, with the worship of "reason," there arose yet another stumbling block. Man abandoned his old beliefs, that is, the precepts offered by organized religion. Such notions as the resurrection of Christ and the belief in transcendence, paradise, and hell were rejected by increasing numbers in the modern world. Once again man became entrapped by time. Time became synonymous with death and death again became a finale.

What remains for those who have divested themselves of religion as an aid and a buffer in facing death? Ways and means of coping with death have, to be sure, come into being throughout the centuries. The stoic is convinced that the more one thinks about death, the less one will fear it. The nihilist is determined to accept the "meaninglessness" and the "futility" of life. The atheistic existentialist becomes his own god, the molder of his own destiny, and assumes responsibility for all of his acts in terms of himself and of society.

Such attitudes are indeed "reasonable," but man is not simply a creature of reason. The irrational forces within him are powerful. Some people, therefore, experience life as prolonged anguish and confront the notion of death with trepidation. Many become alienated from their environment and, as a result of their death-trauma, experience an extreme malaise and live out their lives as virtual strangers, as mere observers of the drama that is life. Life for them seems empty, devoid of meaning—a "waiting for Godot." [12]

Modern man no longer looks for salvation in nature, in myth, in cyclical changes, or in organized religions. He has become his own leader. He feels he can improve his worldly lot through scientific development, industry, technology. He is also convinced of the notion of perfectibility, of biological development. But rejecting the "protective" or "consoling" notions offered in religion (an afterlife, or primordial time) opens up a tremendous gap. The solitary individual stands before it, gasping perhaps, as he peers into its vastness, straining anxiously so as not to lose his balance.

Such were Céline's fears in the early 1920s. Though he experienced these fears unconsciously, in that he did not point to them directly, he was tortured nevertheless by the notion of the hourglass, by the destruction of human life that he witnessed, by the disintegrating corpses he examined daily. The isolation of man, his solitude, his distress, came to be an almost unbearable reality for Céline. And yet as a scientist, he could see a glimmer of hope: there were Semmelweises in the world, there were men willing to devote their lives to conquering death, or at least delaying its approach.

Céline feared death not on an intellectual level but on an emotional one. He well knew that, ontogenetically, man was created, that he developed, and that he had to die when a certain state of differentiation or evolution had been reached. So with plants, with animals, with all living phenomena. "The germ contains the fully developed organism embedded in itself." [13] Céline knew that he would have to die, as all men must; death is ever present, *praesens de futuris expectatio*.[14] He was also well aware of Pascal's profound and wonderful statement on the subject: that man's greatness resides in the fact that, unlike other forms of life, he *knows* he is going to die. He is not unacquainted with his fate.[15]

Yet the more Céline seemed to dwell upon time and its association with death, the greater his anguish became. His experiences in the army, in medical practice, and in science made death all the more vivid and did not diminish his antagonism toward it. Emotionally, he was unable to accept death as an end. Like the Romantics, perhaps, Céline sought to bring time to a stop, or at least to slow it down. For this reason time took on the aspect of a formidable enemy, an antagonist, and death became something to be overwhelmed, conquered, and finally annihilated.

On an intellectual level, of course, Céline realized the impossibility of conquering death. As a healer, however, as a comforter—as a doctor—he could effect its delay, as his hero Semmelweis had.

But why should Céline have feared death to such an extent? Psychologically, death implies a dissolution of the ego, and to fear it obsessively would indicate a weakness in the ego. Such weakness might also explain the need for a hero figure such as, in Céline's case, Doctor Semmelweis.

"The ego," as we know, "stands between the inner world and the outer world, and its task is to adapt to both." [16] When the ego is weak, when man's ability to adapt to both his inner and outer world becomes a bit shaky, life can become a living death. Unconsciously, Céline must always have feared such an eventuality. That he was forever pursuing a life of chance, change, adventure, that he had left his home, his wife, his child, revealed a fear of in-dwelling, a desire to escape an all-encompassing doom. It also indicated a veritable fright of being sucked up by the routine, the humdrum, of existence. He feared being trapped, ensnared, imprisoned, stifled to death. He was not yet ready for either kind of demise on earth, psychological demise or the one equated with the bourgeois way of life (economic security, etc). Céline sought to become immortal, if not physically, at least spiritually, just as Semmelweis had.

Céline was further torn between two ways in life. One was that of the courageous scientist (or writer) in search of the new, the great, the eternal. The other was that of the anguished, solitary individual traumatized by the notion of death, either through strangulation in a pedestrian world or the possibility of the dissolution of his own ego.

The conflict he experienced goaded him, prodded him along in the adventure that would be his life. It also accounted, to a great extent, for his quixotic ways, his inadaptibility, his ill-temper, his complex nature—and his genius.

The second theme that comes to light in the Semmelweis dissertation, that of the hero figure, should be looked upon as a consequence of the first. In general, the creation of hero figures is an expression of dissatisfaction with one's lot and with that of humanity. Heroes, usually born during periods of adolescence or youth, are "helping" figures. They are also bearers of new cultural elements. Symbolically, they are innovators. The hero represents the ideal being, a being capable of extricating individuals from a joyless world or from pressing problems. The hero-worshiper—whether an individual or a collective—projects or identifies with the legendary, historical figure and in this way gives the undeveloped ego the strength it lacks.[17] Once the ego has been strengthened, as is frequently the case during the more mature years, the need for the hero figure diminishes or disappears.

Most heroes, whether legendary, historical, or religious, fall into certain patterns. They must pass certain tests, notably a confrontation with the forces of evil surrounding them. In fairy tales and myths these evil figures are dragons, monsters, and the like (as in the case of Heracles, Theseus); with historical figures (Roland, Bayard) they are the enemy; with religious figures (Moses, Christ), the collective. Heroes struggle with these forces in forests, battlefields, mountains, hills, or any place at all. Psychologically speaking, the struggle as such indicates the fight that the ego (hero) must wage in order to liberate itself from the stranglehold of the unconscious (the enemy in any form), from the deep, from the womb that would drown it. Sometimes the hero succumbs to the forces of the deep (Jonah, Faust, Theseus) and is imprisoned by them for a certain period, before being finally liberated.

Semmelweis, Céline's hero, was never able to adapt himself to school or to society. A wanderer of sorts (if not always physically, certainly in terms of his imagination), he let his ideas penetrate uncharted territories, reaching a kind of no-man's land. It is from this region that he brought back his message, his discovery, in terms of hygiene. The realm of darkness pierced by Semmelweis has its dangers and pitfalls, existing in the form of the void and of chaos. Like the hero of antiquity, Semmelweis cut bravely through the brambles that kept the new world in darkness; like Christopher Columbus, he risked his life to discover uncharted lands.

The hero must possess other qualities. He must be strong enough to defy conventions, which are manifestations of evil. He must be a revolutionary of sorts, at least intellectually: a man able to impose his new cultural canon upon an ungrateful and even hostile society. The hero's real test occurs at this point. It hinges on how successful he is in forcing his ways and ideas upon the world. Semmelweis had failed this test because he gained only the animosity of his contemporaries and was unable to cope with the forces that sought to destroy him; his mind gave way (his ego disintegrated).

As a revolutionary, the hero must also be ruthless, even cruelly so, if he is to succeed in imposing his message. Examples of such ruthlessness are found in many creation myths, those in which all preceding ideologies are crushed to make way for the new force that is to be imposed upon society. The Greek creation myths follow this pattern. When Uranos, for example, ruled the cosmos, he hid his children soon after their birth, fearing he would be overthrown by one of them. Symbolically speaking, he feared dethronement by some new content or force. One of Uranos' children, Kronos, the "tortuous thinker," conceived a plan to deceive his father; he cut off Uranos' manhood and thus succeeded him as ruler of the universe. Once established, Kronos in turn, fearing that his children might seek to destroy him, swallowed them up after their birth. But one of his sons, Zeus, overcame him through force and cunning and reigned supreme, etc. In all creative effort, therefore, the old must of necessity be done away with so as to make room for the new. Such activity usually entails a certain amount of unpleasantness on all sides, as conventional ideas, social stability, and the status quo are torn asunder.

The hero must introduce the new, the turbulent, the unproven—and so the dangerous. It is far easier, or at least far pleasanter, for man to live in a secure environment, rejecting change and resting on the laurels of a hard won reputation, than it is for him to opt for the new and risk losing the material and spiritual forces that he has counted upon for support during later years. The doctors Skoda and Klin were personifications of men who were unalterably opposed to innovation.

Both doctors were seen by Céline as evil-doers, traitors, jealous villains. Both of them considered Semmelweis a threat to their position and reputation, and they preferred to live in darkness and ignorance and to accept the horrendous mortality rate rather than give up a source of income and admiration at court with their colleagues. As for Doctor Klin, he was the epitome of mediocrity, Céline implied, and in a sense he was the less guilty of the two, since he could not even see the ramifications of Semmelweis' discovery.

Semmelweis was in a very precarious position. He would not accept the interdict imposed upon his creative efforts by the doctors Skoda and Klin, but he lacked the courage and fortitude to fight them and to impose his scientific discoveries on the world of his day.

At this point a paradox arises in terms of Céline's beliefs. In matters of science, he was a revolutionary, as Semmelweis had been. Céline was convinced that scientific ignorance was ignoble; he was all for progress in this area, even though it might entail conflict. In matters of politics, however, he condemned revolution and violence. He was against the decapitation of Louis XVI and the liberation of the "masses" (later to become the bourgeoisie). A monarchical form of government, static in quality, was quite acceptable to him. The paradox: he was against change in the political realm and for it in the intellectual realm. But how can one sever the political from the intellectual?

Céline had adopted an illogical viewpoint. He insisted that the status quo should continue, he advocated the old guard in government, the *aeternitas,* on the one hand—and the new, inventive, scientific spirit, the *sempiternitas,* on the other. If looked upon psychologically, such a paradoxical position implies a need for security in the social side of himself, for spiritual upheaval in the intellectual. Céline had not yet become master of his two sides. Semmelweis, therefore, was the perfect hero figure for Céline. He represented both the intellectual revolutionary par excellence and the unfortunate victim of the political turbulence raging through his land and making his life both spiritually and economically unbearable.

Semmelweis, whose messianic message was rejected by society, became its martyr, as Christ had been in his time. Both men had offered the product of genius to mankind; both had been rejected and crucified.

Semmelweis' ego, insufficiently hardened to the rigors of fortune, cracked under the strain. His paranoia indicated an inability to overcome adversity. He could not face the jeering students, the cruel arrogance of the professors, the chaos that his life had become. He retreated into his own inner world, as so many other creative spirits have done: Van Gogh, into the world of the insane, Gauguin into primitivism, Redon, Ensor, Munch into a world drenched with distress.

Semmelweis' inner world erupted into consciousness; the irrational invaded the rational; reality, as we know it, disappeared.

Céline had not yet discovered his own message, his own truth. He knew only that he was disgusted by society and would rebel against it. Rather than withdraw from life, he severed relations with the bourgeois routine and flung himself into the world. He would try to live as intensely, as actively as possible; he would try to tap those sources of existence from which creation emerges.

The question of his own possible martyrdom had not yet been resolved in Céline's mind. Semmelweis, most certainly, could be considered a martyr, an *imitatio Christi.* The Hungarian physician, an idealist, a selfless scientist, had given his all to society. But what of Céline's role in life? Was he willing to do likewise? To be a martyr or a saint implies sacrificing one's personal existence to the ideal or the idea and implies, further, being willing to suffer excruciating torments, physical and spiritual, on behalf of others and to a certain extent, of course, on one's own behalf. To be a martyr or a saint is to spread the messianic message and to be willing to renounce life—it is kind of negation of life. Was Céline the noble soul he considered Semmelweis to be? Was Céline's ideational point of view on a par with that of his hero? Was he capable of doing away with his personal existence and undergoing persecution for the sake of humanity, for the collective? Was he a selfless innovator? Did he possess Semmelweis' humility? Or did he seek gratification on all levels: fame, wealth, eternity?

III

After the completion of his doctoral dissertation on Semmelweis, Céline had most certainly reached a juncture in his life. What path would he follow: the scientific, the literary, or some third path?

One might conclude hastily that science would be all-engrossing. Céline wrote three interesting documents at this period: *Therapeutic Quinine* (1925), *Medicine at the Ford Factory* (1928) and *Social Insurances and a Political Course for Public Health* (1928).

In the first of these articles Céline discusses the medical use of quinine in the treatment of such diseases as syphilis, cancer, erysipilis, puerperal fever, influenza, typhoid, malaria, streptococcus, etc. One detects from this work a keen interest in scientific research and a desire to become a healer.

The second article, that on *Medicine at the Ford Factory*, written upon Céline's return from the United States (1928), analyzes the pros and cons of the assembly-line technique and factory work in general. In Céline's view, there were many positive things to be said about the Ford industrial complex. For one thing, it put to work unskilled labor, war victims, mutilated, infirm, blind, and sick people of all types. Moreover, working conditions in the factory were relatively healthy and hygienic. Ford was looked upon by the workers as a pater familias figure, a benevolent and kindly father. But there were also, certainly, disadvantages to the factory system. No individual worker took pride in his work or experienced any sense of achievement or fulfillment. Other French writers, including another physician, Georges Duhamel, had also noted this negative aspect of factory systems in general and the assembly-line technique in particular.[18] If a man could not experience a sense of pride in his work, life became futile, uninteresting, hardly worthy of the effort.

Céline's third article, that on social insurances, was published in *La Presse Médicale* (November 24, 1928). He took issue, as did many physicians at this period, with the law forcing businessmen to take out social insurance for their workers. He felt that such a law paved the way for socialism and would do away with individualism and personal initiative on the part of the factory owner. The individual, he maintained, was fast giving way to the collective spirit. Most people, explained Céline, were unaware of the ramifications of the changes taking place in their society. Only through medical education could the worker overcome sickness. Doctors, he continued, should go into the factories and teach good hygiene to the workers. The incidence of disease would be reduced and the factory owner would also benefit since the workers would require fewer sick leaves. Doctors, Céline declared, must eradicate centuries of superstition, prejudice, and unscientific attitudes with which workers continued to befuddle themselves.

Céline was convinced that the workers' salvation resided with the doctor. It was the doctor's function, therefore, to spread the gospel of good health, to give up his egotistical and mercenary ways for the good of the people.[19]

The idealism exhibited by Céline in these scientific articles and in his dissertation on Semmelweis would indicate a great interest in science, a feeling of dedication to the betterment of man's lot on earth. One might be led to believe that the Semmelweis type, the doctor as a healer, as medical hero, would be reborn in Céline.

When idealism is too great, however, disappointment in the workaday world can (and often does) become too painful to bear. The innovator finds himself alone; he experiences most acutely the conflict between society and the new message he seeks to bring into the world. He finds himself unable to relate to his fellow men or to the times in which he lives. As such, he becomes alienated.[20] Solitude and a sense of powerlessness overwhelm him; bitterness and a panoply of affects are engendered: rancor, anger—hate!

2

JOURNEY TO THE END OF THE NIGHT

> How does one kill fear, I wonder? How do you shoot a spectre through the heart, slash off its spectral head, take it by its spectral throat?
>
> JOSEPH CONRAD, *Lord Jim*

BY THE TIME OF HIS RETURN FROM THE UNITED STATES, IN 1828, Céline must have concluded that medicine alone was not a sufficiently engrossing *métier* for him. He sought, therefore, to combine it with the literary life, the latter medium acting as a sounding board for his ideas and as an outlet for his affective temperament. He opened an office as general practitioner at 36 Rue d'Alsace, in the working class district of Clichy. But it was during this period, too, that he began writing his monumental novel *Journey to the End of the Night.* By day he would treat his patients; at night he found release in his creative work.

It was not Céline, however, but a friend, Jeanne Carayon, who took the handwritten manuscript to the publishing house of Denoël & Steele. Armed with a bundle of more than a thousand handwritten pages, she went to see the secretary of the firm, urging him to read the manuscript and assuring him, in no uncertain terms, that *Journey to the End of the Night* would revolutionize literature.

Gallimard, one of the largest publishing houses in Paris, had already rejected the manuscript, considering the cost of publication too great to be gambled on an unknown writer. Denoël & Steele, however, accepted the volume almost immediately. Though the necessary funds were unavailable at the moment, Steele, an American-born Jew, borrowed the money from his mother. Convinced of the novel's tremendous originality and brilliance, he was willing to gamble on Céline.

Journey to the End of the Night, one of the great novels of the century, brings into full view a relatively fresh figure, the anti-hero Bardamu. Within Bardamu's complex and chaotic personality there rages a terrible sense of failure, acute anxiety, nihilism, and—paradoxically—inertia. Bardamu, a solipsistic being whose world begins and ends with himself, has never learned to communicate with others and so sinks more deeply into his solitary and miasmic realm. He is a figure who became food for the public of Céline's day and has since become a mirror image of today's society.

Tantalizing themes are also broached in *Journey to the End of the Night:* again, the notion of time and death in terms of the individual and the collective; emotions engendered by fear; hatred for humanity and, by the same token, for self; escape into an illusory state of well-being through sexuality, travel, insanity. Perhaps the most striking theme of all is Céline's assessment of the failure of Christianity both as a religion and as a way of life for twentieth-century man.

PLOT

Each section of *Journey to the End of the Night* is an entity unto itself, with a set of characters, peripeteia, tensions, catastrophes, and *rites de sortie* or conclusions.

The novel, which is essentially autobiographical, opens with Ferdinand Bardamu sitting at a café with a fellow student. A regiment in full regalia passes by. Bardamu is impressed by the intense activity of the parading soldiers; in fact, he is carried away with a sudden patriotic fervor and immediately joins the regiment. A soldier now, he fights in the Balkans, watches the bloodletting and the hideous suffering all about him. He realizes at this point that he must protect himself and that he can best do so by giving the impression of being a fine soldier. He meets an infantryman, Léon Robinson, who is more adept in the ways of the world than he.

Wounded, Bardamu finds himself convalescing in a Parisian hospital. Enter Lola, who becomes his mistress. Fearful of war and its dangers, Bardamu no longer wants to leave the hospital; at one point, he is considered insane. Another liaison, with the popular singer Musyne, whom rich tourists seek out, adds to his pleasures. One day in the hospital he receives the visit of an actress from the Comédie-Française for whom he invents a whole series of heroic adventures that he has supposedly had in the war. The actress is so impressed with his valor that she has a poet commit the heroic exploits to verses, which she recites before an enthralled audience at a gala performance at the Comédie-Française.

Bardamu, meanwhile, discharged from the army because of his wounds and his abnormal mental condition, decides to go to Africa. He embarks on the Admiral Bragueton, a ship carrying military and colonial personnel. A few days out at sea, Bardamu is convinced all on board are plotting to destroy him. He is overcome with fear. He is afraid to leave his cabin. Heretofore he has spoken his mind to all on board. Now he recalls a cardinal rule, a rule that will be instrumental in saving his life: one must give voice to patriotic slogans and one must agree with the majority. He leaves the ship as soon as it docks in the Congo and is hired by the Compagnie Pordurière, for which he will work at Fort-Gono, the capital of Bambola-Btagmanace. Bardamu does some traveling: to Topo, Bikomimbo. A description of life in this region and the meeting of an unusual person, Sergeant Alcide, follows. When Bardamu discovers that the man he had been sent to replace at Bikomimbo was none other than Robinson, his army friend, he decides to give up his job as traveling salesman. He burns the hut in which he stayed (it was riddled with termites anyhow). He contracts a form of dysentery and malaria and is burning with fever, but he finally makes his way out of the forest to San Tapeta, the capital of Rio del Rio. There he meets a priest who sells him to a galley ship captain. Hired on the ship Infanta Combitta as a "slave," Bardamu crosses the Atlantic.

Arriving in the United States, Bardamu is placed in quarantine but escapes and becomes an aide in the immigration service. He then flees to New York City where he rents a room in a shabby hotel, the Laugh Calvin, wanders about the big city, and wards off unbearable loneliness by going to the movies. He discovers Lola's address and visits her. She lends him money to take the train to Detroit, where he finds a job in the Ford factory. There he meets Molly, a prostitute. A kind, self-abnegating human being, she helps him in whatever ways she can. But Bardamu is restless and decides to return to Paris.

Back in Paris, Bardamu finishes his medical studies and finally becomes self-supporting. He opens an office at Rancy, where his clientele is made up mainly of poor people. Cases are now described, giving an inkling as to Bardamu's reactions to them and a picture of a certain society at this period. Bardamu finally abandons his practice at Rancy and wanders about. He meets Parapine at the "Tarabout" and becomes a supernumerary in a theatrical review. He then works for Pompone, a type of pimp, and has a liaison with a Polish dancer, Tania. A priest, Prostiste, lends Bardamu some money for a trip he wants to take to Toulouse. There he visits Robinson, whom he had met again when practicing at Rancy and who had been blinded accidentally. Robinson informs him that he has become engaged to Madelon. Bardamu returns to Paris and becomes friendly with Baryton, the director of a mental institution. He asks him for a job, is accepted, and ultimately replaces him as director of the institution. He takes a Slovakian mistress who also works in the hospital. Robinson, having decided not to marry Madelon, returns to Paris posthaste and, frightened of her reactions, asks Bardamu to hide him in the mental institution. Bardamu complies but Madelon discovers Robinson's whereabouts. Bardamu decides that peace must be made and suggests that the four should go out and enjoy themselves one evening. In the taxi, a misunderstanding arises between Madelon and Robinson and she shoots him three times in the stomach, opens the door of the taxi, and disappears into the night. Robinson dies and there is a funeral. Bardamu and his mistress return to the institution.

THE PICARESQUE

The picaresque technique chosen by Céline offers the perfect vehicle to express his shiftless nature and the lack of direction his life has taken. Exaggeration of disasters, a warped vision of life, a tendency to dwell on the grotesque and sordid aspects of existence, life viewed as a cruelty, are the uses to which Céline puts the picaresque.

The picaresque tradition, so well exploited by such eighteenth-century English writers as Swift, Defoe, Fielding, Smollett, and Sterne; and the French writers Diderot and Lesage, permits protagonists to indulge their bent for wandering, their desire to escape, implying all the while a certain dissatisfaction with self and the status quo. The eighteenth-century picaresque heroes are, for the most part, in search of fortune, prosperity, love, fame, happiness; they have a goal for themselves. Céline's Bardamu has no such visions. He is rather a complex, chaotic mass, ablaze with fears, hatreds, and anguishes of all sorts.

Stylistically, Céline's novel follows Laurence Sterne's dictates to a certain extent. "Digressions, incontestably, are the sunshine," averred the English writer; "they are the life, the soul of reading." An impression of spontaneity, therefore, marks *Journey to the End of the Night.* The influence of Diderot's *Jacques the Fatalist,* a lengthy and deliberately disorderly work, gave Céline a model upon which he could create a figure whose sense of abandon and wanton recklessness would come across in a startling manner. Other influences are also discernible: that of John Locke, for example, who formulated a theory concerning "the irrational nature of idea-association." Laurence Sterne, for one, took the English philosopher's ideas to heart when he wrote *Tristram Shandy,* a turbulent account of a hero's whole life, including his prenatal existence. What was important to Sterne was what passed through his protagonist's mind at a given moment and the reactions accompanying his thoughts. The adventures narrated by Céline in *Journey to the End of the Night* are somewhat similar in that they are set forth with little or no reference to causation. There is no logical, no apparent reason of any kind for certain incidents to happen, and there is no real continuity between them—yet they do happen. This technique has been considered a means of mirroring the unpredictable nature of life, the inexplicable and irrational in nature. Later, of course, this method would be put to superb use by the Surrealists, who structured their novels (*Nadja,* for example, by André Breton) from material released from their unconscious worlds. In this manner new patterns and new ideational contents came into view. Céline used both of these techniques in creating *Journey to the End of the Night.*

ANALYSIS

Bardamu in Europe. Céline's anti-hero, Bardamu, may be looked upon almost as a prototype of many young people today. They live in a world that has no meaning for them, in a society from which they are forever trying to escape, in a land to which they not only do not respond but to which they feel no bond, in a psyche that has no conscious identity and remains undeveloped, limp, broken, divested of fiber, inwardly and externally blind. For this group there are no solutions, no answers, no traditional values, no dignity, no feeling for anything beyond their immediate grasp or gratification. Unable to understand the extreme variety implicit in life, incapable of positive activity, they become a prey to the fantasies of an adolescent ego and, therefore, prone to alienation. They are doomed, solipsistic, drenched in a narcissistic ambiance.

Bardamu is just such a man. He succeeds in almost nothing. He has no illusions, no will to right the wrongs he sees about him. Whatever he touches withers in his grasp and sinks from view into a muck of despair, negativism, and nihilism.

He is a complex blend indeed, an alchemical mixture of passive and active traits. When suffering from lethargy and ennui, he permits himself to be led, like the ebb and flow of water. On such occasions he views life as futile and absurd—a series of meaningless, pitiful, painful, and pathetic moments. The events that make up a life are comparable to so many objects, the one heaped upon the other, always top-heavy and about to crumble with the slightest shift in stress.

He is a precursor of Roquentin, the protagonist of Sartre's *Nausea* (1938), a novel that the existentialist philosopher dedicated to Céline. Roquentin, like Bardamu, feels absolutely no reason to go on living, is horrified by the ugliness and absurdity of life, and does not believe in progress. Unlike Bardamu, however, Roquentin evolves. By the end of the novel he has come to realize that though life may be meaningless, he is free to escape into a creative realm that will give purpose to his existence. *Nausea* ends on a positive note when Roquentin hears an American jazz song: the music acts as a stimulant, encouraging him to write a beautiful book that will enable him to accept both himself and the world about him. Bardamu's struggles have no such finale. Though he does continue to work as a doctor in the mental institution, he is detached from everything about him, as if he were living passively outside of the event.

Bardamu may also have been a source of inspiration for the character Meursault in Albert Camus' *The Stranger* (1942). Like Bardamu, Meursault feels nothing; he is devoid of any goal in life and is wafted along by any current: wind, water, or sun's rays. Only at the end of the novel, when life is about to be withdrawn from him, does he begin to experience its meaning, the realization of the precious gift nature has bestowed upon him.

Bardamu, unlike Meursault or Roquentin, *does* function in society, albeit in a desultory manner. But he has no hope for the future and so is defeated before he even starts. Aware, intellectually speaking, of his turmoils and torments, as are many individuals in life, he is so paralyzed by fear (by that of death in particular) that he is unable to cope with life. He becomes a psychological paralytic, unable to size up situations or to act to his advantage. Still more tragic, however, is the result of such negativity: it divests him of the power to feel anything profoundly. Fear has so impressed itself upon his entire personality that emotions resulting from such anguish arise: rage, anger, hatred.

The chaotic state of affairs that Bardamu sees all about him in the course of his peregrinations may be looked upon both as external or gratuitous, events and as manifestations of his dismal and disquieting inner world. Bardamu is so entrenched in his own concerns and fears that he is quite incapable of relating to others in a serious manner. For this reason he cannot experience love based on altruism and affection. Women for Bardamu, for the most part, are objects—grasping, possessive, lustful types for whom Bardamu feels nothing except the most superficial attraction, which usually ends in disgust.

Because Bardamu is a chaos of contradictions, a being who never achieves any kind of balance or harmony except on the most rudimentary level, his frustrations and dissatisfactions are usually unleashed on outside forces. On a political, social, and economic level, he frequently rants and raves in a highly irrational manner, the event or the object under scrutiny being approached affectively. The war sequence is a case in point.

We first encounter Bardamu at a café. He has just given up his medical studies, blaming his inadequate economic situation for his decision. He tells his friend, Arthur, sitting beside him, that he is against war. Soldiers, he continues, are "talking monkeys" who devote their lives to maintaining the status quo—the rule of money, nationalism, patriotism, and the spirit of sacrifice. All such notions, he says, are meaningless. Moreover, soldiers are devoid of individualism; they are motivated by vanity, their purpose in fighting being to win medals and, thereby, to become an idol of the people—a military hero. As Bardamu spouts his intellectually conceived pacifism, a regiment of soldiers on horseback passes by: fanfare, noise, colors, medals, the screaming of excited crowds, admiring girls throwing themselves at soldiers, passions—all these act as catalyzers, enticing Bardamu into the emotional melee. He is literally swept off his feet; he joins the armed forces. He has thought one way and acted another.

As Bardamu is caught up in the enthusiasm of the crowd, we discern his own lack of individuality. He has become a man who is unable to determine his own destiny and unable to stand by a decision. In this instance, then, he has given up his personal struggle, his credo, and has become submerged in the collectivity.[3]

Bardamu claims that he despises war, and yet he is prepared to annihilate the entire French "race." Certainly he has no wish to help protect a people he considers ignominious, slovenly, unclean, degenerate, decaying, riddled with tumors.

> What you call the race is only that great heap of worm-eaten sods like me, bleary, shivering and lousy, who, coming defeated from the four corners of the earth, have ended up here, escaping from hunger, illness, pestilence and cold. They couldn't go further because of the sea. That's your France and those are your Frenchmen.[4]

Such blanket generalizations, exhibiting no critical faculties at all, are typical of Bardamu's way.

Philosophically, war may be looked upon as a collective act, liberating the aggressive drives accumulated in the participants. It is comparable to a "collective discharge," an excretion of negative qualities, of personal dissatisfactions that render an individual incapable of coping with certain situations and people.[5] War implies activity and as such it is compatible with life. A state of repose is a negation of all that breathes. The cosmos is in a perpetual state of flux because it is made up of a series of antagonistic forces. The basis of life is antagonism, not harmony. It is the degree of the conflict that determines whether the outcome will be positive or negative.

Bardamu is a belligerent in his thought processes; indeed, his thoughts emerge with volcanic rapidity. This is made evident in the continuously dynamic quality of the images used by Céline. During the battlefield scene, for example, shells, guns, fire, and the clashing of metals pulsate. An infantryman, his helmet thrust on his head, his hands filthy and trembling, brings the colonel a message. Moments later, the colonel dies in a burst of shellfire. An infantryman starts to carry him off but as he does so the colonel's head is severed from his body by another shell. The soldier stands there, with the headless colonel in his arms: "only his neck open at the top with blood bubbling in it like stew in a pot." [6] The horror of such an image is reinforced by the statement: "One is as innocent of Horror as one is of sex." [7] The implication is that man is capable of any act that excites him, no matter what the consequences.

What makes the war scene all the more excoriating is the objectivity and the macabre humor with which the facts are related. Stendhal, in *The Charterhouse of Parma,* describes the Waterloo massacre in an equally detached and unsentimental manner that adds to the horror of the things described. Voltaire does likewise with the Inquisition and the bloody battle scenes in *Candide.* By severing feelings from the incident, an element of fantasy and nonbelief is introduced, permitting tension, dialectically formed, to surge forth: action, reaction, challenge, response.

The fire image injected into the battle scene incident not only heightens the fright experienced by Bardamu and all those associated with war but also serves to point up the protagonist's "fiery" or irrational nature. As the battle rages, giant flames burn and scorch everything in sight. Coals, intended to roast human flesh, gleam: "All this heap of flesh was bleeding like the deuce." [8] Each piece of human meat seems to be surrounded by an immense circle of flame—a halo. The energy unleashed by the fire image is a symbolic representation of Bardamus' inner flame and fury, an uncontrollable rage that mutilates and destroys all in sight.

A spiritual aspect is likewise introduced into this same image. The clouds (a heavenly force) are being licked by flames (a force unleashed by man), "with the flames rising up from them, licking the clouds." [9] The gigantic or cosmic violence of this image has its "inhuman" side, therefore, implying that some higher force—God—has been sent to destroy man, as He had once punished Prometheus.

Other images are used to amplify the havoc and destructive force of fire and, by extension, Bardamu's inner tumult. Wind, for example, sometimes looked upon as a spiritual entity (Genesis), also fosters growth on earth, pollinating plants. In this particular episode, however, nothing but disaster ensues, as the flames spread with utmost speed.

> The wind had come up fiercely from both sides of the embankment, the gusts in the poplar leaves mingling with the rustle that was directed against us from up the road.[10]

Wind, spurring the fire on, encourages tremendous activity and howls outright, as it passes through the trees, sounding like so many human cries and sobs. Noises accompany the wind as it sweeps across the atmosphere. Man, powerless in the face of such a cosmic force, remains baffled, encased, so to speak, in a whirlwind or tornado that casts him forth into the enemy's world—death.

The vision of the wasp also comes into play in this scene, reinforcing the atmosphere of tension and pain. The wasp, industrious, cruel, ruthless when confronted, strikes hard, hammers and burns the flesh as it lands upon its victim, like fire or a box of lighted matches.

> . . . it crackled like a lot of big boxes of matches, and infuriated bullets swarmed all around us, pricking the air like wasps.[11]

The superb association of matches, fire, and wind—all viewed as energizers and pain-throwers—heightens still further the vision of man's sordid nature, of his inability to control his instincts, of his combustive forces that burn and corrode his psyche if left unchanneled.

Still other images, those of the tree and of rain, may also be looked upon as visual equivalents of Bardamu's own inner state and his attitude toward the world.

> These trees are as detached, magnificent and impressive as one's dreams. But I was afraid of trees too, since I had known them to conceal an enemy. Every tree meant a dead man.[12]

Trees represent sturdiness, growth, the rapport of matter and spirit. But Bardamu has no confidence in them just as he has none in man and himself. The means that Bardamu will use to escape from reality, from his life, namely hypocrisy, sensuality, and insanity, have to a certain extent cut him off from the tree, that is, from a balanced relationship (as with a tree) vis-à-vis himself, humanity, and nature.

Severed from nature, Bardamu cannot derive strength from it or receive its nourishment and sustaining force. Unlike the tree, which is fed from its roots, giving it the strength to grow its branches and foliage, Bardamu is isolated from his surroundings, unsteady in a world divested of protective foliage. Solipsistic, wandering about, he will keep retreating or running, as if trying to avoid stepping into the quicksand that might engulf him—his own inner world.

The rain image is used expertly by Céline not only symbolically but dramatically as well. It both opens and closes the war episode. As the rain pours down on the soldiers in the beginning, drenching everything in sight, it puts out the "fire" kindled in Bardamu's psyche, the one that had overpowered him and compelled him to join the army despite his fulminations against things military. All his idealism, so to speak, all the fantasy of his visions, is drowned, inundated, liquified, and disappears, like rain, into the giant mass of earth. The entire war sequence concludes with a rain image: "It begins to rain, the fields of Flanders slobbered with dirty water." [14] It is as if a terrestrial conflagration (passion, war) has just been obliterated. The image of the earth lapping up the dirty residue is a visual indication of the fusion of all natural forces. The personification of rain, a cosmic entity, lends both a spiritual and dramatic impact to the picture. As for Bardamu, he is submerged in the flood waters.

Though Bardamu constantly preaches pacifism, his ideas reveal a bellicose and highly energetic temperament. Indeed, Bardamu is a bundle of fiery sparks. His inner world, judging from the previous images, is made up of a series of tumultuous conflagrations. His dynamism is so strong a force that he has difficulty channeling it into fruitful acts. It is projected, helter-skelter, onto people and objects, investing them with intense hatreds. The energy of the emotions expended is released on certain groups (the rich, for example). When this occurs, the violence of the verbal assault is of such magnitude that it creates an accompanying swell of anger in the reader, who becomes emotionally charged by the situation and thus an accomplice of Bardamu.

What does Bardamu hate about the rich? Their lust for money, of course, their possessiveness, their callousness. But he is equally hostile to those who have nothing. An incident illustrating this point occurs when he leaves the battlefield. He sees a mother crying over the death of her little boy. The child's body, dressed in a sailor suit, is described with compassion. Bardamu asks the mother for some fine wine. She has none, she replies. When he offers her money for that same wine, she brings forth the finest vintage, forgetting all about her son's death. The mother's attitude arouses feelings of rancor, if not hatred, in Bardamu.

Patriotism, Bardamu claims, is noxious—a deceit, a lie. Were Paris to burn with all of its hotels, the Tuileries, the ministries, the Louvre and the department stores, it would kindle no emotion in him, he confesses, because nothing would be lost or gained by such a turn of events. "You don't lose anything much when your landlord's house is burnt down.[13] Whether he pays in francs or in marks is no concern of his. What angers Bardamu is that he must pay at all, and that gangsters are venerated the world over: "The poor man's theft becomes a malicious incursion on an individual . . ."[14] When powerful peoples or nations loot, the world stands aside; when an individual or small nation steals, society is ready to pounce. So far as the dialectical historical process is concerned, heroes emerge in every generation: Bismarck, Napoleon, etc. They bring new systems, but to Bardamu's way of thinking, the new is even worse than the old.

Bardamu's emotion-driven views are rarely logical or consistent. At one moment he despises the rich; at another, the masses are equally despicable. The latter are looked upon as stupid, indicating Bardamu's own aristocratic concepts. They are indigent, dull-witted, incapable of rational thought or of insight. Their attitudes, therefore, are flabby and so are swayed any which way by powerful leaders. Feelings of compassion, once expressed for the poor and the meek, have now been transformed into anger.

Bardamu's venom spills over to encompass all of humanity, and the reader who is not careful can be carried along by these verbal tirades. Bardamu's inability to cope with situations and to assess events and political views rationally leads him to seek escape in condemning all of mankind as evil.

What does evil imply for Céline, that he should refer to it so frequently in *Journey to the End of the Night?* Evil is antipodal to good. A person becomes conscious of evil through its opposite, good, and vice versa, as he experiences the polarities of life. The fact that Bardamu sees evil indicates the possibility of his becoming aware of life's fullness. But since he has as yet no understanding of good, he cannot know the real meaning of existence on earth.

From a psychological point of view, evil may be considered an expression of man's negative, inferior, and unadaptive characteristics, more commonly known (in Jungian terminology) as the "shadow." When a person is unconscious of his negative traits, he may project these onto certain external phenomena—people, ideas, whatever. Bardamu is forever doing this: projecting his shadow on segments of society, on concepts, on "externals." Had Bardamu become conscious of what he was doing, he might have been liberated from his resentments and might not, therefore, have felt the need to be so condemnatory. Instead of alienating himself from the objects he so passionately derogated, he might have established some kind of rapport with them. Had Bardamu been capable of making evil conscious, the beginnings of self-acceptance might have followed.

Bardamu's contempt for everything around him succeeds in increasing his solitude and despair. His pain reaches an intensity reminiscent of Greek tragedy. Bardamu feels that he is being victimized, that he is the butt of dreaded Furies who are perpetually unleashing their venom upon him. During the battle scene, he suddenly identifies with the soldier—the sincere and sensitive young man who is succumbing to the forces about him. As the identification grows in depth, a cleavage occurs between himself and the other less naïve men-of-war, and his loneliness becomes still more painful.

Léon Robinson, the reservist that Bardamu meets during this same war sequence, may be considered a shadow figure in that he represents all of Bardamu's unacceptable, unadaptive traits. Robinson has, therefore, many points in common with Bardamu; they both hate death, they both look upon man in general as avaricious, hypocritical, and prone to take advantage of the misfortunes befalling others. Differences, however, are discernible. In the first three parts of the novel, Robinson is an active, aggressive force, whereas Bardamu is relatively passive. In the final part, their positions are reversed.

Though Robinson's appearance throughout the novel is unpredictable, there seems to be a certain pattern in his movements. He appears whenever Bardamu has achieved a certain measure of stability, that is, whenever he has remained at a job for a certain length of time. Robinson emerges in order to alter Bardamu's outlook and to compel him to move on. As a shadow figure, he may be looked upon as a catalyzing agent, like fire, ferreting something out of place, stimulating, arousing aspects of Bardamu's unconscious world that might otherwise remain dormant.

Because Bardamu rejects so much of what belongs to humanity, because he cannot bear the life going on around him, he frequently seeks to extricate himself from his anguish by one escape mechanism or another.

Religion, one of these possible escape hatches, does not offer him the solace he craves. On the contrary, according to Bardamu, God created man in his own likeness: greedy, self-centered, fleshy, piglike, filthy and lazy! Bardamu does not believe in any deity and he derides the manner in which man worships the divine in general.

> A God who counts the minutes and the pence, a desperate God, sensual and grunting like a pig. A pig with wings of gold which tumbles through the world, with exposed belly waiting for caresses, lo, 'tis he, behold our master! Embrace, embrace! [15]

The church, Bardamu maintains, is a hand tool of the politicians. In the past, heretics were burned at the stake for political, economic, or philosophical reasons. Today, heretics of a different type are shot. Only the banners change.

> Flag worship promptly replaced divine worship, an old cloud already punctured by the Reformation and condensed a long time ago into Episcopal coffers.[16]

Nor does sex offer Bardamu an adequate escape route. It affords him only momentary release from anxiety. He has difficulty, after all, in relating to people; his capacity for lengthy rapport with others is virtually nil. Lola, the girl with whom he has a liaison in Paris, resembles "a combative Joan of Arc." [17] She is endowed with a feeble, though enthusiastic heart, but lacks intelligence. It is her body that attracts Bardamu. "I believed in her body, I did not believe in her mind." [18] He disdains her notions of patriotism. They are romantic. She believes in heroes, in chivalry, and in her ancestors who sailed to America on the Mayflower. Her concept of life is diametrically opposed to that of Bardamu's who views patriotism in terms of oozing guts, blood, mutilation. "Everyone has his own fears." [19] To him, her hysteria over having gained two inches around her waist because of having eaten too many fritters is a further sign of her stupidity—similar to that of the masses: "Soon she was as afraid of the fritters as I was of shells," he says with tongue in cheek, as he points to the relativity of attitudes toward terror.[20]

Bardamu's inability to experience a warm relationship with women, to speak truthfully to them, indicates a fear of being rejected. He is literally afraid to tell Lola of his anguish at the thought of being killed in battle. When he does express his concern, humorously, partially masking his real panic, she is revolted by his cowardice. She compares him to a rat—and bares her fangs. Only cowards and madmen, she claims, refuse war. Bardamu retorts: "Then long live all cowards and madmen!" [21]

Insanity offers Bardamu a mode of escape. If he could get himself declared insane, he would not be sent back to the front. In Duval's restaurant, therefore, Bardamu puts on a performance. But is he merely acting? Suddenly he is seized with fear and begins to behave peculiarly. He claims people are persecuting him, aiming rifles at him, trying to kill him. Paranoia takes hold and all semblance of rational vision vanishes. "Poor soldier," mutters an onlooker, as he watches Bardamu trying to clear the phantoms from his sick brain. The police arrive and take him in handcuffs to the hospital.

The fact that Bardamu is considered insane, at least temporarily, raises the question of what "insanity" means. Where does one draw the line between rational and irrational views, normal and quixotic behavior? Bardamu himself ponders the question and answers it as follows: "Bewildered by war, we had become mad in another way: mad with fear." [22]

In the mental institution, Bardamu learns an extraordinary lesson: to get along in this world one must go along with the will of the majority. Unable to relate to people because of his intense hatred for them, he will bury his feelings of anger, for the moment, and adopt a pragmatic attitude, one that will serve him: hypocrisy (diplomacy). He meets a sergeant in the hospital, Branledore, who is recuperating from a perforated intestine. This man has won everybody's admiration. Why? Every time someone passes his bed he cries out, "Victory! It shall be ours" [23] He is on the side of the masses and voices their patriotic slogans. Bardamu decides to try this approach. He tells everyone he meets, including the visiting actress from the Comédie-Française, about his bravery in battle, inventing incident upon incident, and about his intense love for his land. The actress is so moved by his exploits that she devotes an evening at the theater to telling of his braveries in "fine-sounding rhymes and tremendous adjectives." [24]

Can one label Bardamu a free individual? Yes and no. He is free in the sense that he feels no bonds, no sense of belonging, no ties. Yet he is bound and tightly so, prisoner of this world and of his own volatile personality; he is the butt of his emotions, the product of his affectivity, obsessions, and fears. He is quite unlike André Gide's hero, Nathanaël, in *The Fruits of the Earth* (1897), who praises the earth, who succeeds in breaking all family ties, and whose life is a search for experience and fervor. Bardamu is a Nathanael who misfires, a Nathanael come of age; since he never discovers the meaning of life, either within himself or on the outside, he is a victim of his freedom, enslaved by it rather than master of it.

Bardamu in Africa. Our "hero's" boat trip to Africa and his sojourn on that continent are perhaps the most remarkable segments of *Journey to the End of the Night.* The imagery is brilliant, sensual, and exotic, the situations intensely dramatic.

The sense of imprisonment experienced by Bardamu so far becomes even more powerful during his African venture. In Europe, he had been ensnared in war. More seriously, he had been trapped by time in that he was constantly aware of his temporal existence. His life there was lived linearly, with a present, past, future—and an end. He needed to escape from this constricting situation: "to escape alive from a mad international shambles [Europe]" [25] In Africa, the land of the primitive, he seeks new experiences—as a businessman, a dealer in ivory, in rare birds, in the slave market—through which he feels he can escape into a timeless world.

Bardamu is as enthusiastic about his departure from France as Rimbaud was when his "Drunken Ship" was released from its moorings. But his joy is to be short-lived: the ship, symbolically a type of prison for Bardamu, forces him to live in an enclosed area and restricts his activities. Instead of being able to wander about the land and to lead a peripheral existence, as he had in Europe, Bardamu is now limited to the ship. A feeling of constriction, of strangulation, overcomes him. We might make an analogy between his physical situation and his psychological condition: he is no longer able to flitter about, he is compelled to delve within his own depths, his *nigredo,* just as Osiris, Odysseus, Dante, and Genet were compelled to do on their respective "night-sea journeys" or odysseys. As a result, he feels such extreme malaise, such claustrophobia, that he writes, "I felt as if I were living in a case of high explosives." [26] It is always difficult, traumatic, to face oneself.

The days begin piling up one upon the other, like so many uneven cobblestones. To reinforce this acute sense of stifling, Céline calls his stylistic technique into play: he slackens the speed of the events and the conversations. It is as if time were suspended. The temporal image of the boat making its way ever so slowly over a large expanse of water, silhouetted against an infinite sky, gives the impression of time having come almost to a stop. To increase this sensation of motionlessness still further, Céline adds a description of the intense oppressive heat on shipboard and its deadly effect: ". . . a breathless sort of stove atmosphere, disquieting and frightful. The drinking water, the sea, the air, the sheets, our own sweat, everything was warm, sticky." [27]

The more sluggish the ship's pace, the greater Bardamu's excruciating anxiety. Like Garcin in Sartre's *No Exit,* Bardamu is forced to delve within.

No escape, no generalizations, no tirades, no hysteria, no insanity. He is cornered with himself. His situation is critical.

When he looks at the other passengers—he hates. He is, one might conclude, projecting onto the collective certain negative contents of his own, or characteristics of his own toward which he is antagonistic: passivity, laziness, lack of direction, and focus.

Just what does he despise in those about him? As a collective entity, a microcosm of the world, he sees them all as diabolical, gruesome, hepatitic, toothless, syphilitic, flea-ridden, eczema-covered, pimply, fat, slovenly, attracting clusters of flies and bugs of all sorts. This massive creature—the passengers or humanity—looks evil, monstrous, ready to spring at him and lacerate him. Some primitive instinct has been stirred within him and rumbles in his depths. As the days pass, he becomes convinced that he has been placed in their midst, by higher forces, as a kind of sacrifice: "I was the victim." [28] Everyone on board required his death, he thinks. In his imagination the passengers are transformed into an anthropophagous horde about to hunt him down. Bardamu is convinced, for example, that all eyes are cast his way every time he enters the dining room, that whispering campaigns have been started against him, that he has been singled out as the object of a diabolical scheme.

Bardamu feels the passengers are a threat to his safety. He fears them. When feelings of hatred are aimed at the collective, psychic energy pours outward and may reach all-consuming force. Those who hate are in fact destroying, in projection, aspects of themselves. Symbolically, they are doing away with themselves, persecuting themselves. A well-known example of the persecution complex is found in the experience of St. Paul (Saul). The Christ-complex was alive within him, and when he saw it in projection in the Christians, he persecuted them as its representative. He did so only because he was unable to accept this content within himself. He was unaware of its existence within himself.[29]

Likewise, Bardamu cannot accept the ugliness, the slothfulness, the filth of the other passengers. What he is rejecting, in effect, are these very things within himself, things of which he is aware only through their projection onto others. Bardamu is certainly far from unique in this respect. People are always projecting their own ideas or phobias onto others, either adoring or hating them accordingly. A rational and objective attitude is not only difficult to acquire but is almost impossible to maintain when complexes are involved. Passion reigns. The subject is the victim of his illusions or delusions, not the master of them.[30]

Bardamu's persecution complex takes on extreme dimensions and he is virtually paralyzed. He refuses even to leave his cabin. A condition of stasis arises. All activity comes to a halt. The outflow of psychic energy wanes. Now Bardamu becomes thoughtful and begins sounding himself out. The need to save himself being uppermost in his mind, he resorts to what he had learned in the French hospital—to hypocrisy. By agreeing with the majority, affection and even admiration can be won. "Long live France!," he shouts one day, and his situation begins to change radically.

Bardamu begins showing his fellow passengers his wounds, telling them about how he had suffered for his "beloved" country. Ironically, he mused, this was the "only time (that) my country saved my life; till then, it had been quite the reverse." [31] Even Captain Frémizon (a play on the word *Frémissons,* "fear, trembling"—Bardamu's real attitude) begins to admire Bardamu. The captain and the other passengers discern a thousand new qualities in our hero. Indeed, he becomes the most desirable and sought-after passenger on ship. Through a ruse, he has saved himself.

Bardamu has brought about a state of concord between himself and other passengers. One who had always professed pacifism now begins to understand the real meaning of the term. To maintain peace is to permit people to "expand and bask in idiotic self-glorification. Intelligent vanity does not exist. It's merely an instinct." [32] To appeal to the vanity of others is to placate the "enemy" and so bring about a condition of peace. Had Bardamu read Ecclesiastes, he might have understood the extreme dangers implied in adopting a superimposed, cerebrally constructed attitude based on vanity.

Abandoning one's moral credo and one's ethics is surely one way of bringing about peace. Peace with integrity, however, is virtually an impossibility. Philosophically, as we have seen, peace in the sense of rest, inactivity, and finally sterility is a negation of life. War (conflict), on the other hand, implies activity; it generates heat and fire and thus makes for an altered attitude, whether negative or positive. If war (activity) is kept within bounds, it may make for constructive attitudes. Bardamu, as we have already discovered, is a person of extremes who is unable to achieve any kind of inner harmony. His views rest almost exclusively upon affect rather than upon reason.

Fear has driven Bardamu to opt for peace with hypocrisy. It works beautifully on the outside, but what is happening within? He smoulders. In choosing hypocrisy he has overlooked what is most precious to some people: a personal credo, sincere values. To deny these, no matter what they are, is to reject one's identity, or at least some essential aspects of it. The conflict within Bardamu's psyche is not immediately visible on the surface, but on later occasions it will appear in most virulent, hazardous ways. Yet experience may sometimes be the wisest way. As Jung remarked, when a dog finds a door shut, it scratches.

A hero—a Siegfried, a Roland, a Bayard, a Lancelot—overcomes fear through acts of boldness. Bardamu, however, is an anti-hero. His method is devious: passivity on the outside, havoc on the inside. A man paralyzed with fear in this manner cannot hope to find liberation easily.

Bardamu's sojourn on the continent of Africa may be looked upon as a trip into his own *nigredo,* his own depths, or into death. Like Theseus and Pirithoüs, who went down to Hades and were temporarily chained to a rock in the underworld, so Bardamu would live out his own deathlike destiny, undergoing painful, dangerous, and yet fruitful adventures.

For many people, death is the one antipode of life. For the medieval Christian, for example, death was an "unfortunate accident" and the direct result of man's "fall," his imperfection, his original sin: "the wages of sin is death." [33] Because people were so fearful of death, they sought to avoid it either by adopting an ultrareligious attitude and the promise of a glorious afterlife or by drowning their fears in vice. Centuries later man was still attempting to by-pass the notion of death by these means, and also with the belief that "science" would conquer death one day.

To avoid the thought of death, or to deny it in any way, is to harbor an unwholesome attitude toward life. Death is part and parcel of the life process. Each individual must undergo the process of birth, development, and death (or unity). How conscious one is of death is a measure of one's understanding of life in all its states.

To experience the notion of death, through fear of it or otherwise, brings its reality closer to consciousness. When such knowledge is gained, the individual can "mobilize his own inner resources in order to face the challenge and make the decision about his attitude toward life and death." [34] Thus Hemingway's hero in *The Snows of Kilimanjaro,* Harry, tries to face his death and succeeds in so doing in the course of a conversation with his wife.[35] He no longer looks upon death as an object of anguish but rather as part of the life process, as something dynamic, as all else in the cosmos. The protagonist of Henry James' *Middle Years* expresses dissatisfaction with his accomplishments and yet does not feel traumatized by the prospect of death. As an antagonist for these two individuals, death has been rendered virtually harmless and is in the end neutralized because they are able to face it squarely. Other literary examples of positive attitudes toward death may be found in Faulkner's *As I Lay Dying.* Addie writes: "I could just remember my father used to say that the reason for living was to get ready to stay dead a long time." [36] In this same work, Doctor Peabody speaks of death as "merely a function of the mind." [37] These characters experience a knowledge and an acceptance of death as a completion or as another phase of existence.

There is, on the other hand, another extreme, likewise to be avoided: a callous attitude toward death. If an individual is not horrified by death or does not feel some kind of pang or reaction to it, if his attitude is passive, then he still identifies with the world about him and remains relatively unconscious about his state of being, either living or dead. He is, therefore, undeveloped and not (yet) a differentiated individual who has reached "human form."

The capacity to feel a certain amount of terror at the thought of death is one of the things distinguishing man from animal. (This does not include the "instinctive" fear of death, which is characteristic of both species.) Animals do not look upon death as an abyss; man does. For some people death is frightening because it represents an absence; it possesses no form; it is unknowable; it is a mystery, a separation, a change from everything familiar. Terror at the thought of death and a desire to avoid it are normal. What can be abnormal—and unusually so in Bardamu's (Céline's) case—is the extent of the fear.

The inability or unwillingness to recognize death as part of man's destiny, as an essential aspect of existence, indicates a lack of adaptability to outer reality.[38] If the anguish confronting the feeling of death is so extreme, it prevents one from experiencing and enjoying life. As Jung put it, it is as if man were living with the thought that at any moment his house was going to collapse and crush him. All rational activity is paralyzed. Life, as a result, takes on little significance. Living becomes a kind of protracted dread. Though one may be physically alive, in such cases, one is psychologically dead. Such fears as are experienced by this kind of being preclude all meaningful relationships in life. One cannot participate in anything at all, either in terms of oneself or of others, if one is forever being haunted and hounded by the terror of what is about to happen—death.

The ability to accept death as part of life, as a reality, can transform one's stay on earth into a positive experience, into the active and energetic process that living is. To be bogged down with fears, to have the idea of death assume obsessional power, can only create neuroses and stifle emotional growth. Bardamu is conscious of the meaning of death; as a medical student and as a soldier he is intellectually aware of its inevitable occurrence. Yet he is unable to accept the idea of death's being the final answer. Whenever he is compelled to confront this notion, he is thrown into a panic that keeps him from confronting his fear and dealing with it in a constructive way. The energy he expends in the futile search for ways and means of escaping the fear of death reaches untold heights, and is projected outward onto others in the form of hate.

Bardamu's hatred is turned on everyone. To begin with, he holds those of the governing class in contempt; they are vain, arrogant, lords of everything they touch. Those of the military clique fare no better; they are all degenerates. The life of the colonists (in their capacity as governing officials and military men) centers around drink, gambling, the brothel, money. As for the business class, it is made up of avaricious, rapacious, despicable people; nothing that grows, flies, or walks escapes the vigilant eye of these exploiters. Bardamu notes, moreover, that each class is antagonistic toward the other, is bent upon annihilating the other. To stress this atmosphere of acute hostility, Céline conjures up images of rats, scorpions, snakes, mosquitoes, all vying with the others to destroy whatever they happen on: hurting, eating, mutilating.

Bardamu's assessment of the French colonists in Africa, the emptiness of their lives and their goalless existence, is certainly understandable. In certain ways it is reminiscent of the depressing atmosphere enshrouding the protagonists of Paul Bowles' novel *The Sheltering Sky* (1949), who try and fail to communicate with one another and with the world in general; decay greets them under the extreme heat, filth, and poverty of the forsaken area in which they have chosen to live as expatriates.[39]

What is startling is Bardamu's disdain, even disgust, for the Black Africans. He is revolted by their wretchedness, their filth, their ignorance, their sloth, their disease-ravaged bodies. "They stink wretchedness," he says. "They have nothing which makes it worthwhile to approach them." Their primitivism and their cannibalistic ways turn his stomach.

> These niggers are all dead and stinking; you'll soon find that out. They squat there all day; and you wouldn't believe them capable of even getting up to go and piss against a tree, and then as soon as it's night, my God! . . . They go all hysterical, all nerves, all bloody-minded. Part of the night itself gone crazy—that's what the niggers are, I'm telling you. The set of dirty beggars! Degenerate scum . . .[40]

What was the basis for his hatred of the black man? Bardamu must instinctively have feared him, or at least what he symbolized: the blackness associated with death. Bardamu quivers when he hears their tam-tams in the woods, their strange noises, screams, cries, oscillating tonalities—a world of mystery and fright opened up from within that dank realm of the forest. It is as if a world of instinct, wearing the visage of death, has converged upon him and is about to pounce. At such moments, Bardamu's behavior becomes increasingly explosive and hostile.

Something strange occurs at this juncture. Bardamu develops a severe case of malaria and an equally virulent diarrhea (amoebic dysentery). His ailment is physical, and yet it may be looked upon as an indication of his distorted and sick attitude toward life. Indeed, Bardamu himself has confessed that his fevers are so high at times that he feels he is living in a "twilight world," in a realm of fantasy. When running such high fevers, catalizers of sorts, he finds it difficult if not impossible "to make out what was real amid the absurd things." [41] There is a merging of the spiritual and the physical world. Life as a unit is born and with it a period of self-revelation, so necessary to Bardamu's antagonistic and sick psyche.

When his body burns with fever, when conventional limitations and categories vanish, Bardamu's inner world is stirred and new contents rise up into his consciousness. His feeling function, hitherto dormant, is aroused by the first positive figure, Alcide, with whom he comes into contact in Africa. A man who has suffered from intense fatigue, extreme heat, and malaria, Alcide nevertheless has an autonomous will: his profound love for his niece keeps him going. After his brother died, Alcide explains to Bardamu, he vowed to raise his niece, then a little girl, to the very best of his ability. He sent her to the finest parochial school in Bordeaux, and when she caught infantile paralysis he spared no expense in her care. His one desire in life is to give his niece some happiness. "He offered this little girl so far away enough tenderness to remake an entire world . . ." Alcide, inwardly, is the essence of gentleness, kindness, altruism.

For the first time Bardamu admires a human being. Within him, then, something has been agitated. He has responded to the kindness, understanding, and love that Alcide has shown to his niece. Hatred and resentment seem to have vanished, and although Bardamu is extremely ill he experiences a sensation of euphoria. He has discovered something strange in himself: an ability to respond to love and warmth.

Another aspect of his personality now comes to plague him, however: his shadow, Robinson. It develops that Robinson is the dishonest employee that the company has hired Bardamu to replace. When Bardamu meets him in a remote village in the jungle, it is dark and Bardamu is not even certain of the identity of the man with whom he is talking.

> I saw Robinson's face once more, veiled by the haze of insects, before I put the light out. That perhaps was why his features impressed themselves more subtly on my memory, when before they had reminded me of nothing very definite. He went on talking to me in the dark, while I searched through the past, using the sound of his voice as a key with which to try locked doors of many years and months, and finally days, wondering where I could possibly have met this man before. But I could find nothing. No voice answered me.[42]

Blackness engulfs Bardamu. He calls out to the man in the opposite corner of the cabin—Robinson—but no answer is forthcoming.

Robinson, faceless in the absence of light, acts like an unconscious force, a phantasmagoria, appearing without rational motivation. Yet even acausality has its logic. Robinson, as we have noted, always arrives just before some change of attitude on Bardamu's part. What change is it to be this time? Bardamu first tries to visualize his friend, to make sure that it is indeed he. In order to create the image of Robinson in his mind's eye, he has to stir his imagination, to dig back into his past. When Proust resurrected his past, he experienced it as a present reality; it helped him face the world. When Nerval broke open the doors separating his dream from the world of reality, he found the irrational realm more to his liking than workaday existence. Bardamu discovers that his past has always been a stranger to him; now, for the first time, he will try to fathom its meaning rather than continue to seek escape in some elusive present or future. Hitherto, Bardamu's past has been something static, "dead matter." Now, as he tries to sound out those events already experienced, he discovers the limitless nature and fecundating force of his memories. It is an ocean of endless waves, tirades, gyrations, storms, calms, dangers, beauties, and ugliness.

> You can lose yourself groping among these twirling forms of memory. It's terrifying how many people and how many things no longer stir in one's past. Living people whom one has pushed into the crypts of time sleep there so soundly with the dead that one same shadow envelops and confuses both.[43]

As Bardamu regresses into his past he feels as if he were spanning space and time, trying to extract from past experiences whatever might be helpful to him in his daily life. The past becomes something alive, ready to move and affect him. Because he is able to relate back to himself, he also begins to understand the world about him: nature in particular and even death.

In a superb picture, Bardamu expresses the sensations he feels as he first makes contact, indirectly through his own being, with the natural forces about him. He is developing, in effect, a deeply religious sense (*religio*, meaning relating back to), in that he feels himself bound to nature. Strength rather than strangulation ensues from his contact with the cosmos.

> For a whole hour the sky preened itself in great mad streaks of scarlet from end to end, and a green light flared out in the overgrowth and swirled upwards in flickering clouds towards the first stars of the night. After that the whole horizon turned grey, then red once more, but this time a tired and short-lived red. Then that was the end. The colors all fell back in strips like paper streamers at a carnival. This happened every day on the stroke of six o'clock.
>
> Night then opened the ball with all its prowling beasts and its myriad croaking noises.
>
> The forest is only waiting for this signal to start to shake, whistle and moan in all its depths: like some huge, lecherous, unlighted railway station, about to burst. Whole trees bristling with squealing life, voluptuous savagery and horror.[44]

What Bardamu sees constellated about him in the skies above are his own spiritual forces at work, symbolically represented by the stars, the shafts of colors falling in broken lines, in tatters on the trees. Such a downward journey (as seen in the stars' rays) indicates their rapport with the forest (symbolically, Bardamu's unconscious). The direction the spiritual takes is positive, in that it tries to relate to the unconscious. The energy, therefore, is well directed, but it does not yet come into focus, since the rays reach the trees in broken lines or in tatters. When the forest—which is, in reality, Bardamu's being—begins to tremble, as light penetrates its thickest areas, groans, sounds, activities of all sorts emerge from it.

These new contents, coming into existence, urge him to terminate his stay in the *nigredo*—in his primitive, archaic, timeless, and spaceless death-realm. Only an extremely forceful act, however, can give Bardamu the strength to sever relations with such dismal conditions, such oppressive heat and sickness. Heroically, he takes the upper hand. He sets fire to the termite-ridden, rain-drenched cabin that he was to inhabit and to the rotting merchandise he was hired to sell: he destroys all that would have kept him in Africa. Interestingly enough, Bardamu uses flame (intense heat, passion) to do away with what has already begun to decay, purifying, as it were, the putrefied aspects of his own existence and thus paving the way for a return to a new way of life.

Other tests still await him. Bardamu has to find his way out of the forest, which is crawling with dangers, just as the hero of a fairy tale must go through ordeals in order to achieve independence. This struggle for freedom on Bardamu's part can be understood symbolically as a coming to terms with the forces that would have destroyed him, that is to say, with his own antagonistic and decaying functions. Bardamu is, for the first time, becoming conscious of his own strength, of his individuality, and of the meaning of death—and so, life.

Bardamu in the United States: The Feeling Function. The third section of *Journey to the End of the Night,* which takes Bardamu to the United States, is perhaps the weakest part of the novel. Céline's comments on the New World, as expressed through Bardamu, are trite and repetitious. He mouths what every foreigner has said since and before Duhamel: America, the land of the dollar, of sanitation, disinfectants, machines, factories. But he also offers some highly satiric and poignant descriptions, such as that of Bardamu slipping out of Ellis Island (refusing to sit out the quarantine), and that of his arrival in Manhattan and its small, damp, tenebrous streets filled with the poor and destitute, all reminding him of an "immense wound." Perhaps the bitterest picture of all is that of the Bank—an immense Cathedral of Gold into which a Holy Ghost breathes life. The Host, Bardamu suggests, is the money; the parishioners are those who bank within the premises, and God, of course, is the Dollar.

> They communicate with Dollar, murmuring to Him through a little grille; in fact, they make their confession. Very little noise, dim light, a tiny *guichet* set between lofty columns, that is all. They do not swallow the Host. They lay it against their heart.[45]

Writers in all centuries have written of man's attraction to money: Ben Jonson, Molière, Ghelderode, Balzac, Zola, etc. The alchemists, as we know, spent their lives trying to convert base metals into gold, working in secret with formulas of the most esoteric kind. Man's desire and lust for gold has always been a compelling force in his life, an indication of his power drives. Anything possessing such great "virtue" as gold tends to be looked upon as a supernatural force, an omniscient entity, a god. And certainly any god needs a house of worship to pay him respect and homage as an eternal force and power.

Bardamu's own attitude toward money is as involuted as a labyrinth. Though he claims to be on the side of the poor, he admires the large industrial complexes, such as the Ford factory, which he visits during his stay in America. Nor should it be forgotten that Bardamu has stated earlier, back in Africa, that he seeks wealth and everything it can bring him. Bardamu lacks a clear viewpoint on the subject of money; he is too fully immersed in matter (money) to be able to consider it objectively.

In New York, where Bardamu is relatively free from anguish (no war as in Europe, no disease as in Africa, etc.), something new begins to plague him, eating away at his very fiber—solitude. He feels isolated in this vast land in which, he discovers, he is unable to communicate with anyone because he cannot speak English. Even when he sees Lola, who is now back in New York, and they talk together, no sooner does their conversation veer to unfamiliar subjects, people or things he has never experienced, than he feels brutally wrenched from the world he knows, and feelings of extreme loneliness again catapult him into a land of darkness, peopled with frightening monsters, ". . . a sort of sickly, terrifying collapse of the mind." [46]

Bardamu feels like an exile, a stranger. At thirty-seven years of age, he confesses, he is unable to face the emptiness of his life, the desertlike quality of what lives and breathes within him—that arid, unfruitful land which is his. Bardamu has to be on the move constantly, has to be distracted, in order to experience a semblance of peace. What Pascal said of seventeenth-century man can be applied to Bardamu: he is unable to control himself and to build from there. Bardamu states: "Truth is a pain which will not stop. And the truth of this world is to die." [47]

Bardamu chooses an "easy way out" of his troubled state—a land of fiction, specifically that of the movies, which he attends daily, like a drug addict. The movies are a release from the loneliness of his real world; they comfort and warm him.

> Then dreams waft upwards in the darkness to join the mirages of silver light. They are not quite real, the things that happen on the screen; they stay in some wide, troubled domain meant for the poor, for dreams and for dead men. You have to hurry to stuff yourself with these dreams, so as to get through the life which is waiting for you outside, once you've left the theater, so as to last through a few more days of this strife with men and things. You chose from among these dreams those that will warm your soul the most.[48]

The movies have a mysterious power over many people. Their concreteness works upon the viewer not only consciously or rationally but also, and quite directly, in his unconscious realm. Because of this immediacy, they have the power to become a direct experience and thus to have a powerful impact upon the psyche. When personal and intimate relationships are revealed on the screen, they act as a stimulant to the viewer's senses, revealing new dimensions and possibilities. As the viewer's emotions are aroused, his level of consciousness is lowered. Such an idea has been expressed by "European observers," writes Siegfried Kracauer: "In the theater I am always I, but in the cinema I dissolve into all things and beings." Viewed psychologically, such an experience indicates that a dissolution of the ego actually takes place. "If the cinema produces its effect, it does so because I identify myself with its image, because I more or less forget myself in what is being displayed on the screen. I am no longer in my own life. I am in the film projected in front of me." [49]

As consciousness is lowered, the mind becomes more receptive to the dream, to being wafted off into a land of wishful thinking. Like some drugs, cinema can have a stupefying effect. It can also become a habit and so make for loss of identity.[50] The philosopher Gabriel Marcel declared that "the movie goer finds himself in a state between waking and sleeping that favors hypnagogic fantasies." Sergei Lebovici, in his *Psychoanalysis and Cinema,* has noted that films are dreams and as such can encourage the viewer in his fantasies. What is particularly interesting about films is their appeal to collective dissatisfactions or disorders, their ability to satisfy mass desires and needs.

In Bardamu's case, films encourage his reveries. At night in his hotel room, when his loneliness becomes particularly unbearable, he indulges in daydreaming and uses films—and their lady protagonists in particular—as stimulants. Hugo von Hofmannsthal, in an article entitled *The Substitute for Dreams* (1921), declared that movies were made for those who could not get along in real life and needed fantasies in order to pursue their existence.[51] Whatever the merits of this statement as applied to moviegoers generally, it gets right to the heart of Bardamu's attitude.

Bardamu's loneliness is so intense that he tries to remember in his mind's eye the isolated facial expressions he has seen on the screen. Movies, though inanimate, have become real for him, giving rise to actual feelings, reactions, desires. The women he sees on the screen and their exclusively female qualities (relatedness, feeling, etc.) help him fill, at least temporarily, the void within his own being.

Bardamu's need for relatedness indicates his readiness to meet his first positive female figure. He is hungry to experience an aspect of his personality that has lain fallow for all too many years. Alcide stirred those tender aspects during the African venture; now Molly, in Detroit, will evoke similar sentiments.

Bardamu meets Molly when he takes a job with the Ford factory. She is a prostitute, yet a saintly being who displays kindness, altruism, self-abnegating qualities. She is Bardamu's equivalent of Mary, the Mother of Christ, and also another Mary, her counterpart, the Mary who prostituted herself all the way to Jerusalem. Molly is, then, a strange combination of saint and sinner, a composite of extremes, a type of woman attractive not only to Céline but to Genet, Mauriac, Claudel, and many another writer.

Molly, in the brothel, is paid a hundred dollars a day. Bardamu, employed at the Ford factory, is paid only six dollars. But Molly is generous and kind and keeps giving Bardamu money. In fact, she even suggests that he stop working, that she will undertake his support so that he can devote himself full-time to literature. She is the maternal, angelic woman, a superb creature despite her tainted and degrading role in society.

Bardamu has complete faith and confidence in her integrity, sincerity, and devotion. He loves her, he says, in his own way. This means that she is secondary in his life. Yet it does show a marked development in his personality, since up to now he has never felt the slightest admiration for any woman. It is as if his newly emerged feelings have been put to fruitful use and are helping him to relate to and understand his fellow creatures.

Still more important aspects of Bardamu's personality are being stirred. Because he feels love, hatred diminishes and anger virtually vanishes. He fears that he will hurt Molly if he leaves her, and yet he knows that eventually he will have to return to France and to his studies. As consciousness of his own acts begins to appear, as he begins to understand the meaning of give and take in a relationship between two people, he develops a sense of guilt.

What are the implications of guilt? The presence of guilt indicates notions of morality and ethos, the very attitudes that Bardamu had so willingly abandoned in the French military hospital and on shipboard. Bardamu is beginning to emerge from that twilight zone—that world of the primitive and of the adolescent, that undifferentiated realm of darkness—into the differentiated world of the discerning individual, where values can be experienced on a variety of levels.

Bardamu is now ready, in part, to face himself. This is evident in his desire to return to France and to resume his medical studies. A change in his view of the world seems to be taking place and it seems about time for the shadow-figure Robinson to emerge, for it is he who provokes such modifications. Sure enough, Robinson appears there in Detroit, working under false papers, employed in some shady business, and belonging to a "Foreign Legion of the Night." [52] The dark imagery always associated with Robinson reinforces his shadow function and the ambiguity and complexity of his nature. His presence fortifies Bardamu's decision to leave Molly and America. Bardamu no longer wants to live in the dark mysterious world that Robinson's shadow has cast over his life. Now that consciousness has emerged and his rational function has been stimulated, Bardamu wants to further his life's experience.

Escape is no longer the answer, he realizes. He knows what he wants. The fact that Bardamu had, as a youth, cried poverty that he had abandoned his medical pursuits, indicated an inability to face the problems confronting him in completing his studies and practicing medicine. After he returns to France he will be just as poor as he ever was, but he will be strong enough psychologically to settle down to work and study. An apocryphal saying of Jesus explains Bardamu's present situation: "If indeed thou knowest what thou doest, thou art blessed; but if thou knowest not, thou art cursed, and a transgressor of the law." [53]

With the coming of consciousness (feeling function, guilt), Bardamu's life begins to take on purpose and direction.

Bardamu in France: Christianity versus Society. In the final section of *Journey to the End of the Night,* Bardamu returns to France, finds a job, attends and is graduated from medical school, and practices medicine in Barenne-Rancy, a poor Parisian suburb. The variety of patients he treats and the people he meets socially are almost all representatives of decadent twentieth-century society—an indication, Céline intimates, of the failure of Christianity.

Like Nietzsche, Bardamu knows that the Christian precept "love thy neighbor as thyself" is impossible to accomplish in this world. Rather than admit to this, people prefer to give the impression of being holier than thou, at least on the outside. Such an attitude creates facades and makes for all manners of underhanded and hypocritical activity. Bardamu notices this dichotomy in many of his patients, that between the rigid moral codes they profess and put on public display and the viciousness they actually practice. Such cleavage within the personality can lead to extreme tension in some individuals, and to utterly destructive results in others, particularly if they are unaware of the cleavage.

What has society accomplished by erecting such high moral codes? "A denaturalization of natural values" and the "impoverishment of instinct." [54] When instinct is stifled, part of what belongs to man is muffled. Nietzsche declared, "We must liberate ourselves from morality in order to be able to live morally," and encouraged man to free himself from the bonds that were strangling him. "They will call you destroyers of morality, but you are only discoverers of yourselves." [55] When moral ideas become absolute, when they are codified and set down in a series of rigid formulas, instincts and drives are suppressed and man is rendered ineffective, crippled as surely as if his legs had been cut off. There he wobbles about, stunted in his outlook, unbalanced and unsteady in his ways, forever falling and bruising himself.[56]

What resulted from the cleavage between an idealization of moral values and a suppression of instinct? For Nietzsche, it brought about a "transvaluation of values," which meant that "when morality is sought for itself and is considered true, perfect, and good for the collective it may become immoral and evil." An example of this condition is basic to all religions, each one believing itself to be perfect, true, and good for the collective, and each intent upon remaining as is. Only decay can possibly emerge from such a situation.

Life is a growing and changing process and so are values. What might have been meaningful and responsive to people's needs two thousand years ago may not be applicable to the needs of people today. So far as Bardamu was concerned, religion as practiced in France in the 1930s was in no way compatible with the needs of the people. In fact, the church remained a bulwark against change. Since few adhered to its laws, save on the surface, it had become a simulacrum, a device behind which people masqueraded, pretended—and with dire results.

Several of the medical cases reported in *Journey to the End of the Night* must be singled out for discussion, not only in terms of Bardamu's activities but as evidence, in Céline's opinion, of the decay of Franco-Christian civilization.

One evening Bardamu makes a house call on a young girl who is hemorrhaging after a self-induced abortion. Unwilling to have the daughter committed to a hospital, as Bardamu strongly urges, the mother prefers risking her daughter's life to having the neighbors discover the reason for her hospitalization and think ill of the family. "I would die of shame," the mother keeps repeating. She is typical of those who are more concerned about appearing to adhere to a high moral credo than they are about life itself. But when Bardamu receives his fee for the house call, his annoyance at the mother's attitude is transformed into a smile.

Cases of sadism also enter the picture. People are tantalized by evil, incited to indulge in un-Christian activities, aroused by the punishment in store for them. Bardamu observes parents beating their ten-year-old daughter in order to become aroused sexually. First they tie the girl to a bed, then they whip her, then they make love.

Bardamu is himself a product of his environment, of society. When for example, he calls upon a family with an illegitimate infant, he maltreats the child. The parents are aghast and ask him to leave. Bardamu cannot account for his actions, nor does he really try.

Bardamu seems to have developed a devil-may-care attitude toward his patients. Most of the time, indeed, he seems uninvolved, objective, untouched, as if he cared not at all whether his patients lived or died, provided his fee is paid. He rarely if ever gives of himself to his patients, and only on occasion does he participate in their turmoil or develop any kind of pity for the destitute or the dying. He makes no attempt at heroism, no attempt ever to right a wrong. One wonders why he even bothered to study for his medical degree; certainly it was not out of any devotion to mankind! Indeed, in this respect he is comparable to the character Oblomov, in Goncharov's novel, who seems to be devoid of feeling for anyone save himself. Such beings are totally removed from the world of the suffering. Unlike the real scientist, who works long hours trying to discover ways to cure the sick, Bardamu functions, at best, routinely. Only once, and then only when it is too late, does he attempt to save the life of a boy, Bebert, who is dying from typhoid. He fails.

Bardamu is strictly an observer, forever on the outside looking in. He spends many of his moments condemning everything in sight: ". . . evil has become organized like war." He feels a great deal of pity for himself, but none for others. Even when he gets a job working in a sanitarium for tuberculars, he looks upon the inmates with anger and disgust, describing their coughing, their spittle, their emaciated condition, and their all-consuming desire to receive a pension from the government. Money is their only thought, all that keeps them alive.[57]

Bardamu is frequently annoyed with his patients, and most particularly those who do not pay him for his house calls. At times he refuses to go to certain homes unless he is assured of payment in advance. Moreover, he has little confidence in his capabilities as a doctor and confesses to himself that the only reason his services are called for, rather than those of another neighborhood physician, is because his fee is lower. Sometimes Bardamu is overwhelmed by feelings of revulsion when visiting certain homes; fleas crawl over his coat, toilets are flooded, leaving nauseating odors that permeate the buildings and are enough, when coupled with the cooking odors of stews, smoke, and garbage, to make anyone ill.

Bardamu's nonintervention policy vis-à-vis his patients comes across most forcefully in the Henrouille case. Madame Henrouille, tired of supporting her mother-in-law, convinces her husband that the older woman should be interned in a mental institution. She offers Bardamu a thousand francs to sign a paper attesting to the mother-in-law's insanity and committing her to an asylum. Bardamu is prepared to accept the offer when the mother-in-law discovers the plot and becomes belligerent. It is at this point that Robinson suddenly appears on the scene. Unbeknown to Bardamu, he is in need of a job and accepts Madame Henrouille's offer to murder her mother-in-law. He decides to set an explosive where the old woman is sure to walk. It will be called an accident.

Bardamu is not bothered by the immorality of the murder, but rather by Robinson's unexplained reappearance. Since we consider Robinson to be a shadow figure whose previous apparitions were catalyzing forces in Bardamu's life, one can understand Bardamu's dismay: "it was like a sort of illness getting hold of me again." [58]

Still more surprising is Robinson's attitude toward himself. Heretofore, he has been connected with illicit business ventures, shady enterprises. Killing does not disturb him on a conscious level. Yet he now complains of severe burning sensations in the stomach and chest, which give him a sensation of strangling. His discomfiture is real. Its origin is certainly psychological. Robinson is committing murder for money. His values, then, are wholly material. Such an attitude toward money has already been noted in Bardamu, though it is an attitude to which he certainly would not readily admit, and one that he tries to conceal. Unconsciously, Bardamu's materialism is projected onto the shadow figure, Robinson. It is the latter who is struggling to accept this aspect of himself. It creates such tension within him as to give him cramps. Dramatically speaking, Robinson's pain has still other ramifications: it may be looked upon as a prelude to his death: in the end he will be shot in the stomach, in the very part of the body about which he is now complaining.

When Bardamu tries to dissuade Robinson from going through with the murder, arguing that he will surely be caught, Robinson sneers: he is tired of life, he suffers from ennui and the automatism to which his existence has been reduced. Moreover, bourgeois life and an honest career are "business for the innocent." The boredom, the repetitious nature of life, are sentiments mouthed by Robinson but acutely felt by Bardamu, particularly after he opens his office and begins practicing medicine. It is not the poverty or the wretchedness of existence that pain Bardamu most profoundly, but rather a *spleen* of the very kind by which the poet Baudelaire was haunted: a disgust with routine and the impossibility of extracting oneself from a feckless and decomposing world.

The fact that the murder misfires and that Robinson is blinded in the attempt indicates that he (or Bardamu's shadow figure) has not yet come to grips with the decaying and withering elements within him; he has not as yet fully understood their function. Indeed, he is blinded to or by them.

When the explosive intended to kill the mother-in-law succeeds only in blinding Robinson, it forces him to experience intense suffering, to look within (since he can no longer see without), "to put some order into his pain." He is essentially a prisoner of his inner world, as Bardamu had been on board ship going to Africa. Just as a blind person compensates for his infirmity by developing other senses more fully, so Robinson's inner eye is compelled to work. Perhaps he may discern certain dangers involved in leading a peripheral existence. At any rate, he will pay for his ignorance as Oedipus did for his, though he will not necessarily earn redemption.

Robinson's suffering is so real that he weeps. He becomes a living sorrow. His anguish is "so enormous, so multiple" that he cannot understand or react to anything that does not have a direct bearing upon it. Reaching down into the profoundest layers within him, Robinson bridges a gap that has separated him from the rest of humanity up to now. In the primitive and transpersonal region that he has now tapped, the walls isolating him from others vanish, and a sense of solidarity and oneness comes over him—at least temporarily.

> He himself had come to the end of things. There wasn't anything you could tell him now. There is a moment when you are all alone by yourself and have come to the end of all that can happen to you. It's the end of the world. Unhappiness itself, your own misery, won't answer you now and you have to go back, among men, no matter where. One isn't difficult at moments like that, for even to weep you've got to get back to where everything starts, to where the others are.[59]

The important question arises as to how Bardamu reacts to Robinson's failure and to his blindness. A link between the two has already been established psychologically (Robinson as Bardamu's shadow figure); now it is to appear physically, as if Bardamu were vicariously living out or experiencing Robinson's anguish. During this period Bardamu can neither work nor sleep. Only when sick with a cold or when running a high fever can he begin to know some kind of beatitude; at such times a haze blankets his thoughts and dulls his senses, rendering him impervious to truth, fiction, right or wrong.

On one occasion, however, Bardamu does experience a sense of tranquillity: in a bistro in Paris when he hears a melody,[60] the same one he had heard when he was with Molly in the United States. His thoughts wander back to that "happy" period. A feeling of well-being suddenly invades him, distracting him from the crushing task of his present existence. Music, then, has touched his soul, has stirred all the things that Molly represented: tenderness, solicitude, motherliness, affection. At this moment Bardamu no longer feels the sting of loneliness and the absurdity of life.

One is struck by the resemblance of this musical incident to Sartre's description of a similar experience in *Nausea.* Sartre's protagonist, Roquentin, in the midst of despair, hears an American jazz singer bellow out her tune. His emotions are aroused and with them feelings of excitement emerge, a desire to fulfill a destiny by transforming feelings into concrete form—the work of art. Bardamu's experience, however, fosters only evanescent sentiments, which soon fade into oblivion, to be felt no more.

Bardamu suddenly decides to visit Robinson in Toulouse, whence he was sent to recuperate—along with the woman he had tried to murder. It is at the end of this visit that Bardamu becomes no longer the passive observer to a murder, but instrumental in its accomplishment. He is about to leave for the train that is to take him back to Paris when he hears a terrible thump, as though someone has fallen down a flight of stairs, then a scream. Rather than answer the call for help, he runs to the railroad station. He reasons that he would miss his train if he were to stop and offer his services. Once back in Paris he learns that Madame Henrouille's mother-in-law has died in a fall.

The question arises as to why Bardamu failed to answer the call of distress. His fear of missing the train is indeed a poor excuse; there would always be another. He did not look back simply because he wanted the old woman to die. If we consider the mother-in-law symbolically, we may conclude that so long as the unproductive, decayed elements that she represented are permitted to live, Bardamu, who projected them onto her, must feel trapped, hunted, emotionally impoverished. But if he rids himself (and society as well, if the mother-in-law is considered as a collective figure) of these aspects, self-development and progress (in terms of himself and society) may take place.

The murder of the mother-in-law does arouse notions of guilt in Bardamu. Frequently such feelings are accompanied by increased consciousness and further self-realization. Had Bardamu been able to accept his guilt, to live with it and experience it as a productive and positive force in his life, his future might have taken a turn for the better: *sine affictione nulla salus* (there is no salvation without pain).[61] Such is not Bardamu's fate, since he rejects guilt, putting it out of his mind shortly.

Bardamu is never really able to come to terms with his personal evil (his shadow), as manifested in Robinson or as a collective image in society. In Joseph Conrad's novel *The Heart of Darkness* one sees the dangers involved when an individual does not come to grips with his shadow, when struggle or fight does not ensue.

When Bardamu decides to become associated with a mental institution in Paris he is, as it were, closing a circle. It must be recalled that after the war episode, early in the novel, Bardamu was a mental patient. Whether he was merely playing at insanity or was really insane is a moot question. Though he assumes a different position now in his capacity as a doctor, still there are moments, he confesses, when the dividing lines between sanity and insanity are difficult to determine. The cries, grimaces, contortions, conversations, screams of the inmates do affect him—yet there are times when he cannot distinguish their antics from his own nightmares, fantasies, and hallucinations.

> I hovered on the dangerous outskirts of the mad, on their border line, so to speak, always being pleasant-spoken with them which it was my nature to be. I wasn't tottering but all the time I felt I was in danger, as if they were artfully luring me into the purlieus of their unknown city. A city whose streets became softer and softer as you advanced between their slimy houses, the windows melting away, that would not shut, midst dubious rumors. The doors, the ground slipping, and still you were seized by the desire to go a little further, so as to know if you would have the strength even so to recover your reason. . . . Among the ruins, reason soon turns to vice, like good humor and sleepiness with neurasthenics.[62]

What the insane represent for him is the vast world of the imagination, the realm in which thoughts know no boundaries, where time and space are infinite, where reality is the product of one's creation. The fact that Bardamu is tantalized by such a domain, that he succumbs to its riches and excitement, indicates a weakening of his ego and the chaos within his unconscious. Doctors and nurses in institutions do sometimes succumb to the fantasies of their patients; such cases are far from being unique in medical history. Bardamu frequently sees himself slipping into their realm. He understands their world as an extension of his own. As such, it is neither restrained nor limited by either conventions or morality.

During his stay in Toulouse, Robinson becomes engaged to Madelon. It is she who cares for him there and, when he is blind, devotes her time and attention to him. He must feel some kind of rapport with her, since he asks her to marry him. But when his sight returns and she is no longer of any use to him, he breaks the engagement. She is so irate she vows revenge. Robinson flees Toulouse and asks Bardamu for asylum. Weeks pass. Finally Madelon discovers Robinson's whereabouts and one evening, when she, Robinson, Bardamu, and his girl friend are returning in a taxi after enjoying an evening on the town, she shoots him in the stomach and disappears into the night.

What has Madelon killed? Everything that would have represented stability through marriage: bourgeois life. As a shadow figure, Robinson was Bardamu's last tie to the stable and routine aspect of existence. It is also the last appearance of his shadow as a catalyzing force. After Robinson's funeral, Bardamu closes the circle.

> Try as I might to lose my way, so as not to find myself face to face with my own life, I kept coming up against it everywhere, I met myself at every turn. My aimless pilgrimage was over. Let others carry on the game. The world had closed in.[63]

Bardamu has chosen the world of the insane, a type of inner sanctum where values are never absolute and conditions are forever subject to extremes, where worlds of all types merge and converge. From this vantage point, he feels, he will be capable of scrutinizing "a truly appalling, awful world."[64] He will play a double game, observing his sordid surroundings—worlds in collision—and yet keeping his distance. Power must have also entered into the picture since, as the institution's head, he will be master of the domain of the insane, its ruler.

Bardamu's vision of life does not end here. Indeed, he continues to struggle with his own being.

> How many lives should I have had to live to get myself an idea stronger than anything else in all the world? There was no way of telling! It was all no good! My own idea, the ideas I had, roamed loose in my mind with plenty of gaps between them; they were like little tapers, flickering and feeble, shuddering all through life in the midst of a truly appalling, awful world.[65]

Journey to the End of the Night presents an extraordinary portrait of the anti-hero, of the void in which he flounders, of his inability to relate to others or to sustain friendships, of his ineluctable anguish, of his longing for escape into the twilight—the night of the insane.

The picaresque form, with its loosely constructed episodes, is the perfect vehicle through which to express Bardamu's sense of restlessness, his utter dissatisfaction with prevailing social, economic, and philosophical conditions, his own directionless existence. The grotesque distortions and exaggerations, also characteristic of the picaresque form, point up Bardamu's own hatred of and despair with humanity and its condition —and his own condition.

It is Céline's style, perhaps, that is one of the most remarkable aspects of *Journey to the End of the Night.* A discussion of this style will be given in subsequent chapters as it evolves into something unique. Suffice it to say here that despite the episodic plot, which permits Céline's anti-hero to hop around from continent to continent, from incident to incident, the novel has continuity and structure. Céline's "surrealism," or the contents freed from his unconscious that he offers his readers, is given form and molded into comprehensible and rational patterns. Moreover, the autobiographical aspects of *Journey to the End of the Night* are quite apparent. The landscapes and geographical settings of Europe, Africa, and America are authentically realistic. The artist, nevertheless, has his own way of viewing reality, of transmuting it through the wizardry of his pen to suit his own concepts, of imbuing each tree, for example, each patch of sky, each body of water, with its own overtones, rhythms, and sensations, its eternal and cosmic qualities. The forest in the African sequence becomes a land heavy with symbolism, pulsating with mystery, magic, and omens, all focusing upon the protagonist, arousing his emotions or crushing his spirits. A leaf, a blade of grass, a mountain lake are expressions and manifestations of feelings, emotions, adding a whole new dimension to the characters and to the novel as a whole. Since sensations cannot be clearly described in terms of themselves, they must always be compared; metaphors, therefore, are *de rigueur,* and when handled by a poet of Céline's magnitude, a leaf with its textures, its veins or nerves, a blade of grass with its prickly fibers, or a tinder box bursting into flame—all arouse concomitant emotions within readers and protagonists alike, compelling them to recoil with horror or to be drawn toward the hypnotic image.

Céline's style is comparable to a musical scale: it ranges from harsh, strident, tonalities to the more velvety and harmonious ones. Repetitions, onomatopoeias, interjections, alliterations hammer out moods of excitement, humor, aggressiveness, anger, conflict, and rage. The sonorities, as expressed through the visual images, shock and amaze like a burst of rifle fire, strike the reader with their piercing noise, their scorching sensations, like an exploding blast furnace. The reader's complacency is broken. His pat answers to problems, his lofty set of values, no longer seem to be the answer. What he had thought to be secure and steady has withered away. Institutions and people alike have become a series of facades.

Though *Journey to the End of the Night* is essentially a tragic work, humor is not lacking. It alleviates the novel's extreme pessimism, through contrast, reinforcing the mood when returning to the macabre. Céline's humor is of a very special type: lugubrious, cruel—black. It ranges from the laughter of the sadist to the witty statements enunciated by a man observing a degenerate society. Every now and then the peal of cackling laughter is inserted, discharged by a dissatisfied individual hating all in sight. There are no healthy belly laughs. Céline's humor is always tinged with acerbity, despair. It is an instrument used to perfect advantage, a weapon designed to mock and deride humanity—like the gargoyles on Notre Dame in Paris, ridiculing and defying the world they look down upon.

Journey to the End of the Night may be viewed as a type of battlefield, with its volleys of cannon fire and its splattered blood. It is essentially a destructive work, intended to break man of his arrogant ways, to dislodge him from his artificially constructed and illusorily secure plateau, which is, according to Céline, Christian society of the twentieth century. Once such a religious force was a fecundating agent; now it is a wobbly structure with little or nothing to hold it up.

Journey to the End of the Night, published in 1932, was an immediate success. In fact, it almost won the coveted Goncourt Prize. Critics such as Pierre Descaves, of *L'Avenir,* compared it to a burning red pepper with an exotic flavor, offering the reading public a series of audacious and "surprisingly real" images.[66] Ramon Fernandez, in *Marianne,* commented on the novel's "direct" approach. Gille Anthelmar, in *La Presse,* spoke of it as a "hallucinatory work." André Rousseaux, in *Candide,* labeled it a "literature of despair,"[67] Georges Bernanos said it was "comparable to the breaking of a wave in the black of night."[68] Not all critics wrote favorably, however. Henri Bidou, in *La Revue de Paris,* complained of the novel's monotony. Pierre Audiat, in *L'Européen,* dismissed it as a piece of "immense rot."[69] Henri de Régnier, in *Le Figaro,* found only "a satire devoid of lyricism and wit."[70] But Claude Lévi-Strauss, in *L'Etudiant socialiste,* considered Céline's work a revolt against all types of oppression and injustice.[71] Albert Thibaudet, in *Le Reveil de la Marne,* admired this novel because it expanded the scope of the novel in general by including topics heretofore considered unliterary.

When a literary work attempts to attack and destroy, repercussions are bound to occur. Céline would not escape this fate. It crushed him. He would, however, retaliate with all the force and vigor of his torrential personality, and with sufficient armaments at his disposal: anger, hostility, hatred.

3

THEATER/BALLET

Man is subject to innumerable pains and sorrows by the very condition of humanity, and yet, as if nature had not sewn evils enough in life, we are continually adding grief to grief and aggravating the common calamity by our cruel treatment of one another.

JOSEPH ADDISON, *The Spectator*

IN 1928, BEFORE STARTING WORK ON *Journey to the End of the Night,* Céline wrote a play, *The Church,* which was not published until 1933, for reasons to be discussed during the course of this chapter.

Céline was much attracted to the theater. It could be said that he considered this art as Shakespeare had his: life is a stage and each human being is acting his way across it in a series of lies and deceptions. Unlike Shakespeare, however, Céline was no playwright. His drama, if one can call it that, is strictly a "thesis" work. It revolves around one or two central political, philosophical, and economic themes to which the rest of the spectacle is subservient. There is little or no action or conflict within the heart of the protagonists, no psychological study, no character delineation.

The Church may be classified as a bad "naturalist" drama. Theatrical naturalism, it will be recalled, had flourished in the late nineteenth century, when André Antoine founded his Théâtre Libre (1887) and proclaimed his love for all that was "real" in life. When Antoine sought to bring people face to face with themselves and with their environment, he was creating something new and timely for his age. He understood that the theatrical arts must follow the patterns of reality, that actors and actresses, if they were to mirror life with fidelity, had to walk and talk and comport themselves on stage as people did in shops, on the streets, on trains, and in their homes. He created a "peephole theater" that permitted audiences to partake of a slice of life. He favored a "photographic" theatrical reality and almost always used real-life props in his productions. He had a real flair for the theater; he burgeoned with ideas. Céline took Antoine's vehicle, a bit shopworn by this time, and attempted to use it to serve his own ends. The attempt, *The Church,* lacks imagination and fervor and displays an extraordinary ignorance of dramatic techniques. It is a heavy, dull, cold work that might have been more effective, perhaps, as an essay.

There are five acts. The first takes place in Africa where Bardamu, a physician, has been sent by the League of Nations to study epidemics. With his colleagues, also sent by the organization, he talks about tropical diseases, the heat, drinking, the degenerate colonists, and the blacks. At the end of the act, one of the doctors, who has been lying on a bed throughout, is discovered to be dead!

Act II takes place on Broadway, at the offices of the Quick Theater, directed by a dancer, Vera Sterne. Bardamu, now in New York, feels he would like to write a play. The telephone rings incessantly throughout the scene, interrupting the dialogue and supposedly indicating the frantic atmosphere characteristic of Broadway. The conversations revolve around acting, love, money, and general boredom.

In Act III Bardamu is in Switzerland at the League of Nations, an organization dominated by Jews: Judenzweck & Company, and by Mosaic and Moise, directors of the various committees. These men conspire to become rich and powerful by converting monies from one currency to another.

Acts IV and V take place in Paris, where Bardamu is practicing medicine in a bistro. Janine, a young girl of great charm and purity but hunchbacked and lame, is in love with Bardamu. He cannot be attracted to her because she is not physically beautiful. The play ends as Elisabeth, to whom Bardamu is attracted, dances to the accompaniment of a jazz song, *No More Worries.*

Céline's title, *The Church,* the "assembly," has symbolic significance. The word may denote an assembly of doctors (Act I), actors and actresses (Act II), League members (Act III), or of patients and people in general (Acts IV and V). At times these various groups represent something artificial and hypocritical in society. The idea of assembly, however, implies a collectivity and as such is considered intellectually inferior by Céline, who always associated the collective with greed, matter, lucre. It is the collective, the masses, that decides society's rules and regulations, codes of ethics, and patterns of behavior. For just this reason civilization finds itself in a precarious condition.

Bardamu castigates the very principle upon which society was founded, that production is moral and pleasure is immoral.

> To be bored working at an arid job is productive, therefore, to be bored is moral. The Protestants better than anyone else in the world know how to be bored, therefore, they are moral and productive and dominate the world.[1]

From the earliest times, he says, such a view was adopted; he gives the Book of Genesis as an example. To work, to fulfill obligations, to pursue a given task, according to Christian morality, is to follow the righteous way, though such a path might generate feelings of ennui.

Since the "assembly" imposes rigid codes of action, compelling one to limit one's field of activity, such a situation is anathema to Bardamu's character. He is an individualist. He denies being an anarchist, though he is accused of being one by the other protagonists. "The real anarchists are the rich . . ."[2]

As for Céline himself, he too was far from being an anarchist at this period. In December, 1932, he had gone to Germany to study labor conditions and he wrote an article, "To kill Unemployment Will They Kill the Unemployed?," published in *La République* (March 19, 1933), asserting that unemployment and starvation were the results of the "grotesque spirit of anarchy" that reigned in Germany at that time and that had to be put to an end.

> The future? Perhaps a dictator now out of work in Hitler's entourage will finally organize this anarchical group of wretched people and bring about a reasonable level of stability.[3]

Céline was advocating strong-arm methods, dictatorial methods, to repress chaos. The revolutionary spirit, which he had condemned on political grounds in his thesis on Semmelweis, he considered damaging to society. Yet paradoxically, as we have noted, he still supported rebellious spirits in creative endeavors. What Céline had not yet thought out, perhaps, at least not sufficiently, were the lines of demarcation: where did creativity end and political engagement begin? Could one exist without the other?

The collective that Céline wanted suppressed, after studying conditions in Germany, and to which he alludes in *The Church,* is that group, the masses, whose intelligence level is rather low and whose affectivity is frighteningly high. It is the masses who mouth slogans, sing anthems, swallow anything and everything—like bottle-fed infants. Large groups can easily be swayed, after which they indulge in flag-waving, image-creating, idol-seeking. As for the ideals they are eager to further in society, these last as long as the energy generated by those who seek to gain from them. The masses venerate anything and everything that smacks of so-called morality and productivity.[4]

> There is no object in this world which could not become a subject for veneration and I am certain that there are people who have loved shit since there are some who eat it.[5]

Though society proclaims its own virtue, it is in reality corrupt and degenerate. If such is Bardamu's opinion of the collective, then where do his ideals reside? Certainly not with the masses, the poor, and the destitute, the wretched of the earth, for whom he said so many times that he felt such compassion. They are, to his way of thinking, robots, incapable of individual thought, following ideas as a dead leaf is thrust here and there by a brisk wind.

Céline offers no answers. In fact, *The Church* is merely a preview of what he would say so brilliantly in *Journey to the End of the Night:* anti-colonial feelings, man's obsession with money, fear of death, hypocritical attitudes toward his fellow man, alcoholism as a way of life, disease, etc.

From a philosophical point of view then, *The Church* offers nothing new. As a theatrical vehicle, it is also a failure. In Act I, for example, the fact that a man lies dead throughout the scene, unbeknown to the doctors present, is unintentionally ludicrous. The conversations about the colonists and their degenerate ways are tendentious and dull. By way of comparison, Genet's depiction of French colonists in his play *The Screens* infuses life into their deceit and viciousness, their ignorance and pettiness, making for the drama's very blood.

Equally uninteresting and superficial is Céline's depiction of Broadway in Act II. The constantly ringing telephones, the prosaic conversations enunciated by would-be actors, actresses, and comedians are simply dull. It is one thing to be compelled to listen to such conversations in real life, quite another to be forced to watch them on stage or to read them in a book. A playwright must either add to reality or stylize it in such a way as to breathe life into his drama, make it sparkle, dance, and energize, infuse it with a sense of mystery and inspire theatrical illusions.

Act III has been described by some as "Ubuesque," in that its humor is piquant, its caricature incisive and jocular. This is to overstate the position. The scene is neither humorous nor original. It is a caricature of certain aggressive and acquisitive types. Its impact, however, is not droll, but rather pitiful, because the portrayals are more expressions of Céline's personal dislike of Jews than the creation of living theatrical characters. The artist has vanished and been replaced by a man spewing hate.

The three Jews depicted are Polish. They are the typical stereotyped Jew à la Shylock, Fagan, and the like. They wear thick glasses and heavy black coats; they have large hooked noses; they speak with great prudence and look about furtively as they do so; they are deceitful, hypocritical, and conniving.

When Bardamu lashes out at the Jews in this play, an inner glow seems to possess him. He appears to be experiencing some kind of catharsis. Hatred is always a most efficacious manner of ridding oneself, temporarily at least, of whatever is bothering one. It is a way of alleviating one's own feelings of self-rejection.

Whom is Céline destroying by demolishing the Jew? Symbolically, he is doing away with the martyrs, the Semmelweises of the world. People persecuted for their ideas and for their individuality are the very ones that Céline tried to protect, to encourage, to extoll, in his doctoral dissertation. Semmelweis is a martyr type; he is hounded by Viennese doctors whom Céline considers deceitful, ugly, narrow-minded, powerful beings, all of whom exhibit great hubris. When Céline wrote his dissertation he identified with the Hungarian doctor as against those who would destroy him, those who considered him a threat. In *The Church*, the tide has evidently turned. Confusion has set in in Céline's mind—an absence of clarity, perhaps, concerning the issues at stake. When impulses come to the fore, rational thinking must take a back seat. Philosophically, *The Church* is a chaos of confusion. Is Céline siding with the majority or the minority? Is he an anarchist, despite his denials? Is he for dictatorship? Is he compassionate? Does he serve the poor, or would he prefer to do away with them? Except for his hatred of Jews, there is simply no clear-cut point of view in this play.

The most impressive aspect of *The Church* is the interest Céline displays in the art of the dance. Poets such as Gautier, Baudelaire, Valéry, and nations such as the Greeks and the Romans, venerated physical form in motion, that aspect of cosmic harmony in which they sought to participate.

Céline had a veritable one-man cult of beauty, on the one hand, and an affinity for its opposite, disease, decomposition and death, on the other. It is through beauty—not through knowledge or through science—Bardamu exclaims, that man can escape his fear of death, can relieve himself of the drudgery that is life.

> Science is really an attempt to understand, and if one wants to understand so much, I have come to the conclusion that one is afraid of everything. . . We, we are terribly frightened from birth until death; and this never leaves us.[6]

It is, then, the carapace that counts for Céline—the shell, the outward manifestation of beauty, the purity of Greek line as depicted in statues. For this reason Bardamu cannot look upon Janine, the lame hunchback, with any feeling of warmth, even though she is pure, honorable, gentle, and kind, and expresses her love for him. Janine questions him: "You really need . . . just like everyone else, someone to love in this world . . ."[7] Bardamu denies his need to love anyone. He does not care about love, he claims, nor does he want to be loved. "What use is it to be loved?," he replies. "Will it prevent me from having cancer of the rectum, if I'm going to have it!" For Bardamu, love never enters the picture. Only the outer core of the human being, the visual counts: "One knows, at least, that beauty is going to die, and in this manner one knows that it exists . . ."[8]

The history of *The Church* is interesting in that it reveals certain Célinian characteristics. To whom did Céline chose to show this play once completed? To his superior at the clinic in which he was employed, a Doctor Rajchman, a Jew of Polish origin. Indignant, as could have been expected, Rajchman saw to it (though this was never proven) that Céline was relieved of his position. The dramatist opened his own office shortly thereafter on the outskirts of Paris. Céline's growing paranoia was to make itself felt from here on out. He was convinced a plot had been leveled against him by Jews in general, and that they possessed some "mysterious" and "occult" power that would see to his destruction. Intent upon making a career for himself in the literary world, he decided to gain his ends through hypocrisy, as Bardamu would do so successfully on two occasions in *Journey to the End of the Night.* Thus Céline deleted all anti-Semitic remarks from his next work, *Journey to the End of the Night.* Success first, he must have thought, then rout the enemy at the proper moment.[9]

After publication, *The Church* was offered to both Louis Jouvet and Charles Dullin, two of the finest directors of the day, both of whom judged it "unplayable." *The Church* was produced only once, on December 4, 1936, at the Théâtre des Célestins in Lyon by a troupe of amateurs. When Céline wrote to Milton Hindus, eleven years later, he spoke of this production as being "a flop" and admitted that his five-hour play could only be produced by a "prodigious director," if it were to come across. Céline never saw—or never admitted—that he had written a bad play. The blame was always to rest on "the other."

BALLET

Céline, as we have seen, was always drawn to physical beauty, particularly the grace of a body on stage. Dancers, moreover, had always played an important part in his personal life. Elisabeth Craig, for example, to whom he had dedicated his first novel, was an American dancer with whom he had lived from 1926 to 1930. Later, he would marry a dancer. The dance was in his blood.

Several twentieth-century authors have also been inspired to write ballets, most notably Jean Cocteau *(Parade)* and Jean Genet *(Adame Mirror).* Introduced into France by the Italianate Queen Catherine de Médicis, ballet had long been a popular form of entertainment. During the late Renaissance and the Classical period in France, it became a highly elaborate art, with enormous sets, beautiful costumes, and (frequently) weighty and complicated scenarios. In the period after the Revolution ballet became an adjunct of opera. Contemporary French ballet, influenced by Sergei Diaghilev's Russian ballet, has become a synthesis of classic and modern dance forms, ranging from pure dance, without a dramatic plot or incident, to dance drama with fully developed characters and plots.

It was the Dionysian side of dancing, not its Apollonian aspect, that most appealed to Céline. To understand Céline's view one must be acquainted with its opposite.

The soul of dancing, according to the Apollonians (of whom Paul Valéry was representative), resides in pure thought. Mathematical precision, the spirit of perfection, technical prowess, and agility are to be harmoniously blended into a single unique spectacle. In Valéry's dialogue *The Soul and Dance* he depicts a group of exquisitely formed young dancers entering upon the stage in a series of sculptural poses, withdrawing after performing their spacial designs, and returning moments later on tiptoes, extending their alabaster-like legs in rhythmic sequences, in perfect harmony and balance.[10]

> One of pink coral, and bending curiously, blows into an enormous shell.
> The very long flutist with tapered thighs . . . extends her elegant foot, while the toe beats the measure.[11]

Plato, it will be recalled, would have banished all orgiastic dance from his ideal republic, where only spectacles reflecting inner joy in life, physical harmony, balance, and moderation were to be permitted. When dance is executed to perfection, when its soul glows, it can lead to self-illumination. Socrates, a participant in Valéry's dialogue, declares: "The more I look . . . at this inexpressible dancer, the more deeply I experience the marvels within me." [12] Artfully accomplished, the dance leads to expanded consciousness: "I found myself illuminated in a way that I could never have known in the presence of my soul alone . . .," [13] muses Phaedrus, another participant in the dialogue. Dance has yet other attributes, which Valéry describes in another essay, *Philosophy and the Dance.* It permits flights into time/space.

> The Dance is an art deduced from life itself, since it is only the action of the entire human body; but action transposed into a world, into a type of space-time, which is no longer really the same as that of practical life.[14]

Céline viewed dance in an entirely different manner. The aesthetic appeal was there, to be sure, but it was its Dionysian side that attracted him most. Dancing must titillate the senses, must sexually arouse. In *The Church,* for example, at the end of the drama, Elisabeth dances nude on stage, and there are also nude dancers in Act II. It is the orgiastic, frenetic aspect of this art, its erotico-mystical realm, that entranced Céline. For this reason Vera, a dancer in *The Church*, says to Bardamu "as long as you live, you will always try to find the answer to the secrets of the world in between women's thighs!" [15]

The sensations aroused when watching such dancing mesmerized Céline. Feelings of power and intoxication overcame him, as if he had drunk of some exotic libation. What Nietzche wrote of dance in his *Attempt at Self-Criticism* could well be applied to Céline:

> Lift up your hearts, my brothers, high, higher! And neither forget the legs.Lift up also your legs, ye good dancers, and better still: let ye also stand on your heads! [16]

The antirational side of dancing—the very opposite of what Valéry saw in this art—beguiled Céline. To arouse the inner world, to becloud judgment, to incite the instincts, to stir what is most archaic and primitive in man—such is the goal of dancing. The inner beauty, the product of control, the soul of dancing that encouraged contemplation and for which Valéry yearned, was at the opposite pole of what Céline sought: dynamism, eroticism, sensationalism, beauty. Balance for the Appollonian is "an intuition of the world of ideas." [17] For Céline, dancing is a *sacrificium intellectus*. It spurs him on like a drug. It excites him. It is a catalyzer, a force necessary for survival. It is a means of adventure, danger, an open door to a trancelike state leading to the unknown, to the very mystery of life. It implies freedom of movement, release from constricting forces, life.

Céline's first ballet, *The Birth of a Fairy (La Naissance d'une fée)*, was completed in 1932 but not published until 1959. Céline had hoped that it would be performed at the Theater Marinski in Leningrad during his visit to Russia. It was not, however, for reasons unknown.

Judging by *The Birth of a Fairy*, Céline was already a master of the ballet form. He was capable of altering moods at will, of using the entire stage area with exciting sculptural effects. Space tingles and crackles, virtually coming to life. Evil and goodness confront each other, as do the material and the ethereal, matter and spirit, realism and idealism. There are no half measures in this ballet, no calm, no peace; only tempestuous, violent, volatile sequences.

There are eight tableaux in *The Birth of a Fairy*. The action takes place during the reign of Louis XV. The background is a wooded area filled with rocks, crags, rivers, a clearing. Elfs, wood nymphs, goblins, forest sprites all bounce about with unremitting joy. Evelyn and her fiancé, the Poet, are the center of attention. Suddenly, the merrymaking comes to a halt. Animosity takes over as gypsies, farmers, animals all crowd around the various merchants selling their wares. For some reason a fight ensues and a gypsy's table is overturned. She curses, wrongly, both Evelyn and the Poet. Nature unleashes Evelyn's anger at the gypsy's unjust accusation: a storm bursts. The crowd disperses, boisterously. The sorceress dances with her friends: thunder, lightning, rain flood the stage.

A few weeks go by and another fair takes place. Mephisto is present in all his grandeur. The Poet has quite forgotten his Evelyn. He seeks out the other beautiful girls who are dancing about. He dedicates a poem to one of them. The husbands present are all bewitched by the grace, charm, and exquisite beauty of the female apparitions. Death enters. Evelyn is fascinated by this figure and dances with it. The sprites watch Evelyn with despair in their hearts. They help her by giving her a golden ring that makes her the finest dancer of them all. As Evelyn dances in the most extraordinary manner, the other girls grow jealous of her skill, and one of them stabs her in the back. The sprites mourn her death. According to a legend, however, if three "moon rays" drop on the forehead of a virgin in love, she will come to life as a fairy. This happens. Evelyn is now a fairy and as such visits her Poet love, who is enchained in the Devil's castle. She frees him and he seeks to love her again. But such a relationship is impossible: she is no longer carnally attracted to people. She has entered another domain and cannot be reached by any mortal. As Evelyn fades from view, the Poet despairs. He sits on a rock near the water's edge and there begins writing his masterpiece, singing his unrequited love for her.

The Birth of a Fairy is a charming work. The ethereal is represented in diaphonous images. This ballet also includes the chaotic characteristics to which man—and Céline in particular—is prey: jealousy, infidelity, anger, revenge, love, poetry. Evelyn, as representative of a certain type of woman—the fine, the ethereal, the pure at heart—seeks a male counterpart. The Poet, on the other hand, is incapable of prolonged feelings of love. He is in love with beauty in general, not with individuals. Only after his love has been lost, only in sorrow, can his great poem be written.

Certainly the ideas enunciated in this ballet were far from original. The Romantic poets, such as Alfred de Musset in his famous series of poems *The Nights,* had said the same things countless times—that only out of suffering and anguish can the poet create his masterpiece. Yet this ballet is fascinating as a vehicle through which Céline could display his gracious, spiritual side, in which love takes on a certain meaning, at least in terms of the woman. It is only in his ballets, however, that this aspect of his personality will be revealed. Rarely, if ever, did he express it in his novels.

In the ballet, evil is the victor. In life, when beauty and love are within reach, they lose their fascination and cease to be activating forces. At least for the Poet in the ballet, once the object of his longing is out of his grasp, it takes on added allurement. Evelyn gleams and sparkles because she has entered a divine realm from which ugliness, death, and the world of matter have been banished. It is this realm alone that remains the eternal source of inspiration for the Poet.

Man lives in the domain of matter. He cannot penetrate the kingdom of the divine. Mortals cannot cope with the mystery of life. When Evelyn is given the secret of the dance, she performs as if in a mad whirl; color seems to float about in masses of gauze, gestures, and movements twist and turn like vortexes, expressing the very notions of life itself. But Evelyn is punished for her transgression, though it was not of her doing; she has attempted to compete with the gods, and such hubris must be punished. Man must know his place.

Van Bagaden, Céline's second ballet, was written in 1933 or thereabouts but not published until 1937. Céline was under the impression, somehow, that this ballet, along with *The Birth of a Fairy,* would be presented at the Theater Marinski in Leningrad, but it was not.

The ballet takes place in Antwerp and was inspired by Céline's trip to that city. The opening scene is reminiscent of a Flemish painting: the sea in the background mirrors the animation, the noise, the activity taking place on the quays. A whole group of dockers emerges, open cargoes are carried here and there, lovely girls fill the stage. In contrast to gleeful youth, Old Age, in the form of a semi-invalid shopkeeper, known as the "tyrant of the seas," is also present. Boats carrying gold and exotic wares fill the imagination The Old Man, who personifies sadness, possessiveness, and decadence, is juxtaposed with youth, in the form of his employee, Peter, who is excited about life and his future work.

Céline introduces us again to the antagonistic tendencies with which life is replete: old age, standing for greed, destruction, and decay; youth, representing glee, abandon, and independence. Céline's choice of the port of Antwerp as his setting —Antwerp, with its clouds, its winds, and the sun breaking through every now and then, bathing man's earthly antics in an outer wordly light, injecting an aura of semi-illusion and mystery into the ballet—reflects his preoccupation with the dichotomy in nature.

Céline would return to ballet every now and then, but it was never as satisfying a form for him as the novel. The novel, perhaps, was the only genre able to absorb the hatred he felt in his heart and soul—his only real means of catharsis.

4

DEATH ON THE INSTALLMENT PLAN

> Magnificent. Ferocious. He's got more dynamite in him than Hitler ever had. It's permanent hatred—for the whole human species.
>
> HENRY MILLER, writing of Céline in *A Private Correspondence. Lawrence Durrell and Henry Miller*

THE MORE CÉLINE SMARTED OVER SOME OF THE NEGATIVE CRITICISMS of *Journey to the End of the Night,* and over the fact that no well-known director had seen fit to produce *The Church,* the more his hostility grew and the more alienated from society he felt. In his next novel, *Death on the Installment Plan* (1936), he seems to aim his arrows at society in general. In it he demonstrates in dramatic form how parents and society can mangle and very nearly cripple a child, if not physically, then psychologically.

Life is never simple, however, for the man who seeks to vent his spleen, who seeks to speak the truth as he sees it. Céline was certainly aware of this, and for this reason he worried about the success of his latest literary endeavor. Far more outspoken than *Journey to the End of the Night,* his *Death on the Installment Plan* is replete with insidious images depicting man's cruel, rapacious, and vicious nature. This slang-studded novel is a perpetual barrage of hate; it is filled with invectives, epithets, and sordid pornographic descriptions. How would the rather sedate Parisian reading public receive such a work? Would this novel eat into, tear down, or simply offend the highly moral sets of ethics that individuals had established for themselves? Céline had to wait and see.

Though death is of course a major theme in *Death on the Installment Plan,* the novel concerns *life* and, in particular, the resiliency of an adolescent boy in warding off forces that are bent upon his physical and psychological destruction. The notion of death takes on a variety of meanings in this novel, depending upon the protagonist's state of mind. Sometimes it is to be feared; at other times, when despair sets in, it is something to be longed for, a time of rest after a wretched and unpleasant existence, a counterpoise, an outlet, a goal. "Here we are, alone again. It's all so slow, so heavy, so sad . . . I'll be old soon. Then at last it will be over." [1]

Other themes are interwoven into the fabric of this tapestry-like novel: parent/child relationships, the sordidness and vice of pre-World War I Paris. Céline's approach is totally different from that of the naturalists such as Zola and the brothers Goncourt. Their descriptions of wretched neighborhoods and a seamy population are scientifically precise and objectively detailed. Céline creates his forceful and overpowering atmosphere of doom as a painter would, with heavy and incisive brush strokes in the manner of a Franz Kline, with the speed and turmoil of the action painters, and with the ebullience of a Wilhelm de Kooning.

Death on the Installment Plan is an expression of Céline's own hatred and hostility. In part a satire, it is a grotesque novel marked with bitterness, coldness, cruelty, and the grin of tragic laughter. Each of these features is fleshed out on both emotional (rage, passion) and physical planes (nausea, vomiting, excrement). Nausea, vertigo, and vomiting of the most violent kind are described with fluoroscopic vision. The preoccupation, the obsession, with excrement, with diarrhea, filth, smells, as revealed in *Death on the Installment Plan,* is likewise a means of displaying the author's enmity.

The characters are negative, for the most part, with little heart and a lot of brawn. There is something brittle, wooden, about them. They are marionettes who seem to enjoy flagellating each other. We are no longer in the presence of three-dimensional characters such as those described by Balzac or Stendhal. Céline's protagonists are seen through their antics, their gestures, their violence. Barely does one glimpse their soul or penetrate that inner being where feelings and sensitivity abound.

There is in the novel, moreover, a mythlike note that gives it an eternal and transpersonal quality. To underline this aspect of the work, Céline interweaves a legend, that of the Norse King Krogold, into the very fiber of the novel. This myth may be looked upon as revelatory of the ideational content of the novel: the basic cruelty of man when he becomes a conquering force in life.

PLOT

Death on the Installment Plan is partly autobiographical, or so Céline wants his readers to believe. The protagonist's name is his own, Ferdinand. But the parents he describes, supposedly his own, are unlike his real family, and the childhood home he describes is likewise quite unlike the home in which he actually grew up.

As the novel opens, Ferdinand, a doctor, is awaiting death. He tells the reader about his medical career and about a manuscript he has written and seeks to have published. He narrates the legend of King Krogold, which he loved as a child. A movie serves as the instrument for a flashback to his childhood: "The last century, I can certainly talk about it, I saw it end." The novel now reverts to Ferdinand's early years, his mother's haberdashery shop, her legs filled with blood clots and varicose veins, the filthy apartment in which they live, the mother's constantly negative attitude toward her son. The father enters: a heartless man who constantly belittles his son and falls into vile tempers during which he beats both his wife and child. The home atmosphere is stifling, negative, painful. Every now and then this cruel ambiance is relieved by the presence of Grandmother Caroline, the only member of the family to display any kindness toward the child. Uncle Edouard also appears in the picture, his joviality resounding in sharp contrast to the home environment. Ferdinand is a poor student, uninterested in learning, but finally passes the most elementary of examinations, thanks to the generosity of his teacher. He becomes a packer, then a secretary, then an errand boy. He is fired from each of these jobs through no fault of his own, but each time he is castigated and even threatened by his parents, and scenes of violence ensue. Edouard lends Ferdinand's parents the money to send him to "Meanwell College" in England: it is hoped that he will learn English and return a better lad. In England he meets the beguiling Nora Merrywin and her strict husband, the school's director. The school fails and Nora commits suicide—but not before she has expressed her physical attraction for Ferdinand. Her husband goes insane. Ferdinand returns to Paris. He is unsuccessful in finding work. He fights with his father, even strikes him, and is thrown out of the house. Uncle Edouard takes him in and introduces him to his next employer, Courtial des Pereires, an inventor of scientific gadgets who has been forced to leave Paris because of his fraudulent activities. His wife and he open a kind of pension for underprivileged children. Nourished with the idealism of a Rousseau, he seeks to create a new race of productive and happy children. He also harbors fantastic agricultural schemes—a special kind of potato, which will revolutionize the scientific world. All fails. The ideal race is a gang of juvenile delinquents and the potatoes—all are vermin-ridden. Courtial finally makes his "Great Resolution" and shoots himself. Ferdinand returns to Paris. He decides to seek his own way in life.

STYLE

Céline's vocabulary in this novel ranges from the most literary and elegant to the most vulgar. Invectives, epithets, neologisms, repetitions, slang—all enter into the picture and are used with the force and vigor of a Rabelais, the irony and satire of a François Villon. Céline's language bristles with hate.

Language, in Céline's view, had become sick, lethargic, stereotyped, meaningless, inadequate for communicating power and feelings. During the Renaissance, it will be recalled, and during the Classical and Romantic periods, the Symbolist and Surrealist eras, renewed vigor was infused into language. Rimbaud, for example, had created living sonorities, images of fire, by means of a "long, immense and reasoned unruling of the senses," purging words of their former stultified meanings, lending them new and magical notions. Rimbaud had sought to liberate language from the limitations imposed upon it by the bourgeoisie. Céline, in his own way, injected a spirit of rebellion into his narratives, conversations, and interior monologues, indicating his desire to foment, to arouse, to keep perpetually active his revolutionary spirit.

Céline's vocabulary is far from hackneyed and worn; it is devoid of the oft-repeated metaphors, the time-honored images, the conventional and dull epithets and elegant sentences typical of the novels of his day. Mellifluous, smooth clauses, well-placed verbs and adjectives, finely-chiseled phrases are all lacking, as are images of beauty (for the most part), tenderness, warmth, and compassion. One actually feels the impact, the shocking tones, the jarring, brutalizing words that Céline uses as weapons. Sartre wrote, in *What Is Literature?*, that a writer must be truthful and honest in the use of language and must write what he feels and thinks.

> The function of a writer is to call a spade a spade. If words are sick, it is up to us to cure them. . . . If one starts deploring the inadequacy of language to reality, like Brice Parain, one makes oneself an accomplice of the enemy, that is, of propaganda.[2]

For Céline, as for the "primitive," words are acts. The primitive endowed words with feelings, attitudes with an inner reality. Words are the manifestations of what is most archaic in man. When a primitive thinks, he does not rationalize in abstract terms as a "civilized" person does; rather he thinks in visions or in "thought-images." He may, therefore, sometimes mistake the psychic for the real, as he does—perhaps—when he believes in ghosts, in voodoo, etc. Thought is endowed with visionary, auditory force and takes on, therefore, the character of reality. For modern man thinking is not action, words are not acts, because modern man has desensualized the psychic factor. His abstract notions are devoid of body.[3]

Céline has returned to the primitive notion of verbal "thought-images." These arouse the archaic instincts in both character and reader, as if each, almost simultaneously, propelled the other along. When, for example, we watch Auguste in a rage, we are, as are the other characters, transfixed. The words used to describe Auguste's state are a direct outgrowth of his anthropoidal psyche. When on another occasion, we watch Ferdinand's mother hobbling about, her legs a mass of bloodied varicose veins, we empathize immediately. The word is no longer an abstract entity but has a reality of its own. It lives; it is a catalyzer, an instigator, an irritant designed to implant itself physically upon those with whom it comes into contact.

Slang words are also action personified. Slang, for Céline, is language in the making, language coming alive and crackling with excitement. Classical language, he maintained, the language of his contemporaries, is dead. Language is indeed mortal. Words die every day and one must resign oneself to the fact. Syntax, vocabulary, epithets, images, all die eventually. Slang hears its death-knell too, of course, but since Céline's brand of slang was in the process of coming into being at this point, it was still alive, vital, meaningful. Consequently, it "had a slight edge over so many others, it will have lived for a year, a month, a day." [4]

By means of "thought-images" and gestures Céline brings out the farcical, the grotesque nature of his protagonists, as Alfred Jarry had done so superbly in his play *King Ubu* (1896). Both Jarry and Céline are masters at scoring absurdities, underlining brutalities, singling out antics and gestures both cruel and savage.

Gestures are an intrinsic part of Céline's writing style, serving to delineate characters by singling each of them out in terms of a particular tic or phobia. These gestures add dimension and visual impact to the series of scenes Céline depicts, making each of them theatrically potent. The father's rages, for example, are accompanied by precise gestures—vituperative, demonstrative, affective, quixotic. He pirouettes, thrusts, hits, pulls, drags, stamps, bounds forth, pounces.

> I run, passing through an avalanche of glass and debris . . . He charges into the piano that a customer had left us as security . . . he's beside himself. He bashes his heel into it, the keyboard clangs . . . Then it's my mother's turn, now she's getting hers . . .From my room I can hear her howling . . .
>
> I come part of the way down to look . . .He's dragging her along the banister. She hangs on. She clutches his neck. That's what saves her. It's he who pulls loose . . . He pushes her over. She somersaults . . . She bounces down the stairs . . . I can hear the dull thuds . . .[5]

In most of the passages dealing with Auguste's temper, there is a slapstick effect, a whole range of Marx Brothers antics, rendering him pitiful and horrendous at the same time and, strangely enough, far from humorous.

Reactions to people and to ideas are also depicted in terms of gestures. These are all the more powerful since they are accomplished unconsciously. Thus when Courtial des Pereires informs his wife about the failure of his business deal, her entire countenance changes in seconds.

> She collapsed on to her chair . . . I thought she was going to conk out . . . The two of us were standing there . . . we got ready to lay her out on the floor . . . I got up to open the window . . . But she comes to . . . She's frantic . . . She jumps up from her chair, quivering all over . . . She pulls herself together . . . She hadn't been out for long . . . She's up again . . . She wobbles a bit on her pins . . . She steadies herself . . . She gives a hefty clout on the table . . .[6]

There are scenes in which gestures, activities of all types, suddenly come to a halt, in which motion is virtually nonexistent. The portrait of Nora Merrywin, for example, very nearly takes on Grecian beauty in its stillness and repose. The detritus present within the other characters seems not to have sullied her purity. Every aspect of her physique (clothes, hair, complexion) are exquisitely carved and molded as if from stone. Each pose, each stance, comes through forcefully, in curves and mellowed tones, as opposed to the usual cacophonies and brutalities intrinsic to other depictions.

> Her hands were marvels, tapering, pink and white, tender, the same gentleness as her face, just to look at them was like a glimpse of fairyland.[7]

Gestures have a double impact upon the viewer: they fill his mind with spatial images and they serve to impinge upon the protagonist's privacy. By means of gestures one can *see.* Gestures are revelations, symbols, behind which a whole world of mystery vibrates. Once the reader and the other protagonists as well pierce the barrier and learn to decipher the gesture-language, a reshuffling of emotions, of rhythmic sequence of thought waves, comes to pass. Characters are no longer tenuous, vaporous, ambiguous beings but are clearly defined entities. Antonin Artaud wrote, in *The Theatre and its Double,* that every emotion has its corresponding gesture: anger, joy, lust, exhaustion, etc. It is up to the dramatist (the novelist in this case) to extract from within what will best suit his characters at that particular instant. Céline succeeds in attaching to his marionette-like creatures the exact mode of action, the perfect gesture, to bring out their walk, manner, love, anger, eating habits, etc. Gestures, therefore, become active participants, as do rhythms, images, and decors, and force the reader to react to the scene and action depicted. Gestures, once looked upon as autonomous entities, have been made to propel sound and effect, to stimulate. Sartre once said that people are defined by their acts, their gestures. Céline has achieved such definition in *Death on the Installment Plan.*

Gestures denote physical states but also, as we have seen, man's inner architecture. They may be viewed as mechanistic and energetic entities, causing friction, increasing the individual's potential. In modern theater, Ionesco's character the Killer, in *Tueur sans bagage,* reduces his role to a series of gestures—shrugging of the shoulders, snickering, smirking. In Artaud's *The Cenci* mutes gesticulate an entire murder scene. In Genet's *The Blacks* and *The Screens* much of the action is accomplished through miming, bodily movement, and posture.[8]

There are very few tranquil moments in Céline's novels and these are when gestures, rhythmic effects, and action vocabulary are not used. Unlike Beckett, whose novels and plays rest for the most part on immobility, on silence (indicating his disgust with life, his longing for death), Céline's works are *a perpetuo mobile* revelatory of his anguish.

Decor is another source of fascination for Céline. He not only furnishes his readers with very precise background material in terms of the physical environment but makes the very objects in the world of his protagonists manifestations of their life blood.

When Balzac described decor, in such novels as *Father Goriot,* he did so with extreme exactitude: there was a mystic affinity between the characters and their environment, the furniture, the coloring of the walls, the clothes, etc. Though Céline is neither a realist (in the sense that Balzac was) nor a mystic, there exists, nevertheless, a secret rapport between his characters and their backgrounds, as if the one emerged from the other and emptied back into it. Céline's descriptions, however, are not always as precise as Balzac's are, though they can be so when necessary. In Céline's novels decor is usually described with heavy and thickly pigmented brush strokes and thus is delineated forcefully rather than meticulously, impulsively, rather than cerebrally. The descriptions of Ferdinand's home, the seascapes, the boat ride, etc., all play a triple role: they situate the event, they cause it to come into being, and they propel it along.

Consider, as an example, the description of Ferdinand's apartment house in Paris and that of his three-room apartment. It is in this architecturally constructed universe, this nihilistic decor, that the young Ferdinand will have to cope with his parents' slovenly and destructive ways. The building itself is dark, suffocating, drenched with dog urine, human spittle, garbage, smells of all types emanating from leaking gas pipes, rotted food, broken toilets, excrement. As for Ferdinand's apartment, it too, we are told, is rife with filth and unswept refuse. Dried and caked noodles, described in detail, are heaped behind and above the stove and stuck and encrusted on the floors and tables.

The utter chaos in both the building and the apartment and the mixture of decay and detritus could hardly harbor anyone, according to Céline, but the most ignominious and degraded types, those whose lives are spent crawling about in slime.

> I have to admit that the Passage was an unbelievable pesthole. It was made to kill you off, slowly but surely, what with the little mongrels' urine, the shit, the sputum, the leaky gas pipes. The stink was worse than the inside of a prison. Down under the glass roof the sun is so dim you can eclipse it with a candle. Everybody began to gasp for breath. The Passage took cognizance of its asphyxiating stench . . .[9]

As the novel progresses we notice that each of the various decors (his mother's shop, his employer's home, etc.) is personified. Each represents a "human" organism, an active participant in the drama, not merely a place in which things happen. Thus the apartment house has its own personality and conscience (or lack of it). Its atmosphere is claustrophobic, stifling any fecundating force. Its attitude is destructive and aggressive in that it harbors decaying and unregenerate aspects of human society. The building slowly tears down the personalities of its occupants by never encouraging them to bloom or mature.

The rhythmic effects achieved by Céline further the novel's aggressive and chaotic character. *Death on the Installment Plan* is a "polyphonic" work whose rhythms are intricate, dynamic, and powerful. Its stresses, pauses, vibrations, pulsations, accelerations, and cataclysms, acting in unison or in orchestrated patterns, serve to arouse and propel both the protagonist and the reader.

The episodes of confrontation—the word is used here to indicate both an overt and covert antagonism—between Ferdinand's father, Auguste, and himself take on certain rhythmic patterns each time they come to pass. Auguste's anger, for example, usually begins after a pause, a calm; derogating terms are then uttered, and as the tempo increases so does the violence of the language and the accompanying gestures; tones seem to shoot into space, disrupting the previous sense of continuity; finally, rage erupts and engulfs everything in sight, like a giant wave. Auguste, a dynamo, throbs and sways, his words and actions accelerating. Finally, utter chaos sets in.

Auguste's rages, so extraordinarily depicted in terms of rhythm and sound, are like a series of cadences, waves, syncopations, concentricities, accumulations of discordant and cacophonous tonalities—Auguste flies off into a cadenza-like tantrum. Each time he swells with anger, the sentences pulsate and syncopate; staccato effects are achieved. Fortissimos are followed by a blast from the timpani section of the orchestra, after which an atonal or serial passage worthy of a Honegger or a Hindemith emerges into space. Because of the projection of these tones and rhythms into the vast expanse, the individual—in this case Auguste—seems to lose his identity, seems to be overwhelmed by a collective image. It is no longer Auguste who vibrates before the reader but a mythic creature. We focus upon a monstrous being who sweeps all else into oblivion.

> At home it starts up all over again, a tempest . . . My father beats the hell out of me, kicks me in the ribs, steps on me, takes my pants down. In addition he keeps bellowing that I'm killing Him! . . . that I ought to be in jail! that I should have been there from the start! . . . My mother pleads, clings to him, falls at his feet, and screams that in prison "they get even worse." I was the lowest of the low. I was a gallowsbird. That's what I'd come to! [10]

The temper reaches a climax when Auguste's voice becomes a series of arpeggios running up and down the keyboard, unleashing a heavy roll from the timpani once again, after which explosion upon explosion is heard.

> He bellows, he rushes, he explodes, he bombards the kitchen. There's nothing left on the nails . . . Pots, pans, dishes, crash, bang, everything goes . . . My mother on her knees implores heaven for mercy . . . He overturns the table with one big kick . . . It lands on top of her . . .
>
> . . . .
>
> She has blood in her hair. She washes at the sink . . . She's sobbing . . . She gags . . . She sweeps up the breakage . . .[11]

The speed, the momentum, the sound effects hurtle forth. Finally, Auguste throws his wife down the stairs. One can feel the body in flight, thumping in muted tones as it catapults its way down.

The same fury we discern in Auguste's tempers is also realized in nature's eruptions, such as its storms on sea. When the family crosses from France to England, the ocean becomes a giant wave, a heaving, jerking mass pulling, tugging, pitching, jabbing, throbbing, swaying all on board. Few are able to control a parallel motion within their stomachs which, of course, produces vertigo, nausea, and vomiting. As described by Céline in this passage, vomiting has become a communal activity. As each mouth opens up, like a series of giant maws, the regurgitations erupt in a series of syncopated rhythmic effects.

> In the rolling and pitching, people were throwing up any old place, without formality . . . There was only one toilet . . . in one corner of the deck . . . It was already occupied by four vomiters in a state of collapse, wedged in tight . . . The sea was getting steadily rougher . . . At every rising wave, ooops . . . In the trough a dozen oopses, more copious, more compact . . . The gale blew my mother's veil away . . . it landed wringing wet on the mouth of a lady at the other end . . . who was retching desperately . . . All resistance had been abandoned. The horizon was littered with jam . . . salad . . . chicken . . . coffee . . . the whole slobgullion . . . it all came up . . . Mama collapses against the rail . . . She vomits herself up again, all she's got . . . A carrot comes up . . . a piece of fat . . . and the whole tail of a mullet . . . There's a sick mutt, too, so sick he shits on the ladies' skirts . . .[12]

The violence implicit in Céline's rhythmic patterns is characteristic of Gothic novels, so dear to Ann Radcliffe and Matthew Lewis. Like Céline, these authors of horror tales created moods of turbulence and gloom, isolating and endowing nature with aspects forceful enough to inject unheard-of brutalities into the narrative. When Céline describes English weather, for example, it is reminiscent of certain horrendous sections of Lewis' *The Monk.* The rhythms that Céline creates by verbal references to the winds are not only used to delineate character (in terms of their chaotic instinctive qualities) but are also designed to obliterate distance and, paradoxically, indentities. As the velocity of the wind increases, creating a series of truncated rhythmic effects, so man cannot help but be swayed and engulfed in the cosmic flow, losing his individuality in the process, but at the same time enjoying a sense of togetherness with others. At such times the protagonists become one with nature, paralyzed by its immensity, perhaps, but also strengthened by its sustaining power.

> The wind hammered against the house . . . The squalls and storms came bounding over the hill . . . The wind roared through the rooms, the doors rattled day and night. We were living in the middle of a tornado. When the tempest began to roar, the kids yelled like deaf people, they couldn't hear each other . . . Nothing could stand up against that wind! It was bend or break. The trees were stooped over, they never straightened up, the lawns were in tatters, whole patches were ripped up.[13]

One of the most extraordinary rhythmic sequences occurs when Ferdinand almost drowns at Dieppe. His parents have been advised by a doctor to have him bathe in the ocean. Unaccustomed to the tug and the force of waves, Ferdinand is overcome by a breaker. The sensation created by the centrifugal force of the gallons of water rushing in on him, crushing him, leaves him gasping for breath, choking, hiccuping, fainting. When he nearly goes under for the final time, the circular rhythmic effect created by the waves and its withdrawal, the expectation of another onslaught, the choppy, syncopated motion of the water, the child's halting breathing, each following in cadence-like sequences, create parallel sensations in the reader.

> Chilled to the bone, bruised, the child totters and falls . . . A universe of pebbles beats my bones amid the flaking foam. First your head wobbles, sways, staggers, and pounds into the gavel . . . Every second is your last . . . My father in a striped bathing suit, between two roaring mountains, is shouting like mad. He bobs up in front of me . . . he belches, thrashes about, makes wisecracks. A roller knocks him over too, turns him upside down, there he is with his feet in the air . . . He's wriggling like a frog . . . He can't straighten himself out, he's done for . . . At this point a terrible volley of pebbles hits me in the chest . . . I'm riddled . . . drowned . . . It's awful . . . I'm crushed under the deluge . . . Then the wave carries me back and lays me down at my mother's feet . . . She tries to grab me, to rescue me . . . The undertow catches me, carries me out . . . She lets out a terrible scream . . . The whole beach comes running . . . But it's no use . . . The bathers crowd around, all hysterical . . . The raging sea pounds me down to the bottom, then lifts me gasping to the surface . . . In a flashing moment I see that they're discussing my agony . . . There they are, every imaginable color: green . . . blue, parasols . . . I whirl about in pieces . . . And then I don't see a thing . . .[14]

When Céline describes certain meetings between the protagonists (actually antagonists), he speaks of the meetings as *corridas.* These scenes and the characters involved assume the form and tempi of a bullfight, with its attacks, its withdrawals, its furtive, parrying strokes, its thrusts, its vicious leaps, its pirouettes. The impression of tension, irritation, and blood is most apparent, as for example, when Ferdinand and a friend, perched on top of a stove to watch Madame Gorloge and her lover through a hole in the wall, observe the two lecherous buffoons hitting, biting, beating, pulling, twisting each other in rhythmic sequences.

> "Go on, you old cow, shut your trap. Open your basket."
> He didn't listen to her. He put her back on again with three enormous clouts in the gizzard . . . Bam! they resounded. She gasped for breath, the stinker . . . She wheezed like a bellows . . . I wondered if he was going to kill her . . . finish her off on the spot! . . . He gave her another vicious clout . . . right while he was pumping . . . They were both roaring like wild animals . . . She was coming . . .[15]

Rhythms are used by Céline to shock his readers, to destroy their complacency and their worn attitudes, to create a new sense of awareness, to distill what is foreign and to expel his own anger.

HOSTILITY

The feelings of hostility that permeate *Death on the Installment Plan* manifest themselves in diverse ways—through laughter, rage, vomiting, excrement.

The humor, like that in *Journey to the End of the Night,* is tragic, cold, cruel, and in many ways destructive. It is the kind of humor that denigrates, degrades, pains, mocks, humiliates. It is never the belly laughter so characteristic of the popular farceurs of medieval times, or the lively banter of a Molière or a La Biche, or even the derisive humor of a Musset. Céline's laughter is sardonic, cutting, and very nearly sadistic at times. It is designed to accentuate the brutality of certain situations, characters, and points of view and is, therefore, frequently injected into the dialogue or narrative in order to break up the rhythmic flow, the continuity of the emotion, characterizations, and episodes. At times, the laughter is cataclysmic in intensity; in certain scenes it erupts like a volcano, increasing discordant relationships, furthering torment, adding to the already raucous ambiance.

Frequently the laughter is hysterical, springing directly from the unconscious as a reaction to a gruesome event: the father's tempers, Ferdinand's multiple firings, etc. Guffaws also frequently represent the protagonist's inability to adapt to certain circumstances, as when Ferdinand unexpectedly passes his exams. In this case, the laughter is automatic, pathological, a kind of liberation or nervous discharge. Explosive or muffled laughter is also used as a means of expressing embarrassment or derision, or as a mask for fright, as when Ferdinand almost drowns.

One of the many "humorous" incidents in *Death on the Installment Plan* occurs when Ferdinand and his father are delivering some merchandise to a rich lady. She calls young Ferdinand into her bedroom, exposes herself, and tries to seduce him. He runs out of the room in fright and shock. The maid who has witnessed the incident is "doubled up with laughter." [16] In this case, laughter is clearly designed to ridicule. The maid experiences what the philosopher Henri Bergson calls a "momentary anesthesia of the heart." [17] She cannot feel the boy's embarrassment and is totally insensitive to his hurt.

Laughter, under some circumstances, arises when the reader's attention is drawn to the physical image and not to the ethical question involved. When speaking of his father's sister, who ended up as a prostitute in Russia, Ferdinand says: "There was no resistance in her case. She was all flesh, desire, music." In this same vein, Ferdinand speaks of his Uncle Arthur, stating: "Flesh also overcame him." [18] The lovemaking scenes are frequently compared, as we have seen, to *corridas,* and thus are made to appear as a farcical tugs-of-war rather than the uniting of two individuals.

Humor also results from awkward situations such as, for example, the one that occurs when Ferdinand's mother permits a group of actors to use her favorite table as part of their decor. After the performance, she rushes onstage and carries the table off, explaining to those present that it is late, that she must put her son to bed, and that is why she needs the piece of furniture.[19] The mother's act not only underlines her lack of a sense of decorum but also her unwitting cruelty, for she remains oblivious to the shame she is bringing to her son.

In certain scenes the humor is macabre and bitter, such as the one in which Ferdinand describes his mother running down the street, limping along, her sore leg swollen and blue with protruding veins and blood clots. Céline caricatures the pathetic woman—he "seizes her in motion," as Bergson says in his essay *On Laughter;* he "deforms" her by "enlarging her defects." [20]

> But she ran more and more slowly . . . on account of her calves . . . suddenly they were as thin as wire . . . and so hairy they got tangled up in each other like spiders . . . The people up ahead wound her into a ball . . . and let her roll . . .[21]

Céline's humor is frequently and cruelly satirical, and Céline surely must be ranked with the greatest of satirists—Swift, Pope, Voltaire, Proust, Horace, Juvenal, Boileau. For Céline, satire is an instrument of aggressiveness. He develops scenes in which bitter laughter is used to inflict pain by underlining man's weaknesses and his tragic side.

When Ferdinand leaves for England and his mother counsels him to seek out good friends, those with fine manners and of good character, and to work hard, to learn English, to think of his parents. "The English always seem so correct . . ." she added. "So clean! So nicely dressed! I don't know what to say, my boy, to make you behave a little better . . ." [22] The dichotomy between reality and the mother's fantasies serves to evoke a bitter grin.

Names are also used as the butt of Céline's satire. Meanwell College in England, to which Ferdinand is sent, stands for something that Céline dislikes with a passion: those who "mean well" but do not act forcefully, who are unrealistic in their attitudes, and who therefore cannot function properly in society. Mr. Merrywin, the head of Meanwell College, is such a man. He reads the Bible to the children daily and is totally unaware of how bored they are. As he reads, "The kids dug into their noses and wriggled in all directions . . ." [23]

The female of the species do not elicit kind remarks from Céline, either. When Ferdinand meets Gwendoline, a girl who serves fried potatoes in a small shop, and they begin kissing each other, Ferdinand says that he feels dominated, crushed by her power: "She hugged me like a wrestler . . . There was no point in resisting . . ."[24] Concerning women in general: "They'll grow on anything . . . any old garbage will do . . . They're just like flowers . . . The more beautiful they are, the worse the manure stinks . . ."[25]

Absurd situations evoke satirical comments, wrote Théophile Gautier. Thus when Ferdinand describes Madame Courtial des Pereires following her hysterectomy, he speaks of her beard, of her virility.

> Regular moustaches had come out and even a sort of beard . . . They were bathed in tears, which flew copiously as she talked to me . . . Colored streams ran down from her makeup. She had powered . . . plastered . . . and painted like mad! [26]

Johnson derogated satire as a technique because he found it cruel and feared its consequences. "Abuse is not so dangerous when there is no vehicle or wit or delicacy, nor subtle conveyance." [27] Pierre Bayle, in his *Historical and Critical Dictionary* (1697), also expressed a dislike of satire, calling it an untruthful, cruel, and destructive art whose poisons, released by the satirist, always remain with the victim, never releasing him from agony and pain. Céline, however, felt no such compunction and even seemed to enjoy this form of derision. A master satirist, a fine humorist of the "blackest" type, he used his wit to express his vindictive and vitriolic contempt for humanity.

Nausea and vomiting are masterfully used by Céline as images expressive of his hostility toward society. Looked upon symbolically, vomiting is a means of rejection and thus an expression of his distaste for everything about him: family, friends, environment, life itself. If nausea and vomiting are considered merely as organic disorders in *Death on the Installment Plan,* then the real source of the problem, which is psychological, would be masked. Ferdinand's only way, perhaps, of revealing his disgust for everything and his inability to adapt to circumstances, to cope with his environment, to act with courage, determination, and independence, is to rid himself of what is inside of him.

Sartre's novel *Nausea* (1938), dedicated to Céline, makes much of this physical process to point up the protagonist's violent disgust at the thought of man's purposeless existence on earth. As Céline did before him. Sartre rejects all belief in cosmic purpose, in human progress, in illusions and pretenses (religion included) that man erects for himself in order to blur or to obscure the absurdity of life. Sartre, however, differentiates between living (simply being on earth) and existing (being capable of experiencing nausea, of reacting to given situations, of giving physical expression to an inner tumult). Céline makes no such distinction. For Sartre, nausea manifests itself with feelings of anguish and is, to a certain degree, a positive force; for such sensations imply that the individual has become conscious of the painful nature of his existence and is no longer unaware of it or detached from it. Nausea is not a "morbid" feeling; it is rather a type of "awareness" or "consciousness" of the gratuitous nature of life. And when thinking and feeling beings become aware of the contingency, of the gratuitiousness, of all that surrounds them, they experience nausea—they experience life. Such knowledge prevents them from slipping into a nihilistic lethargy and precludes automatic reactions such as suicide. Nausea indicates that one finally realizes that one no longer needs to justify one's existence; one must simply be aware of it, accept it, and do the best one can with it.[28]

Céline's concept of nausea is, in contrast, largely negative. It is only the first step, the expulsion, the destruction of the given situation. Ferdinand is not yet consciously aware of what is at stake. He cannot understand or evaluate his existence as Sartre's hero can. At the end of *Nausea,* Sartre's protagonist finds a meaning to life in the work of art—in the book itself.

Ferdinand vomits for the first time (so far as the reader is told) when he hears his mother talking to a neighbor about how much she has done for her son. "I'd better go to the can to vomit . . .," the son declares.[29] The reaction of revulsion vis-à-vis his mother is immediate. Certainly, it is an indication of their rapport.

Nausea and vomiting occur when Ferdinand looks at his apartment: the detritus, the food splattered about, the daily servings of cold, gluey, pasty macaroni, dished up on filthy, greasy, sticky plates, his father's disgusting eating habits. Eating that eternal macaroni, "it took a good swig of red wine to keep them down."[30]

A similar emotional response is elicited after Ferdinand returns from his grandmother's grave. When the people with him become hungry and begin eating, Ferdinand is so revolted by their spirit of gaiety, their unfeeling natures, that he vomits. This represents a physical rejection of the living, of their notions and attitudes, and may also indicate his disgust with life as such, since food, interpreted symbolically, is a life-sustaining force.

Ferdinand is equally nauseated by the death process—the decay, the worms eating away the flesh . . .

> I felt like throwing up on the spot . . . I couldn't think of anything else but vomiting . . . I thought of the galantine . . . of what Caroline must be looking like now down there . . . of all the worms . . . the big ones . . . the fat ones with feet . . . gnawing, swarming about there . . . All that decay . . . millions of them in all that swollen pus, the stinking wind . . .[31]

Ferdinand's most violent vomiting spell occurs when he confronts his father and strikes him. After this incident, he seems almost to eject his entire being. The vomiting is so acute, so spasmodic, so complete—the ejection of evils, poisons and decayed, infected, unhealthy, parasitic entities—that it seems it will never stop. Up to now Ferdinand has accepted his father's insults and condemnations and the slow eroding of his personality. His giant effort at rebellion, described physically by Céline, indicates that something positive within Ferdinand's psyche is taking root and being born out of the chaos. Other forces also come into play at this time, the realization, perhaps, that his father has acted as he has all these years because his son and his wife have been willing to put up with his behavior. Had they been active and forceful individuals, the father could not have "gotten away," so to speak, with his destructive outbursts. Henceforth, Ferdinand's relationship with his father changes as of necessity: he is no longer to be dominated or stifled by him. Yet when parent/child confrontation does take place openly, the strain on the child can be very great indeed. So it is in Ferdinand's case. The change takes place so suddenly and is so extreme that Ferdinand's entire orientation is disturbed. His father is no longer a paragon of strength to be feared; his image has been reduced to that of a weak, screaming mass, a helpless, degraded entity. He is nothing. Ferdinand's reaction is traumatic: he breaks out into sweat, he shivers, he is crippled with vertigo, anguish, and vomiting such as he has never experienced before.

> I began to vomit . . . I even pushed to make it come up . . . That made me feel a lot better. I vomited up everything . . . The shivers started in again . . . They shook me so hard I didn't know who I was anymore . . . I was surprised at myself . . . I threw up the macaroni . . . I started in again . . . It did me a whole lot of good. Like I was getting rid of everything . . . I threw up everything I could all over the floor . . . I pushed and strained . . . I bent double to make myself puke still more and then came slime and then froth . . . It splattered, it spread under the door . . . I vomited up everything I'd eaten for at least a week and then diarrhea too . . .[32]

This purgation has some positive consequences for Ferdinand. It leads to a total break with his father. Having been thrown out of the house, he will now have to develop and shift for himself—perhaps not immediately or along normal lines, since he has an uncle ready to help him, but at least he will no longer experience the condition of stasis or regression that he would have experienced had this enormous upheaval not occurred.

At the end of the novel, when Ferdinand must decide his future course of action, he is again seized with panic and vomiting. Without family, without friends or his Uncle Edouard, he heaves out his anguish—and chooses the army as a solution to his problem.

Why should the simple decision to find a job provoke such an upheaval? A job implies constriction, limitation. It represents a kind of molding of one's destiny, a traumatic "passage" from an irresponsible adolescence to a responsible and mature adult existence. For Ferdinand, the idea of working hard and paving one's way in life is tormenting. "I threw up in the gutter."[33]

The detailed accounts of the vomiting and the matter ejected[34] are examples of Céline's "fluoroscopic vision" technique, similar in this respect to that of John Barth's novel *Giles Goat-Boy*. Barth, too, introduces concrete (though fragmented) objects in his descriptions, in his attempt to understand the human being. So Céline, likewise, has recourse to "lenses" and to "scopes," trying all the while to look beneath the skin, into the very structure of the individual (his intestines, tubes, veins, etc.), in search for an answer to life's processes and the reason for them.[35]

Céline's obsession with excrement in *Death on the Installment Plan* is another expression of his hostility toward his protagonists and toward society generally.

Psychologically, an obsession with bodily functions such as eating, masturbation, copulation, menstruation, vomiting, and defecation very often indicates a preoccupation with the physical organism per se and an inability to see beyond it—a kind of narcissism.

Excrement in particular has been regarded in religion, literature, art, and psychology in a variety of ways. The ancient creation myths uphold the idea that anything emanating from the body—semen, spittle, urine, excrement, flatus—is a creative element. In some religions there is an association between the "body scheme" and that of the universe. The Greeks, for example, believed the seat of consciousness to be the midriff; the Indians and the Hebrews considered it to be the heart. The liver and kidneys were also important centers of psychic life. Thus Zeus punished Prometheus for his hubris by sending an eagle to feed upon his liver. The visceral centers (the alimentary tract and the intestinal process) also represent psychic centers; the body tone (whether an individual is well fed or not) influences his affective and intellectual outlook.[36]

The alchemists connected excrement with gold, symbolically juxtaposing the "lowest" and the "highest" values. Within its mass, that of excrement, they sought the *prima materia,* one of the arcane substances from which it was hoped the philosopher's stone would emerge.[37]

Martin Luther's preoccupation with obscenity and excrement was symptomatic of his manic-depressive nature. He constantly felt victimized by some kind of enemy that he was forever trying to "eliminate" symbolically. According to Erik Erikson, "Luther's use of repudiative anal patterns was an attempt to find a safety-valve when unrelenting inner pressure threatened to make devotion unbearable and sublimity hateful. . . . The regressive aspects of this pressure, and the resulting obsessive and paranoid focus on single features such as the Pope and the Devil, leave little doubt that a transference had taken place from a parent figure to universal personages, and that a central theme in this transference was anal defiance." [38] When terrorized by the Devil, for example, Luther would say to him: "I have shit in the pants, and you can hang them around your neck and wipe your mouth with it." [39] Such language eased his tension and helped him to express his self-repudiation in terms of the sphincter muscle and the alimentary process. "I am like ripe shit," he declared one evening at dinner, "and the world is a gigantic asshole." [40]

Satirists such as Voltaire did not spare the sanguinary, the cruel, or the excremental. Man, for Voltaire, was ". . . a wretched being, . . . an embryo born in between urine and excrement, excrement himself, formed to fatten up the slime from the area in which he emerges." [41]

Jean Genet—orphan, homosexual, criminal, and all-around pariah—was also preoccupied with the fecal. Such activities, both actual and figurative, permitted him to fill the void, so to speak, which was his life by looking upon everything that he eliminated as a creative act and also as a means of hurling his hatred at society.

John Barth injects a little humor into the fecal situation when he compares Oedipus' "sphinx" to his protagonist's "sphincter" muscle, making "a cosmos into chaos." Barth goes still further in his analogy and echoes the Haeckelian statement "ontogeny recapitulates philogeny," but substituting the word "cosmogony" for "philogeny" and concluding that the "mystery of the universe and the sphincter's riddle are the same because the genesis of the individual and the genesis of the cosmos are aspects of the same process." [42]

Salvador Dali was also obsessed with excrement. On a menu he drew for a dinner party in Paris he depicted one person defecating into another's mouth. In this case, the painter's anal eroticism expressed visually his inability to come to terms with his body and the malfunctioning of his sexual life as well.

All of these associations are relevant to our understanding of Ferdinand's constant preoccupation with filth in general and excretion in particular. The attempt to show his hostility toward society and toward himself is also a creative process, a means of indicating an inability to cope with situations.

Ferdinand, it seems, is always dirty. His hair is filthy and uncombed. In the early years, his face, his clothes, his feet, his entire physical being are embedded in filth. Dirt, in this case, is a means of giving materiality to feelings of physical degradation. The fact that he is the object of his parents' contempt and insults, that they consider him to be a totally worthless and incompetent human being, adds to the visual expression of inner erosion and decomposition. There are times when Ferdinand is so objectionable that he looks like a pariah, is treated as one, and becomes a living replica of moral and physical disintegration.

The fact that Ferdinand defecates in his pants and permits the smells to emanate therefrom indicates, psychologically speaking, a dissociation between his instinctive and his rational sides. The natural orientation between these two aspects of a personality—the most primitive self (instincts) and the spiritual self—is evidently sick and unclean. Such a cleavage within a personality may occur as a result of an excessive rigidity on the parents' part. Dejecta, in Ferdinand's case, represents his inferior side, which he rejects instinctively but which always returns to plague him particularly during moments of stress, fright, and loneliness. His parents are domineering and destructive forces in his life. They represent the overly conventional, the subjugating ways in his world. Without love or understanding they eradicate (or try to eradicate) all feelings in their son. Because of their constant derogation, because of their unloving attitude, Ferdinand feels rejected, alone, sick—cast out into a world even more brutal than the one he has known with his parents. Since he is still a child, is still unformed, protoplasmic, naive, and passive, he can do nothing to rectify this situation except to react regressively—to defecate.

Even at the age of seven he complains bitterly of his parents' regime. They are always trying to hurry him. He never has time to relax and enjoy himself. Because of this state of affairs, "I made in my pants . . . To tell the truth I was in such a hurry all through my childhood that I had shit on my ass until I was drafted." [43]

His only weapon against his parents, his only means of showing his displeasure and thereby eliciting theirs, is by defecating and stinking. When such incontinency occurs his parents are beside themselves with rage and heap further insults upon the lad, thus provoking yet another round of diarrhea, ad infinitum.

> In addition my behind was always dirty, I didn't wipe myself, I didn't have time, that was my justification, we were always in too much of a hurry . . . I never wiped myself properly, I always had a sock coming to me . . . and hurried to avoid it . . . I left the can door open so as to hear them coming . . . I shit like a bird between two storms . . .
>
> I'd go around for weeks with shit on my ass. I was conscious of the smell, I'd be careful not to get too close to people.[44]

After Ferdinand passes his examinations, he is so emotionally distressed, so tense, so fearful that he has no way of relieving his tensions other than through elimination.

> I'd wet my pants and shit in them something awful too, I could hardly move.[45]

When his mother brings him home and his father congratulates and hugs him, the father is greeted by the ghastly odor and is repelled by it. He pushes his son away and very nearly explodes into another tantrum.

Unconsciously, then, Ferdinand uses defecation as a means of keeping people at a distance. He seeks, unconsciously, to become what his parents think he is, to live up to their image of him, to be as revolting, stupid, unclean, retarded, obnoxious, and uncouth as they consider him to be already—or so he thinks. Lonely, wretched, despairing, Ferdinand uses his weapon as a skunk does, to repel those who would hurt him.

How does Céline use nausea, vomit, and defecation as literary devices? Before Sartre and before Genet, but not before the Marquis de Sade and Sacher-Masoch, Céline expressed his anger and hostility by means of the scabrous. The scatalogical became a means of inflaming, repulsing, angering the reader as a representative of the society Céline hated. Paradoxically, Céline sought to win a large reading public; he longed for both fame and fortune. Yet he also sought to insult and revolt his audience.

Céline wanted to beguile his readers, not through the usual means of ingratiation but rather by enervating them and by rejecting conventional values. He sought to revise the accepted notions of what was good, beautiful, truthful, just—views that, so far as Céline was concerned, were meaningless, at least as practiced in twentieth-century Europe. Céline, therefore, set about reversing standards and values in order to force people to think about their lot and their actions, to force them to look within themselves with clarity and honesty.

Though Céline repelled his readers, he did establish a certain intimacy with them. By describing personal details that were hitherto taboo, he exposed man's most intimate regions (both physical and moral) to the light of day. In this manner he let his readers into a secret, sharing his innermost thoughts with them—even the "forbidden" ones, which are always more exciting than the rest. The reader then could enter into complicity with him—either overtly or covertly—and penetrate the inferno of his hatred, anger, and rage.

THE PROTAGONISTS

Céline's characters are not the three-dimensional ones that we meet, for example, in the novels of Balzac, Stendhal, and Flaubert. They are caricatures—extracts or distillations of certain human traits, aggrandized, inflated, or distorted in both form and substance. Céline's beings do not walk their way across the pages; they strut. They do not merely slap at each other; they heave mighty blows. They do not whisper; they castigate in stentorian tones. They are clowns whose humor is sardonic, whose antics are grotesque, whose gestures are mimed; they are macabre creatures whose misery stands out in giant clusters. They are forever embedded, engulfed, in slime. They are brittle, hard, derisive; their suffering is objectified and only rarely subjective. To reveal the inner workings of these creatures, Céline has recourse to several literary devices: dialogues, monologues, confidences, letters, attitudes, gestures, situations.

The characters are for the most part negative: Ferdinand's parents, his employers, the children he meets along the way. Positive protagonists are few and far between: his grandmother Caroline and his uncle Edouard.

The women in Ferdinand's life—his mother Clemence, and his employer's wife, Madame Gorloge—are destructive creatures, though they may not have set out to be. Each in her own way is evil, Eve-like, domineering, egotistical. Each very nearly succeeds in stunting Ferdinand's future, in crushing his *élan*, his lust for life. Nora Merriwyn, the wife of the school director, is more of a phantasmagoria than a reality for Ferdinand. And as for Irene des Pereires, she is a castrator of men.

Clemence, as the name itself indicates, means "clemency," and it has satiric overtones, for she is anything but gentle, understanding, and kind to her son. She works hard, fears her husband's constant angers, and lives in a world devoid of warm relationships. Her days are spent in the futile attempt to earn a living. The boxes she carries to the various stores all over Paris, filled with samples of lace and other materials, weigh her down, both literally and symbolically. She is plagued by bad luck, economic difficulties, and—worse—physical decrepitude: her spindly legs, always inflamed, bending under the weight of her body and the large parcels she carries, are frequently abcessed, the veins standing out in massive clumps. Her life is one long excruciating misery. Constantly rebuked by her husband, she seeks an outlet, unconsciously to be sure, in her son, with whom her relationship has always been bad. Even in the early days she denigrated him and displayed no faith in his capabilities, and her attitude worsens as the years pass. Yet her feelings could be called ambivalent, since she does love him, after her fashion. On the other hand, she sees him as a constant economic drain of which she would like to be rid. The more Ferdinand senses her resentment, the more he withdraws into his own world. The more hostile he feels toward his mother, the more he resorts to defecation, vomiting, and masturbation.

Clemence admires her husband but not her son. For one thing, Ferdinand is not, in contrast to the husband, physically robust. He is weak, puny, and sickly looking, and his stature and demeanor are an indication, to her mind, of the lad's prospects for the future. Her attitude instills a sense of failure in Ferdinand, who knows that his mother will always think of him as "an unfeeling child, a selfish monster, a little brute, capricious, scatterbrained . . ."[46] Though Clemence is instrumental in obtaining jobs for Ferdinand, she always informs the new employer of the difficulties that he is sure to have with the boy—of his laziness, worthlessness, sloppiness, disobedience, and continual nose-picking.[47] Clemence even suggests ways and means of handling her son. "Shame him," she declares, and he will work.[48] Every night when Ferdinand returns from work, his mother asks whether he has been fired yet. Ferdinand has failed before he even starts.[49]

The most painful moment in Clemence's life occurs when Ferdinand fights with his father. Her pent-up maternal instincts and her devotion to her husband both come to the fore. She is a woman divided and of course in tears. Subsequently her leg worsens—she can barely walk, and has to take to her bed; her inner pain has been transformed into physical disability. Her sudden realization of Ferdinand's hatred of his father, of his unconscious desire to rid himself of this devastating and crushing force by leaving his "home" forever, deprives her of what is most precious to a woman: her function as a mother. She will be shorn of her son. The full impact of this colossal loss and of her immense failure in life hits her after the father/son confrontation. When Ferdinand sees her again, months later, she is but a shade, a fiber, a lymph node—not a human being.

Madame Gorloge is a sensual, lustful woman of the Eternal Feminine type. Amoral, sadistic, masochistic, a nymphomaniac, her only interest in life is to arouse and be aroused sexually. She is all flesh. It is she who has Ferdinand accused of theft and fired so ignominiously.

Nora Merrywin gives the impression of being kind and gentle, not of this earth. Ferdinand is captivated by her warmth, by the exquisite beauty of her body, but most of all by what she represents: an understanding and helpful "mother" type. From her, he declares, "emanated harmony." Nora is a kind of "mirage," a phantasmagoria, a vision. She seems not to belong to this earth, and when he is with her it made for "a void in your soul." [50] Brought up under strict moral codes, fulfilling her obligations as schoolmistress and wife, Nora suffers from sexual dissatisfaction. When she seeks Ferdinand out one night, she is so struck by what she considers the magnitude of her crime—her sin—that she is unable to face the fact of her action and commits suicide.

Irene des Pereires is of the androgynic type, a psychological mixture of male and female characteristics. To underline this aspect of her personality, Céline describes her physical characteristics after her hysterectomy: a beard covers her chin, her voice is low, her gestures are vehement and forceful. She is domineering, and also a realist impatient with her husband's inventive fantasies—and yet when he needs her she is "there" to give him affection. In her own brittle way she is also friendly to Ferdinand, who considers her more friend than foe.

The only really positive female character in *Death on the Installment Plan* is Grandmother Caroline. Gentle, understanding, tender, she spends time with Ferdinand, takes him to shows, brings him a little dog so that he will be able to have "a little fun." [51] She is Ferdinand's only real source of comfort in his childhood. While she lives. Caroline sees to it that Clemence's business thrives; she is always there to relieve the family of its economic burdens. After her demise, the world sinks into sorrow.

Each of these women, save for Caroline, is unhappy and unfulfilled. Because joy or real love has been lacking in their lives, their personalities have developed unevenly and, therefore, dispensed kindness fitfully and only under exceptional circumstances. They maim, rather, because they have been maimed.

The most abominable figure of them all is Ferdinand's father, Auguste. The name "Auguste" should inspire awe, reverence, dignity, majesty. It has the opposite effect. It arouses enmity and degradation. Auguste is convinced from the very outset that his son will be a "thief," a vicious creature, a torment, a cross in his life. He castigates the boy for his laziness, his viciousness, his villainy, his egotism, his dissipation. Auguste's tempers, his insults, his floggings increase in intensity with the years and serve, of course, as a barometer of his own dissatisfaction with himself, which he projects onto his son.

> "Ah, you little skunk! You defy me? You little pimp! You swine! The insolence of it! The shame! Do you want to kill us? Is that it? . . . Why don't you say so right away? . . . You little coward! You bum. . . .
>
> "Suffering asshole Christ almighty! My poor dear, what did we do to produce such vermin? As corrupt as three dozen jailbirds! . . . Profligate! Scoundrel! Idler! And then some! He's calamity personified! Good for nothing except to rob us and clean us out! A pestilence! Gouge us without mercy!" [52]

Other negative male characters also come to the fore: Ferdinand's first and second employers condemn his so-called debauchery, laziness, insolence, deceitfulness, lustfulness, perverseness. Mr. Merrywin, the English schoolmaster, is negative in that he never knows what is really going on in his school. He lives in an ivory tower and acts in concert with his own conscience and dignity. When he discovers what a sordid situation he has permitted to prevail, he cannot accept it and commits suicide.

Perhaps the most fascinating character of them all is Courtial des Pereires, the inventor, writer, and jack-of-all-trades. He is imaginative and impractical, materialistic and mystical. He is the first person to speak favorably about Ferdinand to his mother. He tells her of the lad's aptitudes, and that he is discreet, a hard worker, clever, and has a future. The mother is stunned by his positive appraisal of one whom she has considered a total failure.

Courtial is an intuitive type, a visionary who plants a new type of potato that he hopes will revolutionize the potato business. Alas, it does not. The march of vermin spreads like a scourge, a pest, a plague, insidiously enveloping the entire world—perhaps the cosmos. Unable to accept this failure, Courtial commits suicide. Symbolically, his suicide indicates the destruction of this kind of individual by a commercial society. (He is, in his way, comparable to Mr. Merrywin.) Rather than being understood and helped by the collective, he is rejected (symbolically, as vermin is rejected) and destroyed.

Uncle Edouard, the most positive force in Ferdinand's life, sustains him in various ways. He is the one who provides the cash for Ferdinand's English trip, who takes him into his home after his fight with his father, who finds him a job with des Pereires. Gentle, understanding, always willing to lend a helping hand, he sympathizes with, and he understands, Ferdinand's situation and the cruelty inflicted on him.

The children in *Death on the Installment Plan* are pathetic creatures. André is degenerate, lazy, and a liar. Popaul is an alcoholic, a smoker, and a delinquent. Jonkin is retarded. Each in his own way has a negative influence upon Ferdinand.

Ferdinand, an introverted, almost mute child, could have been destroyed by his parents and by those he encountered, but for his lust for life. His built-in hostility, the fight he perpetually wages, the very velocity of his bloodstream all act as barriers or protective agencies and prevent his annihilation. Anger lives within him, revenge seethes covertly, manifesting itself only rarely during his childhood. When his grandmother gives him a dog, he identifies with the animal; when alone, he kicks it, hits it. Ferdinand is acting out his own situation, except that now he is the "father," the strong one, striking the more feeble animal, the little dog. When the animal cowers, defenseless, whimpering under Ferdinand's blows, begging forgiveness as it limps into a corner—as Ferdinand has done on countless occasions—the lad feels a sense of release. To exteriorize pain is to free oneself from it—momentarily.

MYTH

The myth that Céline interweaves into the very fabric of the novel is one of the most exciting aspects of the work. A myth, it must be recalled, is a dramatic narration of the experiences, or a description of the qualities, that are deepest within man. Myths are the outcome of original experiences—not always personal, but rather impersonal or transcendental ones.

Dante, Goethe, Wagner, Nietzsche, Blake—all had recourse to myth. What did the King Krogold myth mean to Céline? What did it indicate in terms of Ferdinand's life?

The narrator, Ferdinand, as a grown man, tells the reader at the very outset of the novel of the joy he used to experience as a child when listening to the legend of King Krogold, the narration of which is then begun forthwith and peppers the entire volume.

Gwendor the Magnificent, prince of Christianity, is about to die, his army having been defeated by King Krogold. But before expiring he speaks to Death, confessing to the shame he feels at the thought of the countless dead lying about, and asking for more time on earth in which to discover the name of the man who betrayed him and to rid the world of such evil, leaving it a place of unsullied beauty. Death answers that Gwendor is living in a dream world, that he is a foolish idealist, that pain is part of life, that life cannot be *only* beautiful. *Everything* betrays, he concludes, not just one man, not just one force.

> "There is no softness or gentleness in this world, Gwendor, but only myth! All kingdoms end in a dream . . ."
>
> "Everything betrays, Gwendor . . . The passions belong to no one, even love is only the flower of life in the garden of youth." [53]

The scene changes, Krogold's castle becomes visible: monstrous, formidable, with dungeons overlooking the sea, "crushing, incised in rock . . ." Its coat of arms is a serpent cut open, bleeding from the neck. Krogold, warrior king, marches forth on horseback, together with his brother the archbishop. Other members of the clergy and court follow. They camp for the night, but Krogold cannot sleep: he has discovered that the gold crescent given him by the caliph is missing. He walks about the encampment all night, despite his painful wounds; he is searching. Finally, he sees a man in a ditch holding the crescent. He smites him, recovers the prized object, and returns to his tent for a good night's sleep.

Later King Krogold marches toward his enemy, ten thousand strong, all of whom are huddled in the immense cathedral. They are kneeling, praying, beseeching the Lord for help. Let the Lord prevail upon Krogold, they ask, not to burn their fields, not to burn their law courts, not to burn their cathedrals. Krogold enters the melee. His might is evident indeed—his brilliant dress, his entourage that makes thundering noises as it clatters toward the cathedral, his pack of dogs jumping in jubilation over his victory. Cities and forests have been rent. The king eats. When finished, he hurls a bone into the middle of the church and his dogs make a lunge for it, screeching, tearing, maiming as they pounce. In the background, religious chants and hymns are heard. People cringe, flee . . . Silence. Krogold takes his sword, makes a gigantic sign of the cross, and hurls it onto the altar. The war has been won. He kneels before the archbishop and sings the credo.

The last scene: we discover that King Krogold has gone on a pilgrimage to the Holy Land, leaving Princess Wanda in the care of a troubadour. Wanda seeks vengeance. She tries to wash away her father's sins.

There is no question that Céline, who loved the Breton landscape, should be captivated by this particular myth, so reminiscent of Celtic and Norse lore. The pattern is usually the same: a fight between beauty and ugliness, spirituality and earthliness, good and evil, life and death, the dream and the reality.

Evil, in the form of King Krogold, has become a cosmic principle. It has become the enemy of life. Like Loki, in Norse mythology, Krogold has turned into a companion piece for the Christian Devil: Satan, Belial, Beelzebub, the pre-Exilic adversary of Yahweh.[54] Krogold is the anti-Christ, the hostile power confronting the love-principle and striving to destroy all of its positive manifestations in the world. King Krogold's situation, however, is quite complex since he, too, is Christian. As such, he represents the aggressive and cruel aspects of Christianity.

As his name indicates, Krogold stands for gold, matter (money, possessions, land, power) and more abstract values as well (the kingly virtues of judgment and wisdom). Rather than becoming master of himself, however, and making the most of the kingly qualities bestowed upon him, he gives in to his material side, to his passion for conquest. He becomes, as his castle indicates, a powerhouse for destructive forces. The castle is described as monstrous, formidable, and crushing. His coat of arms, we recall, is a bleeding serpent. The serpent long associated symbolically with intellectual curiosity (it was a serpent that suggested to Eve that if she ate the fruit of the "Tree of Knowledge" she would gain in acumen and insight), is also considered an evil force, one that foments disobedience and disregard for the status quo. Krogold's bloodied snake would seem to mean, then, the partial destruction of this animal—that is, the annihilation of its (and thus Krogold's) spiritual half (its neck—his neck—is bleeding in the coat of arms) and the solidity of its (and his) physical half, which slithers about in the earth's slime. Thus Krogold has been divested of the spiritual function so important to a king and to a Christian. What remains? His material and earthy self.

Krogold's brother, the archbishop, the soldiers—all Christians—are forceful, strong crusaders. They side with power and strength, not with the meek (that is, the people). According to this legend, then, the church is in the hands of warriors (crusaders) and has become an instrument of destruction. It is no longer the instrument of the gentle, idealistic, righteous philosophy conceived by Christ. The church, Céline implies, has become amoeba-like: it has taken the form and shape of those who head it. In the hands of the spiritually oriented, the church could have become an instrument of justice, virtue, and beauty; in the hands of the Krogolds and their like, it has become a vehicle of greed, lust, and bloody murder.

The fact that Gwendor the Magnificent, a man of the heart, dies early in the story indicates the powerlessness of Christianity to bring out the spiritual aspect, the love side, of religion. And even Gwendor, as he looks at the dead bodies strewn around him, gives in to anger and to the desire for revenge. In his Dialogue with Death, one of the most touching sections of the narrative, Gwendor learns that what he so longs for (goodness, order) is not part of life on earth. If one lives as a member of society, it seems, one must accept its evils. Visionaries are cut down, the meek are crushed. Kingdoms, like religions, are created by visionaries. They live and die, however, betrayed by the mediocre, by the masses. In the sordid world that man has created for himself, in which pity and understanding are so flagrantly disregarded, there is little place for the idealist—the poet, the writer—little place for Gwendor. Who dreams, suffers.

Only in death can illusions be eternal. As Gwendor departs from the world "a beautiful dream takes his soul," indicating his withdrawal from the world of matter, and his entrance into the domain of the spirit. There is no common denominator between the idealist and his vision and what man makes of that vision.

Vindication of sorts does come, at the end, when Wanda (representing the realm of feeling) betrays King Krogold with the troubadour (the poet). Cosmic order is restored, but only in part and only for the moment, since Krogold is already on the march to the Holy Land, campaigning for still more power and spreading still more terror.

What did the Krogold myth imply in terms of Ferdinand? That he was, according to Céline, the product of materialistic and ignorant parents and of an equally destructive society that fed on the ineffective palliative of Christian morality. King Krogold represents the aggressive, near-sighted, materialistic forces with which Ferdinand has to cope, Gwendor, the idealist (a man like Preires or a beautiful woman such as Nora) who cannot survive in an atmosphere of decay.

The Krogolds of this world, and the forceful and repressive powers they represent (the government, the church), are bulwarks against progress. They not only dominate the individual and society but manipulate them. For Ferdinand this implies that he is lost before he even begins: commerce, industry, the church—all are powers that threaten to destroy him unless he "goes along." There is no room in society for the Gwendor type—the pure, the poetic, the intuitive. These creative people are sucked up, demolished in man's greed for power. Yet they too, in the end, may have their revenge.

It is Ferdinand's choice: to struggle against what he believes to be an evil cosmic principle at the risk of being destroyed in the onslaught, or to accept society as it is, with all its evil, and to ride along on the crest of its vices. If he chooses the former, he can expect to lead a solitary life, a life filled with the wretchedness and despair that are usually the lot of poets and visionaries. If he chooses the latter, he may, in the process, lose his identity, his creativity, and his reality.

At the end of the volume, Ferdinand chooses the military. The Krogold side, perhaps. Or is it an escape route?

Considering the fact that *Death on the Installment Plan* was an indictment of France and of its society, what could Céline expect from the critics? For the most part, their response was one of hostility. André Rousseaux objected to Céline's obscenity and his use of slang. René Lalou considered the novel monotonous and cumbersome, though enlivened every now and then with a display of brutality. Marcel Lapiètre dismissed the work as a compendium of trivia and vulgarities. Jacques Bridel called it "mediocre" and "repugnant." Robert Brasillach found it intolerably dull and suspected that the success of Céline's first novel had gone to his head. There were, however, critics who rose to Céline's defense. Ramon Fernandez, for example, considered the novel's style the most "significant" of his time and especially recommended the channel-crossing sequence, which he compared to a "fantastic symphony." [55]

Céline was not one to withdraw when insults were leveled his way. Though a pacifist—technically, as he would have everyone believe—he was a fighter at heart. He answered the critics briefly and pithily: they were stupid, he declared, uneducated, incapable of making any kind of sound judgment. People in general, and critics in particular, Céline continued, are sadistics, weak-kneed, envious, destructive beings—mediocrities who cannot even begin to appreciate a work of art. Céline did not solicit their admiration, he went on. On the contrary, all he wanted was the commercial success of his novel. One could, he further claimed, earn popularity through critical condemnation. Should he elicit the hatred and rage of the critics, should they "cover him with spit," the masses would hasten to buy his book, for anything associated with sensationalism, murder, thievery, and lasciviousness arouses the curiosity of the collective. The masses are like ravenous animals; their appetite for the sordid is never satisfied. Man is after blood, Céline declared, and he would give it to them, enabling them, thereby, to gulp it down.

Céline did not seek the public's love or admiration, he said, but rather their hatred. If only he could earn their animosity, he could be certain of having written a bestseller. It was just for this reason that he insulted his readers. "I suggest, I incite, I titilate. I do everything possible." [56] The more passion he provoked, the greater his readers' reaction and dynamism and the more forceful the impact of his work upon them. To this end distances are obliterated, rational processes suppressed, tempos accelerated, victims devoured.

Though Céline spoke brazenly of seeking to make his readers hate his work, there is no question that he was deeply hurt by the negative criticisms his book received. But rather than admit to his feelings of pain, he sought to repress them; rather than adopt a sincere attitude, he turned to denial; rather than defend his views concerning civilization and literature, he buried them under a barrage of insults.

Céline could not accept his world or himself. He sought a mask. But when a man hides his hurt, his despair, his disillusionment, the sense of defeat and solitude, the restlessness, the inner being within him remains dissatisfied and cries out its own anger, its hatred. And the battle is on.

5

DEATH-TRAP

We used to wonder where war lived, what made it so vile. And now we realize where it lives, inside ourselves.

ALBERT CAMUS, *Note-Books, 1935–1942*

THERE HAD ALWAYS BEEN A TREMENDOUS CONFLICT BETWEEN THE pacifist views iterated by Céline and the irascible, contentious, and violent temperaments of his protagonists. This dichotomy would be expressed, if not more blatantly in *Death-Trap,* Céline's next novel, of which only fragments are extant, then at least as powerfully as in his previous works.

War, according to Céline, is always a distinct possibility and may explode under any type of government. This is so because man lusts after battle, is drawn to bloodshed, thrives on it like a starving dog goes after red meat. What is remarkable, and also quite disconcerting, is the fact that Céline fights the idea of war with such violence: he uses savage weapons (violent images, vicious people, etc.) to *kill* conflict—an ironic situation to say the least.

The question remains as to why he tries to fight brutality with brutality, cruelty with cruelty, murder with murder. The answer is not yet forthcoming. Something, however, seems to be burgeoning within the author's depths, a further dissatisfaction not only with the world about him but also, possibly, with his means of expression. The novel, the world of fiction, may no longer answer his need to expel his anger and hatred. Thus far, however, it has had to suffice.

The Ferdinand of *Death-Trap* is in the army (specifically, in the cavalry), suggesting that the work may have been a sequel to *Death on the Installment Plan.* Only the first two chapters of this novel are extant, however. They were found by chance in 1948 in a Paris bookshop. Additional torn pages have turned up now and again in second-hand shops in Paris, but not enough of them to alter our impression of the work.

As related by Céline in *Death-Trap,* military life takes on a rather special flavor! The work is not comparable, for example, to Jean Froissart's *Chronicles,* which re-create so incisively, and in vast panoramic frescoes, the ideals, the views of the medieval soldiers and officers during their exploits at Poitiers and in Flanders. Nor is it comparable to Philippe de Commynes' *Mémoires*

(1488), in which the historical and military situations under the reign of Louis XII are outlined. Certainly there is inherent in Céline's account of barracks life or the soldiers' ethos none of the zeal that d'Aubigné exuded in his *Universal History* (1620) or in his poems, *The Tragics*, depicting, among other things, the merciless massacres of Protestants by Catholics.

Céline's essential interests lie in the turmoil, the filth, the decay, and the horror of military life, in and out of the barracks, and in the soldiers' attitudes toward death. Alfred de Vigny, who also wrote about military and barracks life, had faith in the soldiers' essential stoicism and dignity. Céline had no such illusions. He did not consider barracks life in terms of sacrifice or renunciation; quite to the contrary. Army life, as depicted in *Death-Trap*, is a life of grotesque horror. The effect of the work is stunning, thanks to the power and the drive of Céline's images and his use of a dual-time technique.

Céline exposes his readers visually to Ferdinand's reactions to the army: his consternation, surprise, and frequent revulsion at the comportment of the officers and enlistees who cross his path. There are many images of soldiers falling down from exhaustion, overcome with fatigue after long forced marches through rain-soaked country, smarting with pain from the gale force of the winds slashing at their faces, images of mud-stained clothes and of boots half rotted with mildew, encrusted with filth of all types, and smelling of dampness and the acrid aroma of the stables. Character traits are also rendered pictorially: the cavalry man's arrogance as he rides his horse, whipping it mercilessly to make it move faster and so proving (to himself) his colossal power over the animal. And suffering is also rendered in terms of the image that gives an indication of the physical stamina necessary to endure, to survive the travail, the cruelties and man's utter ferocity when living together in relatively close quarters.

But the one image that stands out above all others is that of the horse. Céline's depiction of this animal has the power and the energy, but not the beauty, that such painters as Géricault and Delacroix gave to their drawings of horses. Great painters drew the horse with muscles bending, curving and stretching, a body in flight, snorting, panting as the animal seeks to take in more and more breath, increasing thereby the length of its strides. Céline's horses are depicted in another manner: the animal's most elemental aspects are brought to the fore as it defecates, urinates, and injects images of hostility into the entire ambiance.

The symbolism of the horse is indeed complex psychologically. It is an animal long associated with feelings of intense desire, instinctuality, and sexuality. In Greek times, it was dedicated to Mars and its appearance augured war.

Céline's horse in particular may be viewed in both ways: as instinct and as a belligerent force. The variety of pace, the walking, trotting, galloping, and cantering, of the horses depicted in *Death-Trap* gives one an impression of extreme tension, energy, and excitement that is almost too much to bear.[1] The horses drawn by Céline in these chapters may at times take on the speed of a comet or of a flash of lightning, at other times the tempo of a searing thought.[2]

There is no repose in the horses associated with Ferdinand's stay in the cavalry. They are always vibratory and their stamina and power bring to mind Robinson Jeffers' poem *Roan Stallion*, in which the primitive urge, the sexuality basic to every living thing, is depicted. Céline's horses represent unbridled instincts in their rawest, most vicious, and bellicose forms. Indeed, it is war—if not overtly expressed, then covertly felt—whenever the horse enters the scene. Not that Céline was attracted to war per se—he never tires of saying that he despises it; yet the inner man, the author, the creator of such images, belied his ideational or cerebrally conceived views. It was always the belligerent, the quarrelsome, the contentious and insolent aspect of the writer that emerged, not the man of peace.

By means of a dual-time technique, Céline succeeds in increasing the atmosphere of tension and horror already so well incised visually.

On joining the army, Ferdinand is overcome with a sense of imprisonment. Such a claustrophobic feeling is, of course, expressed characterwise, and also in terms of his entrapment in time. Once in the army, he lives on two levels, the first an atemporal, or primitive, time plane, and the second a temporal, or historical, one. The former comes into being before discernment and, therefore, has no past, present, or future. Céline's frequent allusions for example, to "ferocious nature," to the "furious seas . . .,"[3] plunges him into this type of cyclical time pattern, creating the illusion of something eternal and dispelling any notions of death, terror, or fright. There is, however, another level upon which he functions, that of historical time, with a beginning and end and, therefore, with life and death. This historical time he feels most acutely as a gluey, burning substance, a perpetual threat to his well-being. When, for example, he describes his daily activities, army life in all of its unpleasant aspects, he always talks in terms of an end, of death, and because of it seems submerged in the vise-like grasp of historical time.

What is of distinct interest is the effect of crosscurrents with which Céline infuses the entire pattern as Ferdinand shifts from one time level to the other. The dynamism inherent in such (usually unconscious) activity accelerates the pace, introducing an entirely new kinetic experience in terms of the hero. The frenzy of his emotions, his anger, his fears are related to the whirlwind effects of the prose, the turbulent images, the choppiness of the sentence structure. Thought processes—the rational in man—are obliterated.

To increase the reader's sense of Ferdinand's conflicts and fears, Céline adds yet another stylistic effect: he shifts from dialogue to interior monologue to narrative, an interchange that breaks up the flow of events and their chronological sequence. The protagonist and his activities thus appear fragmented, spasmodic, only rarely whole, and comparable in this respect to an early Charlie Chaplin picture played out at top speed. The effect is disorienting: no plateaux are ever reached, no sense of tranquility is ever experienced. *Death-Trap* is reminiscent of a series of slipping and sliding sequences, the monotony of which is alloyed by frequent interruptions.

The impression created by such continuous displacement of focus has, to be sure, psychological ramifications. One may conclude that Ferdinand (in terms of the images, the dual-time technique) is no more master of his outside world than he is of his emotions. Both seem to play havoc with him. The converging time sequences also have the ability to contort the reader's sense of reality. Events and images are transformed into hydra heads, so to speak, with infinite possibilities of acting and reacting to given situations, each perhaps with ignominious portents.

SECRETS OF THE ISLAND

The dual-time technique used by Céline in *Death-Trap* is found also in a movie scenario, *Secrets of the Island* (1936), that he wrote during this period of his development. The decor is the sea, the coast of Brittany, with its steep cliffs, harsh waters, cold, piercing winds—the same coast that inspired Victor Hugo to write so many extraordinary verses.

Céline's coast, as viewed in this scenario, is vicious, arid, shot through with brutal rocks, tempests ever lurking in the distance as constant reminders of destruction and death. As the scenario opens, nature is again in a state of delirium, ready to inflict her damage upon mortals seeking refuge and consolation in her vastness and all-embracing capacity.

The juxtaposition in the scenario of the limitless, interminable expanse and the frenetic activity of the protagonists ushers in a sense of doom and death.

The populace comes into focus. They are poor, passionate, distrustful, sensual, jealous, extremely devout people, whose activity is frenetic, whose personalities are like a series of tinder-boxes, crackling with energy.

A yacht looms up from the distance. Its commander, Erika, a beautiful, imperious, wealthy woman, steps ashore. Deciding to remain in the town, she takes as her chambermaid a young native girl, Yvonnik, who is engaged to the young fisherman Yann. The affection between the two women grows to such an extent that Yvonnik becomes jealous of anyone who pays the slightest attention to Erika. Soon another boat docks and a painter and his daughter, Suzanne, disembark. Erika invites them to her home, and Suzanne and Erika are soon fast friends. Yvonnik is eaten up with jealousy. One day, the fishermen go out to sea. The native women, siding in silence with Yvonnik in her battle to possess Erika, decide to punish the newcomer. They grab Erika's feet and thighs and bite into them until blood gushes out. Suzanne, terrified, takes a gun and tries to protect her friend. In so doing, she shoots Yvonnik. The women, screaming and cackling in a frenzy, rip off Erika's and Suzanne's clothes and tie the two women up. One woman, to show the depth of her contempt and hatred, urinates on both victims. The townswomen then carry Erika and Suzanne to the highest cliff and throw them into the sea. When the fishermen return, they pick up the cadavers and bring them to shore. They learn what has happened during their absence. They remain silent, and a mass is said for the dead.

In this powerful drama, in which hate and jealousy reign supreme, Céline introduces his audiences to the ugliest of destroyers: harpies, female cannibals who feed upon others in the most insidious ways.

What is perhaps the most terrifying element—aside from the intrinsic horror of the whole incident—is that nature acts in complicity with man's (in this case, woman's) most brutal aspects. Nature is no longer designed to bring out man's spirituality, to elevate him to higher realms. Nature has become a mirror image of man's violence and viciousness and encourages his murderous instincts.

Death-Trap and *Secrets of the Island* underscore man's frenzy to kill, either for military reasons or for carnal ones. The virility of Céline's depictions, the harshness of his vision, leads one to believe that fiction will no longer be a satisfying outlet for a man whose inner world, as projected in his protagonists and in the virulence of nature, is utterly chaotic and hostile toward all notions of peace.

Part Two

POLEMICIST

Of this gloomy world,
In what a shadow, or deep pit of darkness,
Doth womanish, and fearful mankind live?

John Webster, *The Duchess of Malfi*

6

THE ANTI-SEMITE

Who is the Anti-Semite?

He is the man who is afraid. Not of the Jews, to be sure, but of himself, of his own consciousness, of his liberty, of his instincts, of his responsibilities, of solitariness, of change, of society and of the world—of everything except the Jews. He is a coward who does not want to admit his cowardice to himself. . . . The Jew only serves him as a pretext; elsewhere his counterpart will make use of the Negro or the man of yellow skin. Anti-Semitism, in short, is the fear of the human condition. The anti-Semite is a man who wishes to be pitiless stone, a furious torrent, a devastating thunderbolt—anything except a man.

JEAN-PAUL SARTRE, *Anti-Semitism and the Jew*

Death on the Installment Plan WAS CÉLINE'S LAST NOVEL, for a time. Rather than try to re-create reality in a fictitious realm, he would seek to partake of it. He rejected the idea of the passive artist living in an ivory tower. His political, philosophical, and economic ideas had coalesced. He had a platform and he sought to bring it to society.

In considering Céline's three polemical works—*Bagatelles for a Massacre* (1937), *School for Cadavers* (1938) and *Some State of Affairs* (1941)—one is immediately struck by the author's seemingly infinite capacity to hate: to hate the French, to hate humanity in general—but mostly to hate the Jew. If Céline had done no more than voice his own ideas, one might not be so inclined to take his message seriously and could, therefore, limit discussion of Céline's anti-Semitism to his personal psychology. Such is not the case, however. The sentiments voiced in Céline's polemical tracts, the picture he paints and the accusations he levels at the Jew, have far greater and more insidious import than merely that of being an expression of one author's dislikes.

To grasp the full import of Céline's polemical works, it is necessary to see them in the context of French anti-Semitism, the French political climate in the period from 1937 to 1941, and the psychology of anti-Semitism generally and as an element of Céline's personal make-up.

FRENCH ANTI-SEMITISM

One of the most favorable periods for the Jew in France during the Middle Ages was the reign of Charlemagne. This emperor was aware of the industrious nature of the Jewish people and understood the economic advantages of having them remain in his domain. His son Louis also watched over their well-being, appointing an officer *(Magister Judaecorum)* to help protect the Jew from the many intolerant clerics of the period.[1]

Such relative security, however, was short-lived. According to Professor Salo Baron's monumental work *A Social and Religious History of the Jews,*[2] with the coming of the First Crusade (1096), a period of persecution began during which killing Jews was not the exception but the rule. Acton wrote: "The men who took the cross after receiving communion, heartily devoted the day to the extermination of the Jews."[3] Around ten thousand Jews were killed during this period. When Godfrey de Bouillon took Jerusalem (1099), he not only killed many of the city's inhabitants but also, quite as a matter of course, locked up the Jews in their synagogue and set fire to it.[4]

Peter "the Venerable" was convinced that the Jews should actually pay for the Crusades. From his monastery at Cluny, he declared:

> Why should not the Jews contribute more than anyone else to the expense of the holy war? Robbers they are; this is the very occasion for compelling them to disgorge. Sacrilegious blasphemers, this is the way in which to punish their impiety![5]

Peter of Blois wrote a celebrated treatise *Against the Perfidious Jews,* in which he characterized them as "brute beasts, incapable of rational argument."[6] If a Jew was permitted to live at all during the Middle Ages, he was treated less well than an animal.

When Philip Augustus became king of France (1180), he extorted money from all classes, trades, and groups, but most particularly from the Knights Templars and the Jews. One of his first official acts was to imprison all the Jews in his domain, freeing them only after having extracted a tremendous "tax." Two years later he confiscated their lands and buildings and expelled them from his kingdom. It is reported by the chroniclers of the period that Philip Augustus "hated the Jews . . ." Even so, they were readmitted to his domain in 1198—but of course their financial status was carefully observed and heavy taxes and duties were imposed upon them.[7]

"Saint" Louis, known to all for his extreme piety and humility, known as one who washed the feet of "Christian" lepers, known as one who served "Christians" with food from his own table, was also known as a Jew-hater. Sire Jean de Joinville (1224–1318), the official court historian, reports the king's point of view in the following statement made by the monarch:

> And I tell you that no one, unless he be a very learned clerk, should dispute with them; but a layman, when he hears the Christian law mis-said, should not defend the Christian law, unless it be with his sword, and with that he should pierce the mis-sayer in the midriff, so far as the sword will enter.[8]

Mass killings of the Jews occurred to such an extent during the reign of Saint Louis that Pope Gregory IX felt himself compelled to declare (September

5, 1236) that the Crusaders had gone beyond the rule of Pope Innocent III in oppressing the Jews. Gregory protested the Crusaders' attempts to "wipe out the Jews almost completely off the face of the earth." And he continued, "in an unheard of and unprecedented outburst of cruelty, they have slaughtered in this mad hostility, two thousand five hundred of them—old and young, as well as pregnant women. Some were mortally wounded, and others trampled like mud under the feet of horses." [9]

Philip the Fair, in 1306, gave the Jews just one month to leave France, under penalty of death. Because of this ruling, over a hundred thousand people had to emigrate, with only their clothes on their back. Several years later, during the reign of Louis X, the Jews were permitted to return, but no guarantees for their future well-being were forthcoming.[10]

Petrarch reports that it was *de rigueur* to blame the Jews for every misfortune, including the Black Death epidemic in France. The Jews were said to have traveled to India for the express purpose of bringing the plague back with them and inflicting it upon Christians. How? Why by poisoning all the wells in France. Because the Jews were considered to be responsible for the plague, Christians had many of them tortured and burned alive.[11] In 1394 the Jews were once again expelled from France.

During the Renaissance and the French Classical period the Jews fared somewhat better. Marie de Médicis, nevertheless, adhered to the medieval notion that the state was created to serve Christianity. With this in mind, the queen-regent decreed in 1615 that the Jews, every one of them (she was convinced) must, as enemies of Christianity, leave France.[12] Not all of them did so, however. There were some—but not many—who remained, either as converts to Christianity or as "Marranos." [13]

The general feeling toward the Jews was one of distaste, dislike, and disgust. Madame de Sévigné, for example, writing to her daughter, Madame de Grignan (June 26, 1689), declared: "I feel horror and pity for them. . . ." Other writers and prelates were not so softspoken. The well-known and influential Bishop Bossuet, one of the most outspoken anti-Semites of the seventeenth century, wrote in his *Discourse on Universal History* of the persecutions of Jews all over the world. He was convinced that when the Jew was tortured and burned at the stake it was because God was angry with him. It was "divine vengeance," he declared.[14] In his famous *Sermon for Good Friday,* he aroused tremendous feelings of hate in his parishioners when he thundered:

> O cursed race! Your prayer will be answered only too effectively; that blood will pursue you even unto your remotest descendants, until the Lord, weary at last of vengeance, will be mindful, at the end of time, of your miserable remnant.[15]

During the eighteenth century a spirit of tolerance manifested itself in two distinct areas: in Switzerland, with Jean-Jacques Rousseau, and in Holland, with Pierre Bayle, the author of the *Historical Dictionary.* Bayle was probably one of the greatest spokesmen for tolerance. It was he who sought to establish freedom of thought and to permit all religions to practice their rituals without interference.[16] Though anticlerical, Bayle was deeply Christian in the finest sense of the word. His work, wrote Paul Hazard, is "the most painful repository ever gathered together revealing man's shame. . . ." [17]

During the so-called Age of Enlightenment, writers of the stature of Montesquieu felt that Christian intolerance was the source of Jewish persecution. In his "Very Humble Remonstrance to the Spanish and Portuguese inquisitors," included in *The Spirit of the Laws* (XXV, 13), he wrote vehemently against the butchers and religious fanatics in both Portugal and Spain, and against the iniquities perpetrated against the Jews. Such humanitarian feelings, however, did not prevent the intrusion of anti-Semitic remarks in such works as *The Persian Letters* (L.X), in which Montesquieu declared: "Know that wherever there is money, there is the Jew." A paragraph later, he assesses the Jewish religion in terms of the other great religions.

> The Jewish religion is like an old trunk which produced two branches which have covered the entire earth, I mean Mohammedanism and Christianity. Or rather, it is a mother who engendered two girls who have harassed her with a thousand wounds. So far as religion is concerned, the closest are the bitterest of enemies.[18]

Voltaire was perhaps the most fanatically anti-Semitic of all the "enlightened" eighteenth-century philosophers. The pages he devoted to anti-Semitic remarks "do not add to the glory of the great man,' wrote Léon Poliakov.[19] Some thirty of the hundred eighteen articles in Voltaire's *Philosophical Dictionary* refer to Jews in such derogatory terms as, for example, "our masters and our enemies, whom we believe and whom we detest" (in the article on "Abraham"), "the most abominable people on earth" ("Anthropophagous"), a people "whose laws say nothing about spirituality and immortality of the soul . . ." ("Soul"), etc. In the article "Jew," Voltaire wrote:

> . . . you will find in them only an ignorant and barbaric people; blended within them is the most sordid avarice, the most detestable superstition, the most invincible hatred for all people who tolerate and enrich them. . . . They must not, however, be burned.[20]

Further on he added, again referring to the Jews: "You are calculating animals, try to be thinking animals." In his *Essay on Mores,* he stated: "We look at the Jew in the same manner as we look at the Negro, as a species inferior to man." [21]

Voltaire clearly suffered from a full-blown anti-Jewish phobia. As the Catholic philosopher Louis de Bonald noted, whereas the eighteenth-century philosophers generally sought to lighten the burden of the Jews, Voltaire displayed throughout his life a decided aversion for them.[22]

Jean-Jacques Rousseau, unlike Voltaire, was favorably disposed toward the Jews. Thus he declared, in his *Profession of the Savoyard Vicar's Faith:*

> Those unfortunate people feel themselves to be at our mercy! The tyrany we exercise over them makes them fearful; they know that injustice and cruelty hardly bothers Christian charity . . .[23]

Elsewhere, however, when referring to the Jews of antiquity, Rousseau must have lapsed from his liberal point of view, momentarily at least, when he went along with his compatriots and judged the Jews as "the vilest of peoples" and "the baseness of this people incapable of any kind of virtue." [24] Even so, Rousseau had admiration for Moses. He expressed this sentiment in his *Considerations on the Polish Government.* It was Moses, Rousseau maintained, who transformed a nomadic tribe "without armaments, without talents, without virtues, without courage" into "a free people." It was this man of God, Rousseau went on, who gave his people the Law—the Ten Commandments.[25]

Diderot attacked all revealed religions and could not, therefore, omit that of the Jews. "This great champion of irreligion" treated all matters touching on the sacred with "a tranquil unrespect, without the least bit of veneration (even for the person of Christ), but also, without iconoclastic fury." [26] It might be said that Diderot, for his time, was the most tolerant of men, a man who advocated freedom of speech for his enemies and permitted them "the liberty of writing and speaking that they want to deny us." [27]

As for the encyclopedia that Diderot edited, one must not forget that there were over two hundred contributors, each of whom expressed his own point of view. Nearly all the articles sought to prove a thesis and in most of them, of course, Jews were not favorably treated. As Léon Poliakov remarked, "Diderot is the Eycyclopedia, but the Encyclopedia is not Diderot." [28]

On January 28, 1791, the creators of the French Revolution promulgated a law declaring that those people "known in France by the name of Portuguese, Spanish, and Avignonnais Jews" would from this time forward be granted "the rights" of citizenship. On September 27, 1791, all the Jews in France were emancipated.[29]

Not everyone endorsed this new trend. The bishop of Nancy, speaking at the National Assembly on December 23, 1789, voiced his fears openly. The French people, he asserted, look upon the Jew with "horror," and a decree "granting them the right of citizenship would set the whole country ablaze." [30]

The eighteenth and nineteenth centuries were, on the whole, ones of relative calm for the Jews of France. The belief in the perfectibility of man was popularized; reforms and laws designed for the well-being of all would serve, people believed, to bring happiness to the world. This would make it possible for each individual to show his good side.

A new era for the Jews was ushered in.[31] From 1816 on, the Jew was part of society; he worked freely, worshiped without fear, and became one with the French nation. The writer and politician Benjamin Constant noted that the Jew might now "figure honorably in the administration, no longer withdraw from an army career, cultivate and teach the sciences." [32]

The acceptance of the Jew into society did not, of course, put an end to anti-Semitism. It merely served to mask it for a time. It cropped up every now and then in such fictional characters as Nunicingen, the "loup-cervier" created by Balzac; in the rabbi, the "fetid Jew, deicide, Barrabas," in Victor Hugo's play *Cromwell;* and in such statements as "to lie and to steal, it's the Jew absolutely," [33] in Hugo's drama *Marie Tudor.* The famous historian Michelet also derogated the Jew, stating "the Jew, foul man . . .," [34] after which he praised him. As for Chateaubriand, he expressed his dislike of Jews in his *Memoirs Beyond the Tomb,* where we read: "humanity has placed the Jewish race in a leprosarium and they will remain in quarantine until the end of the world."[35] Alfred de Vigny, in *The Marshalin of Ancre,* referred to the Jew as "rich and avaricious, humble and false."[36]

It was Count Joseph-Arthur de Gobineau (1816–1882), in his *Essay on the Inequalities of the Human Races,* who introduced racialist anti-Semitism into France. His theses, as we know, would profoundly influence the Nazi theorists. Gobineau believed that man had been degenerating over the centuries and was now weak and evil. Any civilization, moreover, that chose a democratic form of government was, of necessity, decadent. Furthermore, any civilization of value was the creation of the white race alone, and must arise through its "Aryan" branch in particular. Gobineau was not alone. Ernest Renan, for example, believed that the Semitic "race" was made up of an "inferior combination of human nature"—an insight set forth in his *General History.* As for Hippolyte Taine, he advocated a return to monarchy, aristocracy, and the Catholic church, and in his *Origins of Contemporary France* he identified race, environment, and the *Zeitgeist* as the factors that determine the course of history.

Anti-Semitism did not blossom forth from rightist soil alone; the leftists were equally lavish in their condemnation of the Jews. The French socialists, for example, working for the creation of a new society, attacked Judaism on two grounds. The atheististic socialists felt that the Jews were the forerunners of Christianity and as such must be dispersed and assimilated; the Christian socialists saw the Jew as an "international capitalist" who must be done away with as such.[37] What the latter group either did not recall, or never knew, was that the Jewish population of nineteenth-century France constituted only about a fourth of one percent of the total, and that most of these Jews were extremely poor folk, struggling as best they could to keep alive.[38]

The reformer Charles Fourier (1773–1837), a deeply Christian man, was also a violent anti-Semite. In his *Theories of the Four Movements,* he reworked all the old anti-Semitic arguments. First, he accused the Jews of usury, forgetting that usury had been practiced in France long before Jews had ever emigrated there—practiced by Christians. Indeed, the Christians had always demanded a higher rate of interest than the Jews: because it was illegal for a Christian to practice moneylending, the risk was far greater for them, and so were their interest rates. Fourrier also feared the emancipation of the Jews. "The Jew is the plague of humanity, the enemy of all nations," he declared. He was convinced that France, with its Jews emancipated, would become a "vast synagogue," and would fall under the influence of this "parasitical, deceitful" and "avaricious" group.[39] The worst and most humiliating situation that could ever befall France, wrote this philosopher intent upon establishing the perfect society, would be the "admission of the Jews as citizens."[40] Alphonse Toussenel, Fourrier's socialist disciple, continued the attack on Jews in the book *Jews, King of the Epoch* (1844), in which the Jews are depicted as being parasitical and unproductive.[41]

The very Catholic socialist Pierre Proudhon (1809–1865) believed the Jew to be an incarnation of the "Evil Principle" on earth. In his *Caesarism and Christianity* we read:

> The Jew is temperamentally unproductive. He is neither an agriculturalist, nor an industrialist, not really a tradesman. He is a panderer, always fraudu-

> lent and a parasite, who operates in business as he does in philosophy, through lies, counterfeiting, crookedness.[42]

Jews were not human beings, Proudhon declared, since they did not recognize the divinity of Christ.[43]

Anti-Semitic articles peppered the socialist newspapers of the period. In *Revue Socialiste,* which began publication in 1885, in *Cri du Peuple,* and in the other papers the Jews were denounced for speculating, for being parasitical, for being avaricious, for being rich, etc. The editors of these newspapers, for the most part, advocated the "pure morals of Aryan philosophy" and the necessity of liquidating the Jews and their fortunes.[44] Many Christian socialists, including members of the clergy such as Father Paul Fesch, were deeply anti-Semitic. Socialist deputies and poets, as witnessed by Clovis Hugues and François Coppée, were likewise intolerant of Jews.

But it was Edouard Drumont (1844–1917), who considered himself the official spokesman for the socialists, who was the most powerful anti-Semite in France after the Revolution. It was his conviction that all of France's economic and social ills were due to the Jews and that he had been given a mission—by God, no less—to rid his land of the Jewish peril. In 1886, thanks to the help of the popular novelist Alphonse Daudet, Drumont succeeded in getting his volume *La France Juive* into print. This work attempted to prove that France was totally dominated by Jews intent upon destroying Christianity. He was the nineteenth century's "Crusader," he declared, a Crusader fighting and writing in defense of the Holy Roman Catholic Church.

> I have prayed to Christ for resignation if the publication of this book resulted in suffering for me, and for humility if my efforts were crowned with success . . . God had taken the book under His care, because He knew, no doubt, that it was inspired by love and justice.[45]

In another century, in another country, another man would write in a similar vein—in *Mein Kampf.* "I believe today," Hitler declared, "that my conduct is in accordance with the will of the Almighty Creator. In standing guard against the Jews, I am defending the handiwork of the Lord."[46]

It was Drumont who united "religious, economic and racial sentiments into one hatred."[47] He was convinced that if, somehow, the Jews in France could be exterminated, economic and spiritual prosperity would follow. The annihilation of the Jews would mean freedom for the proletariat, and he called upon the French clergy to help him in his crusade to rid France of them. Some clerics complied. Parish priests, Drumont confessed, were of great help to him in his work. Above all others they had "a clear conception of the characteristics of persecution, without parallels in history, which is directed by the manipulators of gold against the poor, by the sons of Judas against the servants of Jesus Christ." He asked the clergy of his country "to denounce the plotting Semites and hand them over to the secular arm."[48]

Drumont applauded the persecution of the Jews anywhere and everywhere. The Spanish Dominicans, who had burned so many Jews at the stake during the Inquisition, were "ardent patriots, who did not hesitate to suppress all Jews." Indeed, he observed, many of the clerics who burned Jews at the stake were subsequently canonized by the church! Drumont was convinced that

France should not only do likewise, in imitation of former activities, but should also initiate a series of pogroms along Russian lines.[49]

Not only were the clerics a great source of help to Drumont, but so was the Catholic press, which attended to most of his publicity. *Le Monde*, the semi-official voice of the archbishop of Paris, the *Revue du Monde Catholique*, the *Action Française*, founded by Léon Daudet, *La Croix*, published by the Assumptionist Fathers, *L'Univers*—all seconded Drumont's opinions. *Le Monde*, for example, declared editorially (May 6, 1866): "All right-minded people will sympathize with the Assistant of Jesus Christ [Drumont!], and will thank him for his intrepidity." [50] Throughout this period letters echoing the most vicious of sentiments were printed: "Jews ought to be whipped . . . given enemas of vitriol . . . skinned alive . . . their eyes put out . . . rugs made of their skin . . ." There were, to be sure, newspapers favorably disposed to the Jews—*Journal des Débats, Paix, Temps, Figaro.*

La France Juive became a best seller among supporters of capitalism, socialism, the monarchy, and the clergy. *Le Petit Journal*, published by Drumont's friends, offered his volume in installments and gave away copies as prizes to contest winners. The work went through more than a hundred and forty printings in ten years and was translated into other languages.[51] Certain groups advocated offering "a premium for shooting Jews, similar to that offered for shooting wolves." [52] The celebrated Catholic writer George Bernanos praised *La France Juive* as a "masterpiece of observation, analysis, and erudition." (Later he would write a defense of Hitler, declaring in 1938: "I do not believe that Mr. Hitler and Mr. Mussolini are demigods. But I merely pay homage to the truth when I say that they are men without fear." [53])

Drumont's great opportunity occurred at the time of the Dreyfus Affair. A Jewish captain, Alfred Dreyfus, had been falsely accused of betraying France. He had been tried in 1894 and found guilty and sent to Devil's Island. It was not until 1906 that the verdict was annulled.

During the early years of the Dreyfus Affair the great majority in France was against the innocent captain. The most vociferous of the anti-Dreyfusards were Drumont, his cohorts, and his newspaper *La Libre Parole*, in which he declared: "It was not a man who was being degraded for a personal fault, but a whole race whose shame was being exposed." [54] Other anti-Semites rushed to corroborate Drumont's assertion. Maurice Barrès, for example, declared: "I don't need anyone to tell me why Dreyfus was a traitor . . . or that he was capable of treachery. I know that from his race." [55] The Jew-hater Charles Maurras did not want Dreyfus to be retried. The poet François Coppée, the critic Brunetière, the novelist Alphonse Daudet and his brother, the journalist Léon, all despised Dreyfus and the Jews. Coppée wrote:

> Ah! Why do they not let us see the foul features of the traitor so that we may all of us, one after the other, spit on his face.[56]

Drumont declared that Émile Zola, the author of *J'Accuse* and a defender of Dreyfus, should be burned at the stake and with no further ado. As for Jews in general, they should be cast into the Seine. Burning them would be too good: "What an evil odor a roasted Jew-boy would make!" [57]

Anatole France, on the other hand, in his *Penguin Island,* satirized the anti-Semite. He fought superstition, intolerance, injustice, demagogy, and dictatorship, and sought to have freedom of thought, liberal education, separation of church and state, social reform established in France.[58]

Perhaps the most outstanding fighter on Dreyfus' behalf was Georges Clemenceau. In 1898 he denounced the judges who had tried Dreyfus and, though fully aware of the man's innocence, condemned him to pay for a crime he had not committed, ostensibly in order to save the reputation of the French army and avoid a scandal. "A nation without conscience," Clemenceau wrote,

> is merely a herd on the road to the slaughterhouse. . . . One may find oneself in a situation where it is necessary to make a sacrifice for one's country harder and more cruel than to give up one's life: the sacrifice of prejudices.[59]

Charles Péguy, socialist, idealist, poet, and also a Catholic, defended the Jews. Not only did he think highly of them as people, he said, because of "their spiritual force which the world, the flesh, and the Devil had never been able to destroy"; he *loved* them.

Though the Dreyfus Affair came close to splitting France into two armed camps, there was a measure of justice in the end. Truth and integrity did become a force powerful enough to determine the future of France. It must not be forgotten, moreover, that France was the first country to emancipate the Jews, and that French government policy with respect to Jews was more liberal by far than that of any other European country save England.

THE POLITICAL CLIMATE IN FRANCE, 1936–1941

The year 1936 was an inauspicious one for France. A "popular front" government, with Léon Blum as its first socialist premier, had come into being and initiated new and positive legislation (revaluation of the franc, a rearmament program, reinforcement of a mutual assistance pact with Russia and Great Britain, dissolution of the fascistic Croix de Feu, etc.). However, hatred of the Popular Front and of its initiator was epidemic. Léon Blum, it will be recalled, was the first Jewish premier that France had ever had. Bitterness, resentment, and anger against him were manifested on many sides. On February 13, 1936, when Blum and his socialist colleague Georges Monnet were riding through the Boulevard Saint-Germain, their car was forced to a halt because of the funeral procession of the royalist historian Jacques Bainville. While the car was stationary, some members of the fascistic Action Française group attacked it, tore off its door, dragged the occupants out, and beat Blum without respite. Some nearby construction workers came to his rescue and literally saved his life. Blum bled so profusely that his recovery took weeks.[60]

The old scourge of anti-Semitism had once again ignited. Hatred of the Jew emanated from rightist groups and from leftist groups alike, and was equally spurred on by Hitler's very effective propaganda machine. Otto Abetz, a former member of the German Democratic party and a pacifist in his youth, was a great help to Hitler in this direction. As a member of the French division of Joachim von Ribbentrop's intelligence bureau, Abetz succeeded in winning many people over to his banner. So suave and subtle a worker, so assiduous and diplomatic in his ways, he served as a professional propagandist for the Nazis in France from 1935 to 1939, funding business and cultural projects, inviting French politicians, writers, and industrialists to Germany—where fine contracts were offered, where peace was discussed, where "solemn" assurances were given of Germany's nonaggression policy toward France.[61]

Jacques Doriot's fascist newspaper *La Liberté,* heavily subsidized by the Nazis, advocated "peace" with Germany. Other journalists had also been bought by the Nazis: the editor of *Le Temps,* Louys Aubin; the manager of the *Figaro,* Poirier. The Vatican aided the Nazis in their work when Pius XII removed the papal ban on the royalist paper *Action Française.*[62]

Writers such as Alphonse de Chateaubriant, the author of *La Brière,* adored Hitler to the point of depicting him as a Christ figure.

> Hitler is immensely good . . . If he salutes the masses with one hand, he holds out the other faithfully toward God. The thoughts of Hitler have their roots deep in the profound waters of the Christian sea. Hitler is trying to raise a Christian temple for Germany . . . The National Socialists are the beginning of the work of God . . .[63]

Chateaubriant's work was widely read, particularly in military circles. General Maxime Weygand commented upon it most favorably.

Charles Maurras, the head of the *Action Française,* wrote of Léon Blum: "He is a man who must be shot—but in the back." [64] Xavier-Vallet, a rightist deputy, was equally unmerciful in his Blum-baiting:

> Your arrival in office, Mr. President, is incontestably a historic date. For the first time this ancient Gallic-Roman country will be governed . . . by a Jew. I have to say aloud what everyone is thinking silently—that to govern this peasant nation which is France it is better to have someone whose origins, no matter how modest, spring from the womb of our soil rather than have a subtle Talmudist.[65]

These statements did not end Blum's martyrdom in France. Maurras drove another nail in an *Action Française* editorial entitled "France under the Jew." Léon Daudet added to the virulence in an article "Blum, the gentle yid," referring to the premier as the "radiophonic Hebrew," the "Cretin-Talmud cabinet . . ." [66] and the like.

The growing dissatisfaction, the strikes, the peasant unrest, the fears of the rightists throughout France all seemed to play into Hitler's arms. Whatever Blum did seemed to divide France still further. When he tried to help the Spanish Republican government, he further alienated a whole segment of the French population. Some French arms were received by the Republicans, thanks to André Malraux' intervention.[67]

On September 7, 1937, Hitler declared his intention of "annihilating" France, after which he would begin the *Drang nach Österreich*...

France was a divided nation and her inner strife blinded her to the reality of Hitler. Blum, though a highly moral and democratic leader, failed to act decisively, feeling as he did that he had no mandate from the people of France: his election victory had been that narrow. Many in France believed deeply in rapprochement with Germany. Defeatism, nihilism, and pan-Germanism permeated many a French circle. Henri Béraud, for example, one of the most outspoken contributors to the rightist paper *Gringoire*, advocated an entente with Germany. Jacques Doriot, the founder of the fascist Parti Populaire Française (after his expulsion from the Communist party), advocated close ties with both Germany and Italy.[70]

When Hitler's *Anschluss* began on March 11, 1938, and Nazi troops seized Austria, the French government seemed not to react. The reason was simple: there was no government. Léon Blum had tried to form a coalition but his hands had been tied. Rightists wanted nothing to do with him or what he stood for. Emotions ran high. Paul Reynaud was almost the only one in parliament to advocate a "renovation" and "modernization of the army." He was a friend of Charles de Gaulle, who likewise fought for a refurbishing of the French army. It was Paul Reynaud who tried to talk sense to the various members of the government, seeking to create a united front. His efforts were to no avail.

Pierre-Étienne Flandin, leader of the centrist party, the Alliance Démocratique, who had visited Germany and had been wined and dined by the Nazis, advocated a "good neighbor" policy. What he was really determined to do, however, was to destroy Léon Blum and his socialist government. And he, Pierre Laval, and other "conservatives" succeeded in this endeavor.[71]

Strikes broke out all over France. Work stoppages hurt the armament production. Employers, siding with Flandin and his cohorts, did nothing to settle the strikes; they preferred to destroy Blum—and, incidentally, their country. On April 6, 1938, feelings in parliament against Blum and his government ran so high that a riot nearly broke out when Duboys-Resney, a rightist deputy, shouted "Death to the Jews!"[72]

In the end, Blum's government fell. Edouard Daladier, a former radical-socialist and now a rightist, became the new premier. Georges Bonnet, who was characterized by General Gamelin as "a foul ferment without morality but with a taste for intrigue," became France's foreign minister and spoke on behalf of peace with Germany at almost any price.[73] Both men, nevertheless, went to London to discuss the situation with Neville Chamberlain, the British prime minister, and made known to him their pessimistic views concerning Germany's aggressions. They feared for Czechoslovakia and sought some kind of guarantee from the English. "The only thing we obtained," Daladier declared, "was that Britain would join us in a common action—but purely diplomatic."[74] Daladier's and Bonnet's pessimism concerning France's military capability as compared to that of Germany was also voiced by some generals: Maurice Gamelin, Alphonse Georges, Joseph Vuillemin.[75] All were convinced that any kind of resistance to Hitler's might would be foolhardy.

On September 26, 1938, *Le Temps* published a letter from Flandin:

> I oppose the military intervention of France in the struggle between the Sudeten Germans and the Czechoslovakian state.[76]

Posters were then plastered on the walls of Paris:

YOU ARE BEING DECEIVED!
People of France, you are being deceived! A cunning trap has been set . . . by occult elements to make war inevitable.[77]

The Big Four met at Munich on September 29/30, 1938. It was at this meeting that Mussolini, Chamberlain, Daladier, and Hitler agreed to Czechoslovakia's demise.

Even after Czechoslovakia's fall, France remained a land divided. Senator Henry Lémery, a friend of Marshal Henri-Philippe Pétain, "the hero of Verdun," advocated peaceful coexistence with Germany. Anatole de Monzie, a member of the cabinet, was also against a declaration of war. Flandin echoed their sentiments. Lucien Rebatet, of the fascist publication *Je Suis Partout*, was categorical about his feelings when he wrote:

> So the war has been launched by the most hideous buffoon of the most hideous Jewish and demagogic regime . . . No. I do not feel the least anger against Hitler, but much against all the French politicians who have led to his triumph.[78]

Though Britain and France declared war on Germany on September 3, 1939, two days after the invasion of Poland, France, this last stronghold of "democracy" on the continent, did not support the war wholeheartedly. Many middle-of-the-roaders under the Third Republic wanted peace. The philosopher Emile Chartier Alain, for example, the trade-union leader Georges Dumoulin, the neosocialist author of the well-known editorial "Why Die for Danzig," Marcel Déat, all advocated a nonaggression pact with Hitler. The communists also felt that a bond between the French and Germans must be cemented because of a Russo-German pact that had been signed in August, 1939. The Soviet Union, they wrote, would be able to assure the world "a just and durable peace . . . and would safeguard the independence of France" against a war begun by "Western imperialists." As for the rightists, their stand had never changed.

Between September, 1939, and June, 1940, Hitler took Poland, Denmark, Norway, Luxembourg, Holland, Belgium—and France. Nine months after France declared war, it surrendered. On June 14, 1940, Paris was declared an open city. The swastika waved in the cool wind on the Eiffel Tower. Marshal Pétain succeeded Paul Reynaud and asked for an armistice. When the Parisians were told of Pétain's request over loudspeakers in the streets, they were, according to William L. Shirer, "almost struck dead." [79]

An armistice was signed in the historic railroad car in the Forest of Compiègne. It was in the same wagon-lit coach that Marshal Foch had signed another kind of armistice with the Germans on November 11, 1918.

Pétain took over as head of a new French "government" at Vichy, a fascist state controlled by the Germans. Pierre Laval operated effectively behind the scenes, taking advantage of the marshal's advanced age at every opportunity. General Charles de Gaulle had already fled France and was setting up a French National Committee (Free France) in London. He and other members of the French army and navy who had also escaped would continue the fight.

And refugees began their flight from Paris. The roads from Orléans and Blois were filled with an estimated two hundred thousand or more people fleeing for their lives. Without food, shelter, water, they ran out of the city literally in droves, amid exploding German bombs. Wounded, bleeding, starving, old and young, from every walk of life, they tried as best they could to keep on living.

> They are just a few of the millions who fled Paris and the other cities and towns before the German invaders. They fled, tearing in fright along the roads with their belongings on their backs or on bikes or in baby-carriages, and their children atop them. Soon the roads were clogged. Troops also were trying to use them. Soon the Germans came over, bombing the roads. Soon there were dead and dying. And no food, no water, no shelter, no care.[80]

THE PSYCHOLOGY OF ANTI-SEMITISM

Why anti-Semitism? A flurry of answers are forthcoming from every corner. Ackerman and Jahoda consider it "a symptom of social pathology, indicating a form of social disorganization that menaces the stability, if not the very foundation of a culture." [81] During periods of economic stability and relative prosperity, anti-Semitism is somewhat somnolent. It is mostly during times of economic stress—or personal tension—that hatred of a minority wakens. Demagogues know that to stimulate hatred within a people for certain groups (or individuals) is a way of diverting peoples' attention away from society's real problems. Just as children are distracted with a new toy, so the masses are made to think of everything except what is really bothering them. Thus anti-Semitism is an escape mechanism, a self-deception.

A person who feels hostility is usually insecure and views the unfamiliar with fright, suspicion, and anxiety. A comparison has been made between hatred and the antibodies that develop in the blood: whenever something strange or new is introduced into the organism, antibodies are created in order to reject it.[82] Similarly, a person suffering from feelings of hostility develops anxiety and comes to be obsessed, whether consciously or unconsciously, with a sense of vulnerability. These people are afraid of foreigners (xenophobia) who might take away their jobs, alter their ways, introduce diseases, etc. In 1814, for example, Ernst Moritz Arndt voiced the German fear of the foreigner: "Everything which is impure in the German philosophy comes from abroad. We rightly thrust all this dung from us, for it comes to us from abroad." [83] Every group is susceptible to similar feelings, given the right circumstances.

The anti-Semite typically looks upon Jews as something "different" and, as such, a threat to his nation and himself. The more inflated the threat seems to be, the greater is the hatred. The more the hater hates what is different, "the greater is his identification with his [own] group." [84] The hater will attribute all the evil qualities he can think of to the "different" group, and in so doing he perseveres in further defining those he dislikes. The Nazis indulged in this practice when they forced Jews to wear a yellow Star of David and began determining the contents of "Jewish blood," writing all types of pseudo-erudite volumes trying to prove the existence of a "Jewish race" and the like.[85]

What Ackerman and Jahoda term the "unselective anti-Semite" uses the group he particularly dislikes to externalize and "diffuse" his own hostility.[86] For the Jew-hater the *actual* qualities of the Jews are of no importance—if they are perceived at all. Whether the Jew is accused of being a capitalist or a communist, secretive or expansive, intelligent or stupid, lazy or compulsively diligent, dirty or clean, etc. is of little import. Some Jews are blamed for not believing in the Trinity, others for believing in a unity, for being materialistic, abstractionist, reactionary, radical, separatist, unproductive, transmitters of values, poisoners of cultures, assimilationists, etc.[87]

Hatred, violence, prejudice, prejudgment, or stereotyped thinking are indications of an "economy of intellectual effort" [88] and of the predominance of the irrational. Indeed, anti-Semites seem to thrive on the irrational. Discussion, argumentation, reasoning has no more appeal for them than garbage has for an overfed goose. One recalls in this connection a story told of Hitler, before he became chancellor of Germany. In one of his speeches he kept blaming the Jews for all the evils that had befallen Germany. Someone in the audience spoke forth: "And the bicyclists?" Hitler then asked the man: "Why the bicyclists?" To which the man answered: "Well, why the Jews." [89]

To reason through a problem with a highly prejudiced individual is not merely difficult; it is well-nigh impossible. One cannot fight "an irrational phenomenon" rationally. To attempt so is to "mistake the symptom for the causes" and must "lead to disillusionment." [90] Perfectly rational people, confronted with an idea or a series of associations to which they are susceptible, can suddenly become totally irrational. Since antiquity demagogues have known how to stir the masses in this way. Adolf Hitler was a latter-day master of the art: he knew instinctively that he could impose his own hatred for the Jew onto all of Germany, and do so quickly, simply by pointing to the Jew as the symbol of evil. When instincts run rampant, hate, violence, loss of individuality, and mob action ensue. As Hitler said to Hermann Raushning:

> My Jews are valuable hostages given to me by the democracies. Anti-Semitic propaganda in all countries is an almost indispensable medium for the extension of our political campaign. You will see how little time we shall need in order to upset the ideas and criteria of the whole world, simply and purely by attacking Judaism. It is beyond question the most important weapon in my propaganda arsenal.[91]

Hitler knew that whereas hatred is not innate, it is as contagious as the most virulent of viruses. His ideas worked so well and with such velocity that some six million Jews were slaughtered before and during the holocaust. In 1945 three truckloads, each with eight to nine tons of human ashes from the Sachsenhausen concentration camp, were poured into a canal, an indication of the rate at which Jews were being killed and cremated.[92] The slaughter was marvelously efficient, despite labor shortages in Germany. Many prisoners, if not cremated, dug their own graves and then were shot where they stood; those put to death in this manner did not have to be carried into their graves since they were already in them.[93]

The historian Theodor Mommsen understood that reason is of no avail when hatred and passions are the motivating forces within an individual. Thus when he disputed the racist arguments and partisan views of Heinrich von Treitschke, as expressed in *Ein Wort über unser Judentum*, Mommsen declared, in his *Auch ein Wort über unser Judentum* (1880), that anti-Semitism could never be cured. To the author Hermann Bahr, he wrote:

> You are mistaken if you believe that I could achieve anything in this matter. You are mistaken if anything at all could be achieved by reason. In years past I thought so myself and kept protesting against the monstrous infamy that is anti-Semitism. But it is useless, completely useless. Whatever I or anybody else could tell you are in the last analysis reasonable, logical, and ethical arguments to which no anti-Semite will listen. They listen only to their own hatred and envy, to the meanest instincts. Nothing else counts for them. They are deaf to reason, right, and morals.[94]

Anti-Semitism is a phenomenon that has permeated many cultures, civilizations, and races. It may be masked at first, but once man's primordial nature emerges, once hatred is stirred, anti-Semitism emerges with all of its vitality.[95]

At bottom, Thomas Sugrue contends, "nothing can be done about anti-Semitism until something is done about Christianity. It is as illogical for a follower of Jesus to persecute a Jew as it is for him to commit any other sin of hate."[96] In an article published in the *New York Times* (January 10, 1971), we read:

> By persecuting Jews while not improving his own moral ways, the Christian anti-Semite feels a catharsis, a cleansing of his own feeling of guilt for failing to meet the high standards of the Bible and the Christian theology.[97]

Sartre, in his essay *Anti-Semite and Jew*, declared anti-Semitism to be a "passion," an "anger," and that it "extended to the psychological realm," as does hysteria. "If the Jew did not exist," Sartre maintains, "the anti-Semite would have to invent him."[98] Hatred and anger are the only entities capable of filling the void in the lives of this kind of person. The anti-Semite fears "solitariness," and by condemning the Jews as "inferior" people he confers upon himself membership in our "elite."[99] He identifies himself with the finest elements, so he thinks, of society.

> The anti-Semite is afraid of discovering that the world is ill-contrived, for then it would be necessary for him to invent and modify, with the result that man would be found to be the master of his own destinies, burdened with an agonizing and infinite responsibility. Thus he localizes all the evil of the universe in the Jew.[100]

Furthermore, declares Sartre, the anti-Semite is mentally "lethargic." He is basically sadistic and understands "nothing of modern society."[101] The anti-Semite is a "coward" who "fears."

CÉLINE'S ANTI-SEMITISM AND HIS PERSONAL PSYCHOLOGY

In 1937 and 1938 France was "ready" for the publication of Céline's viciously anti-Semitic polemical works. He had many allies, haters bent on taking out their personal problems and disappointments on minorities. There was

Lucien Rebatet, for example, the editor of the fascist newspaper *Je Suis Partout*, who declared in January, 1938, after the publication of Céline's *Bagatelles for a Massacre*, that this was "the only book by Louis-Ferdinand Céline to be greeted in our little circle with an enthusiasm barring all reserve." [102] It was a race between Rebatet and Robert Brasillach, of the *Action Française*, as to which one would come out first with his review. Both men, of course, praised the work.

Céline's hatred embraced virtually all of humanity, but in the three volumes under discussion—*Bagatelles for a Massacre*, *School for Cadavers* and *Some State of Affairs*—it centers most specifically on the Jew. Céline's hatred, and hatred in general, can best be understood in terms of what psychologists call "shadow projection" and "complexes."

As we consider the shadow projections and complexes evinced by Céline in these polemics, it is well that we also ponder our own feelings of hostility and sound out our own depths. To substitute for the word Jew the name of the group toward which we may feel a particular enmity—Catholic, Protestant, White, Black, Yellow, Red Communist, Fascist, Democrat—can be a constructive exercise! For some of us, of course, the word Jew will suffice. At all events, our understanding of Céline may then pave the way to an improved self-understanding. As Kant observed in his *Introduction to Logic*, "comprehension" implies "to cognize a thing to the extent sufficient for our purposes." [103]

SHADOW PROJECTION

What *is* hate, that so many people should feel it? As defined by the dictionary, hate is made up "of a group of emotional attitudes associated with a particular object, activity, etc. and remaining partly unconscious but strongly influencing the individual's behavior."

A man possessed by hate, overwhelmed by this force, who sees evil and destruction all about him—always outside of himself—is a man, psychologists say, possessed by his "shadow." The shadow is defined by Edward Edinger as "a composite of personal characteristics and potentialities concerning which the individual is unaware. Usually, the shadow, as indicated by the word, contains inferior characteristics and weaknesses which the ego's self-esteem will not permit it to recognize." [104]

When the shadow's negative characteristics remain unconscious and unacceptable to the individual, they are frequently "projected" onto others. Instead of analyzing such feelings of inferiority and thereby bringing them into consciousness and so transforming what was negative into something positive, the individual refuses even to accept the existence of the characteristics in question and continues to be unconscious of them. He is, therefore, rejecting his shadow, rejecting, that is, an important part of himself. An individual who is forever hating, derogating, finding fault, has what is commonly called a "shadow problem." Céline was such an individual.[105]

When projecting the shadow onto others—minority groups, for example—one believes erroneously that the "others" possess the unpleasant characteristics. It is interesting to note in this context that since everything harmful and unpleasant in the haters' lives is associated with people and things exterior to themselves, the haters seldom suffer from depression. Their self-destruction is focused on an outward object rather than on the self (which is the case of those suffering from depression). The hater, therefore, does not experience despair, but rather a perpetual dissatisfaction, a frustration, but always with the "other."

What happens to someone who is perpetually projecting his shadow outward? He is simply rejecting aspects of himself. His dissatisfactions, his negative qualities, rather than being aired out and understood, are misunderstood and neglected. They are literally imprisoned within the individual. The natural response to imprisonment is rage. These negative characteristics, enclosed within the psyche, seethe, as do the feelings associated with them, such as fear, anguish, and hate. Blocked within the unconscious, however, they act and react, sometimes violently, and wreak havoc. The more such feelings of hate and rage are repressed in this manner, the greater becomes their virulence. Instincts are also aroused. An analogy here may be drawn between repression and a dog. If a dog starves—if his master pays no attention to it—the dog becomes vicious, aggressive, and destructive. If well-fed and given some attention, the dog becomes malleable, pleasant, lovable—a positive entity.

When an individual rejects part of himself, his instincts—the primitive forces within him—are aroused. An analogy may also be drawn here. When a man kills in a burst of passion, one often feels that the primitive has taken hold of him. When Céline wrote *Bagatelles for a Massacre* and his other polemical works, he so hated the Jews that he declared himself ready to tear their "globulous" eyes from their sockets, to have the Jews exterminated, to force upon them the most ignominious end. One might assert, in this case, that Céline had been overwhelmed by the primitive forces living within him.

What was Céline accomplishing by spewing forth his hatred as he did? He was eliminating, through the projection of his shadow, his own dissatisfactions, his own guilt feelings, his own moral conflicts—all of which remained, of course, quite unconscious. The negative aspects dwelling within his psyche were simply transferred to external objects and as such were "combatted, punished and exterminated as 'the alien out there' " instead of being dealt with on a personal level and thus being made conscious.[106]

Such shadow projection explains, to a great extent, why at intervals throughout history certain minorities have been persecuted: the Cathars in the Middle Ages, the Jews in Spain during the Inquisition, Protestants and Catholics in France during the Renaissance—and in wars generally. At these moments the conscious mind is overwhelmed by the shadow, which empties itself out or erupts in wars, revolutions, etc.

In olden days, the collective shadow, the evils of a community, was projected or heaped onto a goat by a priest; the animal was then sent out into the wilderness and the clan was purged of its sins: the evil of the community supposedly disappeared along with the animal. But so did the pain that facing and trying to resolve tensions and problems necessarily entails. By merely rejecting a painful situation, one escapes a conflict that could have had salutary effects. Christ was a scapegoat. He took upon himself the sins of the world and was rejected as an "evil" force. So Jews generally have been looked upon by many as an irritant, as an embodiment of evil, and as such deserving of being done away with and the world purged of all trace of them.

When Céline cursed the Jew in his polemical writings, he sought to destroy an entire population and thus was exhibiting his scapegoat mentality. He identified all the evils of French (and world) society with the Jew. No guilt, no discussion of morality, no sober assessment of political, economic, or social situations is to be found in his works. Céline was in effect ridding himself—but not really—of all the unacceptable sentiments lodged within his own unconscious and projecting these onto an outside group. The Jew then became the scapegoat.

When blame is focused upon a minority group there is little fear of retribution, for the hater identifies with the majority: "Take it out on the dog." [107] It is, therefore, a safe manner of purging oneself of fears and anxieties. The Romans, we recall, used the Christians as their scapegoat. As Tertullian observed: "If the Tiber overflows into the city, if the Nile does not flow into the countryside, if the heavens remain unmoved, if the earth quakes, if there is famine or pestilence, at once the cry goes up: 'To the lions with the Christians.' " [108] It is interesting to note in this connection that Tertullian himself used the Jews as a scapegoat in order to be relieved of *his* hostilities. Projection works both ways. In later times the Christians returned the compliment and held the Jews to be responsible for all of their misfortunes. In 1021, for example, a minor earthquake temporarily disrupted the Easter festivities in Rome; the Jews were blamed for the incident and many of them were put to death.[109]

Céline's fanatical attitude toward Jews is an indication of his own doubt and insecurity. When beliefs—religious, psychological, social, literary, etc.—are sturdy, recourse to execution, annihilation, massacres, burnings at the stake, is unnecessary. But when faith or belief in self is in doubt, when insecurity reigns, then hatred and fanaticism result.[110]

Dangers are in store for those like Céline, whose attitudes are shaky and remain repressed and unconscious. Unaware of his shadow projection, Céline displayed in his novels a great propensity for sadism and destruction.[111] As the split between the conscious attitude (fanaticism) and the unconscious view (doubt, insecurity) is reinforced, a "systematized" projection of the shadow results. In *Bagatelles for a Massacre, School for Cadavers,* and *Some State of Affairs* we find perfect illustrations of such a situation. Paranoiac reactions can be observed not only in terms of the individual but of the society, of which Céline is the representative. At this point the persecution of the "alien" becomes the individual's and the nation's uppermost concern. Slogans and advertisements proliferate in an attempt to repress the aggressive tendencies of "that other" (race, religion, political) group. War, for example, can only be waged if the enemy becomes "the carrier of a shadow projection." [112]

A paranoiac such as Hitler is convinced that all Jews are plotting against him and his country; the megalomaniac is positive that he understands the "mystic notions of the cosmos." [113] Hitler believed he had been chosen by God to be the leader of his people. "Paranoid thinking is a disease and can be caught from another person; it is an inflammable potentiality that can be easily ignited." [114] An interesting example of the contagious nature of such attitudes is the case of a gentle and kind Austrian Catholic. He had always been against Hitler and his group. Yet one day, when he saw some Jews being kicked and beaten in the street, he was mesmerized by what he saw; his thoughts wandered, and he even began thinking of the Jews as "guilty criminals who deserved what was happening to them." At this moment he felt himself superior to them, but fortunately he mustered his common sense and did not join the tormentors. Later on, however, "when he had calmed down, he was stunned by the thoughts he had had." [115]

When a shadow projection runs wild, "inflation" (hubris) can occur. Céline's novels were mere literary expressions of his political, philosophical, and aesthetic ideas; as "fiction", they were not taken seriously in social and political circles. By 1937, however, the situation in France (and in the world) had changed. Céline no longer felt the need to have recourse to symbols, images, or fiction. Now he could express his anger and hatred openly and in terms comprehensible to all. Céline believed that he was a kind of "spokesman" for certain groups. Psychologically speaking, he was identifying with collective values.[116] Thus, he looked upon himself, unconsciously, as a type of psychopomp, as a "message bearer," as a leader of souls.

When Céline began identifying himself with the collective (the identification of his individual ego with transpersonal contents), he was suffering from "inflation." [117] In *Bagatelles for a Massacre,* for example, he sees himself (half mockingly at first, but then seriously) as a possible and even probable future dictator. He will begin his "leadership," he writes, by promulgating a series of laws, all dealing with the annihilation of the Jew. Céline had become so caught up in the idea of power that he could no longer see any limits to his might—no considerations of morality, no pangs of conscience.

When such megalomaniacal views are adopted, damage lies in store for the individual. On the psychological plane, the ego is overwhelmed by unconscious forces of which it is totally unaware. A restriction of consciousness usually follows suit and an *idée fixe* takes root. Once this notion begins to grow, it distorts all perspective and blurs all vision. When Céline saw himself as a dictator, he was not the ruler but the ruled—ruled, indeed tyrannized and overwhelmed, by his shadow.

Céline was being swallowed up by his dark, evil, demoniacal side—a region in which archaic forms live, breathe, and strengthen themselves. His inability or unwillingness to recognize and accept his negative side sequestered its contents within him. When they erupted, it was always through shadow projection, unconsciously experienced, symbolically in his novels (frequently as horrendous, destructive, dismembered, grotesque individuals or entities), as the most insidious form of invective in his polemical works.

Céline's shadow worked nefariously, as something external to him in the form of an enemy—the Jew, with whom he equated the Negro, the Asiatic, the communist, the imperialist, the democrat, etc. Céline saw himself as a hero, a latter-day Bayard, brimming with self-righteousness and devoid of any sense of guilt.[118]

Scapegoat psychology is dangerous to society: it leads to wars, inquisitions, pogroms, and other horrors. It is equally catastrophic to the individual. When a person does not experience his shadow—when he remains unaware of his negative characteristics—he never comes to know himself whole. He is, therefore, the more likely to be overwhelmed by the "powers of darkness" that lead to mental breakdowns. And yet confrontation with the shadow, with the ugly, evil, sick aspects corroding one's psyche, is also a shattering experience.

Self-encounter for one who has been accustomed to blaming "the other" for the evils within oneself is undeniably traumatic. But such self-encounter can have positive results.[119] As one becomes conscious of one's negative side, as one analyzes these characteristics, accepts them and assimilates them, new contents rise out of the unconscious and into the conscious personality. New roads may open up. What was repressed up to now, what was destructive, can become positive. With larger perspectives and renewed vision, what had formerly been looked upon as a threat to the ego and to the conscious mind—in Céline's case, the Jew—may no longer seem to be quite so dangerous. It might even be recognized as beneficial.

COMPLEXES

Céline always experienced his shadow in projection. His unconscious negative contents, therefore, never became integrated into his total personality. Rather they became autonomous entities within his subliminal world, each going its own way.[120]

Such autonomous psychic entities are known as "complexes." In a "well-adjusted" and relatively "normal" person, the ego (the "center of consciousness") is made up of many complexes—of a "whole mass of ideas pertaining to the ego." This ego-complex, as it is called, is able to cope with most problems relating to the individual in question and is considered "the highest psychic unity or authority." [121] Moreover, the ego-complex gives direction to "associations and ideas." When a person is deeply disturbed, the psychic totality may become fragmented and split up into various complexes.[122]

When such a split-off occurs, each complex may be looked upon as a kind of "miniature self-contained psyche which . . . develops a peculiar fantasy-life of its own." [123] When the complex becomes virtually autonomous, the resulting fantasies may assume abnormal proportions. They become a kind of "vassal" who is no longer willing to give "unqualified allegiance" to his suzerain.[124] When one is asleep, fantasies are manifested in dreams. When one is awake, they pursue their course in actions, attitudes, writings, frequently under the domination of "repressed or other unconscious complexes." Autonomous complexes may be looked upon as "toxins" because they do not fit into the "conscious mind" harmoniously. They may resist all attempts on the part of the will to cope with them.[126]

Complexes may be looked upon as having a type of electric current: they possess affective charges and feeling-tones. The affects given off by a complex are sometimes so great as to be capable of acting physically upon the person experiencing the complex. Respiration, blood pressure, the circulatory system may all be altered, depending upon the power of the complex over the individual. When certain exceptionally deep-rooted complexes break through into consciousness, they can erupt with such extreme violence that they invade the entire personality. This kind of situation occurs in cases of psychosis.[126]

There are passages in *Bagatelles for a Massacre* and Céline's other two polemical works in which his hatred for the Jew pours out with such intensity that one can actually feel his entire physical system tingling with affects.

What happens to a person who comes to be dominated by a hate complex? The complex inflates and distends, growing like a cancer. As it invades the psyche, its energy, released in affective charges and feeling tones, bombards rational attitudes and thought processes. As the complex increases in dynamism, the entire psyche falls under its dominion; almost everything the individual does, thinks, or feels (if he is capable of feeling) is centered on the complex. Distorted views, even a power complex, may take over at this juncture. Words, places, associations of every kind evoke the hated being or group. When a person is disturbed by a word, mood, event, or situation, his feeling tones are aroused and his entire psyche loses its balance. In such cases, little or no growth of personality is possible.[127]

The complex, the autonomous psychic entity, keeps attracting to itself energy that properly belongs to, and that should nourish, the psyche as a whole. With what result? As the complex gains in strength and vigor, the rest of the psyche starves, atrophies, and finally disintegrates. Such a situation is manifested in the following manner: things that are actually very important to the individual in his daily life and yet do not pertain in some way to his complex are sluffed off, whereas relatively insignificant statements or acts that the individual feels are related to his complex become all important. Under such circumstances, a situation, a word, a glance may elicit a burst of anger or some other response all out of proportion to the overall situation. In *Bagatelles for a Massacre,* Céline informs us that his works have been analyzed by a psychiatrist. Céline's reactions to the doctor's statements were instantaneous, violent, and far more extreme than the incident warranted. Indeed, Céline reviled the doctor, labeling him an imbecilic, delirious, idiotic, perverse, sick, "monstrous, obsessive, rotten sub-nigger,"—among other things.[128] Obviously the raw nerve of a complex had been touched—and Céline jumped.

Such intense reactions may assume pathological proportions, as indeed they later did in Céline's case, following the publication of Jean-Paul Sartre's essay "Anti-Semite and Jew" (*Les Temps modernes,* 1945). Sartre had written the following statement:

> Look at Céline; his vision of the universe is catastrophic. The Jew is everywhere, the earth is lost, it is up to the Aryan not to compromise, never to make peace. Yet he must be on his guard; if he breathes, he has already lost his purity, for the very air that penetrates his bronchial tubes is contaminated. . . . If Céline supported the Socialist theses of the Nazis, it was because he was paid to do so. At the bottom of his heart he did not believe them. For him there is no solution except collective suicide, nonreproduction, death.[129]

Céline's ferocious rebuttal, published under the title *L'Agité du bocal,* is so violent, so irrational, as to be a perfect example of an instantaneous complex reaction. The essay is a series of meaningless invectives and irrelevant scatologies. Not a single flicker of lucidity is discernible in it. The following is typical of the rest:

> Damned piece of rubbish filled with shit; you emerge from between my buttocks to dirty me on the outside! Anus! Cain pfoui! What are you looking for? Let them assassinate me! Let me crush you! Yes! . . . I can see him on a photo . . . his big eyes . . . that hook . . . that drooling air-hole . . . What wouldn't he invent, that monster, to assassinate me! Hardly emerging from cack himself, there he is denouncing me . . .
>
> He makes my abode in my ass so you can't ask J.-B. S. [sic] to see clearly or to express himself distinctly, yet J.-B. S. seems to have foreseen the notion of solitude and obscurity in my anus.[130]

Céline's essay neither refuted Sartre's statement nor did it support his own views. But it clearly revealed Céline's chaotic state of mind.

Those experiencing incessant hatred, anxiety, worry, and anger are never free to think clearly. Their viewpoint is always colored by persistent feeling-tones and affective charges that are constantly cast outward, like waves, from the complex.[131] Jung compared the associations and feeling-tones associated with a complex to Wagner's leitmotifs, which are a "complex of ideas" related to and part of the dramatic whole. The variations that Wagner wrote into his music, always based on the principal theme, may be compared to the feeling-tones of complexes: "Our actions and moods are modulations of the leitmotifs."[132] When the various complexes, releasing their effective charge and feeling-tones work harmoniously, as they do in Wagner's music, a magnificent structure results. In an individual, however, when an autochthonous complex runs rampant, inflates, injects its force into the psyche, it levels down consciousness and *un abaissement du niveau mental* (a lowering of the mental level) takes over.

Let us analyze the workings of such activities. When a person experiences danger, for example, or hate—or thinks he does, which amounts to the same thing—the harmonious relationship of ideas within the psyche is altered. A complex, a medley of powerful feeling-tones, forces itself upon the psyche, pushing everything else into the distant background. Only the ideas, feeling-tones, and affective charges relating directly to the complex are permitted to grow. A superb example of just such a situation was described by Flaubert in *Madame Bovary.* Emma Bovary is telling of her love for Léon, who has left town shortly before, in terms of the various pieces of furniture in her home. Each chair, table, fireplace arouses within her a feeling-tone that sets up an affective charge within her and nourishes, stimulates, and keeps her love-complex alive. In Céline, a similar network is set up and continually stimulated in his polemical works. Whenever the Jew is mentioned, or an idea actually or supposedly pertaining to him is alluded to, Céline's hate-complex churns.[133]

Autonomous ideas erupt into consciousness whenever there is a disruption between the individual's emotional life and his ideational content.[134] Thought-deprivation then takes hold.[135] The result: confusion in speech, repetitiousness, meaningless reactions, sudden impulses, series of nonconnected verbal associations, assonances, a disruption of logical sequences, contraction of words and sentences in an attempt to express one or more ideas.[136] The individual's normal thought processes are, to say the least, impeded. Certain word formations are so "strange" as to be reminiscent of the neologisms of sufferers of dementia praecox.[137] These verbigerations will be found in Céline's later novels.

Such thought-deprivation occurs when a person senses danger. At that moment sensations are aroused; they alert the corresponding complex and the affective charges and feeling-tones seem to grow out of proportion. As the ego loses its stability, it likewise experiences a loss of clarity and loses its hold on the other sensations and complexes. Though the ego may not be totally annihilated, it may, under such circumstances, be considered an "affect-ego," far weaker than the complex that dominates it at the moment.[138] When the fear passes, the complex may or may not fade back into its proper place and permit the restoration of rational perspectives. If the fright persists, however, new associations are born, feeling-tones and affective charges are further aroused, each looming ever larger in the personality and paving the way for an even more serious psychic imbalance. The complex may remain constellated if the feeling-tones continue to be strong enough to nourish it. In Céline's case they were. The symbols and imagery, the vocabulary, the *abaissement du niveau mental* all indicate that in every one of Céline's novels and treatises he was overwhelmed, in one degree or another, by the pull of his complexes.

When one is under the dominion of a complex (anger, hate, love, jealousy, fear, power, etc.) reason, as we have said, is to no avail. Logic does not count. Emotions are far more powerful than any cerebral thinking. Narrow-mindedness and lack of thoughtfulness become a predominant part of the personality, which soon verges on the pathological.[139] Such sluggish illucidity of mind, such *engourdissement,* is fertile terrain for the growth of prejudice, delusion, hallucination, and obsession. One who has such a point of view can never base his arguments on logical reasoning; his "reasons" are always slanted to fit his complex. If, for example, someone meets with a disappointment, he may conclude summarily that he was victimized on purpose, that he is the butt of people's anger, that he is a martyr—the paranoic tendencies are obvious here. In such cases, not only is gross misjudgment in full force, logos is totally absent. Such is Céline's thinking process in the three polemical works that are now to be considered: *Bagatelles for a Massacre, Some State of Affairs,* and *School for Cadavers.*[140]

BAGATELLES FOR A MASSACRE

Bagatelles for a Massacre is a work seemingly designed to stir the French people to hate, to adopt a fanatical, irrational, negative attitude toward the Jew. Céline declares, forthrightly: "I became an anti-Semite and not just a little bit, to laugh about, but ferociously, to my very depths, enough to blow up all the kikes!" [141]

The torrent gushing from Céline's pen, the cataclysmic prose, the endless invectives, his entire emotional outlook become quite comprehensible in the light of our understanding of shadow projection and complexes. All of the mental activity, all of the ideological, political, aesthetic, and economic concepts touching the Jew in *Bagatelles for a Massacre,* reveals thought-deprivation. The generalizations, the falsifications, the warped manner in which thoughts are elaborated, the blindness of the hatred, reveal far more about Céline's psychological plight than they do of the situation in France and Europe at the time. Though readers of Céline's previous works were, to a certain extent, prepared for such a tremendous onslaught of hatred, as prefigured in the ferocious, disruptive, and dismembering imagery of his novels, perhaps only a few were aware of, or were willing to admit, the full extent of Céline's *engourdissement.*

But what of our own hates? Are we not a bit pleased at times, when someone in power meets with adversity? Do we really love the poor, the weak, the sick, the old, the failures in life, the rich? What exactly stimulates our feelings of anger and hatred? What excuses do we offer? What rationalization do we invent? Is our hatred instinctive?

Only by dealing with our own shadow projections and complexes can we experience something positive from so a negative diatribe as *Bagatelles for a Massacre* and Céline's other polemical works.

Bagatelles for a Massacre falls into several categories relating to Céline's hatred of Jews: literary, economic, political, racist, and psychological.

Céline declares that he hates Jews because they are all literary critics and, as such, utterly foul. It was the Jews who wrote against his novels *Journey to the End of the Night* and *Death on the Installment Plan,* which they condemned because they wanted to take out their anger on him, to seek revenge.[142] Critics, Céline continues, are stirred by hatred; poison oozes from their pens in unending streams. Moreover, they are all impotent, megalomaniacal, decadent, tyrannical, rancid, failures, etc. They are comparable to "dung." Critics are rich because they are Jews.[143] Because of them the writer Céline will be neglected and forgotten. He declares that he has suffered humiliation and outrage at the hands of his "Jewish masters"—that "Jewish shit." [144]

A rational answer to such an irrational outpouring is difficult to offer. Suffice it to say that the critics who condemned Céline's novels most vociferously—Henride Régnier (*Figaro*), René Lalou (*Les Nouvelles littéraires*), Georges le Cardonnel *(Le Journal),* Jacques Debu-Bridel *(La Concorde)*—were not Jews.

Céline goes on to say that French literature is bad because most French writers are Jews. Racine, he writes, was one-half of one-quarter Jewish and an exhibitionist besides.[145] Racine was in fact, as everyone knows, a devout Catholic; where Céline discovered information to the contrary, he does not say (of course). He further asserts that Renaissance literature is vapid, and that it "had splendidly prepared its judeified fanaticism." "Naturalism" is the product of "Freemasons," who are associated with Jews. Positivism is a bundle of "calamitous prejudices," as are other literary conceptions, because the Jews who adhere to them are sterile, conceited, monstrous, megalomaniacal, etc.[146] Throughout the centuries the Jews have "systematically and totally" annihilated the most "natural and instinctive emotions in French painting, poetry, and the theater." The Jew, Céline continues, "has replaced the Aryan emotion with the negro tam-tam." As for Surrealism, it is merely a "Jewish imposture." [147]

Céline attacks such writers as Zola, Bordeaux, Gide, Giraudoux, Proust, and Valéry with lists of prurient words.[148] Thus a series of ignoble adjectives follows Proust's name, for example, because Proust was a Jew and, as such, should never be placed in the same category as Balzac.[149] Later, in a show of great rage, Céline claims that *all* French writers were Jews.[150] No sooner does he make this blanket statement than he contradicts himself—as he so often did—with the claim that there are very few Jewish poets because, unlike Aryans, Jews are incapable of experiencing emotions directly; [151] they are mere imitators, copiers, gesticulators.

As for French music, Céline's "Aryan sensibilities have been negrified." [152] French music had been ruined by an invasion of Jewish music from Africa. The tam-tam, introduced into civilized lands by Jewish Negroes, has destroyed what is intrinsic to the French—to the Aryan—and has substituted something degenerate and rotten.[153]

Such statements as these indicate that Céline's reason must have been deeply affected by the shattering power of his complex.

The second hate category is based on economic principles.

Céline claims—and these statements are repeated ad infinitum throughout the volume—that "gold dirties everything," [154] that all Jews have money and are, consequently, filthy, that they run the government and indeed the universe. Yet in the next breath he claims to have known many poor Jews in England, those who had worked in the dockyards, and he hates them too, and also the poor ghetto Jews in Lithuania, Croatia, and Roumania, and with equal fervor, because they are forever seeking to better their lot by working hard, arguing, fighting, conniving, trying to get ahead.[155]

What is Céline here condemning in the Jew? What is generally regarded as a rather positive and healthy social attitude: the desire to forge ahead in life, to amount to something. Such an outlook, such activity, makes for creativity and progress. One discerns a note of sorrow, however, in Céline's condemnation.

Céline accuses the Jews of being powermongers; it is they who are the bankers, the businessmen, the government officials, etc. In this connection it is interesting to note that Céline himself was always obsessed with money. As we recall, he wanted to create, and he succeeded in doing so, a myth about his lack of interest in material things—about the great poverty he had suffered as a child and the unhappiness that had resulted therefrom. Whenever he was interviewed by a writer, journalist, or scholar, he would bring up the subject of his poverty and affirm his lack of interest in money. Even such astute critics as Robert Poulet, Marc Hanrez, and Roger Nimier were deceived by Céline's claims along such lines.

The myth has been debunked by Céline's childhood friend, Marcel Brochard; Céline, it seems, was never poor. Indeed, both of his parents earned fine livings, and their son lacked nothing. When asked why he indulged in such mythomania, Céline answered:

> You must choose, to die or to lie.—You create reality by arranging, by cheating the right way.[156]

This is Céline's way. In writing novels such fabrication is of course not only permissible but desirable. In interviews, however, and in philosophical and literary treatises, it is neither.

The myth concocted by Céline concerning his complete lack of interest in monetary matters was no true myth. Céline was a man actually obsessed with material things, a man preoccupied throughout his life with questions of money. His novels are drenched with evidence to this effect. More important, however, are the pains he took to see to it that the royalties from his novels *Journey to the End of the Night* and *Death on the Installment Plan* were changed into gold bullion and placed in a safety deposit box in a Copenhagen bank. Céline quite evidently needed to know that whatever his country's future might be, he would personally be secure in a financial way.

It is interesting to note in this connection that when Céline went to Russia to spend his royalties from the translation of *Journey to the End of the Night* (which had been made in 1936 by Elsa Triolet and Louis Aragon) he was in a state of agitation throughout the journey. First of all, he was annoyed because he actually had to pay for his trip (as if this were an unusual situation). He spoke about his largesse, saying that he had not "hesitated to spend his money . . . that he had payed full fare . . . two hundred fifty francs a night" for a second-class hotel room at the Hôtel de l'Europe, including bed bugs, that he received no discounts anyplace in Russia, that the Russians still owed him two thousand rubles, that no highly placed government official met him at the station or showed him around, that he mixed with "the people" on his trip, etc. Céline never forgave the Russians for not having permitted him to take his royalties—his money—out of Russia. In a vitriolic pamphlet entitled *Mea Culpa* (1936) he declared: "I am still missing a few hatreds. I am sure they exist." [157]

Céline's constant refrain of "money, money, money" owed him by the Russians is reminiscent of M. Jourdain in Molière's *The Would-be Gentleman.* Jourdain, too, wanted to give the impression of being "above" money, of being interested only in culture and refinement. His business sense was extraordinary, however, and motivated most of his actions. Certainly, there is nothing intrinsically harmful in being preoccupied with money. The danger resides in one's inability to admit the fact to oneself—and this was the case with Céline.

The preoccupation with gold, Céline tells us, exists not only in Russia and in the Jew but has even invaded the world of the theater in France! Céline had recently written two ballet scenarios, *The Birth of a Fairy* and *Voyou Paul. Brave Virginia.*[158] Hoping to have these ballets produced by Jacques Rouché in Paris, or elsewhere, Céline had solicited the aid of a mutual friend—a Jew, oddly enough—in order to have a better entrée to Rouché. When Rouché told Céline that he did not want the ballets without appropriate musical accompaniments, Céline screamed "Jew" and accused his friend of having deliberately sabotaged his chances with Rouché. Céline rationalized and concluded that his ballets would not be produced simply because Jews ran the opera.[159]

Céline asked some musicians to compose music for the ballets—of course they were Jews, he claimed, because "all great musicians are Jews"—but after looking at the ballet they hemmed and hawed and nothing came of the meeting. Céline was irate. He was being "judeified," he said. When his friend suggested that he offer his ballet to the Arts and Techniques Exhibit of 1938, Céline suddenly flashed: since all engineers, contractors, and directors are Jews, there would be no point. And referring to his "Jew friend," he said, "I would have liked to have turned his eyes around in their sockets . . ."—those "globulous Jewish eyes." [160] The Jews, Céline stated, were responsible for his suffering, and indeed for all the pain experienced by all "people on the earth."

When one considers the fact that Céline had tried to use "influence" to have his ballet produced, exhibiting the very *arriviste* ways that he was wont to condemn in the Jew, particularly the poor Jew working in the London dockyards, it becomes quite clear that Céline was unconsciously projecting his shadow onto others.

Céline further accused the Jew of hypocrisy, of cleverness, of trying actually to succeed in life! In this connection it is interesting to note that his first two novels are virtually free of anti-Semitic remarks, whereas *The Church* is filled with them. Why? One writer believes that it was because Céline knew he had to have one smashing success before he could dare to reveal himself plain. Though *The Church* was written several years before *Journey to the End of the Night*, it was not published until 1933, after the appearance of his novel. A theory has been advanced with regard to this issue. Céline believed, according to this theory, that *Journey to the End of the Night* had assured his success and that any vituperative remarks concerning Jews or others that he might make in the future would not harm his career. But when his play *The Church* was criticized not for the anti-Semitic remarks in it (though these were looked upon with disfavor by some) but simply as a wretched play, Céline felt himself under attack, and the Jew was of course to blame. Céline had learned a lesson, or so he thought. When *Death on the Installment Plan* was published in 1936, he was primarily concerned about his future as a writer and for this reason he omitted most anti-Semitic innuendos or references.[161] He did not want to have any such remarks interfere with the success of his work. His career was most important to him. Saving the world from the Jewish plague would have to wait for the proper social and political climate. The atmosphere was perfect in 1937. To accuse the Jew of ruse is, perhaps, to be artful oneself.

What were Céline's own politics, that he should denounce all Jews as communists?

Céline had once been interested, or so he stated, in the common man, and he had been attracted, therefore, to communism, a philosophy that had promised so much to so many. But he was not one to join parties. He was too much of an individualist for that. He maintained, in fact, that he had never in his life even voted; "idiots are the majority," [162] he declared, and "fools" always win. Why, therefore, should he bother to vote? Nor had he ever signed any manifesto for martyrs, for the wounded, the tortured, because

Jews or Freemasons are always at the bottom of such petitions or maneuvers.

The Jews run the Soviet Union, Céline maintained, that land of jailers and torturers. The Jew, the "scum from Asia, scum from Africa . . ." [163] are the provokers of all revolutions and other disorders. According to Céline, Lenin, Kerensky, and Stalin were all Jews. The entire Comintern, he insisted, was made up of Jews. We know this to be untrue, of course, and ironically enough Stalin was himself a violent anti-Semite.

The only "Christians" in the Soviet government, asserted Céline, were those who had belonged to the old clique and were permitted, for reasons of form, to remain.[164] But even they, he continued, must grovel before the Jew. These last statements are fantasies on Céline's part. For centuries pogroms had existed in Russia and anti-Semitism remained a problem even after the advent of communism. Moreover, some members of the Comintern were noted for their dislike of the Jew. These are facts. But for Céline, the Soviet Union was a *Jewish* imperialistic state.[165]

For Céline, "Jew" and "communist" are synonymous. Such an identification is ironic in view of the fact that the Jew has always been (and still is) persecuted in Russia. He has no possibility of educating himself as a Jew, he has no freedom of worship, and until recently he was not even permitted to emigrate.

Democracy, according to Céline, is likewise a creation of the Jew. Evidence? It was the Jew and his cohorts who fought fascism in Spain in 1935 (much to Céline's displeasure). Moreover, Jews are revolutionaries. They are dictators who seek to rule the world,[166] and dictators are ignominious, vermin-like people. Yet in the next breath, surprisingly enough, he declares that if only *he* were the dictator, he would know how to cope with those masses! What people need, he writes, is ten years of silence—and these years should be imposed upon them! [167] And, getting down to specifics, he would know exactly how to treat Jews! He would have the following three laws passed, immediately:

1. All Jews, half-Jews, quarter-Jews, those married to Jews, etc., would have to fight in the front lines. No infirmity, no excuse would be possible; no Jew would be allowed to rise higher than Captain.
2. The Jew would not be permitted to be a doctor, aviator, politician, chauffeur, etc. He would never be permitted to remain further than twenty meters away from the front lines—the line of fire.
3. Any infraction of these rules would be punishable by death. There would be no discussion, no arguments.[168]

Such a ruthless program seems all the more ironic given the fact that Céline himself, accused of complicity with the Germans during World War II, fled France in 1944 and thus escaped the firing lines, and given the fact that he squirmed with fear for years to come.

Céline voices his admiration for Hitler in *Bagatelles for a Massacre.* He prefers Hitler to the Jew because Hitler is sincere. If Hitler had said to him, "Ferdinand, it's the big division now. We're going to divide everything," then, Céline continued, "he would be my pal. The Jews have promosed to divide, [but] they lied as always . . . Hitler does not lie like the Jews." [169] Céline knows, so he declares, that Hitler believes that "might makes right," but that is quite all right; at least he is not hypocritical about it, or "subtle," as the Jews are. Céline has certain ideas in common with Hitler. "Hitler doesn't like the Jews, neither do I." [170] Céline would prefer a dozen Hitlers "to one omnipotent Blum!" [171] He can understand Hitler, whereas he cannot even begin to comprehend such a type as Léon Blum, his worst enemy, a man "he could hate to death." Never once does Céline question Hitler's morality, his right to kill so many millions, to fill concentration camps with innocents, to plunder, to gas the countless.

Would Céline kill a Jew? "If necessary, yes," he answers with aplomb.[172]

Céline hates Jews because they were the inventors of patriotism, of the Crusades, of the Reformation—all intended to kill Christians.[173] Our hero's contradictions abound. On one page he claims the Jews are internationally minded, on another page they are the promulgators of patriotism. As for the Crusades, we need only glance at the details concerning this movement to discover the tremendous number of Jews who were killed or mutilated, their homes razed to the ground, in both the Holy Land and in France—by the Crusaders. The Reformers were, for the most part, Calvin and his followers, Luther and his . . .

Céline accuses the Jew of being a "racist" and he despises him as such. Judging from Céline's statements to follow, few could have outdone or even matched his own ultramilitant and ultraracist attitude. He considers the Jew to be synonymous with the "Asiatic"—with the foreign. The Jew has "Judeo-Mongolian bad blood," he is part and parcel of "Asiatic vermin." [174] All Jews are Negroes, Céline writes. They are trying to destroy the Aryan race, and this through communism.[175]

> The Jew is a Negro, the semitic race does not exist, it is an invention of the Freemasons, the Jew is the product of a cross between the Negro and the Asiatic barbarian.[176]

The Jews, Céline writes further on, are worse than Negroes.[177] They have invaded France! "The negrified-Jew is not at home in our land. We are in their land." [178] In France—in the land of the Jew-Negro—the "white" man, the Aryan, can only indulge in manual trades or be a soldier, nothing more. All intellectuals, all artists, all heads of state—all are Jewish-Negroes, because "France is a Jewish colony." [179]

Jews are Africans. They are Africa-oriented and for this reason unable to understand spirituality. They possess only "a fraction of very vulgar sensitivity . . ." [180] Their nervous system is rudimentary. They are degenerates, like the Negro, and have added nothing to European art or culture.

Céline's complexes, at this point, seem to have overwhelmed his conscious mind completely.

What, psychologically speaking, does Céline hate about the Jew?

He hates him because, according to Céline, the Jew seeks to elicit pity from the world. But isn't this pity the very emotion that Céline has sought to inspire in his readers with his pseudo-myth of the impoverished child, the tortured, the tormented little boy? Isn't this the very pity that Céline had tried to evoke when he complained of all those critics who were intent on crucifying him, and also when he wrote of his poor health and other trials and tribulations throughout *Bagatelles for a Massacre?* Céline denies that he seeks or needs compassion: "I adhere to myself." [181] However, notwithstanding this ostensible desire to remain heroically aloof, Céline did take the slightest opportunity in his novels, in his interviews, and in conversations with friends to try to arouse "pity" for himself.

Céline hates the Jew, he says, because the Jew is a stranger in France, a perfidious person, an adventurer, a dentist, a hairdresser, a parachutist, a pimp, an artist, a politician, a vampire, a sewer, etc. The Aryans—the true Aryans—cannot breathe in such an atmosphere of envy and mutual hatred.[182] Hitler was right, Céline goes on, to try to rid his land of Jews. France should do likewise.[183]

Céline is quite correct, of course, when he says that society cannot even function, much less improve, when it is drenched in an atmosphere of hate. Hatred is indeed a stultifying, destructive force in society, just as it is in an individual. But what Céline despises in the Jew is what he projects onto him: feelings that live within Céline himself and are his own.

More important, however, is Céline's claim that all Jews are paranoiacs. They are convinced, he writes, that the world is against them, that they are being perpetually persecuted. But is this not precisely the conviction that is eating away at Céline's own organism? He is in terror of everything: strangers, foreigners, governments, war, the world. Unable to face and assimilate his fears, he seeks a scapegoat—the Jew. Céline fears the Jew as some fear the Blacks and others fear dogs, cats, birds, etc. Destroy them, they believe erroneously, and the fear will vanish.

The Jew, Céline believes, is not at all inventive; he is merely parasitical. Endowed with a robotlike nature, he is to blame for bringing "standardization" to civilization. Because of this there is now a sameness in French taste. Céline had probably never read Adam Smith when he made such statements, and he had forgotten that the Industrial Revolution was not a Jewish enterprise, and that Henry Ford, said to be the creator of the assemblyline, was not only not a Jew but was himself anti-Semitic.

Céline failed to notice, among other things, that by repeating his hates ad infinitum, he was creating a sameness in his work, a monotony, a "standardization."

Céline's anti-Semitic complex had so absorbed his thoughts, had so clouded his vision, that when writing *Bagatelles for a Massacre* he suffered from thought-deprivation, from an *idée fixe.* Such a situation is neither unusual nor strange. Many intelligent people, seemingly rational on most subjects, go blind when a complex is struck. A person suffering from the disease of hatred "in general," but directed against the Jew in particular, clearly experiences *un abaissement du niveau mental.* No amount of logic, as we have seen, can alter his convictions.

Whether Céline's hate-complex was triggered by some unpleasant event, such as an unfortunate or unhappy incident in childhood, or whether he had been exposed to an anti-Semitic ambiance during his younger years, is thus far not known. We know only that the hate principle existed, that it grew, that it filled the void within his personality. Like the bull who rushes at the red cloth, Céline sought to destroy the Jew. Whenever the word Jew is mentioned, it triggered some hate-complex within him.

Victimized by his hate-complex, Céline's energies were drained. His interest in objects not intimately associated with his *idée fixe* was diminished. His thoughts lacked focus. His writing became turgid, muddled, superficial, monotonous. When we speak of the writer who fails to renew himself, who writes one or two books of import but thereafter merely repeats in a variety of ways what he has already said, he may be said to be under the dominion of one or several very powerful complexes. Such was Céline's situation at this period. Rather than free himself of these complexes, permitting them to flow back into their rightful place, into the ego-complex, he merely restated himself. His creative output, therefore, became dull, routine, subject to the same obsessions, the same associations, fantasies, contrasts. Great writers have understood this condition, perhaps unconsciously; Arthur Rimbaud and Jean Genet, for example, both stopped writing once their need for self-expression disappeared. But not Céline. He continued his polemics in two equally destructive and trite works: *School for Cadavers* and *Some State of Affairs.*

SCHOOL FOR CADAVERS

School for Cadavers, dedicated to Julian the Apostate, piles up series upon series of adjectives and nouns in a frenetically topsy-turvy series of unrelated and innocuous sentences. The "arguments" of *Bagatelles for a Massacre* are reiterated—that Jews are Negroes, Asiatics, communists, etc. Again he praises Hitler, Franco, and Mussolini, those "fabulous" people, so "admirably magnanimous, infinitely pacifist," and worthy of two hundred fifty Nobel Peace Prizes.[184] "Fascist states do not want war. They have nothing to gain from war. They have everything to lose. If peace lasted another four or five years, all of Europe would be fascist." [185] "Death to the Jews . . . Rise Aryans!" [186] Hitler had saved all right-thinking people from Stalin and the Jewish hangmen. "You owe Hitler a lot!" [187] It is almost as if Céline were echoing Hitler's words when, in Berlin on March 7, 1936, the Führer harrangued his audiences and said:

> I will not have the gruesome Communist internation dictatorship of hate descend upon the German people! This destructive Asiatic *Weltanschauung* strikes at all values! I tremble for Europe at the thought of what would happen should this destructive Asiatic conception of life, this chaos of the Bolshevist revolution, prove successful! [188]

France is floundering, Céline continues, because it has been too lenient with the Jews. Democracies such as Czechoslovakia should not be permitted to flourish; Eduard Beneš, the president of this land, is a Jew, Céline maintains (erroneously): "filthy little talmudic scum . . ." [189] Céline's answer to all problems?

1. The expulsion of all Jews.
2. The forbidding and closing of all Lodges and secret societies.
3. Forced labor for all dissatisfied peoples, those who are hard of hearing or otherwise disabled, etc.[190]

SOME STATE OF AFFAIRS

When *Some State of Affairs* was published (1941), France had already been defeated. In it, Céline's manifest hatred for the Jew, for the French, and for all of humanity has not abated. Judging from *Some State of Affairs,* it has invaded his entire organism. He is filled with pleasure and contentment when he speaks of the extermination of the Jews, who have finally paid the penalty for the troubles, misfortunes, and disruptions they have caused. It is about time, Céline suggests, that France, the real Aryans, find their own "white" religion, rather than continue to follow the lucubrations of a faith founded on what twelve Jews had prescribed.[191] The Jews are good for only one thing: "Eat the Jew." [191]

As we have already seen, there were many in France during the late 1930s and early 1940s who shared Céline's beliefs. Léon Daudet of the *Action Française,* writing in praise of *Bagatelles for a Massacre* (February 10, 1938), considered Céline's polemic "against the Jews" a very courageous and great work. Charles Plisnier of *L'Indépendence Belge* declared Céline's work to be a "masterpiece and a tour de force" (March 19, 1938). Robert Brasillach of the *Action Française* commented on the brilliance of Céline's polemical work and on the fact that Céline had already felt the spirit of "revolt" that lived in the heart of the "natives of the land."

It is in Céline's polemical works that his hatred really seems to bloom, that his dictatorial and authoritarian tendencies take root. Gone is the humor and the semicoherence of his novels. Michel Beaujour, in a superb article, has compared the Céline of the polemics to some of his characters, in particular Auguste, who always gave vent to his instincts and his rage and never considered anything lucidly, humanly. Céline, it seems, had become his characters.[192]

ORDEAL

In December, 1937, following the publication of *Bagatelles for a Massacre,* Céline was asked to resign his post at the Clichy dispensary. The free time that he now enjoyed permitted him to complete his second polemical work, *School for Cadavers* (1938). In 1939, after France had entered the war, it seems that he volunteered his services as an army doctor but was rejected on grounds of ill-health. Despite this setback, Céline served in a medical capacity on the armed steamer *Shella,* going from Marseille to Casablanca. En route to Marseille, the ship was sunk by a German submarine. Céline returned to Paris after this incident and found work at the Sartrouville dispensary. In 1940, deciding to leave there, he took the dispensary's ambulance and drove his future wife, Lucette Almanzor, an old woman, and two babies to La Rochelle, where he worked in a hospital for two weeks. He refused an offer to join General de Gaulle's Free French in England. Instead, he returned to Paris in October and settled down in an apartment on rue Girardon. He was appointed chief of the dispensary at Bezons (Seine-et-Oise), where he practised medicine off and on until the arrival of the Allies in June, 1944.

Céline's third polemical work was published in 1941, during the German occupation. The following year he went to Berlin, ostensibly to visit German hospitals. He had some good friends in the German medical corps: Doctor Karl Epting, a Doctor Haubolt, and others whom he had known in Paris both before and during the war.

Fearing Allied reprisals, Céline decided to leave France in July, 1944, a month after French and English troops landed in Normandy. Céline, his wife and cat, and the actor Robert Le Vigan left Paris for Denmark. Some years before, it will be recalled, he had converted his royalties into gold bullion to be held for him in a bank in Copenhagen. He said that up until 1944, his novels had brought him a million francs a year and twice that to his publisher, Denoël.[193] Since Céline had to pass through Germany to reach Denmark, a *Passierschein* was necessary. Céline and his group sojourned for a while at the Park Hotel in Baden-Baden; Doctor Haubolt then sent them to Kränzlin, near Neu-Ruppin (Brandenburg). From November to March, 1945, Céline and his group lived at Sigmaringen, where many collaborators and members of the Vichy government (including Pétain and Laval) had been given asylum by the Germans. In March, Céline and his group were given permission to leave Sigmaringen. They crossed Germany under difficult conditions, finally arriving in Copenhagen on March 27. They were given shelter and hospitality by an old friend, Karen Marie Jensen, and lived for several months more or less in hiding before Céline was denounced to the Danish authorities as a French collaborator. The French representative in Denmark asked for his extradition in a letter dated December 18, 1945. The extradition, however, was denied.

On April 19, 1946, Céline was arrested in Copenhagen. On November 6, he answered *pro domo* the accusations, giving his side of the story: "Answers to the accusations of treason formulated against me by the French Court and restated by the Danish police during my interrogation." On December 20, Céline's wife was arrested. She remained in prison for two months and he for fourteen, at Vesterfangsel. On February 26, 1947, the Danish minister of justice permitted Céline to go to the Ryshospitalet at Copenhagen, provided he gave his "word of honor" not to try to leave the country. On June 24, he promised "not to leave Denmark without permission from the Danish authorities" and he was permitted, therefore, to live at Konprinssessegade with his wife. In May, 1948, Céline and his wife left for Körsor, a small port town on the Baltic Sea, where they remained until 1951.

In February, 1950, Céline was condemned by default in France "to one year of imprisonment and fifty thousand francs fine." He was declared "to be a national disgrace" and "half of his monies were to be confiscated." By 1951, however, Céline was able to take advantage of the amnesty law of August, 1947, and in June he and his wife returned to France.

Céline's case has continued to be a source of great controversy and heated debate among patriots, intellectuals, philosophers, politicians, and even the man in the street. Many friends and admirers of Céline attest to his innocence, admirable character, sincerity, integrity, perspicuity, and forthrightness. Others are not so lavish in their praise. Some consider Céline to have been a betrayer of France, a vicious, cruel, sadistic person, a man consumed by unconscionable rage and hate. Because of his international reputation as a writer, it is argued, his polemical writings did great harm—much more harm than did the lucubrations of less well-known and less gifted pro-Nazi journalists and writers. Céline's writings spread dissension and bred antagonism.

The French Resistance opened its files on Céline after the war. What follows is a résumé of the principal documents brought to light in the case against him, together with his answers to various allegations.

Céline was brought to trial in absentia in 1945, accused of fomenting anti-Semitism, of advocating a Pan-German policy, of having sought to create, by publishing three polemical works *(Bagatelles for a Massacre, School for Cadavers, Some State of Affairs)* and contributing articles to collaborationist newspapers *(La Gerbe, Au Pilori, Emancipation Nationale),* a climate favorable to Hitlerism in France.

In the three polemical works, it was asserted, Céline had not only distorted facts (when he stated, for example, that there were twenty million Jews and "mixed-breeds" in France when there were only six hundred fifty thousand) but had also plagiarized from the works of such notorious racists as Houston Stewart Chamberlain, Edouard Drumont, and others. Not quoted in the testimony, but appearing in the magazine *Esprit* (No. 66, 1938), in an article by its editor Emmanuel Mounier, was a detailed account of Céline's plagiarisms: on one side of the page Mounier printed Céline's words and on the other side the phrases and sentences he had copied from such works as *The Reign of the Jews, The Next Workers Revolution,* and *Israel: Its Past and Future.*

Céline declared that he had never advocated any kind of rapprochement with Germany. Yet one reads in *Bagatelles for a Massacre:* "I prefer German peace any time." [194] In this same work he further stated that he liked the Germans because they belonged to the white race,[195] and he supported an alliance with the Aryan race.

> I want an alliance to be made with Germany, and right away; not a small, precarious alliance. A real alliance, solid, colossal, with lime and sand! Unto life! Unto death! Man needs hate to live. People need only hate the Jews and not the Germans. To hate the Germans is to hate against nature. France is Latin only by chance. Really, she is Celtic, three-fourths Germanic.[196]

According to Lucien Rebatet, editor of the fascist, pro-German publication *Je Suis Partout,* Céline advocated a total alliance with Hitler—military, political, and economic.[197]

The prosecution further asserted that during the German occupation of France Céline had been present at meetings of the pro-Nazi organization "Emancipation Nationale," that he had contributed to pro-Nazi newspapers and magazines, and that he had delivered lectures encouraging friendship with the enemy.

Céline answered his accusers as follows:

1. "As soon as the Germans arrived, I became completely disinterested in the Jewish question . . . I don't remember ever having written a single anti-Semitic line since 1937."

To this affirmation the French court offered the following facts to the contrary. On December 18, 1941, in *La Gerbe,* the pro-Hitler paper founded by Alphonse de Chateaubriant, Céline had written: "One must take a stand against the Jews. Let us not compromise ourselves!" His *Some State of Affairs* (1941) is filled with pro-Nazi remarks such as: "The clauses of the true pack, the only one respected: Vote for the Aryans. Urns for the Jews." [198]

2. "I have never, at any moment, in any sentence in any of my books," swore Céline, "encouraged anti-Semitic persecution. . . . Jews should erect a statue in my honor for all the evil I could have perpetrated against them but did not."

More evidence was offered by the government, some of which reads as follows. "Eat the Jew," wrote Céline, and by Jew, he declared in a footnote, he meant all people having even one grandparent who was Jewish.[199] "The Knights Templars, the Jews, and the Freemasons must be retried." [200] "Luxate the Jew to a post!" [201]

3. "I have never in my life written for a newspaper," Céline declared.

The court offered articles written by Céline in 1941 and 1942 for such pro-German newspapers as *Au Pilori* and *L'Emancipation Nationale.* The latter paper was the one to which the collaborator Drieu la Rochelle had also contributed articles. Some extracts of Céline's articles were offered.

> All the anti-Jewish French, without exception, feel as I do, think as I do. They no longer understand. . . . Each time Hitler begins to talk, he blames the Jews formally for having unleashed this European war. Why then, don't you, who want to be incorporated into the National Socialist fold, blame the responsible ones officially? [202]

4. "I have never in my life delivered a lecture," Céline affirmed.

Yet on January 11, 1942, the pro-Nazi newspaper *L'Union Française* published a report on a lecture delivered by Céline in which he examined, point by point, the aspects of French life that the Nazis sought to destroy and *should* destroy. He made the following points to those present.

a. The Regeneration of France through racism. No hatred of the Jew, simply the desire to eliminate him from French life. There must not be any anti-Semitism but only racism.
b. The church must take a position concerning the racist problem.

The reporter declared further that Céline "had exposed the urgency with which this program must be carried out, with his usual torrential verve, truly his own."

5. "Have I ever," Céline asked, "exhibited any anti-Semitic works in anti-Semitic Institutes? No."

The prosecution introduced a photostatic copy of a letter written by Céline to a Captain Sézille, secretary of the Institute to Study Jewish Questions, in which Céline complained bitterly that neither *Bagatelles for a Massacre* nor

School for Cadavers had been exhibited on the shelves of the institute. He hoped that the omission would be rectified and that it had merely been an oversight.

6. "I have always carefully kept my distance from all Kollaborators'! . . ."

The court again brought out the evidence: an article printed in *L'Emancipation Nationale* (November 21, 1941) in which Céline wrote:

> I didn't wait for the High Command to bedeck the Crillon with flags to become a collaborator.

Other articles were also offered by the court. In *Au Pilori* (December 11 and 14, 1941), for example, Céline had written:

> I have been anti-Jewish from the very beginning. I sometimes have the impression that I have been surpassed by certain new elements. At least, their ideas concerning the Jewish problem are different from mine. That's why I must meet them and explain my ideas to them.

Collaborators such as Alphonse de Chateaubriant, Jean Luchaire, Marcel Déat, Maître de Monzie, Bernard Fay, Captain Sézille, Lucien Rebatet, Drieu la Rochelle, Ramón Fernandez, and others met to discuss the question raised in Céline's article.

Céline further clarified his position in another article in *Au Pilori* (January 8, 1942) entitled "Deserters? We? No, You!" More evidence contradicting Céline's assertion that he was not a collaborator was brought forth in a note sent from Ambassador Otto Abetz to M. Zeitschel, assistant to a Captain Dannecker, who was in charge of "Jewish questions" in the Army of Occupation. In this note, Abetz informed his correspondent that Ferdinand Céline's name could be added to the list of the people on whom they can count (Paris, January 3, 1941).

7. "The banning of my works pleased me greatly," Céline affirmed.

Articles in *Au Pilori* (January 8, 1942) and *L'Emancipation Nationale* (November 21, 1941) attest to the fact that Céline was not only writing but was being published and widely read.

8. "Since . . . I didn't receive the least bit of 'bon de kilos' from them [the Germans] . . . my books could not be printed because of the lack of paper."

In point of fact, it seems that one of the earliest acts of the German occupation forces was to lift the ban on a number of books, including Céline's *Bagatelles for a Massacre* and *School for Cadavers.* Céline and his publisher Denoël "triumphed," not only in terms of reputation but financially as well. Céline's two polemical works were reprinted in 1941, with new editions following in 1943, including an illustrated edition with twenty photographs. *Some State of Affairs* was published by Denoël in February, 1941, and by May of that year had gone through fifty printings. Except for Lucien Rebatet's pro-German *Les Décombres,* no other such large editions were authorized by the German authorities.

9. "I never took any position against the French Resistance," Céline said.

In *Some State of Affairs,* Céline described heroism (that of the Resistance) as being made up of a hundred "hooligans, half-breeds, Jewish courage, those who have nothing left in their carcass but bile, profit-seekers." Other assertions of a similar nature appeared throughout this volume and in an article published in *L'Emancipation Nationale* (November 21, 1941).

10. "I who have never helped the Germans in any way," Céline went on.

Yet Céline's dossier contains quotations from *Some State of Affairs* indicating that he not only did not advocate war with Germany but strongly favored an alliance with that country. His distaste for both England and America encouraged this stand, as did his racism. As for the German press, journalists considered his anti-Semitic works to be revelations and of great help to their cause. In *Der Stürmer (The Stormer),* a pornographic, anti-Semitic German weekly, whose managing editor Julius Streicher, the *Gauleiter* of Nuremberg, was Céline's friend, the French writer's work was highly praised. In fact, a special edition of a half million copies, with the first page devoted to Céline, was printed.

In French newspapers, Céline's comments were printed in *Notre Combat* (1941), in articles "Céline Speaks to Us of Jews"; in *Cahier Jaune,* "Louis-Ferdinand Céline, the Capital Contemporary"; "The Powerful Anti-Jew Visionary!" in such papers as *Pariser-Zeitung, La Gerbe, Je Suis Partout, Gringoire,* etc.

Céline's name was mentioned with respect by such racists as Montandon in his *l'Ethnie française* (Paris, April, 1941), Querrioux in *Medicine and the Jews* (Nouvelle édition française, 1941), Pemjean in *The Press and the Jews* (Nouvelle édition française, 1941), the count of Puységur in *What was the Jew before the war? Everything! What must he be? Nothing!* (Ed. Baudinière, 1942), Jean Drault in his *History of Anti-Semitism* (ed. C.I. 1942), and Lucien Rebatet in *Décombres* (Denoël, 1942).

11. "My novels were banned in Germany and this ban remained strictly enforced during the entire Nazi regime. German literary critics passed over my literary and political works."

To this claim, the French court offered pictures of various German editions of Céline's works, together with articles and advertisements praising them.

The prosecution summed up its case as follows:

> The frenzy of his formulaes, the vehemence of his entreaties, of his call for pogroms, surpassed those of Streicher, hanged for his crimes against humanity, and his [Céline's] insane anger was comparable only to that of the Führer.

Because Céline enjoyed such a formidable literary reputation, the court asserted, what he said throughout the war and the occupation had extreme impact. He was therefore doubly responsible, more so than any of the mediocre writers who voiced pro-Nazi opinions. Other defendants, the prosecutor continued, had spoken the truth about their activities during the occupation, and "some even displayed a certain amount of dignity in their indignity." The same could not be said of Céline who, if he did not lie outright, was struck with a sudden and extraordinary lapse of memory when he declared, for example, that he didn't "remember ever having written a single anti-Semitic line since 1937."

Part Three

OUTBURST

Today violence is the rhetoric of the period.

Ortega y Gasset, *The Revolt of the Masses*

7

GUIGNOL'S BAND I

Your soul will be dead even sooner than your body: fear nothing more!

FRIEDRICH NIETZSCHE, *Thus Spake Zarathustra*

Guignol's Band I, PUBLISHED IN 1944, IS A FRIGHTENING WORK for two reasons: its premonitory nature and its revelation of the extreme tumult and mental erosion being experienced by Céline at this stage along his life's way.

Céline had already experienced the War and the Occupation. Certainly solitude and rage must have possessed him most severely. He had been rejected by the fascists because he had not been sufficiently outspoken in their favor. He was even more distasteful to the patriots because of his pro-Nazi polemical works. He emerged from the holocaust a broken man, a man cornered and not knowing where next to turn. The chaos intrinsic in *Guignol's Band I* mirrors this inner situation and also marks a type of prefiguration of the horrendous experiences he was to know in Germany during his wanderings and after his arrival in Copenhagen and his imprisonment there.

Guignol's Band is a spring from which gush gallons of endless hatred, violence, and terror. It is the work of a soul sick and enshrouded in fear and anguish, of a psyche torn apart, each fragment undergoing one emotional crisis after another. It is the kind of novel that the alchemists of old would have considered revelatory of the "horrible darkness of our mind," the blackness of chaos, the *massa confusa* of *prima materia*. Nothing is positive in this work; nothing is clear, whole, or alive—save for pain. Céline, as the author, reveals himself to be shattered, fragmented, splintered like crushed glass. Not a single instant of repose is reflected in *Guignol's Band*—only feelings of entrapment, enslavement, and hurt. We are introduced to a man's chthonic realm, to his most primitive side, to that unformed world of instincts and the potential for evil.

Céline was a man against the world, against the cosmic order. The German swastika, the symbol of the land he visited, stands for destruction, and in Céline's case it seems to have been an outer manifestation of an inner picture. The swastika originally symbolized cosmic order, since it represented the "sun," and in Sanskrit *su* means "well" and *asti* is defined as "being." The

Nazis, however, reversed the image, indicating their desire to turn *against* the sun and the cosmic well-being—their desire to annihilate.[1]

The destructive and frenzied quality of *Guignol's Band* is expressed not only in terms of the novel's content but also, and most effectively, through Céline's kinetic hero, who enacts his fitful antics in three different media: the literary, the pictorial, and the musical. By uniting the three arts, Céline not only enlarges the novel's scope but accentuates its visceral rapport with the reader, the protagonists, and the author. This stylistic technique enabled him to create a veritable mimodrama, a guignol, in which the marionette-like creatures gesticulate their fruitless and absurd lives upon the paper.

PLOT

Ferdinand is making his way out of the Orleans area in an ambulance during World War II. The district is being bombarded by Stukas. Tanks and military transports are everywhere. Suddenly, the scene changes: London during World War I. Ferdinand meets Borokrom, whose nickname is Boro, a chemist originally from St. Petersburg. They become friendly and together invade the Soho district, where they mix with prostitutes (Angèle, Véronique), a Doctor Clodovitz (Clodo), who worked in the London Freeborn Hospital, the pimp Cascade, pickpockets, murderers, a pawnbroker (Claben), and his governess Delphine. The novel closes with Ferdinand and his cohorts murdering Claben and burning his home.

THE KINETIC HERO

In this semipicaresque novel, Ferdinand is quite "uninvolved" throughout. He adheres to no cause, has no ideal, flits from one sequential episode to another, thereby giving a false impression of "becoming." Paradoxically, though he moves about with frenetic speed, his very motility gives him a static quality. He is actually not budging an inch; his philosophical concepts remain stationary. He does not become; he is.

Ferdinand is not the "alienated" individual of Sartre and Camus, whose heroes are forever probing metaphysical and ontological questions in the hope of finding some kind of rational explanation for their "absurd" existence. Ferdinand is not alienated because he has never belonged to any society or political or religious group from which to be alienated. He is equally at home (or not at home) everywhere. Because of this complete adaptability, he becomes a passive type—not the victim-hero of Franz Kafka's *The Trial* or Saul Bellow's *The Victim.*[2] Ferdinand's life never takes on purpose. He experiences what might be termed a "structured chaos."

In *Guignol's Band,* an exploratory and uncommitted work (if one considers a lack of commitment less binding than adherence to a belief), one detects a Schopenhauerian veneer. Like the German philosopher, Celine believed that man is forever living under a veil of illusion and delusion, that he is duped into thinking himself master of his actions, ideas, and life's course. What is man, really? Merely an instrument of greed, or to use Schopenhauer's word, of his all-powerful "will." It is the will that determines all the body's activities and functions: thoughts, eating, bowel movements, generation, nervous system reactions, etc.[3] The will, moreover, is autonomous, and as such it lives and exists from and within itself. Nothing outside it can compete with its power and insatiable hunger. It is the will that compels man to desire, forces him to be forever dissatisfied. Reason, according to Plato, Descartes, Pascal, and others, is supposed to distinguish man from animal in that it is capable of understanding and formulating abstract notions. But reason needs the will to function and therefore follows the will's dictates. Only if man can escape from the world of desire, through contemplation, can he hope to transcend the frustrations and pain of mundane existence. While Schopenhauer considered this condition of contemplation to be a distinct possibility for everyone (he supposed that if Orientals were capable of achieving this ideal state, Occidentals should be able to do so too), Céline thought it impossible for Occidentals. The Oriental has been taught from birth to dispel, diffuse, or transcend the ego, whereas the Occidental has been taught to develop his self, his individual existence. In Céline's view, such a dichotomy, so far as the psyche is concerned, cannot be breached.

The nihilistic atmosphere of *Guignol's Band* is even more pronounced than that of his first two novels. In *Journey to the End of the Night* and *Death on the Installment Plan* the narrators are involved human beings, relatively speaking, trying ontologically, spiritually, and materially to extricate themselves from the nonsensical maze that is their lives. They are thrust hither and yon from one continent to another *(Journey)*, from one job to the next *(Death)*, in a series of escapades, but always are seeking some kind of fulfillment, are seeking to answer, in terms of themselves, life's seemingly irrational side. The details are realistically described on the surface, but the exaggerations, repetitions, and rather strange creatures that find their way into the narrative lend a surrealistic and outer-worldly atmosphere to both novels.

Guignol's Band may be described in a similar fashion but with one great difference: its kinetic hero is solitary and uninvolved. He never searches for an answer because he knows that none will ever be forthcoming. In many ways Ferdinand is an expression of the ultramodern world that man has created for himself, a world in which science and speed are the motivating forces. Motivated by what? A "will" that asks no questions about consequences for man and society, that relates to nothing, that always acts impulsively, illogically, in fits and starts. Though Ferdinand may think, at times, that he is acting in a rational way, actually he is merely pushed from one series of negative incidents to another. He is a man driven by his will, his instincts, and for no reason. His body, blood, gestures, muscles are the tools of an insatiable appetite for life, but a life lacking direction and devoid of past, present, and future.

When Ferdinand's passions are satisfied, at least sexually (and temporarily), he is no happier than he was before. He finds no sense of fulfillment in anything he does. He is always outside the situation or else so inextricably within it that he cannot see it plain. A void, therefore, always settles about him, causing his every action to swing back and forth, like Schopenhauer's pendulum, from pain to ennui.[4]

Ferdinand is desperate; he is also unconscious of this fact. He is incapable of any thought, any evaluation. He feels a crushing sense of inadequacy, life is painful for him, but he has no idea why. He contemplates the suffering about him, he sees the poverty, the disease, the prisons, the hospitals, the battlefields. Yet his agony, suffered alone, is always fleeting, since he is forever diverting himself in one adventure or another.

He is motility personified. He bounces here and there like a puppet, lacerating, mutilating, striking, jabbing. His kineticism adds to his chaos, increases his already fragmented personality by drawing his attention away from his problem to someone else. His psyche could be described as being made up of a series of "faults" in the geological sense of "lines of fracture." [5]

Yet it is through his kineticism that he finds a certain amount of release from a gloom that would be unbearable if it were prolonged ad infinitum. Young, vibrant, Ferdinand thinks that joy is for the asking and he finds it (at least he finds excitement) in confrontation with enemies (quarrels with anyone and everyone) and in sexual adventures. His insatiable energy is channeled in a series of fruitless attempts to circumvent his pessimism. Like Proteus, he is always transforming himself, escaping—so he erroneously believes—from the world of causality to which he has been chained. Each adventure, he thinks, will cut the cord that holds him to the land of bondage, to his "band" of friends, symbolically speaking. It has the opposite effect: he becomes more deeply entrenched in their ways.

The endless series of fustigations that make up *Guignol's Band* is a symbolic representation of nature at odds with itself, of the strife, competition, and conflict inherent in every form of life, terrestrial or cosmic. Every species in the world struggles for matter, space, time. Immobility spells death. Ferdinand is alive in the sense that he is always struggling, always moving about. Yet he is, psychologically speaking, dead, since nothing he does has meaning or direction. He is like a jack-in-the-box, forever popping up and down to no purpose.

PICTORIAL AND MUSICAL STYLE

The fruitlessness of unguided activity, the extreme dynamism of *Guignol's Band*, as revealed in the protagonist's fight, in his lust to kill and in sex, is expressed stylistically, pictorially, and musically in a rather spectacular manner.

The opening paragraphs describe the excitement of exile: a whole population is in flight, as individuals and as a collective entity. Fear and trepidation are imprinted in everybody's heart. These emotions are described visually: people running about, pushing, hiding, falling, trampling; children, babies crying out, men shouting, carts, ambulances stalling; motors starting at various pitches; vehicles of all types cluttering the road, bumping into each other, screeching to a halt.

> Everything! the carcasses! the junk! the tanks! piles upon the crunching and rattling caterpillar-guns that smash all interference under the direction of a quartermaster! It's the saraband of fright, the fair under the crawling-dislocating thunder! It's the rubber-man who wins! Ah! hooray for the cosmic scoundrel, the unscrupulous bachelor with the corkscrew bicycle, the armored stinker! [6]

Bombings and shelling from the enemy add to the rhythms and timbers. The heavens finally enter into the túrmoil, accelerating the cacophonies, as they pour forth, in concert-like fashion, tons of water of a variety of opacities. The action becomes triunal: sheets of liquid dropping from above, deafening sounds from man-made machines, bombings that tear open the earth below, transforming it into a series of gaping abysses.

How does Celine achieve the effect of extreme motility in this and other passages? In the same manner in which the Futurists (in Italy and France) and the Vorticists (in England) expressed speed in painting. The Futurists were struck by the dynamism of twentieth-century civilization. No matter what the themes they chose to depict on canvas (automobiles, wheels, trains, explosive machines, dance halls, etc.), they infused their paintings with excitement and speed, attempting in this manner to express man's preoccupation with the dynamics of motion. In Umberto Boccioni's *The Riot* (1911), for example, powerful rhythms and a variety of activities are revealed by breaking up the composition of certain forms in given areas on the canvas. Once form was shattered, the illusion of motion could be created. Giacomo Ball and Carlo Carra, other members of the Futurist group, expressed this same motility by disrupting what had been considered whole—by contracting objects into a series of multiple, unidentifiable, and overlapping entities. They reasoned that when a train or a car rushes by, the object gives the impression of being "condensed," sometimes even dissolved into nothing, certainly of being "telescoped." Vision, therefore, seems fragmented, even fractured. The object, whole when stationary, is shattered in motion. In Balla's *Speed of an Automobile + Lights* (1913) the lines delineating the car are not only fractured but overlap. To give the impression that the car is going in a certain direction, light is introduced into the scene. It shines from behind the object, lending a certain feeling of transparency to the scene and forcing the eye into one or another direction. Color, then, is divided, just as form is. In Boccioni's *States of Mind* (1911) tonalities are so shattered that they come to symbolize aggressive movement. Linear time and spatial concepts, once broken up in terms of light, lose their significance and impact as objects. They enter into the larger picture. They are caught up in the universal flow, the dynamism and sweep of the pictorial surface.[7]

For the Futurist, motion never achieves a condition of stasis. Objects and subjects are forever broken up, distorted into a series of geometric forms, designs, frequently unidentifiable, repeating sequential episodes, in rhythmic patterns. The impression of speed created on canvas is frequently so great that entire segments of the picture seem to be warring with one another. In Carra's painting, *The Funeral of the Anarchist Galli* (1910/11), the rays of light shining from above are suddenly interrupted, breaking up the images upon which they focused, injecting a sense of motion into each of them. Form and shape, as such, are nonexistent.[8]

Just as the Futurists were caught up in the dynamics of motion and sought to express on canvas the impact of industrial development and the immense mechanizations of society (the speed, excitement, and fragmentation that ensued), so Céline depicts objects in motion, shattering and distorting form.

There is still another reason, however, for Céline's attraction to fragmentation. Images of objects cut open or reduced to their component parts were a means of expressing his feelings of horror and pain as he witnessed the play of events and the course society was taking. Céline had recourse to abstraction, as had Paul Klee, as a means of escape. In 1915, soon after the beginning of World War I, Klee had written in his diary: "The more horrifying this world becomes (as it is in these days) the more art becomes abstract, while a world at peace produces realistic art." Franz Marc also turned to the abstract realm for solace. "Very early in life," he wrote, "I felt that man was ugly. The animals seemed to be more lovely and pure, yet even among them I discovered so much that was revolting and hideous that my paintings became more and more schematic and abstract." [9]

And so Céline will have recourse to abstraction and distortion. His protagonists—Ferdinand in particular—are forever busy in multiple activities, perpetually expending their energies. As a result, the narrative sections and of course the dialogues seem blurred. Nothing is clear or concise; everything is shattered, ambiguous, tenuous. The reader is forced to glimpse multiple headlong activities that tumble in and out of view on a second's notice. In the exodus from the Paris scene, for example, early in the novel, motion dominates at the expense of recognizable physical forms. Throughout the novel, indeed, during the various fights, fires, killings, the frenzy of motion very nearly overwhelms realistic delineation. As a result, one has the distinct impression that it is not a story which is being related, but rather a giant hovering mass—a horrendous excrescence—gaining momentum all the while, polluting the air.

The impression of motility, fragmentation, and distortion are particularly discernible in the fights between the prostitutes.

> Then the big hysteria broke loose. . . . Angèle threw a fit, she was foaming, and with a nervous laugh . . . Boy, she started snorting! and twitching! . . . she couldn't stop . . . She was ripping her clothes, shrieking, tearing at herself, kicking in tears, on the floor! at her cruel man's feet! . . . What a Trafalgar! Her bun came off, and flew apart . . . He was walking in her hair, tangled in it! . . . What screams! He didn't know where to stand! . . . She yelled worse! [10]

The fight gains in momentum. The figures blur. Light becomes brittle and fragmented all at once as the continuous physical motion is viewed. The tempo slows momentarily, only to accelerate seconds later, accompanied by drastic contraction of images, overlapping figures, each pulling and tossing the other, telescoping every gesture, condensing form until each figure virtually dissolves into the other.

> Joconde's choking! . . . Hooked up together like that! . . . But Angèle's stronger, she twists the old one's arm, she flattens her on her back! . . . Now she's on top . . . Biting her cheeks with her fangs, like that . . . grr! and grr!
>
> The old gal's waving her arms, squirming . . . Angèle grabs her again full of blood! . . . She's going to turn her upside down . . . bang her head. . . .
>
> The old one gets away, tucks up her skirt, capering about, dashing between the tables . . . the girls run after her! . . . she gets away, jiggling, fluttering, it's wonderful to watch! stumbles, stops! She stands there, planted . . . she

> winks . . . she takes out her castenets . . . Ah, it's a big challenge! . . . And stamps her heel! . . . and she's a fury! it's a dance! . . . a trance! . . . her fingers all nerves! . . . her hands quivering all over! . . . crackling, spluttering! . . . small . . . small . . . tiny . . . still smaller . . . grains . . . grains . . . mill, even still smaller . . . trr! . . . trr! . . . grainy . . . grainy . . . Rrr! . . . that's all! . . . silence! . . . and tzix! . . . she's off again! . . . The devil's tail! . . . the tail's caught! . . . trr! . . . rebounds! . . . hump! . . . her whole train! . . . and roundabouts! and twirls! hounding like a panther! at the end of the room! her train running after her! . . . over there! . . . hop it! . . . she's here! . . . a kick at her furbelow! . . . hup! sweeping off! Angèle's foaming . . . That's the limit! She can't take any more! [11]

The fierceness of the rage, the passionate desire to kill, the jealousy that invades these two figures as they hurl themselves at each other, are expressed in terms of motion, blurring all configurations. The two prostitutes, who have no code, no ethics, no morality, indulge their hatred to the very limit, until it reaches whirlwind dimensions. They are, in this respect, not only fragmented visually but are split off from the female principle, in that they represent only one aspect of the eternal feminine: the sensual, the animal-life, always fascinating, always destructive.

> And then, hup! Without time to. say off! She's up in the air! She sprang up! a knife in her fist! I see the blade! . . . Plop! . . . she launches out! . . . plunges it sideways! . . . Plup into the old one! right in the ass! . . . in the old one's ass! What a shriek! . . . It cuts through everything! tears everything! . . . the walls! the blinds! . . . the streets! . . . Joconde sure bounded! . . . with the knife in her ass! She's jumping all around screaming . . . she's running all around us! . . . she's yelping "Help!" She's squeezing her ass in her two hands . . . flying all around! . . . all around the table . . . Ow! Wow! Wow! [12]

As the action loses momentum, the reader can see the prostitutes scratching and clawing at each other, two felines attempting (rather successfully) to lacerate each other. The entire gamut of animosities inherent in womankind are enacted visually. The scene ends with the prostitutes, knives in hand, nails and teeth at work, mutilating and bloodying each other.

Many other scenes in *Guignol's Band* are also imbued with extreme momentum. The giant fire which destroys the pawnbroker's home literally sweeps across the horizon. The blaze, reminiscent of a giant dust storm, speeds by, shatters form, truncates the flashing rays of light, telescoping the entire scene.

> The house was crackling horribly . . . from top to bottom! . . . the firemen couldn't get at it any more . . . not even approach it from a hundred yards! . . . it was just a torch . . . a wild enormous torch . . . the flames were shooting from all the windows . . . The crowd was getting bigger and bigger . . . they must have come from all neighborhoods. . . . a terrible jabbering in addition to the crackling of the flames . . . all around the burning mass . . . they must have seen it from far off . . . from farther off than the devil . . . They'd come rushing up in crowds . . . a storm of jabberers! [13]

The fire's uncontrollable growth gives the impression of panic, to be sure, but also of breathlessness, as it devours all in its merciless embrace. Fire, the instrument of an unknown will, perhaps divine, perhaps evil, is sent, symbolically speaking, to purify, to scorch the putrid state of affairs, the venom-paved buildings and streets, making way, possibly, for growth and productivity.

Céline's descriptions are conceived aurally. Entire passages are reminiscent of a musical score, with its preludes, expositions, rhythms, tonalities, contrasting vibrations, pulsations, color tones, stresses, repetitions, counterrhythms, contrasts—as if musical instruments had been called into play to underline the throbbing and swaying atmosphere and the velocity of a heaving mass as it hurtles through space.

Céline achieves his effects through alliterations, onomatopoeias, assonances, rhyme schemes, harsh, brittle, and jarring consonants, modulating vowels, and pauses, the latter usually indicated by his omnipresent three dots. The discordant nature of some sequences (such as the fight of the prostitutes), creates the impression of an individual battle, and also of a giant war involving everything in sight. The episode conveys a sense of cosmic terror, implying that man is dominated by his situation, that he is passive, absurd, shunted here and there by some unknown transcendental force. The fire scene is another example of man at war with his universe. Fire, bursting and raging out of control, flaying the atmosphere, is expressed visually, as we have seen, but also musically. Its tonalities are never harmonious or moderate. They emanate as a series of blasts, repetitions of clashing consonants, not along classical lines (that is, with the passage resolving its conflict in tonic tones) but rather smarting from the elements, continuing its tonal gyrations. Discordant, chaotic, brittle sounds accelerate or diminish in pace, accompanied by unresolved and undetermined atonal intervals.

In none of the descriptions involving fights or antagonisms does the sequence ever become balanced or evolve into a whole composition. The images are made up of glaring, harsh, blaring, explosive tones, with cacophonies and atonal notes constantly infusing a macabre, disturbing and nerve-racking noise into the whole. At times, musically speaking, *Gignol's Band* achieves such unbearable clashes of jarring tonalities that it is something of a torture to pursue the reading of the novel.

Other elements also enter into the picture. Céline had always been much drawn to slang and made masterful use of it in his writings. Now, however, we notice that his vocabulary is filled with verbigerations—the constant repetition of "stray" words that seem to have a certain hypnotic power over the individual uttering them. Words such as *Vraoum!, Ding!, Dang!, Derange!,* and *Ouis!* [14] are used to express excitement, anxiety, or any other turbulent emotion. Odd word associations add to the reader's impression of volcanic emotion implicit in the protagonists: "To your stations, men! Swarm of cables! traps shut, bolted, dumbfounded, transposed, agog with excitement! . . . prostrated at the prodigious spectacle of the fragilities of landing, of the subtle miracle! . . ." ("Hommes à vos postes! Grouillots des câbles! bavoir calés, férus, esbaudis, transposés, immobiles d'émoi! . . . prostrés aux prodigieux spectacle . . ."). [15] The entire spectacle is a feast of neologisms: borrowed, invented, created words of all types. To add to the disjointed and disorienting effect of *Guignol's Band,* Céline indulges in speech confusion. In the narrative and dialogued parts of the novel, words describing the activities of the protagonists cascade out of their mouths. In some passages the verbiage seems devoid of meaning.

> Besides I've got my albumin . . . with a checkup and everything . . . just let 'em try and kick me out! . . . that Matthew won't get my hide, he'd sure like to see me yanked in! . . . For me to clear out! Ha! Small-timer! . . . he'd treat me to a drink in Waterloo! . . . after that . . . he can have the cuties! . . . Big-shot dealer and everything! The police don't worry them! . . . hypocrites! . . . All the gals in bunches for the Corsicans! . . . for the Belgians! . . . for anyone . . . Ah! that matter! Business fine! . . . I know what the fox's got in the back of his mind! I haven't been on the Strand since yesterday! Beg your pardon! . . . No fog! He says to himself . . . he'll be drunk like the others . . . They're all wacked up at the moment . . . They're all bitten by the war! . . . I'm going to make him ashamed! He'll beat it! . . . Zim! Boom! Patriotic, those frogs! Beg your pardon! . . . A bone! . . . Just wait! [16]

Endless passages of words are piled one upon the other in meaningless sequences, disconnected and entangled.[17] Lucidity is virtually nonexistent. This lack of vision gives rise to a narrowing of consciousness and to extreme suggestibility. A series of clang-reactions occurs—superficial verbal and motor associations, repetition of "stimulus words," constant distractions, all indicating a kind of regression into an infantile world, an archaic realm of raw, undifferentiated instinct.

The endless conflicts, the physical struggles between young and old, men and women, women and women, that fill the pages of *Guignol's Band* are, of course, an indication of the inner chaos implicit in the characters involved. There is no repose, no silence, no room for any kind of meditation. Action, speed, contest are the volume's by-words.

Though Céline may well have despised war, as he was wont to say he did, his characters seem always to be at war with themselves and with others. Not one of his characters transcends the violence of the atmosphere. War, erosion, disintegration, maiming, debris, and broken, shattered, and bloodied bodies make up the bulk of the material of this work. The impact is cumulative, the upheaval complete. The characters, repulsive both physically and morally, bring to mind the ugliest of the figures depicted by certain German Expressionist painters, most importantly George Grosz in his *Funeral of the Poet Panizza* (1917) and other works.

As vision after vision emerges from Céline's unconscious in a variety of speeds, timbres, and verbigerations, one factor remains constant: the frightful, nightmarish, sadistic quality of each of the sequences. The novel brings to mind certain of Salvador Dali's canvases, in which disconnected images alternate at different speeds, ushering in an atmosphere of horror by means of distortions and disfigurements. His *Paranoiac Face* (1935) may be looked upon as his visual impression of what has been called "man's unconscious, with its strident luminosities, its frightening shapes hovering here and there, creating the visually excruciating anguish the sick man must feel." Céline's detailed description of the pawnbroker's face, as he is being taunted, assailed, and finally murdered, is a verbal transposition of an emotion—fear. One can actually feel the change in the pawnbroker's facial expressions, ranging from bonhomie, humor, to utter horror, as he sinks lower and lower into the world of terror.

> Fell flat on his back with his mouth open . . . Then Boro starts cramming him . . . he stuffs him . . . he stuffs him . . . he rams it down! . . . coins by the fistful . . . like that, by force . . . The old guy swallows it all! He puffs for a second . . . and poof he rams in another . . . another fistful! The old guy feels like throwing up too . . . He's making horrible efforts . . . he's barking! He's beating the air! . . . waving his arms around . . . All you can see is the white of his eyes! . . . He wants to vomit but he can't! . . . not a single goldpiece! . . . he's convulsing, even disgorging! but only drool! . . . only gurgles . . .
> We jump on his belly . . . We bounce up and down on it . . . to see if he's going to puke! . . . Go fuck yourself! . . . We bend down to look at his face . . . we put the globe lamp right against it . . . his head's split! Wow! . . . a hole right between the eyes . . . A crack! . . . A noseful of snot dripping . . . It's all white . . . all gooey. . . .[18]

At the end of the sequence the characters are mutilated, their clothes are in tatters, their bodies are a mass of festering wounds, their world is depraved, as each in turn stares at the pawnbroker's lifeless body.

Who better than Céline could depict verbally what he had experienced emotionally: degradation? Céline's goal was not merely to compel his readers to shudder; it went far deeper than that. The novel was the only means he had of ridding himself of his inner turmoil, of exposing his sick soul to the warmth of daylight. The malaise the reader experiences when reading this volume is comparable to reactions that one might have when viewing Ivan Albright's canvas *The Temptation of Saint Anthony* (1948), in which the saint's physical dissolution is depicted by means of surface eruptions, blood stains, lacerations. Céline reveals degradation through this same medium: bruises, cuts, disease, and distortion.

Guignol's Band is the product of a deeply disturbed man who lives, for the most part, in his unconscious realm, perpetually at the mercy of deformed and terrorizing forces.

GUIGNOL'S BAND

Who and what was "guignol?" Why did Céline use this term in the title of his novel?

The guignol, the puppet, was known in ancient China, Japan, Egypt, Etruria, Greece, Rome. Chaucer made reference to puppets, as did Cervantes. Marionettes were being used in medieval mystery plays at Lübeck and Dieppe as early as 1443. The word *guignol* is thought to be of Italian origin. A weaver from a small town in Italy, Chignolo, settled in Lyon, France, in 1750 or thereabouts. He had made some small wooden marionette-like figures. He wrote brief plays for them and began giving theatrical spectacles using them, rather than human actors, to portray the events. As Chignolo's fame spread, imitators created similar puppet-like creatures. Puppet shows became the rage of Paris. In the eighteenth century, the dramatist Le Sage wrote plays especially for marionettes.

In 1897 a horror theater named Le Grand Guignol opened its doors in Paris. Its aim was to frighten people, to terrorize them to the utmost. Its founder, Oscar Méténier, as secretary to a police commissioner in Paris for over six years, had observed the worst elements in Paris and had witnessed murders, knifings, suicides—crimes of all types. He had frequented the lowest dens. The violence and the tragedies intrinsic in the lives of these people had been fixed in his mind, and when he founded the Grand Guignol (Theater of Horrors) he sought to shock his spectators. His actors were living puppets, big mechanical-minded puppets. Though they were human beings, they set out to exploit man's basic weakness—fear!

Man has always been haunted by fear, reasoned Méténier, and the best way to diminish its pangs is by a sort of vaccination, by putting tragic events and excruciating dilemmas right under the public's nose. The stage of the Grand Guignol was in itself awesome. Dread would overwhelm the spectator as the curtains parted: screams would split the air, blood would flow and spurt, cadavers would appear and disappear; strangulations, murders, knifings would enliven the incidents depicted. Strangely enough Parisians and foreign audiences would flock to see more and more sadism and brutality in this theater. They used to enjoy watching young girls held down on their beds, struggling to free themselves as horrendous-looking men began mutilating them, as ghastly hags took out sharp knitting needles and began separating the girls' eyelids only to pierce them with these instruments a few moments later.[19] Oh what a joy was horror!

What did the guignols, puppets, and marionettes have in common? Their bodies, their heads, and their limbs—whether they were made out of wood or not—were designed to imitate man's actions. They were grotesque in appearance, frequently timorous by nature, boastful in attitude, speaking their minds in proud or shrill voices as the play required. They were always manipulated by others, either through strings from above or with fingers from underneath the stage. It was customary for the guignols to fly into a rage, kill, bludgeon, imprison, escape, outwit enemies. Inhuman in their manner and personality, mechanical in their gestures, unfeeling in their brutal ways, they were forever repeating their rituals, their childlike antics. Such beings did not respond to warmth; they were brittle; they had no soul and for this reason their tales of woe, strife, pathos, violence, and rebellion did not inspire true feeling. Even so, they were made in man's image.

Céline's characters were manipulated by him in a similar way. They were created in his likeness, as man is a reflection of God's image. Neither man nor his creations, his puppets, possesses free will; neither has the slightest notion about direction, accomplishment, or fulfillment. Each man, each puppet, frets "his life upon the stage."

There is, nevertheless, a difference between Céline's guignol and that of others. The French, English, and Oriental guignols present a microcosm of the world: good and evil, beauty and ugliness, light and darkness. Céline's, on the contrary, stand for the dark, chthonic realm. They are one-sided, a manifestation of man's evil nature only: the ugly, the deformed, the sordid, the degraded—the lowest depths. In Céline's work, good is not warring with evil, nor light with darkness. There is, therefore, no hope of understanding between the people depicted, no rapprochement. Ferdinand and his band are incapable of feeling, of building friendships, of interchanging sympathies. Céline's creatures offer no contrast in mood. They are guignols, to be sure, but only one aspect of them: their hard, robotlike quality, devoid of any nuances of personality. Undeveloped, primitive beings, like the roughly-hewn wooden creatures of old, so Céline's creatures are guided by instinct, manipulated by some outside force (in his case, Céline himself), reacting fiercely and spasmodically to each other's dictates.

The fact that Céline chose the guignol as his medium, a medium that permitted him to accentuate the effects, to aggrandize the turmoil, to reduce man to dwarf size—like the inhabitants of Lilliput—underscores his inability to cope with his own fiery and belligerent nature, as he tears himself and the others to pieces.

As we observe the diabolical activities of Céline's characters, listen to the visceral language shooting forth from every page, hear the brittle, provocative, and repetitive phrases bombarding our ears, watch the mechanical gestures and the expressionless faces, we will turn away with feelings of revulsion. We will have seen beings created in the image of our own soul—a morass, a black pool.

SYMBOLS

Guignol's Band is by no means lacking in pain. It does not reside, however, in the characters or in the events depicted, but rather in the descriptions of London and of Nature in its various manifestations. Here we find reflections of Céline's poetical flights and his metaphysical anguish.

Céline looks upon nature as a type of *pleroma,* as an infinite expanse that holds the answer to man's suffering. One has the distinct feeling that Céline seeks to reduce the individual to an inordinate small size, to have him vanish from sight, to have him evaporate, so to speak, in the immensity of the giant mass which is the universe. The individual, then, is absorbed by the cosmos, as the penitent who begs for forgiveness is dissolved into God. In such instances pain and anguish also vanish. It is by means of this kind of assimilation into nature that the individual may draw from its wisdom and its strength the forces necessary to keep him going as a unit, to prevent his fragmentation.

Céline's description of London in *Guignol's Band* is personified. The Wapping section is represented in terms of man's creations, his machines, his industry, his scientific achievements. This material, or mechanical, aspect of his world is juxtaposed with beauty, timelessness, and spacelessness—that is, with the ineffable quality implicit in the vast expanse of nature. The sun's rays, for example, shine down upon the ugly, dungeon-like houses. As they pierce through the bleakness of the environment, the rays seem to warm and comfort the loneliness of the sordid world man has created for himself.

The Wapping section as depicted by Céline seems not only unfriendly but extremely dull. The streets and houses are all alike. One wall rises after another, analogous. Giant ramparts of red brick, monster stores called "citadels of merchandise" with miles of goods, furniture, "mahogany forests," carpets large enough "to cover the Moon, the entire world . . . all the floors of the Universe"—emerge in swift succession. Though Céline is filled with disgust at the mountains of matter that clutter man's world, impede his vision, and stifle him, there is nevertheless something spiritual that enters the picture, relieving man of the atmosphere of doom. A sense of the cosmic, as symbolized by the moon, the forests, the sun, enlarges the entire visual picture. The universal and the eternal forces, it is implied, may one day help man overcome his blindness, illuminate his involuted ways. Because man is limited and constrained by his personality (desire, greed, anger, hatred) and by his creations (the proliferating matter that has invaded his existence) he seeks liberation. Céline's vision in this particular image begins with specifics (the city, the houses, the stores) and ends with a collective and metaphysical view. The implication is that the answer lies in man's rapport with the transcendental.

The water image always fascinated Céline, who used it time and time again in all of his novels as background for his characters and also, frequently, as a protagonist. In *Guignol's Band* this image is introduced in terms of the River Themes and the London fog hovering over it. A sense of motion and of perpetual flux accompanies the ripples of water as they flow downstream as far as the eye can see. The greyness of the clouds, as they cast their gloom on the entire panorama, injects a series of macabre luminosities into the scene.

> The sky . . . the gray water . . . the purplish shores . . . it's all so soothing . . . No control of one or the other . . . gently drawn round . . . in slow circles and eddies, you're always charmed further off toward other dreams . . . all to expire in lovely secrets, toward other worlds getting ready in vails and mists with big pale and fuzzy designs among the whispering mosses . . .[20]

The vastness of this picture is as striking as its atmosphere of sorrow and of forlornness. A sense of dread and of doom, of pointlessness, envelops the entire landscape.

Guignol's Band was not a popular success. Even Céline's publisher, Denoël, was not enthusiastic about the novel. "I see only fights in your book!"[21] he commented. Most of the critics made mention of the repetitiousness of the work, both in terms of its vocabulary and sequential events. They were more than a bit weary of the sordid milieux, the revolting images, the seamy side of life that Céline was forever choosing to depict.

Céline did not attempt to justify his choice of subject. He did, however, defend his writing style and his vocabulary. The stark, aggressive, and visceral language, which was intrinsic to all of his novels, he declared, was an expression of life itself. Action, upheavals, antagonisms, conflicts, aggression, excitement, the volatile, the vibrant . . . all these are expressions of man's existence on earth. Tension, Céline believed, must always be extreme, nerves always taut, anger kept at a high pitch, violence everyone's by-word. A novelist must avoid the stereotyped, the standard, the vacuous, the overused language; no emotions are aroused by writers who keep enunciating the same platitudes, those pseudo-lucubrations, found in the novels of his contemporaries. Céline wanted to inject a kind of breathlessness into his work, the very fear and trembling that he experienced when facing situations beyond his control—people stronger than himself.

> Nothing is more difficult than to direct, dominate, transpose spoken language, emotional language, the only sincere language, everyday language, into written language, to stabilize it without killing it . . . Try it . . . This is the terrible "technique" where most of the writers just collapse, a thousand times more arduous than so-called "artistic" language . . .[22]

The highly charged, brutal, sensational type of writing that Céline advocated is evident in *Guignol's Band.* This negative and destructive work may properly be looked upon as a literary manifestation of the author's extremely chaotic and disturbed frame of mind.

8

FAIRY-PLAY FOR ANOTHER TIME I

. . . I mean that personality . . . which suffers from the underworld fate—the man in him who does not turn towards the day-world, but is fatefully drawn into the dark; who follows not the accepted ideals of goodness and beauty, but the demoniacal attraction of ugliness and evil. It is these anti-Christian and Luciferian forces that well up in modern man and engender in all-pervading senses of doom, veiling the bright world of day with the mists of Hades, infecting it with deadly decay, and finally, like an earthquake, dissolving it into fragments, fractures, discarded remnants, debris, shreds, and disorganized units.

C. G. JUNG, *The Spirit in Man, Art and Literature*

Fairy-Play for Another Time I, PUBLISHED IN 1952, IS NEITHER a novel, a novelette, a short story, an essay, nor a pamphlet. It cannot be categorized. It is an outpouring—even more violent and irrational than *Guignol's Band*—of raw material from the unconscious in the form of fantasies, visions, dreams, obsessions, and revelations, all set down helter-skelter. Rational judgment is very rarely if ever exercised. There is no sifting, no evaluation. It is as if the author were being drawn and quartered and then expelled from his dungeon-like world in obedience to some creative impulse within him—a daemon perhaps. The flood of autoerotic, sadistic, masochistic, voyeuristic fantasies, each pounding away at the other blindly, frequently appears senseless. And yet despite the fact that the linguistic rhythms increase in speed and viscosity, arousing and dulling the reader's senses, the book as a whole is dull and repetitious.

This is the work of a man fighting for his sanity, a man trying to extricate the pain, anger, resentment, and unassimilated feelings that have built up within him and curdled in his subliminal world. The energetic charge that accompanies the severing of this tangled inner "stuff" is so great as to defy any rational sifting of such material. The unending and confused series of images—some of them archetypal—that emerge in *Fairy-Play for Another Time*

I are comparable to those observed by Doctor Marie-Louise von Franz in schizophrenics:

> There the collective unconscious is seen as a kind of chaos of contents all of which have the latent possibility of something meaningful to human consciousness. But instead there is confusion, and consciousness is too weak to stop the flood. One could say that a good mind was needed to sort out that stuff, but that does not help because one cannot bring mental order into these things. What is needed is the feeling function, the function of choice, which says "Now I will pick this and discard the rest," and, "I will relate to this consciousness and store it away." Without the feeling function's evaluation one does not know what is important, and what is not. One cannot sort the chaff from the corn in the unconscious. What the schizophrenic pours out is a mixture of the most beautiful, meaningful, archetypal material mixed up with banalities and cynicism and nonsense. It is just all one heap.[1]

Fairy-Play for Another Time I is just such a product, that of a mutilated psyche. It is a manifestation of the physical and psychological distortions experienced by the author in his twisted and tormented world.

PLOT

Fairy-Play for Another Time I begins at the end of the German occupation of France. The narrator receives a friend's wife (Clémence) and her son in his seventh-floor Montmartre apartment. The reader never knows why they came nor what they are doing there. The monologues and dialogues that make up this volume shift back and forth in time and space from the various sections of Paris to the Danish prison in which the narrator had been incarcerated, to his exile from Paris, to pre-War days, to world history including events as played out in France, America, Germany, England, Africa, etc., to erotic thoughts, dancing girls, paintings, etc. Only one rational sequence of events is related: the story of Jules, the crippled painter who lives on the ground-floor apartment of the narrator's building. His models are always beautiful, healthy, young dancers from fine families. Frequently, Jules uses them for other than artistic purposes. Indeed, his sex life is carried on both in his studio, with its windows giving right on the street, and his back room, with its criblike structure. Finally, the narrator gives his wife, Arlette, permission to pose for the painter, indulging the cripple's fancies.

ONTOLOGY OF THE CHARACTERS

The characters, who are forever spewing forth venom, include Clémence (the name itself is ironic), her son, and a host of others, and of course the narrator.

As the work begins, the narrator comments on Clémence's former beauty, as contrasted to her present ugliness. Indeed, she is as insidious as the rest of humanity, as vile as the son she has brought with her, who "stinks falsehood." [2] The narrator talks to the lad, who refuses to sit down. He stands rather with his back to the wall, awkward, surly—a typical ingrate, says the narrator. He will certainly turn into a killer, he concludes, because he resembles the rest of humanity. The narrator further predicts that this lad will follow the trends of his day, will do what is à la mode. If the easiest road to follow is to side with the Vichy government, then the boy, when grown, will do so—a typical collaborator type. Now that the liberator has arrived in France, all those who had sided with the occupying forces will be punished, because "hatred is stylish." [3] Friends of the former government (including the narrator) are to be hounded and declared guilty. Others, equally culpable, upon whom the label of "Nazi" has been pinned, have succeeded in slipping away or joining the ranks of the powerful.[4] Life, the narrator concludes, is a chameleon-like process. Everything depends upon one's gestures—the *persona*—or mask worn vis-à-vis the world.

The lad depicted by the narrator is a mirror image of himself at that age: rude, ill-tempered, resentful of all convention. These characteristics are revealed both in the boy's facial expressions and in his physical demeanor. His refusal to sit down, for example, and to listen indicates his rejection of parental authority and the status quo. The fact that he stands alone, near the wall, implies a sense of solitude and isolation. That the narrator predicts that the young lad will become a murderer, falling into the well-worn paths of others, also fits the picture.

Other traits emerge as the novel pursues its course. Feelings of self-pity are aroused in the narrator. As linear time and rational attitudes vanish, he sees Clémence and her son sniffing about in his things, trying to acquire his old rags, "pillaging" his cooking utensils, while he is incarcerated in a Danish prison. "Destiny has taken everything from me." [5] Yet the impact of Céline's chimerical vision is not nearly so forceful as that of the breathtaking picture drawn by Charles Dickens in *A Christmas Carol,* when Scrooge views human rapacity at work after his demise, or that drawn by Kazantzakis in *Zorba the Greek,* where acquisitiveness is viewed in the guise of a horrendous brood of Cretan women who, like vultures, not only take the objects belonging to a dead woman but very nearly dismantle the entire house in the process. Céline's fluoroscopic account of greed falls flat because there are no contrasts. All the characters are evil, all are murderers scratching and trampling over each other in rapid succession. It is all most *un*dramatic.

As the narrator's resentment festers, confusion sets in and with it an onslaught of affectivity. Concepts of time and space and notions about the characters and their identities are all swept away into the melee of fleeting pictures that ensues: the narrator in exile, the sick fleeting Paris, the German conqueror taking over, the pre-War sea coast, the Liberation army. Even the narrator confesses: "Confusion of places, of times! Shit. It's fairy-play for you, you understand . . . That's fairy-play . . . the future! The past! The False! The True! Exhaustion!" [6]

The multirooted, multisegmented and multistoried tirades that float about, bearing the reader to Africa, Paris, Denmark—and with such alacrity—leave us gasping in a pool of ambiguities. Mention is made, for example, of innocent people killed in 1914, of the narrator's role as a doctor, of the Danish prison. Each of these undistilled and unsifted images triggers off another barrage of digressions in which the narrator pictures himself as both victim and martyr in an *imitatio Christi.* The narrator's world seems to be toppling about him, crushing him like an avalanche, smothering his very life energy, pinning him down until he screams with pain. The contrast between the narrator's lack of control and the control as experienced by the poet Alfred de Vigny, who lauds stoicism, is plainly discernible. Indeed, Céline satirizes one of Vigny's poems, *The Wolf,* when he writes: "The wolf dies without howling, not I."

At one point the narrator sees himself hanging on a cross being picked at by vultures, condors, and dragons, all seeking to devour him. He thinks of himself as being like Christ, as an innovator, as a prophet of a new way of life and a new world to come. The narrator sees himself at Golgotha, amid jeering crowds happy at his suffering, then during the German occupation of France in the role he played as a pamphleteer. There is no question as to his feelings of innocence. Not a smudge mars the pristine purity of the narrator's soul. But his vision becomes blurred at this point. He is so alienated from reality that the sequences following verge on the pathological.

The narrator does not realistically reassess his actions during the German occupation of France. He does not see himself as part of the jeering crowd that has conquered France, a replaying, perhaps, of what had taken place two thousand years previously at Golgotha. He sees himself as society's victim and is invaded by unending feelings of self-pity in this regard. Oblivious to the world about him, he sees life only in terms of his suffering in the Danish prison. An irrational medley of hostile imagery emerges.[7]

A review of historical situations is given in hodgepodge form: half-truths, half-thoughts, half-tones. Dictators, collaborators, aggressors, martyrs from the time of Darius to that of the Knights Templars, from Montmartre to Copenhagen, bubble out one after another. After the emergence of these gloating and airborne historical visions, a counterpoise takes root: a young dancer, rose-colored, strong, well-proportioned, and beautiful, smiles and laughs. No sooner does this chimerical vision of health make its appearance than a series of prison scenes ensues, replete with scatological invectives and a host of phantomlike creatures.[8]

One has the feeling, frequently, that the narrator has lost all contact with reality, that he has regressed into his own subliminal world. There is one scene in particular in which the irrational dominates almost completely. It begins with cadavers strewn about the Place de la Bastille where Louis XVI was beheaded. Other sites in Paris are then mentioned, fictitious and real (Place du Thrône, Place de la Révolte, etc.), where even more horrendous crimes have been perpetrated. The narrator, who spans both time and space, has participated in all the events described. Sometimes he tries to flee his surroundings, at other times we see him fighting off people he considers to be Avengers, Destroyers, Annihilators, all intent on killing him. As the vision fades into the distance, dancers take over the scene, whipping up the light fantastic. Views of burning houses, blackmarket activities, a witches' sabbath, half-born figures now emerge: "It was blacker than in the mines!"[9] Blackness has enveloped light.

The narrator's world has become opaque, dark, dismal, more frightening than the most sinister dungeon in medieval castles, with their iron spikes and torture chambers.[10]

The ontology of Céline's characters may be observed only in terms of the evanescent images that are replete in *Fairy-Play for Another Time I.* These are formless at one moment, take on girth, weight, and amplitude seconds later, only to vanish into the darkness. Feelings are nascent in this same fashion; amorphous essences grow about, explode only to take on new dimensions afterward. Life seems to have become a self-procreating process lacking all rhyme or reason. Like amoebas, the creatures of Céline's fantasy are born, increase in size, split apart, only to form new existences, new associations, and so on endlessly.

EVIL AS A COSMIC PRINCIPLE

The "problem of evil" is implicit in *Fairy-Play for Another Time I.* Evil, like Lucifer, the "light-bringer," may be looked upon as a highly productive agent, a type of paving of the way for enlightenment. A sense of evil plagued Picasso in his Blue Period. The artist at this point looked away from the light of the world into darkness, into a realm of decay and fragmentation, into the blackness of his own universe.[11] He distilled and transformed this material, creating some of the greatest canvases of all time. William Blake, too, was terrorized by forces of evil. In his allegorical drawing illustrating Harvey's *Meditations Among the Tombs,* which depicts a group of dead bodies living in foetuslike form, evil is rampant.[12] Blake's mystic visions became positive forces by means of the creative process. Blake succeeded in relating to his environment and to the people surrounding him. Céline did not. Evil, as it appears in *Fairy-Play for Another Time I,* serves only to further Céline's destructive penchant. It is not assimilated into the work of art.

The instinctive and highly volatile energy that emerges in *Fairy-Play for Another Time I* gives the work a tattered and terrifying glow. The irrational no longer seems to be used by the author as a literary device to sting and pierce the reader but is rather a part of a kind of madness that has made its way into the very deepest layers of his world. Evil seems to have taken him over in this realm.

Evil has reached such proportions as to be a cosmic principle, spreading hate, rage, despair, doubt, malevolence. "Think! Centrifugalization of hatreds!"[13] Evil is uncontrolled and falls into every phase of this volume, impinging upon its artistic fabric. It sucks up whatever notions of understanding or enlightenment might otherwise have come to the fore. Its offshoots—the creatures ranting about throughout the work—verge on the demoniacal, like Goya's creatures as they cackle their lucubrations. Words and images explode and trample each other. Evil stalks about much as it does in Edward Bond's play *Saved* (1965), in which one scene features a group of Teddy-Boys stoning an infant in a landau. Céline's equally repugnant depictions, his lacerating, cutting, and melting down of human beings, manifest his own predilection for the macabre and the vicious.[14]

The narrator's conscious mind has been very nearly submerged by the onslaught of his unconscious realm. His ego can no longer function as a discerning mechanism. A kind of blindness ensues, and one can understand why the narrator is unable to "see" anything beyond his own psyche and, consequently, is unable to relate to others, to events, to history, to any kind of political or philosophical situation or structure.

Céline, at this period, must have been experiencing a series of "dangerous" extremes that could have led to insanity, or at the least to some functional disturbance. One may well ask where the dividing line is to be drawn between the mentally deranged and the visionary. The answer is vague. If the ego is no longer capable of judging, sifting, or giving direction to the emergent unconscious material, then equilibrium will be destroyed. The ego is then no longer the center of the conscious personality. In the case of the deeply deranged person, the mind never stirs from the object that obsesses it. Céline's vision does change to a certain extent, though it focuses mainly on one sentiment: evil, with its offshoots of hate, rage, and violence. Such an obsessive attitude implies a definite lack of perspective and could lead one to believe that he suffered from some functional disturbance. Moreover, there was no real working relationship between his ego and the collective unconscious. A harmonious relationship between these two aspects of the psyche permits expanded vision. Artists, for the most part, draw upon the *prima materia* to produce their works of art. Bosch, Breughel, Blake—great artists whose works revealed traumas—had sufficiently well-developed egos as to permit evaluation and sifting to take place and with it the birth of works of art.[15] The artist then reigned supreme. In Céline's case, his world had been invaded by darkness. He lived in an abyss that he had dug for himself, perhaps unwittingly, and it was in this dark realm that the artist was concealed.

THE CRIPPLE

There is, surprisingly, one rational sequence of events narrated in *Fairy-Play for Another Time I*. It is worthy of being related because of the insights it sheds on the entire situation.

Jules, the hunchback and crippled painter, lives on the first floor of the narrator's building. His models are strong, beautiful young dancers from fine families. He has them go through a real ritual every time they come to pose for him. First he has them undress and pose for him in various positions, after which he immortalizes them on canvas. Passers-by peer into the window and sometimes watch their antics. At other times, Jules takes his models into his windowless back room, has them pose for him in a criblike structure, and then indulges himself sexually. Jules wants the narrator's wife, Arlette, to pose for him. Since Arlette is devoted to her husband, she asks him for permission first. He is delighted, even insistent upon her posing for the crippled painter. And he also wants to know the final outcome.

Jules suffers great pain from his stubs (reminders of what had once been his legs). He picks at them all the time, masturbates, infects his entire genital area.[16]

The fact that Jules is a painter indicates the importance that hands play in his world. They touch and feel. It is by means of them that form and shape may be delineated on canvas. During the course of the narrative, we learn that Jules is also a sculptor. Active tactile sensations are aroused by the objects he seeks to mold. For the ancient Egyptians, we recall, hands symbolized action as well as a certain mental attitude. If we consider hands from this point of view, each gesture becomes a transforming agent for feeling, moods, and ideas. A further analogy may be made between the hand, with its five fingers, and the human body, with its four limbs and a head. Such an image represents balance, courage, and sturdiness, all the qualities that Jules seems to lack.

Jules' hands serve three purposes: to cause pain (a spiritually creative act), to arouse himself sexually via an exterior object (the dancers who pose for him), and for autoerotic activity (masturbation). In the first instance, energy is creative and driven outward by the strength of the hand, gaining stability, and becoming a form of expression. In the second instance, there is an alliance with the beautiful that could bring about health in an active and normal individual. In this case, hands represent a source of well-being. In the third instance, infection invariably sets in, causing Jules extreme discomfort and pain. If one is to regard the last example as a symbol for introversion (since the individual "works" upon himself and not upon an outer object), the results are withdrawal and regression from a world to which he cannot relate and for which he therefore feels antipathy. Disaster can ensue in the last case.[17]

Feet also play an important role in this story—by their very absence. Symbolically, feet enable man to stand erect in contact with the earth, that healthy, vital, and nourishing force, bringing him solidity and relatedness. When this function is dead or sick, it is expressed in literature and in art most frequently by cripples, people with clubfeet or suffering from some kind of ailment of the feet or legs. Jules has no legs at all, a fact that implies that no normal relationship with reality, his fellow beings, or even himself can come to pass.

The Jules-type of cripple brings to mind some of Samuel Beckett's characters. They too have extraordinary difficulty relating to the world about them and instead of confronting society, they regress, withdraw into their own circumscribed realms, there to rot. Beckett's characters are usually placed in an environment in which they find themselves degraded and decomposed little by little. They are pitiable beings who can barely move about, impotent invalids who must remain in bed. Some of them live in a jar, with only the head visible, and this is "covered with pustules and blue flies." The rest of the body has withered away—no thighs, no legs, no feet. There is also no fight left in Beckett's creatures. They live in a void, in a realm drenched in nihilism. They are all dying or dead, devoured by filth or disease, in the process of suffering unbearable metaphysical pain. Beckett's creatures possess nothing but their sick bodies. They have no desire left—or love. No positive force emerges from them. Only a type of progressive enlightenment into the futility of life.

Unlike Beckett's characters, Jules feels longing for the healthy, beautiful dancers. This longing for his opposite *could* result in something positive. The outcome of an alliance between ugliness (crippled painter) and beauty (healthy dancer) is the painting. But the question now arises whether the painting will depict the grotesque and sick artist or the beautiful dancer. Will the painting Jules makes be a work of art or a fragmented and distorted mirror image of the gnome that he is? The answer is never forthcoming.

Other facets of Jules' personality also come into focus. Psychologically, he has never developed above the anal level. He is, therefore, continuously indulging in sensory stimulae. More important, however, is his attraction to voyeurism. Mention is frequently made of the window in his apartment, of passers-by who watch him either painting and observing a nude model or indulging in sexual activity.

Voyeurism/exhibitionism is nothing new. One of the earliest mentions of this disease appeared in Theophastrus' *Characters* (ca. 370–287 B.C.). It has existed in one form or another throughout the centuries.[18]

It would seem that each time Jules indulges in some form of exhibitionism, he rids himself of a terrible burden and, at the same time, experiences a certain amount of pleasure. Though many exhibitionists do not need companions, only spectators, both were important to Jules.

What is of particular interest in Jules' case is the role played by the visual, which did more to excite him than any other sense. His art, unlike that of many other pictorial and literary creators, may be considered not a sublimation of his instincts but rather a "de-sublimation" of them.

It is through the visual experience that the narrator also lives out his existence. When he grants his wife permission to pose for Jules, he sees himself in a series of sadomasochistic and autoerotic fantasies. He is titillated by them. He also suffers a certain anguish and at times even revels in the joy of "self-sacrifice."

If we look upon Jules as the narrator's mirror image, we might ask: to whom has the narrator given his wife? Symbolically, he has given her to his sick half, to whatever is mangled, infected, and diseased in his own subliminal world. The beauty and health his wife represents may, by means of a *coniunctio oppositorum*, heal what is sick, and in this way refurbish certain aspects of the narrator's personality.

THE TURNING POINT

Fairy-Play for Another Time I represents a turning point for Céline the writer. His prose in this volume resembles a scatter of pebbles, globs of dirt, and fistfuls of sand being catapulted out of some abyss—stinging the eyes, nose, throat of the reader. The constant listing of rhymed or unrhymed words with few or no rational associations (*amoureuses, voyeuses, discuteuses, curieuses, religieuses*); the switching from French to foreign words (pedigree); the constant enumerations, alliterations, obscenities; the gratuitous shifting of tenses (future, present, past, imperfect subjunctive, etc.); the ellipses, the altering of word order; the strange punctuation, the question marks, the exclamation marks, the italics, the parentheses, the unexpected junctures; the non sequiturs; the false analogies; the puns—to mention but a few of Céline's literary devices—serve to increase the madness of the narrative as well as its repetitive nature.

There is certainly a devaluation and dislocation of language in *Fairy-Play for Another Time I.* When a dramatist of the stature of Eugène Ionesco indulges in such literary antics, his prose is alive and vibrant. It becomes a veritable diabolical experience. This is not the case with Céline, at least not in this volume.

Yet Céline was convinced that he had created something new, a fresh language with its own rites, rituals, and rules. In *Conversations with Professor Y* (1955), an unconventional essay, he states that language should be emotion personified:

> Emotion in the written language! . . . I'm the one who put emotion back into language! . . . as I told you! . . . it's no small accomplishment . . . I swear it . . . that thing, the magic; any fool today can move people through "writing"! . . . but to find emotion in the "spoken" word, in actual writing! It's infinitesimal, but it's something! [19]

Modestly, Céline admits that he has invented only a tiny little "thing," just in terms of style, like Lavoisier, for example, the inventor of a couple of little numbers, or like Pasteur, who gave a few names to the smallest of things he could barely see under the microscope.[20] Céline also predicted that thousands of writers would one day copy his "emotion"-packed style, "embellish" upon his ideas. One day it would even be discussed by members of the French Academy.

Yet when emotion remains unchanneled, when its pitch is never altered, it becomes boresome. In such instances it is the archaic aspect of a being that functions—not the artist in man.

The forces necessary to temper the gushing violence implicit in *Fairy-Play for Another Time I* should have led the artist to ponder his work, to impose some order on the tangled mass of material that burgeoned forth from his unconscious. Had the artist in Céline been in control, then the free associations, the interior monologues, might have been strikingly developed. Significant images might have emerged, as they did, for example, in James Joyce's *Ulysses*, most particularly in Marion Bloom's visions after making love.[21] With Céline, however, the thinking principle was never put to use. The creative effort resulted in a blend of one or two diamonds scattered about in a moldy mass of dust.

Had Céline experienced a real struggle between reason and affectivity, a kind of adaptation or at least a compensation for the inadequacies he felt might have taken place. Though Céline sought to give the impression of innovation, he merely trod the well-worn path of the "hyperemotional." He was convinced he could dazzle with frenzy, blare with his trumpet blasts, numb with his agony, and compel identification with his suffering, but he failed in all these endeavors. His technique grew frazzled at the edges. He lost his legs, his balance—as his protagonist Jules had done.

The barrage of images, the cold application of certain stylistic rules, an emotion-packed vocabulary transformed what might have been original into something routine, repetitive. *Fairy-Play for Another Time I* is comparable to a series of percussive, metallic, vibrating tonalities, guttural and blurred sounds. One might quote from René Char's poem, *The Masterless Hammer,* to illustrate this point:

> The step withdrew, the person walking became silent
> On the dial of Imitation
> The Scale casts its weight of reflex granite

Céline's prose had become just that—a reflex—an imitation of past endeavors.

Céline was now living in the dim, fearsome, mysterious world of the autistic, oscillating as it were between an undifferentiated inner world and an equally foggy conscious realm. It was as if he were alone on a mountain peak or buried within a volcano, peering down or up—no matter, the world was malevolent.

9

FAIRY-PLAY FOR ANOTHER TIME II

> I have always observed that people who are always ready to suspect certain crimes in others indulge in these themselves . . .
>
> DE SADE, *Aline et Valcour*

JUDGING BY CÉLINE'S NEXT LITERARY ENDEAVOR, *Fairy-Play for Another Time II,* subtitled "Normance," his mental condition was getting worse. He had begun this work in 1945, while in Denmark, and completed it in 1953. In the interim he must have sunk even more deeply into the morass of his subliminal world. Unable to extricate himself from the powers of his instincts, his drives and his extreme nervous energy, he became their prey. He was trapped within them. When they erupted, it was with torrential power. No ability to evaluate, to judge, to differentiate was ever manifested. Sensations, sequences of events, individuals were all blurred as if in a maze. Acting and reacting had become an almost automatic or mechanical process. Céline was no longer aware of the fact, or perhaps he ignored it, that writing is an art and not a release mechanism.

Fairy-Play for Another Time II, is a fragmentary, ambiguous, discursive work that could, to a certain degree, be characterized as a war chronicle. The action takes place in the narrator's apartment building in Paris. It is from this vantage point that the Allied bombardments of the city are described: the noises, upheavals, bursting flares, sirens, blinding antiaircraft lights. More personal aspects of the narrator's existence are likewise detailed: his dog Piram, his cat Bébert, his wife Arlette, the tenants of the building (among them the crippled painter Jules), the strong man of the markets in Paris (Normance). Céline juxtaposes the relative stability of apartment-house living with the extreme motility of the falling bombs, chaos, and destruction on the Parisian scene. He attempts, in this manner, to bring out the drama intrinsic in such a horrendous situation, and also to describe the material and spiritual demise of a society.

What could have been an extraordinarily exciting work—hallucinatory descriptions of Paris aflame, of searing flares, of nerve-racking gunfire, of fright, of contrasting activities (motion and stasis)—is in fact a painfully dull and routine one. The endless verbigerations, the constant noises forever holding the same pitch, the similarity and redundancy of the imagery, the lists and further lists of disconnected words, clauses, sentences, the meaningless repetitions, all fail to kindle any reaction, either cerebral or visceral, in the reader.

WAR CHRONICLE

Since the second volume of *Fairy-Play for Another Time* deals with the Allied bombing of Paris and day-to-day life in one apartment house there, it can be approached as a type of war chronicle. The narrator gives us a detailed account of his lodgings, of the furniture thrust about as a result of the multiple explosions, the perpetual blasts that crackle the walls and cause ceilings to come tumbling down, of plaster and dust invading the atmosphere, dimming both vision and senses alike. Frequently, the narrator, a doctor of sorts, rushes about the building—one never knows quite why—and listens to the tenants' heartbeats with his stethoscope. All individual activity seems futile, doomed.

Unlike the usual war chronicle, however, the events depicted in this work emerge as if experienced in a nightmare, or as if the dream had been perpetuated into real life. One never knows, therefore, what is real or unreal, what has been destroyed and what remains intact. The narrator—typically Célinian in this respect—is instinctual, demonstrative, and barely coherent. He seems capable only of reciting the same complaints over and over again, the same hates and desires for vengeance. Constant intrusions of invectives, gasps, screams, obscenities, and brutalities interrupt the continuity of the narration, stylistically paralleling the nervous shock caused by the detonating bombs. All is murky and turgid, emerging from a cesspool and falling back into it.

Prolonged cries of anguish such as those uttered by Céline's protagonists have also been emitted by the heroes of other authors, but with far more felicity. Kyo Gisors, for example, one of the heroes of André Malraux' tremendous "war book," *Man's Fate* (1933), was fully aware of life's horrors. He had few if any illusions, but neither did he burrow his head in the sand and bemoan his fate or indulge in futile hysterics or dementia. He knew the absurdity of the world and the horror of man's plight, yet he acted with lucidity, courage, and energy in an effort to bring to fruition the one *act* in which he had faith: the revolution. By means of an extreme tension of will, Kyo Gisors completed the act that gave his life meaning.

It is through positive and direct action, then, that Malraux circumvents what could have become nihilism. His heroes, unlike Céline's, look within themselves, assess life as lucidly and as objectively as possible. Malraux, like Céline, condemns all types of evasion from solitude and from the fear of death. Gisors, for example, accepts his solitude, declaring: "There is no such thing as knowing people." Another character, Tchen, openly expresses his very human fear of loneliness. But he experiences this anguish not as a negative force but, rather, as a positive one: "One always finds horror within oneself . . . one must merely look sufficiently deeply. Fortunately, one can act." Malraux rejects any kind of escape, even in religion, whether Christian, Buddhist, or some other. All spiritual panaceas preach the spirit of resignation, leading people to prostrate themselves before a transcendental God, preventing them, thereby, from acting with forthrightness and independence. Opium and love are equally deleterious to the man who seeks to assume man's fate fully and by direct action. By expending energy in creating a new social order, a "fraternal community"—or through the works of art that individuals leave to humanity as their legacy—man can better his lot on earth and life can take on meaning. One must note also in this connection that there was no disparity between the attitude that Malraux preached in his works and his actions in real life—in World War II, for example. His activities in the face of the enemy during that conflict were courageous. His determination and heroism when confronted with death, deceit, and destruction were extraordinary.[2]

Like Malraux, Céline condemned such escape mechanisms as religion, alcohol, drugs, etc. When it came down to activities in real life, however, the comparison with Malraux ends most abruptly indeed. Céline fled France after the Allies landed in Normandy, when it was rumored that attempts had been made upon his life. A vast difference, therefore, existed between Céline's theories (there is no escape) and his acts (I shall escape, if I can), a further splitting of what had already been severed. The tumult caused by the increased conflict—certainly experienced unconsciously—was directly expressed in the spasmodic nature of both volumes of *Fairy-Play for Another Time* and *Guignol's Band.*

Departing further from Malraux, Céline did not believe that any act of any nature might be capable of bettering man's lot. Indeed, he preached a philosophy of negativism, pointing up all the social and political evils, demanding annihilations, constraints, drawing incessantly upon racial arguments as an explanation for evil.

In *Fairy-Play for Another Time II* Céline harps incessantly on the horrors associated with the bombings—on man's evil and despicable nature. He seems quite content to keep reiterating the same castigations—in psychological terms, projecting his own innumerable dissatisfactions upon the world at large. The question remains as to why he did so. It must have given him a frame of reference, a certain security. In following, at least philosophically, the same arguments ad infinitum, he lived in his own circumscribed world, maintaining his own status quo, his own condition of stasis. Fresh points of view were forbidden. Céline's negativism might be compared to a religion that clutches its worshipper in a vise, never permitting him to stray from the straight and narrow path. Doubt never enters the picture.

Had Céline really accepted such a negative position, he would never have pounded away at man in his novels, reminding him constantly of his hideously cruel and degenerate nature. Had Céline acquiesced to utter hopelessness, he would not have written at all. To what avail? His volumes attest that he could not accept the very philosophy that he enunciated in his works. He kept pointing to man's evil nature in order to illuminate him, to acquaint him with his own ugliness, thereby, perhaps, solving certain problems. It was just this dichotomy in attitudes (a disgust with life and a desire to ameliorate man's condition) that caused him such utter confusion. This conflict was made even more dangerous by the intrusion of another factor within him, one that seemed to grow increasingly more outspoken. We have already noted that the evils Céline saw all about him were a projection, to a great extent, of his own shadow. Céline could no more accept society's evil nature than he could his own. Unconsciously, therefore, he was rejecting both. Céline was a fighter—without weapons!

Norman Mailer is another inveterate pessimist. In his war chronicle, *The Naked and the Dead,* he portrays a sick society spreading its own disease. The reader is confronted with a metaphorical work: the landing of American troops on the small island of Anopopei during World War II and the "taking" of it. But though the novel attests that society is sick, it exonerates no one from his responsibility toward the group.

> . . . no matter how crippled and perverted an image of man was the society he had created, it was nonetheless his creation, his collective creation (at least his collective creation from the past), and if society was so murderous then who could ignore the most hideous of questions about his own nature? [2]

Mailer was not an optimist in the sense that such pre-World War II writers as Farrell, Hemingway, Faulkner, Dos Passos, or even Steinbeck were. These writers believed, for the most part, that if society's ills were to disappear, or at least be ameliorated, then man's lot on earth would be improved. Mailer's vision of man is pessimistic because he is convinced that character is unchangeable. Even so, man does have a capacity for courage, in Mailer's view, a desire to challenge life and fate, thereby seeking ways and means of achieving something—of fulfilling himself. He must, however, proceed with lucidity and search constantly for means by which to improve his lot. Mailer does not condone the man who wallows in a state of euphoria, in complacency, nor does he approve of the eternal negativist, the man who forever complains and does nothing to improve situations.[3]

Though Malraux and Mailer, among others, consider life to be absurd and anguishing, there is a positive aspect to their writings, a light that might perhaps lead man to experience some semblance of salvation, or at least a bit of self-satisfaction. Céline offers nothing of the kind. His world is enshrouded in utter nihilism. His hatred blinds him. His fear curdles within him.

The rage Céline felt at his imprisonment in Denmark, the resentment he expressed at having been treated like a collaborator by his French compatriots, fostered feelings of ever increasing hate. The bombings he describes in *Fairy-Play for Another Time II*—the toppling of buildings, the gutting of roofs, the chaos within the apartment house in which the narrator lives—must be judged not merely in terms of a realistic description but must be considered symbolically as the picture of a man's inner destruction during a period in which perspectives have vanished and reality has lost definition. It is the work of a man thrashing about, gasping for an answer, tremulous, timorous, voicing his anguish in irrational speech patterns and thoughts.

IMAGERY

Most of the imagery in *Fairy-Play for Another Time II* revolves around the bombings of Paris—flares, guns, glaring lights, noises, chaos, upheavals, shattered buildings, crackling walls, furniture pushed about . . .

Fire, flame, and conflagration are the images that prevail. These harsh colors and violent pictorial representations symbolize energy that has always plagued Céline's protagonists in one degree or another. It triggers such feelings of hate, rage, and vengeance that not one moment of repose can be experienced. Tension, nervousness, anxiety sizzle and pop on each page, sending endless messages in rapid, staccato succession.

Let us examine the fire image more closely. Fire, as such, is a life-giving force. It is often associated with solar symbolism: health and growth in both a spiritual and an animal sense. Fire can also be considered an "agent of transmutation" that brings about purification and rebirth. The legend of the phoenix attests to this: when this bird realized that its death was near, it exposed itself to the sun's rays and burned itself to ashes—but from the marrow of its bones it would rise again, reborn.[4] The great Paracelsus associated fire with life, both being parasitical in that they live off other things. Fire, then, is good, it gives off vital heat. And yet it is evil, as well, since it destroys everything with which it comes into close contact.

For Céline, fire-bombings, flares, explosions, bundles of light flashing about rapidly all represent something essentially destructive. He sees them only as an exterior force.

> Look at the bombs Lili! Look! They're on Renault . . . The planes are discharging tons of explosives . . . white . . . white . . . butterflies of planes . . . one of these is blazing on Renault . . . The heights of the clouds . . . the blue . . . orange . . . green flames . . . giant candles zig zag . . .[5]

> Another load surges forth from them . . . there are at least ten . . . they're sliding up. They've spilled their horrors . . . one sees their lanterns . . . under their wings . . . a blue lantern . . . a violet one . . . they are flying low over our roof . . . vrrr . . . vrrr . . . they're spraying arrows from the ravines with an enormous whistle of air . . . the entire cluster undulates between the stars . . . it looks like jonquil stars . . . the sky is a sea of jonquils . . .[6]

What does fire (energy, electricity) imply as an inner image? Since the blaze Céline describes throughout the work is virtually continuous and helter-skelter—since it is without direction—it might very well indicate unchanneled, uncurbed emotions experienced within the narrator. We have already noted such a situation in terms of the narrators in the first part of *Fairy-Play for Another Time* and in *Guignol's Band:* always at the mercy of their emotions, victims of their own tremendous energy. Neither their thoughts, their acts, nor their points-of-view are ever guided, coherent, or assume any kind of depth. They are peripheral, spreading about in a wild blaze of fury, in fiery outbursts or simply smouldering, flaming up every now and then. If this inner picture is allowed to pursue its course, the healthy aspects of the narrator's psyche will either wither from lack of fresh air, or burn up from the heat, or simply turn to ashes. Whichever the alternative, sterility will ensue.

Fire, then, as viewed in the second part of *Fairy-Play for Another Time,* is an agent that tears continuously at all aspects of life: material (destroying buildings and furniture) and spiritual (creating havoc within the narrator's psyche, stimulating such emotions as fear, anger, revenge, hatred).

Fire may also be considered as a dismembering force. It cuts to pieces everything that is unified in both society and in the individual. When reviewing certain myths, such as that of Set and Osiris, we learn that Set (Evil) sought to destroy Osiris (Good) by cutting him up and distributing his limbs hither and yon about the world. In the destruction of Paris, as recounted by Céline, we find a similar situation: flares, incessant fires, blazes that break out throughout the city, all work diligently to dismember every material object. In the Egyptian myth, Osiris' wife, Isis, searches out the various parts of her husband's body—except the genitals. The procreative parts, symbolizing vital energy, are missing. The old society that Osiris stands for can therefore no longer function positively, since it is incapable of renewing itself. Horus, his son, becomes the leader of the emerging order, paving the way for future development. Unlike the ancient myth, Céline's account offers no possibility for renewal. The fragmentation and dismemberment approach totality in terms of both the outer (city) and the inner (narrator) worlds. There is no coming together of anything, no rebirth seems possible: the rot and decay have gone too far.

The same sensation of "breaking up" is also felt in a series of images revolving around the narrator's furniture and assorted objects in his room and in the apartment house. Every time a bomb is detonated, with accompanying conflagrations and blaring noises, the building sways, furniture flies off in all directions. Closets, commodes, chairs, tables, papers, ink—everything budges, moves, bumps about with such alacrity that one would think these objects were on a capsizing boat.

From the narrator's description of the motility of the objects one might conclude that they possess, or are at the mercy of, some higher force, or that they are obeying some inner logic of their own. Many of the objects seem to be lost in their flight, in both a material and an ontological sense: the former, because they no longer belong to the possessor, since they seem to be endowed with a will emanating from some higher order and seem to be obeying its dictates; the latter, because they no longer serve any function and have, therefore, no real being or reason for being.

Looked upon in this fashion, tables, chairs, beds, and the like, become replicas of man. They are pawns who feel abandoned and forsaken, having lost sight of both the spirit within them and of their own identity. They experience a sense of estrangement and alienation. They are, moreover, so obsessed by their minute size, as compared with the immensity of the cosmos, that they are seized with a notion of powerlessness and futility and are unable to relate to themselves or to anything about them. They have lost their being. Like the sticks of furniture Céline describes, they are at the mercy of higher forces—the bombs falling on a war-torn Paris. Each object goes its way, hitting, striking, breaking up, shattering—and for no earthly reason.

> I look around . . . the dresser is no longer against the wall . . . it's waltzing that unruly one . . . it's going through the door . . . it's polkaing on the landing . . . The entire building is shaking . . . this commotion . . . all the floors . . .[7]

The furniture, the walls, every object in the building moves about with cumulative force, underlining the impression of insecurity, instability, and fragmentation.

The objects in the above descriptions are impersonal, mechanical, and technical (to use Theodore Dreiser s expression); they play no role in shaping lives and are merely "serviceable" objects—they are there in order to make a point. Rather than measure the relative affluence of an individual, for example, as they would had Balzac or Flaubert depicted them, they indicate the owner's inability to handle them (himself) and to cope with exterior forces as well. Instead of acting upon the objects surrounding him, showing his and succumbs to their wills. He is, then, a pawn observing the various aspects of himself (as symbolized by the furniture) as they tear about in senseless activity.

Frequent mention is made of another image, the deluge. Phrases such as "deluge" of clouds, of fire, of water, "conditions of deluge,"[8] "a deluge moves sky and earth"[9] have cosmic implications. It would seem that Céline's use of this word would indicate that the world was being devoured by some tremendous, omniscient, and omnipotent force over which man had no control.

Traditionally and symbolically, a deluge is associated with catastrophes in that it destroys forms and structures, both material and spiritual. Such annihilation paves the way for the emergence of a different kind of life. Though there is a connotation of punishment in the word "deluge," there is also a feeling of purification and of regeneration. In the narrator's case, however, there is as yet no indication as to what the new order will be—if there is to be one. Only the imminence of sweeping change is implied thus far. The nature of the change is unclear.

The energy expended in the constant upheavals, in terms of the imagery (fire, furniture, deluge), brings to mind a type of war of the elements, as if earth, water, air, and fire were clashing and the very basis for spiritual and physical existence were in danger of utter collapse. Certainly a frightening thought, particularly when no future is in sight.

THE ABNORMAL

Many a writer has included dwarfs or freaks of nature in his writings to indicate some kind of imbalance or lacuna within a human being, or to illustrate certain inner motivations that may otherwise be invisible to the naked eye. For example, a dwarf and a mentally deficient man, respectively, figure in Carson McCullers' *The Ballad of the Sad Café* and in John Steinbeck's *Of Mice and Men.* In *Fairy-Play for Another Time II* the abnormal appears in the characters of Normance and Jules (the latter, the crippled painter, appears in the first volume as well). Though Normance is a husky from the Halles (markets) of Paris and represents physical brawn (man's earthly, instinctual self), his head is kept covered to hide an enormous blood clot. Just as Jules lacks balance because he has been shorn of his legs, so Normance is also unequipped to face life due to a brain prone to malfunction. Normance's head remains hidden, symbolically speaking, to prevent his tragic aspects—the maiming of his spiritual values—from being discerned.

Normance's instinctuality, his brute force, is made manifest several times, but most particularly in his fight with the narrator. After they have come to grips and Normance finds himself on the floor, the narrator watches him as he attempts to rise. He is stunned by the impression the husky from the Halles makes upon him. He seems much fatter than he had seemed before the fight—more bloated. Suddenly, he assumes gigantic and monstrous proportions.

> . . . he's getting bigger! . . . even bigger! . . . his chest . . . his stomach! . . . I'm not moving, me! . . . I'm not moving! . . . he walks backward . . . he staggers backward . . . he rocks backward . . . his blood-clotted head trembles, oscilates . . . his package-head! . . . he walks back! . . . he's going to spring from the wall . . . he's leaning . . . he lunges! . . . he charges at me . . .[10]

Normance represents the aggressive individual (or society) who turns on the less fortunate and crushes—brawn rather than brains.

UNANIMISM AND DISPARITY

Though great disparity exists in *Fairy-Play for Another Time II*—in terms of imagery, the characters, and the writing style—unity is also present, oddly enough, in the chronicle's very disparity. Similarity exists in the divergent characters (Jules, Normance), in the lack of variety in the writing style, in the constantly blaring imagery, the continuous turmoil.

A secondary aspect of unity is also to be found in the location of the chronicle's action: the narrator's house—unity of place. Jules Romains and Michel Butor have also constructed novels adhering to this same unity, creating many visions and extreme variety from but a single area.

Romains was the inventor of a technique that he labeled "unanimism" and demonstrated in many of his novels and plays. He believed that human groups, though disparate in all ways, may experience collective sentiments. In a theater, for example, audiences can participate in a single idea or emotion, can be aroused by a single feeling, a single character, can experience a communion of the spirit. In Romains' novel *Someone's Death,* which takes place in an apartment building, a tenant, Jacques Godard, has just died. Soon afterward he becomes the only topic of conversation for the tenants, most of whom had not known him in life. The dead man has come to life in the minds of the collectivity and brings them together. What had formerly been disparate individuals, participating in their human adventure as solitary beings, now know unity of thoughts, and because of this they enter into an instinctive communion with one another.

Céline created, perhaps unwittingly, a similar situation in *Fairy-Play for Another Time II.* Not only does the action take place in the narrator's building but the tenants' preoccupations are all focused on one subject—war. Each character reacts affectively according to his nature: bestially, angrily, and hatefully.

Unlike Romains' novel *Someone's Death,* which may be considered both a "vertical" work, in that it analyzes in depth the souls of the protagonists involved, and a "horizontal" work, in that it engenders a series of concentric circles resulting from the activity centering about the initial "thought," *Fairy-Play for Another Time II* never probes at all. It resembles a sponge cast on the water's surface, creating a series of ever-widening concentric circles but never sinking beneath the visible surface.

Michel Butor, a "new wave" novelist, also wrote a work, *Milan Passage* (1954), in which life is described in a Parisian apartment house. The classical unities of time, place, and action are all observed to the letter in this novel, which begins at six at night and ends with the coming of dawn. The work is structured around a series of parallel lives, those of the tenants. It is unanimistic in that each individual or family is described almost simultaneously by the novelist. In this manner a communal type of living is evoked, with activities crossing and overlapping one another. *Milan Passage,* however, is a far more complex work than Céline's novel. Its characters are so structured that they resemble "geological stratas," a microcosm of society as a whole.

Milan Passage, with its extreme objectivity and detail, is as monotonous in its way as Céline's perpetually taut emotional attack. Butor is the cerebral author par excellence, one who describes in realistic terms everything the protagonists see, feel, or think. Céline, his opposite, details whatever he observes in an excitable, irrational, and tempestuous manner. Neither author's depictions afford relief or drama.

Great art, whether pictorial, musical, or verbal is concerned with "the mystery of existence in the metaphysical sense." [11] Céline was certainly tormented and disturbed by the mystery, but his inability to find a satisfactory answer to life's problems, in terms of himself and the society in which he lived, led him to an impasse. As a result he experienced extreme alienation and solitude. Often he felt as if he had been set adrift on an unfriendly sea.

Céline was filled with that vital energy which artists know only too well, but not with the harmony that makes for unshakable monuments in the domain of the aesthetic. He was unable to give expression to the energy within him. For this reason, what might otherwise have been meaningful in terms of the written word took on the frenetic and quixotic form of the ephemeral. Céline was trying to give expression and form to what was tearing at his vitals—fear, anger, hate, and revenge. He was casting about trying to catch hold of, and to transform, unchanneled energy into some artistic mold. He failed.

Céline's novels could be called examples of "action writing" in allusion to "action painting," of which Jackson Pollock was a master. This American artist described his technique as follows: he felt physically immersed in his canvas during the actual act of creation, but then was able to abstract himself from it.

> When I am *in* painting, I'm not aware of what I am doing. It is only after a sort of "get acquainted" period that I see what I have been about. I have no fears about making changes, destroying the image, etc. because the painting has a life of its own. I try to let it come through. It is only when I lose contact with the painting that the result is a mess. Otherwise there is pure harmony, an easy give and take, and the painting comes out well.[12]

The first half of the above statement may be applied to Céline. He is "in" his writing just as Pollock was "in" his painting. What Céline depicts, however, is a state of undifferentiated dissolution, a *massa confusa,* a primitive condition before the state of consciousness has taken hold or after it has disappeared. Pollock's last sentence is not applicable to *Fairy-Play for Another Time II.* Céline never experienced the necessary harmony with his creation to assess it, to structure it, or to give it depth.

Fairy-Play for Another Time II is regressive rather than evolutive. It is like a tornado, wreaking havoc wherever it goes, then falling flat at the end, once the tremendous winds of energy have blown themselves out.

10

GUIGNOL'S BAND II, OR LONDON'S BRIDGE

> In nature's infinite book of secrecy
> A little I can read.
>
> WILLIAM SHAKESPEARE, *Anthony and Cleopatra*

THE SUBTITLE OF *Guignol's Band II,* THE SEQUEL TO *Guignol's Band I,* is *London's Bridge.* A "bridge" implies a link between two opposing polarities, two aspects of life (good and evil, rich and poor, spirit and instinctuality, etc.), a transition from one state to another, an inner change. Physical events that were looked upon as mechanistic in *Guignol's Band I* have led to a transformation of energy in the sequel and thus to an equalization of opposites. The tensions between Ferdinand and his gang, once so great and always leading to friction and death, have now been replaced, to a great extent, by philosophical and political discussions, satire, burlesque, farcical interludes.

Such a metamorphosis in concept may reflect a parallel inner change in Céline. A kind of modus vivendi seems to have been established whereby his psychic contents, though still not harmonious, do manage somehow to live together—if not productively, then at least not destructively.

The change of focus in *London's Bridge* is most apparent in terms of Céline's protagonist, Ferdinand, and his relationships with women. Ferdinand is now, it seems, capable of love. Important personality changes therefore come to the fore. Feelings of being wanted, appreciated, and loved arouse genuine affection within his being. The hard, wooden, puppet-like Ferdinand has become a more malleable, warm, and understanding person, one capable of sharing his life with a partner.

PLOT

The plot of *London's Bridge* is rather complicated. Ferdinand has escaped from the "band" and his sordid companions of *Guignol's Band I.* He meets Sosthène de Rodiencourt. Both men find employ with a retired colonel who is entering a competition, sponsored by the war office, to produce the best gas mask. They live in his luxuriously appointed home with servants and the fourteen-year-old Virginia, the colonel's niece of whom Ferdinand becomes enamored. Interesting episodes follow, including Sosthène's panic at the thought of being enclosed in a gas mask and long discussions concerning religion, philosophy, the theater, and politics. One evening Ferdinand takes Virginia to the Touit-Touit Club and seduces her. He wants to make her his life's companion. The uncle is furious. Ferdinand renounces Virginia. The colonel, strangely enough, simply vanishes from the picture: no one ever hears from him again. Ferdinand sees Virginia and she informs him she is pregnant. He is touched by the news and swears fidelity, but the words are evidently not entirely meaningful to him because he soon accepts a job as ship's cook and forgets his promise to Virginia. Meanwhile, the pimp Cascade, of *Guignol's Band I,* discovers Ferdinand's whereabouts, kidnaps him just as he is about to set sail, and takes him to his den, along with Virginia. There he meets other members of his old gang. A night of frantic merrymaking ensues, with much dancing and drinking. Suddenly, everything comes to a halt. Boro and Clodovitz (of *Guignol's Band I*) bring in a long, foul-smelling box. It contains a decomposed body—that of Claben, which had not burned in the fire.

Ferdinand finally succeeds in escaping, together with Virginia and Sosthène, and the volume ends as the three walk about London.

THE LOVE THEME

Until Ferdinand meets Virginia, his life is devoid of any positive love figure. This girl, a cute, charming, mischievous, fourteen-year-old blonde, will be the vehicle by means of whom Ferdinand will liberate aspects of his personality hitherto constricted, and thus be able to experience a sense of relatedness. But liberation also implies its opposite—constriction. Ferdinand's attachment to Virginia limits his own freedom. Yet such restrictions as he now imposes upon himself will have salutary results. For the first time he will be able to experience both aspects of life (liberation, on the one hand, construction, on the other) and be more conscious of the meanings and values inherent in each.

As Ferdinand's love for Virginia increases, so does his consciousness of self. He has never been interested in his dress, manners, vocabulary. Suddenly, in his new milieu, he realizes the importance of etiquette, charm, and neatness. He is now on guard with Virginia at all times (in terms of his vocabulary) and inhibits himself voluntarily. It is a difficult task.

> Look at Virginia once again! . . . to look at her always! to adore her. . . . my eyes are heavy, they are burning! . . . Ah! . . . I can't be amiable . . . frisky . . . how my heart palpitates . . . My heart is light . . . I want to be proper.[1]

The self-imposed discipline compells Ferdinand to develop other facets of his personality. It is as if a dam has been set up, channeling the flow of various currents, enriching the riverbed still further. A modicum of reason has penetrated a totally impulsive nature. Ferdinand begins rationalizing about life and contemplating his activities and his future. With love as a motivating force, the world of vice is no longer necessary to generate excitement.

As Ferdinand's love for Virginia deepens, other qualities emerge, Formerly, he has been a being driven hither and yon, as if he could not stand still for a second. He has been like Don Juan in this respect: anything that smacked of attachment or security has been anathema to him: ". . . constancy is good for ridiculous people, that's all . . . and love's pleasure is based on change."[2] There is no question that Ferdinand's natural bent for adventure is still alive within him. Life has something spontaneous and chaotic about it that Ferdinand needs. What distinguishes Ferdinand from Don Juan, to a great extent, is the fact that the Spanish nobleman was not able to adapt to society, to focus his energies on a single idea. Ever responsive to a variety of stimuli, he followed their bent. Ferdinand, on the other hand, has now become attached to Virginia. His life has taken on focus.

What has attracted Ferdinand to Virginia? Her naïveté and her innocence brings a new cast to his life. Life has become a game, a joyous, humorous, jubilant spree. Ferdinand relates to Virginia's childlike aspects; these evidently find a responsive chord within his own psyche. When, for example, Ferdinand inadvertently makes Virginia cry by questioning her about her dead parents, he is sorry for what he has done and sets out to rectify the situation. How does he accomplish this feat? He distracts her as one would a child: he gets down on all fours, barks like a dog, hops around, nuzzles close to her, groans, whimpers, rolls about on cushions, on the floor, and each time he approaches her his heart palpitates a bit more violently. Virginia howls with glee.[3]

Why does he chose to imitate a dog? The choice is certainly unconscious. Yet it is highly meaningful. Most important, he wants to amuse her. When a human being takes on an animal's characteristics, he becomes ludicrous. The dog, however, has specific attributes. Frequently appearing at women's feet in paintings and photos, he symbolizes faithfulness as well as subservience. This animal may be looked upon, then, as the guardian of the weaker sex and the guide or leader of the flock. Ferdinand will be all these things to Virginia.

Though his love for Virginia has brought him happiness (insofar as he is capable of this experience), it has also caused him fear. Life, therefore, will no longer be experienced merely as a one-sided affair, but as a composite of all-inclusive opposites. Ferdinand thinks of Virginia's adorable little face and moments later with anguish at the thought of losing her some day.

> Oh! if I lost her one day! . . . I don't dare move about! . . . I want to embrace the world . . . Miracle. . . . My anger has vanished . . . my wickedness, all of it . . . I am entranced . . . happy . . . That's all! . . .[4]

Tremendous satire and comedy are implicit in Ferdinand's love episodes. Such weapons are designed to mock romantic, sentimental, maudlin love. They are also vehicles used to mask feelings of relatedness. Since love is something new in Ferdinand's life, he is unsure of how to handle the fresh emotions coming into consciousness. Uncertainty breeds oversensitivity. He fears being ridiculed, as does any adolescent when admitting to his first love. Ridicule may be parried by masking it—through comedy.

The scene, for example, of Ferdinand's marriage proposal to Virginia is comical, satirical, and yet very touching. In certain ways, it is reminiscent of episodes in Raymond Queneau's *Zazie in the Subway* (1959), about an impish little girl. Both novels deal mortal blows to conventions, deriding their inconsistencies, their hypocritical and sordid aspects.

The marriage proposal scene begins with Ferdinand confessing his love for Virginia in simple terms. Then all of a sudden, he is struck down by a vision and so deeply stirred by it that he is convinced he has experienced some kind of grace. He describes this vision. Everything has become light and aflame. Joy and happiness glow within him and within the trees that now light up all about him, rising, trembling, palpitating. "The entire bush of fire palpitates," a delicious perfume emanates from the "spirit of the flowers, tenderness, charm."[5] He knows ecstasy: fire, light, and birds flutter about him.

Such a scene may be viewed either as a giant parody of romantic love, with its effusiveness, exaggerated gestures, verbal prowess, overly expansive ways, or as a mockery of religious visions.

Ferdinand's desire for Virginia is, according to the above passage, infinite and his longing is insatiable. He is comparable, in this respect, to both a hungry animal who never ceases to want and to a child who longs for an unattainable toy. As his feelings become more and more overt, Ferdinand expresses them with increasingly voluble and grotesque tonal effects. The sentences are no longer structured, as they were in previous passages, no longer built up in balanced and harmonious fashion. Verbal virtuosity, brilliance, and bravura follow helter-skelter. Polyrhythmic and polytonal effects are introduced to demonstrate strain, conflict, and desire. Intertwining beats, clashing rhythms (low sounds juxtaposed to strident ones in this passage) serve to increase the tense atmosphere. The punctuation, the three dots, and the exclamation marks so frequently used in this passage, accelerate the violence of Ferdinand's passion. As he verbalizes, the flow of language is interspersed with images, onomatopoeias, harsh tonalities, alliterations, assonances, dissonances: "flambe, fremissantes, fleurs, . . . piquées, branches, buisson, feu, palpite, douceur, bouffées, extrase, ravi, ardeur, flammes, virevole, hurle . . ."[6] Oddly enough, though Ferdinand is speaking of love, very few mellifluous, velvety harmonies are to be found in this passage. Rather, harsh, boisterous, robust, energetic registers are sounded—cacophonies reminiscent of Hindemith. The dichotomy between the feelings expressed and the brittle tonalities indicates the existence of a split within Ferdinand's personality. He loves Virginia, to be sure, but he cannot accept the responsibilities that such a relationship imposes. Though he seeks to protect her from the inevitable cruelties of the real world, he cannot compel himself to remain constant, to live a fixed and regimented life. Such a schism is also apparent in the fact that he seeks to be frank with her and yet speaks in symbols she is unable to understand. "I am a bird . . . I spin around . . ."[7] Like a bird, he tries to explain, he hovers from one plant to another. Virginia, still a child, is unaware of the depth of the cleavage within him. What he offers her—prolonged love and relationship—is in direct opposition to his personality, which is that of a wanderer.

Perhaps this scene's most arresting feature is its visionary aspect or, rather, its mockery of religious visions in general. The burning bush, of whose glowing light Ferdinand speaks and which has been witnessed by so many saints as they become one with God is comparable to an epiphany. Whereas St. Francis of Assisi, St. Ignatius Loyola, and St. Theresa of Avila all described their contact with the Divine and His ministers in the most reverent of terms, Ferdinand concretizes his vision by assuming a variety of ludicrous and scornful stances, posing in a very devout manner at one moment and, seconds later, with extreme abandon, and finally staring deeply, longingly, and lasciviously into his beloved's eyes.

Satire also figures in some of the love scenes. For example, Ferdinand returns to the colonel's house and searches for Virginia, calling out to her frantically. Finally, he bellows forth with operatic vigor: "I am looking everywhere for my Virginia." [8] These words are an echo of Orpheus' agonizing call in Gluck's opera *Orpheus and Eurydice,* when the poet searches for his beloved in the underworld and sings forth in mellow and poignant tones: "I am looking for my Eurydice."

When Ferdinand hears no response from his Virginia, he begins trembling, shivering, and panting in anguish, and horror sets in. A touch of twentieth-century speed is now included. Ferdinand's gestures, like inflamed emotions, become highly accelerated. Within seconds he touches the depths of despair. Each gesture, owing to its extreme speed, seems distorted and, like a Charlie Chaplin film unreeled at a gallop, is transformed into a series of spasms.

Despite the variety of satiric inuendoes, Ferdinand's attachment to Virginia indicates a step in his development, a consciousness of his own identity, and the realization of his role in society. The real test of his evolving personality occurs when he learns of Virginia's pregnancy. His reaction to this news is ambivalent, as it well might be. He dances with glee at first, as he thinks of the human being he has helped create. His joy simmers down when his thoughts wander off onto the economics of the situation: he has no job with a future. His mood becomes tinged with pathos.

Ferdinand's thoughts do not smolder in pathos for long. His mood changes quickly as he talks to Virginia. He puts her to bed that night, tucks her in like a child, looks about her room and sees the dolls, the toys, the little cradles strewn around. He watches her and realizes that she too has changed. Now that she is to become a mother, she is less prankish, less childish, more reserved and more sedate. Feelings of responsibility, of fear for the future, have enveloped her existence and diminished her flightiness, as they have Ferdinand's.

The conflict Ferdinand experiences upon learning of his impending fatherhood makes him realize that joy, in and of itself, is merely an illusion, that the young live within this framework because they are not yet aware of life's negative side: the possibilities of failure, danger, loss. Youth is energetic, enthusiastic, easily swept off its feet, sustained by ideas that stimulate and arouse. This very dynamism prevents an assessment of their true situations and their true selves.

Adolescence has come to a close.

THE FORTUITOUS

Ferdinand's newly developed sense of constancy and responsibility does not eliminate his longing for freedom, for a life of adventure, excitement, and the fortuitous.

The desire to escape the drudgery of mundane existence is discernible in several water images. In *Guignol's Band I,* we recall, the River Thames had assumed lugubrious overtones: it was an expanse of never-ending motion, a reflection of wind-swept, dreary skies. In *London's Bridge* the Thames is personified as a composite of opposites: vibrant, harsh, mysterious, lovable, fascinating. It is also a blend of natural and man-made elements: clouds, water, wind, as well as the ships, the dirt, the grating and jarring sounds and images of a technological society. Ferdinand, we may say, is part of his environment, judging from within the image rather than from outside it. He looks upon the river as a stepping-stone for his drama and seeks to embark on a boat leading to the enchanted land of the unknown.[9]

Ferdinand, the man who longs to roam, has also been personified in terms of the water image. His notions of departure and his fascination with the fortuitous are expressed in water's natural aspects (its beauty, color, contours, etc.), and not in terms of its disruptive and painful side, as manifested by industrial society (smoke, soot, noise, factories, etc.).

The disparate sensations coexisting in Ferdinand are also expressed musically. Repetitions of words may serve to amplify the protagonist's emotions; they may also have the opposite effect, increasing the monotony of the passage, as electronically magnified music does at times. Parallels, therefore, may be drawn between Ferdinand's subjective experience and their concretization in accompanying sonorous tonalities, each generating a variety of very nearly endless possibilities and ramifications of moods, ideations, and tendencies. By varying the rhyme scheme (bachots, canots, souquer, border, etc.), as well as the alliterations, assonances, and hard consonants (f, t, d, etc.), there emerges a medley of reverberations that catapults the reader, whose nervous system responds to the diverse tonalities, into another atmosphere.

Céline's prose, an extraordinary phenomenon, is an expression of his characters' need for the fortuitous. Each word, based on "indeterminants" or "chance," seems to find its way onto the page in an unexpected manner. An analogy may be drawn between Céline's prose in *London's Bridge* and Karlheinz Stockhausen's *Piano Piece XI,* which consists of seventeen different sections that the composer wrote out on a single cardboard sheet. The pianist performing the work is free to begin where he sees fit. So with Céline's prose. Though there is a story line, particularly in this volume, a reader may begin anyplace, during the marriage proposal scene, the epiphany, the dog imitation—no matter.[10] It is the extraordinarily unpredictable nature of Céline's prose, in terms of its musicality, that makes for its versatility.

THE FARCE: RELIGION AND THEATER

One of the most extraordinary farce sequences[11] in all of Céline's works is the "Book of Vega" episode, in which we find Sosthène indoctrinating Ferdinand into the beauties, mysteries, and rituals of Oriental religion.

The "Book of Vega," to which the protagonists refer, is certainly to be understood as a parody of both the *Vedic Hymns* and the *Bhagavad-Gita,* as well as other less well-known Hindu religious works.

The religious ritual in the "Book of Vega" episode begins with Sosthène and Ferdinand, the participants, closing the apartment windows and drawing the curtains. Sosthène dons a Chinese robe to lend flavor to the atmosphere and to indicate the role he will play in the ritual: that of priest, thaumaturge, magician. To get in the mood, he begins gesticulating, conjuring up spirits. Ferdinand sits near him, beats out a rhythm on the border of the book, first with his finger, then with a piece of copper, then with a spoon, finally with a toothbrush. Sosthène begins his dance, in wide-sweeping gestures as the outset, then in more rhythmic and spasmodic motions. His entire frame is contorted with religious ecstasy. Ferdinand's accompaniment takes on the dancer's nervous beat, emphasizing each of Sosthène's gestures. Suddenly it is no longer Sosthène who is dancing; it is Shiva, the representative of cosmic energy, the god who is both creator and destroyer. He is doing the war dance, enabling man to free his soul from the "veil of illusion" that is his life.

Sosthène stops and takes a moment out from his dance to explain the significance of the ritual. He analyzes the value of his gestures, which may be looked upon as hieroglyphics—images in space—as well as the various positions and postures of his body, his knitted eyebrows, his grimacing face.[12]

Sosthène resumes the dance. He changes his impersonations. At one moment he becomes a dragon spewing flame, a demon battling the enemy, a roaring, devouring monster. At other moments he is a god ready to annihilate his antagonist, ready to throw him to the ground, ready to watch him writhe with pain. A battle ensues with the dragon. Frenzied now, Sosthène tries to lure the demon his way, to attract him, to win his confidence; he does so in a series of swirling and cajoling movements. Sosthène finally disrobes, having paraded before all manner of gods and angels, whose affection he has sought to win in his fight for survival. He begins by flagellating himself, trying to amuse, to enlighten, dazzle, dizzy the demons and, finally, to possess them. Ferdinand, meanwhile, has been beating out rhythms at a fulminating tempo, as Sosthène gyrates, rotates, whirls, spits, recites, accentuates, elongates, hammers out a variety of syllables in harsh and metallic tones, and in velvety and tender ones as well.

Sosthène has become Shiva incarnate—the Shiva who killed the demons, flayed them, donned their skins. Sosthène repeats all the acts required of the worshipper and at this juncture he feels capable of transcending the human condition, of experiencing immortality, of immersing himself in both god and nature and, thereby, of experiencing *apokatastasis,* a return of all things to their place in the natural cosmic order.[13] Sosthène, in accordance with the mythologems attached to the dances of Shiva (in this case as expressed in the "Book of Vega"), experiences rebirth and liberation.

As narrated by Céline, the religious ritual has become a broad farce whose implication is that the practice of Yoga and of Oriental religious beliefs may be salvation for the Easterner, but not for the Westerner. For the Occidental, who seeks to escape or who longs for peace of mind, Buddhism and Hinduism may well bring on emotional or psychic disaster, the extent of which will depend, of course, upon the individual in question. To try to emulate the

Oriental in his religious concepts and practices is to destroy what is inherent to the Occidental: his ego, the part of his psyche that enables him to evaluate and determine his position in terms of the world about him. The Occidental's ego is the vehicle with which he relates to life and reality in terms of himself as an individual, not as a collective figure. The Oriental, on the other hand, seeks Atman: a suprapersonal, transcendental state that enables him to achieve selfless detachment. His ego, therefore, is purposefully undeveloped and diffused. The Occidental does not require such spiritual detachment. He needs, instead, to experience "the phenomenal world in his own way," that is, through the development of his ego. The Occidental who adopts Oriental religious devices destroys what is basic to him. He maims himself and compels himself to limp through life rather than to walk through it at a brisk pace.[14]

Céline further implies that religion per se, created originally to ward off fear and to bring about spiritual fulfillment, is no long effective. Today's religious ritual is devoid of profound meaning; it is no longer a living force in people's lives. Whatever the ritual demands—dancing, kneeling, whirling, twirling—it is a series of empty gestures having extremely humorous side effects. Religion, as observed in the "Book of Vega" episode, is a farce.

The "Book of Vega" episode, in addition to being a religious spoof, may also be considered as a satire of those modern theatrical innovators who have drawn heavily on Oriental religious experience in creating their new brand of theater.

It would seem that Céline was arching his bow in the direction of Antonin Artaud, that he was ready to puncture Artaud's "Theater of Cruelty" ideology. Artaud, it should be recalled, believed that there was as much a poetry of the "senses" as there was of "language"—that feelings have their own reality and cannot always be translated into words. To express sensations in terms of vocabulary is, frequently, to betray them. It is for this reason that allegorical figures on stage, with or without masks, can reveal certain impressions that words may fail to make manifest. Oriental theater—that of Bali, Japan, China—according to Artaud, has restored the visual or plastic elements to theater. Such theater is a nonverbal performance that touches the very depths of life by means of gesture, sound, facial expressions, and movements. Artaud knew that the impact of the visible action on stage can have a tremendous effect upon man's unconscious. Gestures looked upon symbolically, for example, were to be considered as transforming agents, communicating the mysterious and hitherto unrevealed contents of the unconscious of the author, the director, and the actor. Objects themselves, he said, chanting, costumes, gestures, words, imitative harmonies (buzzing), are all-powerful in stimulating a visceral reaction in the spectator by lending a metaphysical and awesome quality to a production. When a spectator sees a strange and horrifying wooden form appear on stage, he *feels* he is viewing a manifestation from beyond, but what he is actually experiencing, through projection, is his own inner world. When dragons or other inhuman manifestations enter upon the stage, dread and awe are aroused in the audience, not by language but by form. Space for Artaud was, therefore, alive, full, active, part of the cosmic flow and not distinct from it. For Artaud, Occidental theater is a branch of literature, whereas

Balinese ceremonial art has the quality of a religious rite. The latter serves to arouse the spectator mystically and restores cosmic balance to his world.

Artaud looked on the drama as a "curative" agent to man. For Céline, this modern palliative was no less a failure than religion as a means of combatting evil on earth and in transforming pain into joy. Céline believed that no ritual, save perhaps the sexual one, could spare man from suffering. Whatever religious or theatrical notions were offered to society by visionaries, none had been effective in alleviating man's pain. Religions had not stemmed the tide of wars, nor had they transformed man's bizarre and cruel ways.

Despite the fact that the "Book of Vega" episode satirizes not only religious rites but Artaud's concepts as well, it is nonetheless a remarkable example of "Theater of Cruelty" production translated into another medium. While deriding Artaud's theory—the theory that by bombarding the audience with a variety of noises and fearsome visions, enacted in space, one would shock them into a new state of awareness, shatter their facades and compel them to reject their complacent attitudes—Céline was actually accomplishing verbally, "fictionally," what the theatrical philosopher had set out to do in the domain of the dramatic arts.

The "Theater of Cruelty" aspect of the "Book of Vega" scene deserves closer examination. Céline conveys through gesture and sound what Artaud, the psychedelic theater, and the theater of the ridiculous have sought to accomplish and succeeded in accomplishing. A composite of lyrical, erotic, mystic, and violent tonalities, each interrupting, intertwining, and overlapping the others, enters into the picture. The nerve-racking quality of the entire fresco gives the impression of the discontinuity implicit in modern life. Because of the repetition of strident consonants (f, t, s, z), chromatic tonal sounds, so reminiscent of the twelve-tone compositional technique of Schönberg and Webern, are also injected into the atmosphere. Juxtapositions of adjectives, nouns, and verbs (or their omission), and bizarre punctuation (exclamation marks, series of dots) increase the dissonances, the violence and aggressivity of Sosthène's battle with the demons. The clash of beats from Ferdinand's accompaniment (with the spoons, sticks, tooth brushes, all manner of things) lends a wild, hysterical, frenetic madness to the entire scene. An analogy could also be drawn with John Cage's "chance," or aleatory, music. Cage frequently places an object (a bell, for example) directly on the strings inside a piano, causing the instrument to have a more percussive sound, like that of a Balinese gamelan. So Céline's frantic scene introduces impressions of the fortuitous in life, the unknown, the mysterious and highly emotional.[15]

Other mimodramas occur in the course of *Guignol's Band II.* Thus the sequence in Hyde Park, for example, in which a member of the Salvation Army speaks out her idealistic concepts. Ferdinand and Virginia are standing in the crowd listening to the Salvation Army woman beseeching, screaming at her audience in her terrible voice: "I say the rich must pay!" Whereupon the audience chuckles. "Christus is at war! We bleed with him." The audience trembles a bit, then laughs. A light rain begins to fall at this point, as if it had been preordained. All the umbrellas open up instantaneously. The speaker pursues her valiant diatribe, sings hymns, chants, prays, asks her audience to join in. She bellows forth, wiping the water from her forehead, begging the audience to continue singing loudly. Suddenly, just as hymn three hundred four is being sounded, the heavens open up. The voices become garbled, strained, hoarse, as sheets of water pour down from above. "Women of Britain win the war," [16] shouts another suffragette. The rain calms no one's enthusiasm, remarks the narrator.

Thus the Salvation Army, so poignantly described in Bernard Shaw's *Major Barbara,* is mocked by Céline.[17] He cuts down idealism and underlines the utter uselessness of statements such as "Christ suffered for humanity, his blood will redeem us all." These words and thoughts, once weighted with meaning and spirituality, now fall on dead ears. They signify nothing for twentieth-century man, implies Céline. Another message must be forthcoming—something valid for those who so desperately search for identity and a way of life.

Other interesting devices are noteworthy in this passage. As the speaker begins enunciating her ideas, the scene shifts from her to the audience and to Virginia and Ferdinand, who are huddled in a corner. The constant spotlighting of various people, the alteration of the focusing procedure from long shots to close-ups, succeeds in disrupting any sense of continuity, the implication being that nothing—neither political nor religious belief—is stable or eternal.

THE MACABRE

The most sordid episode of all occurs when Boro and Clodovitz bring Ferdinand the sour-smelling box containing Claben's decomposed body. This morbid joke has important symbolical overtones. The notion of murder and decay is introduced into what could have become a positive and productive turn in Ferdinand's life.

Though such a macabre scene spells regression for Ferdinand, his attitude has changed so drastically that it serves to make him even more conscious of life's dichotomy and, consequently, the better able to face both aspects of life. In *Guignol's Band,* we recall, physical events took on a mechanistic and energetic form; they acted with regularity and reacted with cause and effect. In *London's Bridge* we are offered a new type of energy, one leading to a kind of equalization (at least momentary) of opposites. Tensions, therefore, are not so strained, energy is channelled into relatively positive fields, friction no longer cancels out all of life's constructive features. Ferdinand adopts a new way of life and functions rather well within its structure. No longer solipsistic, he evolves from the embryonic and automaton-like individual into a man able to live a comparatively full life.

But once the macabre (Claben's decomposed body) has been injected into the scene, a demoniacal attraction for ugliness and for evil is again aroused within Ferdinand. This new feeling ushers in a mood of doom that infects the entire atmosphere. But Ferdinand now refuses to permit death and decay to overwhelm him (contrary to his previous behavior); the shock of viewing the putrefaction, the stench from the box itself, brings him to his senses.

No longer the fighter, nor the flighty lovebird, nor the adolescent who seeks to escape in a thousand different directions, he realizes that he will have to come to terms with life, will have to sign a pact with humanity. Henceforth, Ferdinand accepts the fact that he must lead a double life by donning the mask of the guignol (as the book's title indicates) when in the company of others, that he must inspire them with laughter and jubilation, must indulge in a series of ludicrous antics and rituals, while inwardly experiencing solitude, despondency, and pain.

As Virginia says to Ferdinand at the end of the volume: "Ferdinand dear! Make your face." [18] To survive in a world filled with strangers, cataclysms, and cruelties, Ferdinand will have to play the clown, the Pagliacci, hiding the erosion within and in the end dying with his secret!

Part Four

TRILOGY

There is no old age for man's anger,
Only death.

Sophocles, *Oedipus at Colonus*

11

FROM CASTLE TO CASTLE

Collective crimes incriminate no one.

NAPOLEON I, *Maxims* (1804–15)

THE TURBULENT AND CHAOTIC EXPERIENCE THAT HAD BEEN Céline's life took on collective stature in his next novel, *From Castle to Castle* (1957). This work is the narration of Céline's "myth."

From Castle to Castle takes us to Germany after Céline's flight from France in 1944, then to his stay at Sigmaringen, a refuge for French political figures (Pétain, Laval, Abel Bonnard, Lucien Rebatet, Paul Marion, etc.) who sought and received protection from the Nazi government. According to Céline himself, it was at Sigmaringen that he cared for the sick in a small hotel room that he had transformed into a type of hospital. Judging from Lucien Rebatet's statement on the subject, Céline was accorded many privileges. He owed his special standing to Doctor Karl Epting, former director of the German Institute in Paris during the Occupation. Doctor Epting, whose admiration for Céline was great, had given him the place of honor in his newly formed association for French intellectuals living in Germany at this period. Meetings were held at the city hall of Sigmaringen. Céline was equally well treated by German officers and most particularly by the S.D. Colonel Boemelburg, the police chief at Sigmaringen, known as the terrible "Bouledogue." By the end of February, 1945, Céline received official permission from the Nazi government to go to Denmark. In organizing a farewell party for himself, attended by those staying on at Sigmaringen, he offered beer to all—and the bill to a Doctor Jaquot. Céline, his wife and cat, and two hundred kilos of luggage departed from Sigmaringen by train.[1]

Céline uses myths (based on the *Völsunga Saga*, the *Eddas* and other Scandinavian legends) to create the cold, harsh atmosphere of northern lands. He brushes his canvas with icy tones, somber color effects, lugubrious cloud-filled skies, snow-laden mountains and roads, grey, foggy visions—a fitting background to the "twilight" stages before man sinks into oblivion.

From Castle to Castle is vastly different from *Fairy-Play for Another Time* and from *Guignol's Band*. The depression, the despondency, the feelings of utter emptiness that Céline had experienced at the end of the German occupation of France and during his journey to and incarceration in Denmark, had forced him into his own depths, compelled him to experience extreme introversion (drawing upon his psychic force, or libido, within his unconscious). When this energy was finally released, it burst forth like a torrent of chaotic, heaving, undifferentiated masses. When the simmering-down period came to pass, when discernment emerged, conditions for productivity likewise came into being.[2] In *From Castle to Castle,* then, we see that the artist has been permitted to gain in importance, at last.

The first section of *From Castle to Castle* is typical of Céline's previous works. We encounter the familiar angry pronouncements and accusations leveled at individuals, societies, and nations. Once these conventions are out of the way, Céline offers up the first in a series of startling apocalyptic visions.

PLOT

The narrator (Céline) is in Paris, looking out of his apartment window at the Seine. He sees a houseboat, is fascinated by it, and walks down to the quays. At close range he observes what now appears to be an ancient wooden frigate, *La Publique.* He goes on board for a moment, meets some old friends, one of whom is the actor Le Vigan, dressed in a gauche costume. The ship's admiral, Charon, is a strange creature with a monkey's head and the body of a tiger. He assumes gigantic proportions. It is he who demands gold from the passengers for safe passage. Whether he receives it or not, he takes out his oar and smashes their heads in, after which he twists his fingers in their brains. The ship then sinks beneath the water.

Another vision emerges. Céline, his wife, and his cat are at Meudon, where he has a small clientele.

The reader is then wafted off to Sigmaringen in Germany, the former dwelling place of the Hohenzollern family. There are descriptions of this domain as it was in former times, but superimposed upon this grandeur is an up-to-date vision including such figures as Pétain, Laval, Alphonse de Chateaubriant, Heinrich Hoffmann, and General Abetz. Other types pass into this heteroclitic work: an insane Cathar Bishop, Valkyrie-like women, etc. Finally Raoul Orphize, a film director, arrives at the castle and decides to make a movie of daily life at Sigmaringen, the final Götterdämmerung of the Third Reich.

THE SHIP OF DEATH

As we recall from *Journey to the End of the Night, Guignol's Band I,* and other works, Céline was fascinated by water. Any large expanse of water and things associated with it (barges, houseboats, canoes, steamers) held some mysterious power over him. The images in *From Castle to Castle* are no exception.

In an early image in *From Castle to Castle,* the narrator gazes at what seems to be placid waters and is mesmerized by the upsurgence from its depths of a strange ship carrying what could be described as a group of monstrously mutilated and already dead beings, who, paradoxically, "begin to become agitated."[3] Céline's hallucination is so vivid, so believable, that he cannot distinguish it from reality: "I went down to try to figure out whether it was a dream or not a dream."[4]

Symbolically, bodies of water, because of their fluidity and the immense riches in their depths, are usually thought to be representative of the unconscious. The ship emerging from the sea could thus be described, in psychological terms, as representing the contents of the unconscious breaking through into consciousness, or the unreal entering the domain of reality.

Since the ship carries dead people we may allude to it as the "Ship of Death." As such, it moves about aimlessly and becomes a vehicle or instrument that transcends the world of phenomena. In many respects it is reminiscent of the Flying Dutchman's "Phantom Ship," which sailed the seven seas and was considered a bad omen whenever it was encountered. Originally, this spectral ship, as interpreted by Walter Scott in *Rokeby*, was a vessel laden with precious metals. After a horrible murder had been perpetrated on board, a plague broke out. No port would permit the crew to land, and for this reason it was doomed to sail forever. As narrated by Wagner in his opera *The Flying Dutchman* (1843), this same myth took on cosmic proportions. A Dutch captain struggling against the elements vows to the gods that he will sail around the Cape of Good Hope if it takes him until the end of eternity. His hubris is such that a curse is visited upon him: he will remain a traveler forever unless he finds a wife willing to sacrifice herself for him.

Céline's vision is a composite of these two legends. His ship wanders about the high seas. Its cargo does not contain precious metals, but rather a symbolic "plague" made up of abnormal, destructive, heinous, incontinent, rotting human wrecks. The vision of the ship does not bring bad luck; it represents rather an individual contemplating his shadow. There is no struggle or antagonistic reaction to what he sees.

The fact that the narrator (Céline) is watching his own inferior characteristics in their destructive enterprise brings to mind Joseph Conrad's *The Heart of Darkness.* In this novel, one recalls, the narrator Marlowe tells of his experiences as captain of a small river steamer in the Belgian Congo. High nightmarish visions reveal, in psychological terms, his regressive primitive world, his shadow. Marlowe, unlike Céline's narrator, confronts the image he sees and when he recognizes "dark aspects" of his own being—that is, the savage within him (the unassimilated primal energy that is wreaking havoc within his personality)—he is fascinated at first, then demoralized. After he undergoes suffering of the most excruciating kind, personal growth in depth and wisdom is forthcoming. Conrad himself noted that this experience, which he related in his novel, had changed his entire existence.[5] Céline's narrator, unlike Marlowe, reacts passively to his vision. He never confronts the forces he sees. He merely observes them.

Let us examine Céline's vision more closely. As the ship draws nearer to the narrator, a kind of monstrous form, a Leviathan type, a Behemoth-figure emerges from its wooden frame. It is the ship's captain, Charon, who has the head of a monkey and the body of a tiger and wears a uniform embroidered with silver and an admiral's hat bedecked with gold. As he stands there on deck he assumes enormous proportions, and as he strides about the vessel, it tilts.[6] When standing erect, etched sharply against the horizon, he takes his oar and begins smashing the heads of the already mutilated passengers, decapitating them (in a way), crushing their craniums, after which he runs his fingers through their brains, forcing the blood to gush out: "jams from the head . . . massacre with an oar . . ."[7] Mothers, children, all receive the same treatment, whether they have paid Charon his fee for safe passage or not.

Who was the original Charon? If we return to the Greek myth, Charon was pictured as a dark, grisly cranky old man wearing a sailor's cloak. He was miserly in that he demanded the "obolos" carried by the dead in their mouths to ferry them across the river Styx. The Greek Charon represented the archetypal image of the "old man," a just and positive figure. In Dante's *Inferno,* Vergil leads the poet through the gate of Hell and Charon is also viewed as an old man with white hair. In Dante's account, Charon complains because the poet is not a "shadow" and thus weighs more than his other passengers and is heavier to ferry across.

Money pacified the Charon of the Greek myth, assuring the soul of safe passage. Céline's monster is rapacious and ravenous. Money is not enough. He needs blood with it. Céline's Charon, therefore, emerges as a Destroyer, a completely negative Father Principle, a demonic figure, a savage beast, standing, as it were, on the "Lip of Hell." He is the symbol par excellence of man's negative principles, of unassimilated primal energy—a monster ready to devour anything and everything in sight.[8] There is, moreover, no possible association to be made with any human element, since Charon is devoid of feelings. There is no similarity between him and man save for the fact that both stand erect.[9]

Since Charon is described as having a monkey's head and a tiger's body, his spiritual half, which resides in man's head (according to the Platonists) is nonexistent. His head, in that it has taken on the form of a monkey, represents man's baser forces, a lower level of intelligence. The tiger, symbolically a fearful, bloodthirsty animal that never permits its prey to escape, represents cruelty. When associated with the cult of Dionysos, the tiger is ready to dismember and devour anything that crosses its path. In China, the tiger represented darkness and unchanneled instinctuality. Though the tiger is imbued with other qualities, namely courage and heroism, Céline's view of this animal is one of unmitigated evil, wrath, and darkness. It is interesting to observe that "if a human being behaves like an animal he is not in harmony with his instincts. An animal which behaves like an animal is in harmony with itself."[10] Céline's Charon was in no way "in harmony" with himself; he was at odds, indeed, with every aspect of his inner being.

Charon possesses other characteristics. He is a giant and, being of much greater than normal stature, symbolizes power and strength. Giants, along with their relatives the Titans, Cyclops, etc., are looked upon in myths as antidiluvian monsters, as fabulous animals possessing primeval natures. These powerful, untamable forces usually struggle with the gods and are in the end defeated by heroes. In Norse mythology, for example, the giant Ymir sprang from the clouds and from him a whole race of giants followed. When he was killed, the heavens emerged from his body, the earth from his flesh, the sea from his blood, the mountains from his bones, the trees from his hair, and the sky from his skull. This cosmogonical myth symbolizes man's desire, through sacrifice, to reawaken or to stimulate certain cosmic forces.

In this manner he attempts to right an evil situation or to eliminate an imbalance.

When monsters or giants emerge in myths and legends (Minotaur, Goliath, Gargantua, Hercules, Cyclops, Satan, Grendel) it is an indication of some kind of cosmic upheaval, of a need, perhaps, to deal with a tyrant, or with some hostile force or psychological situation (dominance of the beast in man) within the land or people. When a monster appears, therefore, it creates disorder, chaos, shock. From such a "reshuffling" or rearrangement of elements within the structure, a new community may arise, a fresh state, one that will be better than the former one (or so it is hoped).

Céline's Charon represents the animal in man, a preconscious state prior to differentiation. He is an expression of primordial wholeness, a huge mass of flesh possessing enormous power but associated only with the earth. There can be no rapport between his spiritual and his chthonic sides since the former is nonexistent. Hence he represents the instinctual forces within man that are absolutely alienated from the world. He is an amoral, blind entity and incapable of distinguishing anything at all. Suffused, moreover, with hubris, he goes about his destructive work with gusto. A person viewing such a mass of matter reacts either passively (as did Céline's narrator), or else fights what he sees (any hero), creating, thereby, tension and chaos from which new and fruitful attitudes may emerge.[11]

What are Charon's activities? Since Céline's giant has nothing in common with the old man as depicted in the Greek myth and resembles, rather, the "Terrible Father" archetype, the darker side of the personality appears to be in a state of dissatisfaction and rebellion, provoking him constantly to destroy everything about him. Charon decapitates his passengers by smashing their heads with his oar, running his fingers through their bloody brains. When Jarry introduces a decapitation ceremony in his play *King Ubu,* he does so with humor and irony. Céline's narration, on the contray, is fluoroscopic, sparing us none of the gory details. Because Céline dwells on man's viscera, his image is reminiscent of William Burrough's depictions, in *Naked Lunch,* of "mangled insects," of "trailing the colorless death smell," of lingering odors and the taste of the "afterbirth of a withered grey monkey." [12]

The decapitation ritual has been known to man since ancient times. In Western civilization the axe and the guillotine were instruments used for this purpose. Crowds usually watched the ceremony with screams of joy, frenzy, and excitement. Such decapitations usually indicated a rejection of the mental attitudes of the persons being killed. Since the head is the container (or receptacle) of man's spiritual or divine aspects, it is usually treated with love, respect, and awe, as witnessed in the cases of St. John the Baptist, Julien Sorel, etc. In Céline's case, however, the heads are mutilated and destroyed, a symbolic indication of Charon's desire to rid society of whatever orientation to life's forces these heads represented.

Céline's Charon is, strangely enough, a destroyer of the already dead. If we look upon the dead people in the ship as representative of sterile forces within man and society, we might conclude that Charon is annihilating whatever is unproductive, whatever has attained the last stage of moral and physical decay. But though he destroys what is unfruitful, no fecundating agents arise from the debris, because what he annihilates is already dead. His acts, in this context, can be considered as adding negation upon negation.

Monsters and giants, as we have noted, frequently represent unformed potentialities, that is, a potpourri of both good and evil qualities. Céline's Charon, a horrendous apparition bursting forth like a volcano from the sea, represents only evil—madness, perversion, decapitation. He is the anti-hero, the anti-Christ, the amalgam of all demoniacal forces.

To fight such a monster would indicate a positive desire to decry the mismanagement of man's political, economic, social, and spiritual affairs and a desire to free man's conscious and unconscious forces from the stranglehold of arcane powers. But no hero—no Siegfried, no David, no Beowolf—ever emerges from Céline's vision. Nietzsche had already warned against a heroless world when he wrote: "By my love and hope I conjure thee, cast not away the hero in thy soul." Céline pays no heed. The narrator of *From Castle to Castle* does not fight the monster. He displays none of the virtues of the "hero" personality. He is not the vanquisher of chaos. He merely stands by and watches the destruction. The demon is in unchallenged command, while the narrator—Céline—stands onshore, safe and out of reach.

The narrator's safety is further assured by the presence of his dog, Hagar, which is described as having a frightful snout and as being mute and discreet.[13] It is interesting to note that Hagar, according to Biblical tradition, was Abraham's Egyptian servant who was cast away into the desert with her son Ishmael, who would become the father of the Arab people. When Hagar was dying of thirst, the Lord's Angel pointed out a spring of water to her, saving the lives of the outcasts.[14] Céline's dog is likewise a faithful-servant type: he watches and protects his master, keeping him out of harm's reach—and keeping him from doing much of anything. The dog is, therefore, in this respect, like a wall preventing any disturbance of Céline's vision or of his passive attitude. Though Céline's dog is never cast away, he does view the sea and its contents, sniffing about the corpses and every now and then, when thirsty, imbibing the water and, with it, that most enriching of all beverages, blood.

Céline's Hagar may also be compared to the Greeks' three-headed Cerberus, a creature who guarded the door to the underworld, never molesting any of the "shades," provided they did not attempt to leave. In Christian symbolism, the dog may take on another aspect, that of the faithful and courageous guardian of the flock. In Egyptian mythology, the dog is the companion of the dead.

Céline's dog is the guardian of the living—the author—and is faithful and subservient to him at all times. Hagar, then, has both a positive and negative function. He "protects" his master against the world, preventing any kind of productive activity that might otherwise have emerged from heroic confrontation with the ship, its monstrous captain, and its mutilated passengers. In this respect, Hagar resembles the over-indulgent parent who smothers the child with care, never permitting him to experience life in its frantic, dangerous, and yet growth-giving aspects. Hagar plays a positive role, however, in that he does not permit his master to be submerged or drowned by the overwhelming archetypal images that he sees (the ship, the monster, and the passengers). Since in ancient times the dog belonged to Aesculapius, the doctor, he is a fitting companion to Céline's narrator, who is also a man of medicine.

Who are some of the passengers in Charon's boat, aside from the multitudes he destroys with such alacrity? There is Emile for one, a collaborator that the narrator knew in Paris. As a collaborator, Emile had been lynched by a Parisian mob as he was leaving a post office. Everything within him had been broken—"de-boned." His eyes had been gouged out, his legs nearly crushed. When he walks about he moves "like a spider, rotating." [15]

When Céline associates the spider with Emile, he stresses the forces of destruction. Spiders, forever weaving their webs, symbolize the world of phenomena (for the Hindu, Maya's veil of illusion), which entraps and ensnares the unwary, destroying any concept or notion of the world that lies beyond the visible. The spider, weaving its web in rotating fashion, represents Emile's wobbly walk and his lack of equilibrium, his unbalanced rapport with heaven and earth, his inability to adapt to circumstance, and his repetitious way of experiencing life.

When maimed or otherwise abnormal beings appear in myth or in literary works, they usually possess some magical or other compensatory power that makes up for what is lacking in them. Cassandra, for example, though blind, possessed inner vision, and Hephaestos, though lame, was the finest of forgers. In Emile's case, however, there is no redeeming feature. He represents mutilated man in a state of decay. He has become, according to the narrator, a sacrificial agent, a single man paying for a collective crime. From him, therefore, there emerges blood, for which humanity forever thirsts. Blood relieves people of feelings of guilt and ensures—so they believe—future growth and possibilities for rebirth, at least symbolically. *"Die Natur verlangteinen Tod,"* wrote Goethe: Nature demands a death. Blood must be spilled, whether in religious services (the wine becomes Christ's blood), in wars (with the unleashing of carnal instincts), or in the street (when momentary insanity overcomes an individual).[16]

The narrator's old friend, the actor Le Vigan, also appears on shipboard. Ready to be filmed in a historical movie, he is dressed as a gaucho, with spurs on his boots. Le Vigan is one of the few to escape Charon's oar. This might be due to the fact that, unlike the other passengers, who are passive, he, as a cowboy, is at least outwardly ready to fight, to lead an active life, to keep the herd in check.

What is the significance of the Ship of Death image? Is it an attempt, perhaps, to "reinvent the world," to use John Barth's expression? Certainly Céline gives us an insight into man's inadequate adaptation to life, a concrete figuration of a situation deteriorating both in terms of the viewer and of his society. Charon's activities are cruel. They lead to death and rotting of the flesh. As a representative of man's ego-dominated psyche, his desires must be gratified instantly. Charon also represents that aspect of the universe (or of the personality) which is in a constant state of antagonism, tension, and combat. As Rudolf Steiner wrote in *The Philosophy of Liberty:* "The process of the universe is a perpetual combat . . . which will end only with the annihilation of all existence. The moral life of man, then, consists in taking part in universal destruction."

The monster Charon indicates a dissatisfaction with the status quo, a desire to rid the world of its present political, economic, and spiritual structure based on nineteenth-century pseudo-idealism. World War II is but one manifestation of the "European sickness" that has now become a "world ailment." Man, if the monster within him is to continue its destructive bent, will sink into a regressive state, dominated by all the negative forces lying buried within its unconscious, forces that are transforming him into a criminal, into a one-sided, sordid being. Nothing in *From Castle to Castle* indicates any possibility of rebirth. It is a totally negative vision in which man, his civilization, even his destiny must be destroyed—his brains spread forth all over the "fluid" world—as a lesson for those who would try to rule such a conglomeration.

On an individual level, Céline's death-ship image, its crew, and its passengers represent, as we have seen, his shadow—always a problem to him because it never became integrated within his psyche. Since the narrator is protected by his dog, what this animal represents is not dragged under with the ship as it withdraws into the waters at the end of the scene. One might conclude, then, that the narrator's conscious attitude does not change. He is not swallowed up by the powers of darkness but merely views them as unassimilated negative agents. It is as if the author/narrator were standing at the edge of his conscious realm, peering into that deep maw which is his unconscious, a world of mystery.

Death, in the form of the passengers and of the entire hallucinatory vision, represents in this context the end of an epoch. Charon's destructive nature, as experienced through the narrator's projection, may be looked upon as a desire for self-destruction. The narrator's many death fantasies, of which the spectral ship is but one example, indicate an unconscious desire to withdraw from the world. But since he plays no active part in the vision, it implies a yearning for only a "partial suicide." [17]

THE CASTLE SIGMARINGEN

The castle of Sigmaringen, as viewed by Céline, leaves one with the "troubling power of an undiscarded nightmare." [18] The reader follows the narrator on to another level where thoughts, emotions, sentiments, after having been thrashed out, survive as self-contained figures forever gliding about in a boundless and timeless realm.

Céline's castle Sigmaringen is modeled after the one inhabited by the Hohenzollern family. It crowns a high rock from which one can see the right bank of the Danube, about fifty-five miles south of Tübingen on the road to Ulm. Its interior, furnished with rococco accoutrements, is dark. It is all very impressive but a bit frightening—as if some formidable spiritual power were contained in every room, watching and observing the world as it evolves about it.

Symbolically, darkness has frequently been equated with matter, with primordial darkness and primigenial chaos. In hermetic language, blackness or obscurity indicates a path leading to the profound mystery of the "Origin," an *obscurum per obscurius*. In *From Castle to Castle*, and particularly in the castle sequence, we find this chasmal condition to be present: a regressive area where evil curdles in a series of base forms, an oasis of unsublimated forces.

The Hohenzollerns had lived in this area ever since the eleventh century, as unimportant counts in the early times, as the imperial family of Germany by the nineteenth century. The family flourished because of its formidable army of soldiers, its capable officials, and its extremely severe, self-demanding ethical code. The family gave Germany a series of rather unimportant and uninspired rulers, as well as two relatively "unusual" monarchs: Frederick the Great, sometimes termed a "philosopher king," and William II, whose reign put an end to the entire kingdom. The Hohenzollern rule was based on absolutism and militarism. For this reason the empire, built on a thirst for glory, seemed bellicose. Even Frederick the Great, who was supposedly an intellectual, provoked a war to conquer Silesia, over which he had no rightful claim, and this, as he wrote, because his "age, the fire of [his] passion, [and] the thirst for glory" were uppermost in his personality.

The castle of Sigmaringen, as described by Céline, has a sinister look about it. It is marked by a cruel, aggressive, sadistic atmosphere. There is an absence of light, and the creatures who inhabit this domain are mutilated beings—dead people, deformed children, generals (Pétain, von Raumnitz, Abetz), government officials (Laval), mad surgeons who enjoy operating without anesthesia so they can watch their patients wail and moan, a female devourer, Aicha, who stands with her hounds outside of Room 36, waiting for her victims to enter and never reemerge, cancer patients, bands of nymphomaniacs, an insane vicar, and Jews who, Céline writes, "deserved to be arrested" because *they* have turned the entire area into a "ghetto." [19]

Céline's castle has no redeeming factors. It is his conception of hell: an enclosed area with a series of rooms with or without windows, false doors, false compartments, false closets, built over uneven floors in zig-zag formation, caves, trap doors, mazelike areas. The castle is comparable also to the catacombs, with their infinitely deep stairwells filled with the sick and dying.[20] In addition to the diseased (lice, fleas, syphilis) and the mentally deranged who live in and about the castle of Sigmaringen, there is a whole population of decapitated beings who run about the mazes gesticulating madly, screeching, and grunting (though they have no heads). The castle has a moat around it, a drawbridge, all manner of strange chimneys and crenelations, fantastic and irregular in aspect—like a fairy-tale castle inhabited by demons and gnomes.

Céline's nightmarish castle is reminiscent of the one featured in Wagner's *Götterdämmerung:* high on a mountaintop from which the Rhine is visible, a realm where the gods assemble and are finally consumed in flame, a type of premonitory symbol of future disaster.

In Céline's realm, a *massa confusa* of dark, ignominious, ominous forces, a region where depravity, decay, and degeneration, cohabit, one experiences thanatoid forces at work: death-wishing, death-dealing, comparable to the chthonic powers conjured up by the early Greeks (Harpies, Erinyes), the Arabs (Djinns), and the Germans (Valkyries). The destructive energy inherent in the thereomorphic deities worshiped in ancient times is also present in Céline's inhabitants. They exercise a subtle fascination over the narrator, mesmerizing him into a state of receptivity during which all attempts at judgment and evaluation fail. He seems to be caught in their destructive web.

For all its strangeness, the castle of Sigmaringen possesses a unique art gallery. Here paintings and statues of all types are preserved for future generations: equestrians, heads, nudes, portraits of the "sacred family" in all of its grandeur and decadence. They are a bizarre group, Céline intimates, creatures of dynasties who felt no shame, hunchbacks with bloated bellies.[21] The Hohenzollerns were comparable, Céline writes, to the famous murderers: Landru, Tropman, etc. "Here are the mugs . . . in series . . . fascinating . . . of a sick man . . ." [22] Five stories of paintings and statues! The tour through the galleries of Sigmaringen is reminiscent of Sartre's description, in *Nausea,* of the paintings hanging in the Museum of Bouville. Sartre, however, makes much of the remarks and attitudes of the self-satisfied, arrogant "bourgeois" viewers. Not so Céline.

Intellectuals also make their home in Céline's castle, which has fantastic library facilities for their use. The image of the various readers climbing ladders, pulling out books on so many periods in history, is striking. Many volumes are depicted in detail; they treat of momentous events such as religious and political revolutions and the brilliant tortures perfected by the Spartans, the Girondins, the Templars, the Communards, the Spaniards, the Nazi collaborators, the Hungarians fighting off the Russians, Saint Louis, Hitler . . .[23] Man is offered cruelties in all forms.

The library is depicted with verve and point and reminds one of the library that Rabelais featured in his Abbaye of Thélème. By way of contrast, however, it must be noted that whereas Rabelais' beliefs were positive in almost all domains, Céline's are negative. Rabelais, as a man of the Renaissance, believed that fine books elevated souls, that education helped man improve, that beautiful surroundings added to humanity's *joie de vivre.* Céline feels that man uses books (knowledge of all kinds) to destroy, defame, and crush, that despite the fact that man has existed for thousands of years, he has not really grown in the sense of perfecting his lot on earth. Nor does Céline believe, as Rabelais did, in the perfectibility of man.

Though the castle of Sigmaringen has its physically beautiful aspects (fine tapestries, china, magnificently carved wooden pieces, silver, glassware of the most exquisite designs), it also possesses objects that encourage vice, license, and murder (trophies, armaments, standards, emblems, bunkers, armored tanks, etc.) [24] Nine centuries of Hohenzollerns, driven by greed for gold and power, committed all kinds of transgressions, strangulations, hangings, mutilations, drownings.

The novel's long passages describing the material contents of the castle are an indication of the value that Céline himself put on matter and things monetary. Indeed, the word money itself is used so frequently in *From Castle to Castle* that it becomes quite obvious that the author has become its slave. Though he iterates his belief in aestheticism, he admits that "life costs a lot of money," [25] and that money itself possesses many "virtues." Moreover, he continues:

> Oh, if I were rich, I tell you, or if I even had Social Security, I'd watch all this disorder, all this dilapidation of hydrocarbon, lipides, and rubber, this crusade of gasoline, duck, and super-booze with Napoleonic calm! mamas, papas, jalopies . . . let them all be swallowed up . . . why not? Three cheers! But the trouble is . . . I haven't the wherewithal . . . can't afford it . . . that's all . . . and you're taken with resentment, bitterness, hatred . . . being splattered by those swine . . .[26]

Anger, resentment, hatred all vanish, Céline argues, once you have money; when money is plentiful, problems have a way of disappearing. Wagner, it is interesting to note, entertained similar notions and likewise suffered from the money disease.[27] Gold is of course the very subject matter of Wagner's *Das Rheingold,* and the entire Ring Cycle centers on the recapture of this treasure. Unlike Céline, however, Wagner was a compulsive spender who was convinced that money was meant to be "admired" and "enjoyed" and felt rancor when he had none. Like Wagner, Céline hated those who had money—people like Claudel, for example, who spent so many hours of so many days reading the stock pages, investing his gold, intent upon lucre—though the religion he claimed to profess extolled poverty.[28]

The castle of Sigmaringen and its residents may be looked upon as a microcosm of the world. It might be interesting to note, at this juncture, the difference between Céline's views of Sigmaringen and the views enunciated by Madame de Staël. Almost a century and a half had passed since she wrote her volume *On Germany* (1810), in which she offered a comparison between French and German culture, politics, and mores. A germanophile, she depicted the Germans as a sentimental and tender people, as a nation of scholars, musicians, philosophers, and poets—Lessing, Schiller, Goethe, Kant, etc. The Germans not only possessed creative spirit, but a profound soul. The French, she concluded, were superficial by comparison, cerebral and limited in their concepts.

Céline's view, as we have seen, is totally different. He sees the Black Forest region not as "romantic" but in terms of its gloom. The snowy realms, the striking beauty of the landscape with its high mountains, its ruler-straight trees jutting into the skies, are for him portentous, oracular pronouncements of doom. Hitler, too, was mesmerized and excited by the "awesomeness of the abysses" rather than by the "harmony of the landscape." [29]

For Céline, the castle represents negative forces at work. Its inhabitants have reached the "twilight" of their lives, and for this reason the castle is in a state of delapidation and decay. Since it no longer answers the needs of its people, there is no longer any reason for it to exist.

An edifice built high on a mountain, the castle descends deep into the bowels of the earth. It is a composite of forces at work in society as a whole and in Céline's subliminal world in particular. Its lower levels may be associated with a type of cave, an underworld, to which Céline has descended, a *katabasis eis antron,* or initiation ceremony, of the kind that Aeneas experienced when he entered the Temple of Apollo guarded by the Cumaen Sibyl. Aeneas emerged stronger in his outlook after his encounter with terrorizing forces.[30] Céline does not.

Who, or what, are the forces encountered by Celine's narrator?

What do they represent?

PERSONAL EVIL TRANSFORMED INTO COLLECTIVE FIGURES

One thousand, one hundred forty-two historical, mythological, and hallucinatory figures cohabit in Sigmaringen castle. Each lives in a room or else in an apartment, a "closed-off" area that can be viewed, psychologically, as a complex or phobia (those aspects of a man usually incompatible with his conscious attitude). The inhabitants, including Céline's narrator, are frequently hesitant about entering a room, just as one is anguished when trying to understand or experience a phobia or complex. There is, paradoxically, a certain ambivalence in attitude, a two-way action, which pulls one toward and pushes one away from one's goal. The energy created in this fashion can well be excessive, as we shall see.[31]

Pierre Laval lives on the second floor of the castle ("Thus are dynasties installed"), in an apartment well suited to a man who lusted after power: it is furnished in Empire style, with bees, eagles, velvets. Laval, a former member of the Chamber of Deputies (1914) and premier of France (1931–1936) had been unjustly accused by his compatriots, Céline's narrator implies. Verbal castigations are leveled at the inhabitants of Sigmaringen when they label Laval a Jew, a kike. Laval was a patriot, a pacifist, a "great conciliator," the narrator avers. It was Laval, was it not, who disclosed certain secrets concerning Roosevelt, Churchill, and the intelligence service? And although Laval was not overly enthusiastic about Hitler, he was convinced, nevertheless, that "one hundred years of peace" would ensue if the Führer ruled Europe.[32]

The narrator admires, then, a man whom Pétain had removed from office as vice-premier of the Vichy government in December, 1940, who was reinstated, through German pressure, as administrative chief-of-state, whose leadership encouraged extraordinarily repressive measures, and who was executed for high treason by a firing squad on October 15, 1945. It is difficult to understand Céline's reasoning when he calls pacifist a man who was willing to accept domination by the war-minded Nazis, at the expense of honor and integrity. One wonders also how pacifism can be equated with the activities of a nation whose very modus vivendi was based on conquest and genocide, who honored such types as SS Brigadeführer Heinrich Lämmerding, who had hundreds of innocent French men, women, and children slaughtered and then burned at Tulle and Oradour-sur-Glane (1944).[33]

Another "great" living at Sigmaringen is Henri-Philippe Pétain, whom Céline alludes to as "Philippe le Dernier, king of France," [34] and who lodges in no less than seven salons on the sixth floor. His apartment is filled with carvings of all types, rosewood tables, extraordinarily beautiful accoutrements and objects worth millions. He is France's World War I hero, a great of Sedan: "Oh, how you incarnate France, Monsieur the Marshal!" [35] According to Lord Lloyd, mentioned by William Shirer in *The Collapse of the Third Republic,* Pétain was "vain, senile and dangerously ga-ga." [36]

Céline has little admiration for this World War I hero, who had been commander-in-chief of the French army under Marshal Foch and president of the Council during World War II, who had signed the armistice with the Germans (1940), and then headed the Vichy government until 1944. The narrator feels that he was not forceful enough in bringing about a state of peace within his own government. Moreover, he is not overly impressed with Pétain's delusions of grandeur, his vanity, which so frequently blurs his lucidity and makes him self-satisfied with the laurels he has already won, rather than striving to create a giant and peaceful realm.

Other "admirable" dignitaries grace Sigmaringen. Admiral Darlan, for example, former commander-in-chief of the French navy who had proposed scuttling of the fleet during the early months of the German occupation so that neither the Germans nor the British could acquire it. As Minister of Marine under Pétain, he pursued a policy of collaboration with the Germans. Yet when he saw the tide turning, he left for Algiers to join the Allies. He was assassinated on Christmas Eve, 1942. It is understandable that the narrator should describe him as having a "haunted look." [37]

Baron von Raumnitz, the Nazi commandant, has his secret headquarters on the second floor. His rooms are always filled with flowers for himself and his entourage.[38] Judging from the flowers decorating his room—azaleas, hydrangeas, narcissus, roses—one might infer that he resembles one of those young "flower gods" of the Greeks (Hyacinth, Narcissus), all of whom were homosexuals (having been emotionally castrated by the destroyer-woman type). The name "Raumnitz"—a composite of *Raum,* meaning room, a female symbol, and *Raumnasz,* signifying a measure or capacity or strength—might indicate an affinity with Ernst Röhm, the homosexual thug responsible for organizing and training the "strong" *Sturmabteilungen,* the storm troopers. Once one of Hitler's close friends, Röhm was murdered when he was of no further use to the Führer.[39]

Von Raumnitz, like Ernst Röhm, is a brutal individual having little if any warmth in his make-up. His wife, Aicha, a type of death-goddess, symbolizes the castrating feminine principle. One usually refers to this type of man as a *puer aeternus,* as a psychologically undeveloped person who has evidently experienced a "delayed puberty" and for this reason displays courage only very spasmodically.[40] Both von Raumnitz and Ernst Röhm are comparable to the modern British "Teddy Boys" and the American "Hell's Angels" (and similar motorcycle gangs) who hide inner weaknesses under facades of courage, bravery, and cruelty.

The Militia also make its headquarters in the castle. This group of soldiers, described so brilliantly by Jean Genet in his novel *Funeral Rites,* is seen in *From Castle to Castle* as having covered itself with glory under the German occupation of France.[41] The members of the Militia never felt any pangs of conscience when shooting down and mutilating their countrymen. Indeed, killing was their sport and, according to Céline's narrator, they had even fewer scruples than the invading Germans.

General Abetz, Hitler's ambassador in Paris during the German occupation, also lives in the castle. He invites the narrator to dinner. They eat in a small dining room because the general, a bit paranoiac, fears bomb attempts, particularly since Hitler's life was jeopardized in this fashion some years back. Abetz is a stout man, well shaven, and when he speaks he commands everyone's attention. He is a visionary, the narrator declares, who seeks to re-create an empire out of the disparate states of Europe, an empire like that of Charlemagne. This empire, about which the narrator is very enthusiastic, would bring peace to the world. In many ways, what Abetz suggests is reminiscent of Hitler's "Teutonic Empire of the German Nation." Abetz plans to erect stone statues to Charlemagne and to his peers on the Place de la Défense in Paris, and also statues to von Rundstedt, Goebbels, and other heralds of things-to-come—modern counterparts, he declares, of Roland, Olivier, etc.

Heinrich Hoffmann, Hitler's personal photographer, is likewise invited to Abetz' dinner. It was Hoffmann one recalls, who introduced Hitler to Doctor Theodor Morell, a man in whom the Führer had much confidence until 1937, when Morell's "quack methods" began to fail.[42]

The third guest, Alphonse de Chateaubriant, the author of a pro-German book, *La Gerbe des forces,* was a "fanatical worshipper" of Hitler. He saw him as a "Christ-like being" and in 1937 he made a pilgrimage to Germany to look upon this god. Chateaubriant was convinced—absurd as it may seem—that National Socialism was based upon Christian humanism and Christian ideals. He was determined to see peace established with his German neighbors, whom he believed to be noble in spirit. After the Liberation he was condemned to death *in absentia.*[44]

The fact that the narrator dines with Abetz, Hoffmann, and Chateaubriant, indicates, symbolically speaking, that a communion is felt among these people and their ideas. The sharing of food, whether actually or in fantasy, implies a type of "ceremonial union." In former times people believed that when you dined at someone's house you were responsible toward your host and he, likewise, to you. Dining, then, indicates a kind of harmony, a positive and dynamic relationship.[45] Such an interpretation is certainly applicable in this case, since Céline's narrator does believe in a unification of the European states under the wings of the German eagle.

As for the narrator, he claims never to have concealed his feelings of hatred, contempt, and disgust for the Jews (among others), and when feeling particularly dejected, he rants and raves against them—just as Hitler did.[46] He is not an opportunist, he claims, as so many other Frenchmen were when they saw that the Free French forces were gaining the upper hand, and when the Allies landed in North Africa, turning the tide of the war. He is not, he feels, an Admiral Darlan, who sided with Pétain at first and later entered the Allied fold, or a Flandin, who served in Pétain's government as foreign minister and then changed his opinions, or a Camille Chautemps, who acted for the Vichy government in a semi-official capacity in Washington. Nor is he comparable in his outlook to such writers as Paul Claudel, who composed "an impassioned ode in praise of Pétain" in the early days of Vichy—and another ode, "in almost identical words," to General de Gaulle when it began to appear that he would emerge the victor. Nor has he changed his opinions, as did François Mauriac, who went into ecstasies at the sound of the voice of the hero-marshal calling upon the country to accept defeat and to get back to work. Mauriac had indeed written, in *Le Figaro* (July 3, 1940): "The words of Marshal Pétain on the evening of June 25 had a sound that was almost intemporal. It was not a man who spoke to us, but something out of the profound depths of our History. This old man was delegated to us by the dead of Verdun." [47] Mauriac too, like Claudel and others, had switched his allegiance to Charles de Gaulle when this leader came to power. Paul Valéry, André Gide, and how many more had shared in the unmitigated admiration of Pétain. The narrator refers to these people as hideous opportunists. No reference is made, of course, to Céline-the-narrator's flight from France after D-day.

Finally a movie director Raoul Orphize (Orpheus?) arrives at Sigmaringen. He wants to make a film based on daily life in both castle and town. The narrator wants no part of the enterprise. He is despondent and expresses negative views concerning the whole project. Orphize, on the other hand, feels strongly about the endeavor and tries to inspire the narrator with fervor. The picture will be shown all over France, he declares, and will arouse favorable reactions. It will be a lasting memento, a testimony to those living at Sigmaringen, a defense of their activities. And it will likewise satisfy people's need for illusion presented as reality.[48] It is interesting to note in this connection that when Hitler viewed a film of the bombing of Warsaw in 1939, he was absolutely transfixed as he watched the sky blacken, the bombs being released, the explosions sounding. At the end of the film, when a "montage" was shown of the planes diving toward the British Isles with ensuing flames, Hitler's enthusiasm was unparalleled. He spoke out vehemently: "That is what will happen to them! That is how we will annihilate them!" [49] Such is the reaction Raoul Orphize anticipates, once his film is shown to Parisians.

Other festivities are also planned at Sigmaringen, including an apotheosis to German victory, a type of *Walpurgisnacht*, a Witches' Sabbath, in which the Devil himself will be present and thrill to the occasion.

Along with the parties, the political issues, the films, there is a cancer ward in Sigmaringen. Cancer seems to be invading the entire scene. It is in the narrator's capacity as doctor that he cares for the advanced cases. The descriptions given are so vivid, so detailed, that each word carries affective power and may be defined as that type of "compound code" which John Barth described as something with a "simple surface" but with "enormous complexity beneath," that is, like a "maze of termite tunnels" in "joists" or "intricate cancer" in a "perfect breast." [50]

The narrator describes tumors of all sizes and shapes—bulbous, bloody, growing like parasites, excrescences, some so elongated that they can be pulled; some women can even be hung up by "their tumors." Hysterectomies are always in order: women are in need of being emptied like "rotted rabbits." [51] Cancer has become a scourge.

When depicting the cancer ward at Sigmaringen, the narrator associates, in typically Surrealistic manner, with analogous experiences he has had in Denmark. A shifting of scene, therefore, occurs. The reader finds himself in the Danish prison in which the narrator had been incarcerated, and in Sonby Hospital, also in Denmark, where he had been forced to work in the cancer ward.

The narrator speaks of his own sickness, of the dampness of the cell in which he had been imprisoned, of the months of solitary confinement, of the loss of weight (forty kilos), of the pellagra, of the lugubrious Baltic land with its cloudy skies, its lightless days, its high seas. Solitary, anguished, he writes that he used to look across the sea from his prison cell to Malmö, a small Swedish town, yearning for freedom.

The very mention of the city of Malmö is interesting from two points of view: the first, because the narrator looked upon this land as an escape route, a liberation from the humiliations of what he considered to be an unjustified incarceration; the second, an ironic association indeed, because it was to this very town that the Danish underground, in 1943, smuggled eight thousand Jews in two weeks. The latter momentous event took place shortly after Hitler had given the orders to deport Danish Jews to extermination camps. Hitler's men had chosen the High Holy days as the perfect moment to carry out their plan. The Danes, in an extraordinary show of courage and heroism—literally at the risk of their lives and those of their families and friends—refused to permit the murder of their people—of "Danes of Jewish religion." In the blackness of night, the people huddled together in small rowboats and made their way in silence to Malmö and to freedom. The trip was exceedingly difficult and dangerous. Not only was it completely dark, but German submarines infested the area. So that the boats would not lose their way, one person in each boat held hands with someone in the next. And so they were saved.[51] The narrator probably did not know of this incident, perhaps one of the most heroic in history. Even if he had, he would have castigated the Danes all the more for having dealt so severely with him, a "guiltless" individual.

Other medical prodigies besides the narrator live at Sigmaringen: Czechoslovakians, Germans, and twelve French doctors, ten of whom are insane. One in particular, however, is outstanding: a mad surgeon who operates by cutting peoples' heads off. His method: first, sever the ear, then gouge out the eyes, and finally cut the entire globulous mass away from the torso. He is always pictured with scalpel in hand, very nearly salivating as he watches more and more patients pass by. Indeed, it is he who single-handedly creates the headless population that runs about frantically at Sigmaringen.

Also to be found in this mad array are children with bloated bellies who rush about in the Black Forest gathering wood, screaming, groaning, and giving voice to their hysterics.[52] There are special camps for the internment of collaborator's children.[53] For the most part, the children in *From Castle to Castle* are depicted as disgusting, ugly, dirty, sex-obsessed little creatures, and yet worthy of some small measure of pity, since they are, after all, the victims of egotistical and demoniacal parents.

Generally speaking, children are traditionally equated in literature and art with joy and with hope; they are an awakening force. The children who figure in *From Castle to Castle* are despairing and decaying forces. Symbolically they may be looked upon as unconscious, unformed, unprotected entities having few if any propensities for a positive existence and incapable of attaining any kind of consciousness. They lack brains (they have no heads); they are all brawn—and not too much of that. When they laugh, it is hideously grotesque, raucous; their features are contorted, distorted—a rictus engraved on their "headless countenances."

The insane—if we may distinguish them from the grotesques mentioned so far—also have a place in the monstrous castle of Sigmaringen. Céline, as one might well imagine, had always been preoccupied with the question of insanity. In his very first work, that on Semmelweis, he had declared that this courageous doctor had been driven insane by society's failure to understand him. And in *Journey to the End of the Night*, we recall the protagonist is interned in a mental institution and later on works in one as a doctor.

The narrator of *From Castle to Castle* depicts the visions of the insane in an extraordinary manner. One of the most striking and perhaps fascinating portraits in the entire volume is that of the Cathar Bishop of Albi who tells the narrator that he has been persecuted ever since 1209. He then asks the narrator whether he is a Cathar. When the answer is negative, the man of God asks him to help him acquire a permit giving him permission to attend the Synod of Fulda.[54] The image of the bishop walking through the crowds, blessing each and every one just before the worshipers are to be led to slaughterhouses, is awesome and unforgettable.

The women peopling Sigmaringen and its environs, as perceived by the narrator, are mere functions. They are, for the most part, highly sensual, aggressive, ruthless, cruel, and domineering types. Strictly biological in their outlook, they proceed instinctively, with little or no spirituality. Because of their virility, they are comparable to the Valkyries, the offspring of Wotan and the earth goddess Erda. The Valkyries, it will be recalled, were warrior-maidens whose function was to retrieve fallen heroes and bring them back to Valhalla, where they would fight as an army in defense of the gods.

A variety of Valkyrie-like females live at Sigmaringen. Some are old, decrepit, ugly, paralytic; others are young, bold, beautiful; some have ticks, others warts on their noses; some are sexual deviates, others not. Since most of these women inhabit the lower depths of Sigmaringen, their madness might be reminiscent of the concoctions dreamed up by Jean Giraudoux' Madwoman of Chaillot, but with one significant exception: the latter's endeavors served to bring forth love and peace in the world; Céline's madwomen are agents of destructions and symbols of hate.

Aicha von Raumnitz, the wife of the commandant, wears red boots and when she walks her hips are forever undulating provocatively. She is as strong as her name indicates: *Eiche,* an oak tree in German, and *Aichen,* a gauge or standard, may be associated with the fact that Aiche measures the worth of human beings much as did Isis and Osiris in the Egyptian underworld.

Aicha is always accompanied by her hounds, which obey her orders instantaneously. They show their fangs when necessary, they growl, and at a second's notice will tear someone apart, like "hyenas," if she so wills.[55] In this respect her dogs are "devourers of soul." When Frau Aicha enters a room panic sets in.[56] Everyone moves away, slowly at first, then with greater alacrity. It is she who holds the keys to Room 36, a "superprison" into which people such as a garage mechanic, the insane bishop of Albi, two old men, and a nurse, among others, are compelled to enter secretly at night, never to be heard of again. The narrator is curious about the contents of this room but he never dares enter it because there is no exit.

Dogs and other animals (monkeys, centipedes, tigers, cats) figure in all of Céline's works, either as protectors or destroyers, as dark forces emanating from a subliminal world, as representatives of instincts. Hagar, in the ship episode, is the narrator's protector, his servant. Aicha's hounds are also protectors, to be sure, since they do not permit anything or anyone to harm their mistress. They may also be looked upon as scavengers, warriors of sorts, comparable in strength to Cerberus in Pluto's realm, whose function was to prevent any of the "shades" from returning to the upper world (thereby demolishing any possibility for atonement or salvation). These animals are to a certain extent Charon's counterpart in the Ship of Death sequence.

Aicha's dogs are negative forces in that they represent a certain kind of "madness." Symbolically, dogs are looked upon in this manner because they are the carriers of hydrophobia, which represents unassimilated evil in the psyche. Like the Valkyries, who possessed their horses, so Aicha has her hounds, who execute the death sentence upon whom she chooses, as the Norse women did when spying a hero on a battlefield.

Aicha can be equated, then, with the Goddess of Death in that she sentences others to their doom. Indeed, Aicha possesses "divine" aspects because she exemplifies the merciless and inhuman characteristics in women, the "superhuman" and transcendental qualities that belong to the gods alone.[57]

The "door" through which Aicha's victims enter, never to reappear, is also indicative of her nefarious points of view. The door may be seen as a facade, a cover or wall hiding the room's contents, a feminine symbol. The room, symbolic of a womb or hole, is frequently looked upon as Mother Nature's representative, the implication being that Aicha is the guardian of all the beings and forces that return to Mother Nature and are devoured by her—nourishing, sustaining, and restoring her to power, at the expense of the sacrificial victims she sends through the door into Room 36.

Who are Aicha's victims? What forces do they represent? A garage mechanic, symbolizing the modern industrial society; the insane, namely, the vicar standing for all those who are unable to relate to society and whose religion is no longer valid; two old men, sterile forces without any procreating capacity; a nurse, the female healing principle that has vanished from the world.

Another inhabitant of the narrator's realm is Frau Frucht, whose name, associated with *Furcht* ("fear") and *Frucht* ("fruit"), is indicative of her personality. She is both fruit-bearing and fear-instilling. Men serve her as men served Circe, Astarte, and Ishtar. The Female Principle that she represents has overpowered the Male forces in society. The sexual symbol as represented by her is, therefore, impersonal, unrelated to anything, similar to the rites practised by the followers of Dionysos. Heraclitus' statement equating Hades and Dionysos is applicable to Frau Frucht.

The men and women permitted in Frau Frucht's apartment, Room 15, are virile. She is a degenerate, in Céline's view: a sexual deviate, a nymphomaniac, a lesbian.[58] Her rooms, a fitting background for her orgies, are furnished in Second Empire style, symbolizing the rococco and the decadent, the end rather than the beginning of an era. Antique dealers in France, who depend so heavily upon this period of *ameublement* to further their trade, would be overjoyed to view Frau Frucht's quarters, with its circular sofas, its ornate bathtubs, its sculptured dragons, its Muses, etc. It is here that the sexual rites take place. Frau Frucht is madness personified, a reincarnation of the Maenads, the Furies, and the Bacchantes all wrapped into one. War excites her sexually; danger and excitement tantalize her.

Young girls are much in evidence in the castle and environs of Sigmaringen. Alluded to ironically by the narrator as "the young flower girls of Sigmaringen," they are reminiscent of Hitler's "League of German Maidens." These girls, ranging in age from fourteen years on up, are permanently pregnant. They are whores, the daughters of fine military or diplomatic families, who have gone mad sexually. Hilda, the sixteen-year-old daughter of Aicha von Raumnitz, and her band frequent railroad stations waiting for fresh troops to arrive. They love to make love and certainly are convinced that "life on earth must have started in a railroad station . . . you see girls in droves . . . Hilda and her group, services immediately rendered." [59] War titilates these girls and provides them with a raison d'être.[60]

There is one scene in which the fleshiness of these young girls, their lethargy, their idleness, their dissoluteness is described in terms flamboyant enough to dissuade any sane woman from ever engendering. A group of these pregnant Valkyrie types, happy to serve the Fatherland in their procreative capacity, are standing around the piano, or lolling about on sofas, in the living room of the castle. They are all in their sixth or eight month. Their double and triple appetites, the ugliness of their configurations, their ignorance, their utter instinctuality is just one more indication of the narrator's opinion of women in general, one aspect of a horde of humans who deserve to be destroyed.[61]

The only "decent" women who figure in *From Castle to Castle* are a receptionist, Madame Mitre *(miter),* who patiently listens to peoples' complaints,[62] and Lili, the narrator's wife, equally innocuous. Passive in all respects, they both emerge as amorphous entities.

Women, as depicted by Céline, resemble only one aspect of the Eternal Feminine, the destructive aspect. They are primary images of the Great Mother archetype. His women are destroyers who seduce men and make them mere instruments of pleasure (Frau Frucht), who devour men (Aicha), and who arouse the nubile (young girls) for procreative purposes. Women are positive only in their procreative function. Yet even this aspect, though considered an asset, takes on negative overtones in *From Castle to Castle.* What they give birth to are more monsters, more deviates, more maimed beings who will pursue the sordid game of life.

When women are viewed as negative aspects of the Great Mother archetype they can also be looked upon, symbolically, as devouring aspects of the unconscious. In this capacity they have been equated, because of their physical and psychic energy, with the Greek Furies, since they are associated with vengeance, conflict, insanity and death. Women of this type are manics: conveyers of energy, wildness, intoxication. Because of their destructive nature, their virulence, and their inability to feel or to understand, they may stand for an area within the male psyche that is "split off," unrelated to the whole, dissociated with consciousness. They are autonomous in their acts and attitudes and therefore possess little or no understanding of eternal or spiritual values. They take on an obsessive existence of their own, one that leads to schizoid tendencies and psychotic disturbances.

The female types created by Céline, and upon whom he projects, have lost all capacity for discernment and for feeling. Women add to the darkness that has invaded his soul, to the lugubrious atmosphere of the Sigmaringen episode: to the twilight of the gods who dwell within—to the Götterdämmerung.

As we have already noted, Céline's approach to both history and people was irrational. By constantly castigating the "others" as being responsible for his problems, he tried to rid himself of the blame for his inertia during the war, his acceptance of German ways, and his flight from France (among other things). Céline felt no sense of moral conflict. He refused to acknowledge any kind of personal guilt, any kind of personal responsibility toward other individuals and toward society.

Céline's view of himself and others had not changed with the passage of time. What had changed was the fact that he now could live with his shadow problem, with his hate. The anger he had once felt *(Guignol's Band I)* was no longer a self-destructive force. It no longer corroded his very fiber. It had become part of his blood and flesh and being.

Intuitive, like Hitler, Céline both knew and sought to force emotional responses from his readers and was always able in this way to give vent to his overpowering hatred. Like the German dictator, Céline was a master at arousing hatreds, creating conflagrations, using primitive, archaic, dynamic arguments.

Céline's realm is reminiscent in many ways of that depicted by Breughel in his *Madmen's Feast,* a realm that harbored the monstrous and engendered the perverse. Céline was a kind of fisherman who dredged up his subliminal materials in the form of fantasies and hallucinations and served them up to his readers in all their sinister, destructive, demoniacal horror.

12

NORTH

The artist's eye should always be turned in upon his inner life and his ear should always be alert for the voice of inward necessity. This is the only way of giving expression to what the mystic vision commands.

Kandinsky in C. G. JUNG, *Man and His Symbols*

North IS THE QUINTESSENCE OF CÉLINE'S POSTWAR WORK. Though written in 1960, after *From Castle to Castle* (1957), it relates his peregrinations through Germany (Baden-Baden, Berlin, Kränzlin) before he reached Sigmaringen.

North is a final ecstatic, explosive thrashing-out of the wreckage that was Céline's inner world. The spectacular nature of the terror-imparting images reaches searing proportions; ugliness and hate are experienced visually and aurally (with accompanying accoustics, resonances, and vibrations) as well as concretely, as metallic or wooden objects shooting through space, bruising anything in their path. A world clothed in horror and drenched in vice rises up and jars the reader. More important, however, than the breadth of the hallucinatory vision portrayed in the novel is Céline's revelation of the Great Mystery.

North deals with a solemn initiation into Céline's cult, in which the outcome is not fertility—as it had once been in the Eleusinian or Kabeiroi rites celebrated in ancient Greece—but sterility, not atonement and purification but depravity and decay, not light but darkness.

Surprising differences may be discerned between *North* and *From Castle to Castle, Guignol's Band, Fairy-Play for Another Time I and II.* In the earlier novels we noted the tremendously accelerated rhythms with which the events were related, rhythms reflecting the author's chaotic inner world. Coherent passages were the exception. The events related were usually spun out in fits of menacing rage, in irrational spells, in bouts with tremulous and ambiguous forces within him. Anxieties, repressed by the author in Germany and in the Danish prison, gushed out after his return to France, and did so with such vigor and violence as to incapacitate his rational function—always weak at best—rendering it unable to withstand the onslaught. The result: the very nearly complete inability to peer through the turgid waters of his unconscious, to unravel the raw emotions. In *From Castle to Castle* we noted a change. The primitive forces, though still welling up within him, had simmered down slightly. With a concomitant slowing down of pace, images became more sharply delineated.[1]

The relative quiescence of *North* (particularly the first two sections, the third being less tempered) reveals the breadth of Céline's skilled literary techniques. The novel has taken on the stature of a structured work, with an outline, organization, and recounting of events along relatively fixed lines, an assertion one can certainly not make when referring to either *Guignol's Band* or *Fairy-Play for Another Time.*

PLOT

The author, his wife, and his cat Bebert stay at the Hotel Simplon, a luxury establishment located in Baden-Baden, Germany's famous thermal station. It is here that the elite—the high Nazi functionaries, magnates of the Ruhr, aristocrats, collaborators, exiles—are housed. Though the rest of Germany suffers the rigors of war, the inhabitants of the Simplon Hotel eat extraordinary foods (caviar, champagne) brought in almost daily by parachute. They dwell in an atmosphere of ease and plenty. The narrator—Céline—is asked by the hotel management to dispense medical care. He is taken to see the sick in the various hotel rooms and witnesses feastings, sexual orgies, etc. One day, the chancellor orders the evacuation of the hotel.

Céline, wife, and cat are on their way to Berlin. They meet the narrator's actor friend Le Vigan. They live in a bombed-out hotel for a few days, eat poor food. Finally Doctor Harras, a high Nazi official, helps them obtain their papers.

The third and longest phase of the narrator's odyssey is perhaps the most spectacular. Doctor Harras takes the narrator, his wife and cat, and his actor friend to Zornhof (Kränzlin), a vast domain owned by members of the German nobility. There farmers, peasants, Polish and Russian deportees, French prisoners of war, collaborators, conscientious objectors, prostitutes, a policeman, a pastor, and an SS man all live together; each feels an unbridled hatred for the others. Doctor Harras gives Céline the key to the supply closet, admonishes him to give nothing away, and returns to Berlin. Under pressure from the inhabitants of the estate whose rations are skimpy, the narrator doles out cigarettes, liquor, and whatever else they wish. Strikingly sordid incidents are depicted: a spectacle given by gypsies, the violence and murderous instincts inherent in a paraplegic's personality and his death in a cesspool, prostitutes beating up old men, the cutting up of dead horses, scenes of lasciviousness, etc. Finally, the narrator, his wife, and other survivors are told to leave the estate. Traveling on a weird cart drawn by twenty cows, they make their way out of this strange land.

Gaston Gallimard, the publisher of *North,* incurred a lawsuit fifteen months after the volume's publication and two months after the author's death. A Berlin lawyer demanded that *North* be withdrawn from circulation. His client, a Mrs. S—z, claimed that she and her entire family had been slandered by Céline and that his assertions allegedly concerning them, in *North,* were false.

Her husband, she declared, had suffered infantile paralysis at the age of fourteen and had been left a paraplegic. He had not been insane and had not wanted to kill her—nor had she tried to poison him. She was, moreover, not a nymphomaniac, as Céline had depicted her. Her father, a captain of cavalry who had died in 1947 at the age of eighty-three, was an honorable man and had not had himself whipped by young female Polish deportees living on his estate, or had children by them, or ever "urinated" with them, as Céline had asserted.

Gallimard withdrew *North* from circulation and suspended all translations. The legal battle dragged on for three years. The press, ironically enough, gave the case enormous publicity, naming real names and incidents—the very ones that Mrs. S—z had tried to conceal. On March 22, 1965, a third judgment from the West Berlin court was handed to Gallimard, compelling the publisher to pay six thousand Deutsche marks to Mrs. S—z and three thousand Deutsche marks to each of her children.

BADEN-BADEN

The interest of the Baden-Baden episode is two-fold: it analyzes the types to whom Céline's narrator relates and it reenacts the first of a series of mystery cult rituals.

Baden-Baden, one of the most beautiful areas in all of Germany, lies on the outskirts of the Black Forest. It is a thermal station, in vogue ever since the eighteenth century, where such illustrious figures as Madame de Staël, Benjamin Constant, and Hector Berlioz partook of the waters. The dichotomy existing between the beauties of nature and man's mutilation of this giant force is brought forth pointedly by Céline: the Black Forest, with its huge pines, its mountains, its strikingly blue skies, its bold and courageous forms, is contrasted with Allied bombings in the distance, blazing fires, reddening skies, incendiary rockets pouring out like so many drops of coagulated blood—making the earth shake with rage.

In the Simplon Hotel (known in former editions as the "Brenner," meaning to burn, as if Céline were burning his bridges behind him) there live only people of wealth. Their lush existence, their bloated bellies, their prodigious consummation of caviar, salmon, cognacs of all sorts, and other delicacies underlines the social inequities existing in societies and among nations. Céline, it must be recalled, was far from adopting a socialist or communist point of view. Convinced that the poor were as ignominious as the rich, he did not favor any redistribution of wealth; given wealth and material possessions, the have-nots become as possessive, domineering, and aggressive as any aristocracy. Céline might be called an ethical nihilist. He is convinced of the perversity of social, political, and economic institutions as they stand, have stood, and will probably stand in the future; yet to destroy these institutions would serve no purpose, since they are made up of human beings who, if not evil at the outset of their project, become so as their power increases.

Céline's ethos, in this connection, could be likened to that of Jean Genet. Both men are convinced of man's basically evil nature. When Genet wrote *The Blacks* (1957) it was not to glorify this race. He was under no "illusions." Nor for that matter would he shed tears over the fate of any minority group.

If Black society were supreme, he reasoned, it would be no different from White society. In fact, it would be merely a mirror image of it.[2]

To whom does Céline relate? With whom does he sympathize? The insane, the passive, and certain animals.

Frau von Dopf, an older woman who lives at the Hotel Simplon, is pleasantly insane. She speaks incessantly of Metternich, whom she thinks is still alive; of her husband, the general, who had taken her to Italy, Spain, and China (where he helped Mao reorganize his army); and of her jewelry, furs, and tapestries.[3] Clearly, Frau von Dopf lives in another realm, a world of fantasy, and can in no way relate to the sanguinary events troubling her era. When she talks of the past and of her husband, she seems to slip into another dimension where contentment, warmth, and security reign. Céline's descriptions of her are handled with finesse and unusual warmth, indicating a certain sympathy—mitigated to suit his personality—for the weak, the passive, the sick.

Clearly, Céline has nothing to fear from the mildly insane. They cannot hurt him and, as a doctor, he knows he can handle them. In fact, he has something in common with people who live in a realm of fantasy, who are not governed by logical rules, who do not proceed rationally in their evaluation of people and things. Their minds escape the constrictions of mental processes, as his does. He has always been incapable of Cartesian thinking. His feelings are constantly vacillating and his points of view are arrived at summarily.

To be sure, the insane observe the world in a rather primitive manner. But "normal" people can slip into such a world of fantasy when their concentration lapses. At such times, individuals play the roles that real life might deny them. They can also experience sensations they might wish to express in their daily existence but cannot. Fantasies enable the participant to repudiate what he fears or wishes to annihilate, without necessarily experiencing punishment or guilt. Fantasy also acts as a compensatory factor for people suffering from feelings of inadequacy.[4]

When fantasizing, an individual is actually selecting his own emotions, sifting them out or bringing them together in new ways. Such activity may help him adjust to the world about him. A writer may create a whole new world through his fantasies, as Céline did, revealing in symbolic form whatever is intolerable to him or whatever might be longed for—moments of extreme pain or ecstatic joy.

Céline expresses, through his fictional characters, certain ambiguities in his personality and in society. Each figure in *North* represents a "wide spectrum of emotional associations."[5]

Mlle. de Chamarande, a gorgeous, voluptuous, sensual French girl who goes swimming daily in the Hotel Simplon pool, represents an aspect of the Eternal Feminine. Each time she parades at the pool, she wears a still-more-revealing bathing suit, attracting every male eye. Once she had been in love with a lawyer, a member of the French Militia, but a few days before their marriage, her fiance was killed by French patriots. She was able to flee France, thanks to the help of the SS; had the French caught her, she would most certainly have been condemned to prison or worse. The Germans treated her with the utmost graciousness, enjoyed watching her bathe, and were captivated by her undulating form. Indeed, Céline writes, she had conquered the entire German contingent.[6]

For Céline, such a woman represents youth, health, vigor—everything Hitler tried to create in such movements as the "League of German Maidens." Her body weaves arabesques in space as she walks by. Her exquisite physical lines are a joy to behold. Her soul is unimportant.[7] In some ways, the narrator identifies with Mlle. de Chamarande: they both fled France fearing reprisals from patriots and were well received by German dignitaries. But unlike Mlle. de Chamarande, a type of youthful fertility goddess, the narrator is neither healthy nor strong.

The narrator also identifies unconsciously with another character, Fräulein Fisher, Doctor Schulz' secretary. She is ugly. She was a collaborator during the war and has a red spot on her cheek. Céline compares her to Quasimodo and, to increase her unaesthetic nature, he makes her near-sighted. One might look upon Fräulein Fisher as a creature whose attitude toward life has been bogged down in her own pettiness. Her lack of courage, her deceitful nature, her inability to adopt to a forthright and clear-cut point of view during the war—all this is, so to speak, written all over her face. The inner world, amorphous in nature, became concretized once it emerged to the light of consciousness. Fräulein Fisher might be considered a type of "memory character," a phenomenon that has emerged within the narrator's psyche and that he recalls to consciousness when necessary. Consciously, of course, the narrator is convinced that he is totally unlike Fräulein Fisher—convinced that he was not a collaborator.

Symbols, such as the key, also play an important role in the first section of *North*. Doctor Schulz has asked one of his trusted officials to accompany Céline on his visits to the sick inhabitants of the hotel and to use the passkey to let him into the various rooms. Though Céline is not the holder of the key, he is, symbolically speaking, a type of thaumaturge—a magician or miracle worker. It is his task to unravel the enigma—that is, to diagnose the patients' illnesses. He therefore becomes a type of father image, a supreme manipulator, a figure of importance, rather than society's victim, a pariah, which he feels (unconsciously) that he is at this period.

Doctor Schulz has made one proviso: the narrator must never discuss his patients' illnesses. This interdict may be associated with others famous in mythology: the order given to Orpheus when conducting Eurydice out of Hell, or those so freely handed out in fairy tales.

What do such interdicts imply? They usually indicate some kind of test that a hero must pass. But there are no heroes in any of Céline's works, no powerful men or god-men capable of overcoming evil, of freeing people from destruction, death, or decay; no Theseus to kill the Minotaur, no Perseus to destroy the Gorgon, no David to annihilate Goliath. The hero myth, so important throughout history as a symbolic representation of an individual's growth, maturity, and increased consciousness, is totally absent.

In going through various difficult tests the hero gains insight into himself through confrontation; he assesses his worth and becomes more aware of his own inner strengths and weaknesses. Looked upon as part of an initiation ritual, such a test would imply the necessity for a revelation of sorts, an initiation into a mystery. Adherents of the Dionysian cults were initiated into their orgiastic rites by means of fasting and the imbibing of wine or a magic brew. The wine brought about a lowering of consciousness, making it possible for the novices to perceive the secrets of nature. The followers of Orpheus, on the contrary, underwent a more spiritual initiation ceremony and experienced their religious joy inwardly.[8]

Céline's role or function in the Simplon Hotel is ambiguous. He is confronted with an enigma, an obligation, and at the same time he is invested with power. He has a key-bearer at his disposal and thus possesses a *rite d'entrée,* the equipment necessary to unravel and perhaps solve the mystery. When he enters the various rooms he is, psychologically speaking, entering closed-off areas within his own subliminal world (or complexes), areas usually incompatible with conscious points of view.[9] Yet he does not act, despite the fact that he is equipped to do so; he remains passive, an observer.

What does he find when he enters Room 113, the first on Doctor Schultz' list? A bacchanalian orgy. The room is dark except for a single flickering candle. A woman, naked under an open robe, makes her way to him and begins kissing him. Slowly other forms become discernible: a bus boy from the hotel, a manicurist, a commander, etc. As the narrator's eyes become accustomed to the darkness, he sees people massaging each other lasciviously and uttering incantations. The odor of incense permeates the atmosphere. A large photograph of Hitler hangs upside down on the wall, draped with pieces of black crepe across its frame. The participants in the orgy are celebrating Hitler's death, though he may not be dead after all: they realize that the bomb they set (or perhaps only imagined they set) may never have gone off.[10]

What Céline is describing is his version of the Eleusinian mystery ritual: an entrée into another phase of existence. In ancient times, to participate in the mystery meant to liberate oneself from one's personal ineffectiveness and wretchedness and to be endowed with strength, with an almost godlike quality. By worshiping the fertility deities (Demeter, Persephone, Dionysos) one was imbued with the strength and power of Mother Earth.[11] The rites of the Eleusinian and Dionysian mystery cults, celebrated by women and men, respectively, were frequently enacted in a bloody manner, with the eating of a dismembered goat or bull, a symbol of fertilization. In the Orphic ritual, "the victim must be torn asunder and devoured." [12] The worship of the Great Mother goddess, of which the mysteries were a manifestation, permitted man to become a fecundating force, a dispenser of power and joy. Christianity suppressed these ancient mystery cults.

When the narrator enters the hotel room he sees a microcosm of a matriarchal society at work—a fertilization rite in which each individual draws for himself from an eternal source of strength. The fact that the room is very nearly dark indicates the absence, symbolically speaking, of the light-bringing factor—of rational or conscious controls. Darkness, as part of the ancient ritual, is the "nocturnal element," or that "power residing solely in the night—the power to engender the light." [13]

Slowly, however, the narrator's eyes become accustomed to the darkness and a flicker of light appears. Light, which is frequently equated with the solar principle or the cerebral process, renders the volcanic temperament impotent; it also paves the way for an analytical approach to things, an approach that unravels mysteries and divests them of their magic force and power. What the narrator sees in the darkness is the *prima materia* of man, elemental forces rising forth from an unconscious realm, sexuality as a potent and fertilizing agent—in Cicero's words, the *principia vitae.*[14] The fact that the narrator does not participate in the revelries indicates his objective view of the sexual. A similar attitude was expressed in *From Castle to Castle,* (but though not in Céline's other works, *Journey to the End of Night, Death on the Installment Plan,* etc). It would seem that the narrator is unable to relate to nature, to feed upon it, to draw strength from it, at least in a sexual way. Sexuality, then, is no longer a source of creativity for Céline.

As his eyes watch the participants whirl about in mad frenzy, he sees Hitler's picture hanging upside down and decorated with black crepe. The fact that the portrait is hanging upside down indicates a topsy-turvy relation with it—his own. What is taking place in this small "madhouse" is the very opposite of the "order" that Hitler had ordained. These orgiastic descendants of the Dionysian mystery cults have tried to kill their leader, Hitler, just as Agave, in a savage outburst of passion, had torn her son, King Pentheus, to pieces. But Hitler's murder has not been successful. Even so, the revelers enjoy their feast: it is just as if their plan had gone through. They refuse to accept reality and prefer to live a life of fantasy in which their goal has been fulfilled.

Hitler's picture, hung upside down, reflects the reversal of the actual situation. The Aryan superrace, Hitler believed, would be distinguished for its health, vigor, courage, and beauty. What has the narrator actually observed? Degenerate, sordid, ugly beings, similar to those depicted by Visconti in his film *The Damned.* The Germans' idealization of the *Übermensch,* an overidentification with the male society, is a compensation for their own weak, sick side—a grotesque masquerade of themselves.

In another room, Number 117, the narrator sees tables set with the most marvelous roasts, fruits, ices, cakes, champagnes. Everyone there indulges himself, gratifying his senses to the utmost and sacrificing nothing for the good of others. Beatific melodies emanate from the room. Here, too, is the exact opposite of what Hitler had envisioned for his people. The actuality is reminiscent of ancient Roman society at its most decadent.

What do all these rooms have in common? They are all far removed from the horrors of the war. There is practically no common denominator between what is going on inside the "vaults" and the political scene in Germany at the time. It is as if the author were taking his readers through a madhouse, an entangling and confusing representation of a matriarchal world.

It is quite clear that Germany is losing the war but that the idle rich are enjoying the fruits of the earth in all senses of the expression—and everyone will take advantage of such a situation if he can.

BERLIN

Céline's depiction of Berlin brings the reader into contact with a war-torn city as seen from three different levels: the earthly realm, the upper sphere, and the underworld regions.

The earthly level deals most particularly with Céline-the-narrator and his physical condition. He complains constantly of dizzy spells and buzzing in the ears, and he walks about in zigzag fashion, like the spiderlike character in *From Castle to Castle.* The two canes he uses to help him hobble about in Berlin bring some kind of equilibrium to his condition.

If the narrator's sickness is to be looked upon symbolically, as well it may be, the inference is that since balance is lacking, adaptation to the realities of life is unhealthy. The fact that he experiences "dizziness" indicates that "his head" is no longer really in control of his actions, that his view is blurred, his orientation vague.

Because the narrator has no papers, he is forbidden to practice medicine. He cannot relate to the Germans. For the first time in his life he feels like an utter stranger. More serious, perhaps, is his political situation: to be a Frenchman in Germany at this time was dangerous, even for Frenchmen sympathetic to the cause of the Reich. The feelings aroused by his equivocal position aggravate the narrator's paranoia. He feels hunted by his own countrymen. Accused of collaborating, he is certain that wherever he may be the "others" will try to do away with him.

> . . . as hated by people from one end of the world to the other, suspected by all, a traitor to France and to Germany . . .[15]

With the passing of days, the narrator's thoughts center more and more on himself. Fear makes him cringe, not only from the destruction going on about him but from the incessantly terrorizing feeling of being the focus of hatred. Some people, he writes, are talented for the piano, others for the guitar, others for mathematics. As for the narrator: "I have the talent . . . of making myself excommunicated." [16]

The narrator's paranoia, his notion of himself as victim, might in certain ways be comparable to what Genet experienced, with one great exception: the latter's situation was determined by his destiny, not his will. Born an orphan, Genet always felt that he had been rejected by society. Once he accepted the fact that people considered him a pariah, he sought to earn, to deserve, society's hatred of him by seeking social ostracism through criminality and capital homosexuality. Genet never wanted pity. Rather he chose to thrust himself into situations that would arouse the hostility of others. He sought to ascend through degradation, to strengthen himself through exercise. He was spared nothing, therefore, in the domain of human suffering. He turned himself inside out to lay his smudged, sickly, suffering soul bare for all to scorn and stone: homosexual, dope peddler, male prostitute, betrayer, thief! Genet lived intimately with life and with excrement. Nothing was too low for him, just as nothing was too vile for Saint Marie Alacoque, who "gathered up the dejecta of sick persons with her tongue." [17] Genet's odyssey, as narrated in *The Thief's Journal* and in *Funeral Rites,* was dangerous because he earned society's hatred of him and in so doing armed himself inwardly against any hurt the world might aim his way. Genet had, thus, submitted himself to all the ignominies known to man, had played out his own version of Job's saga. Genet was fully aware of what he had done and experienced, and he had grown through suffering, which for him was a beneficent agent.

The author of *North,* on the contrary, never faces his inner world objectively, clearly, or decisively. Were he able to do so, he would observe his own faults, and among them his lack of courage in the face of adversity. He would be strong enough to remain in France despite the threats made on his life, strong enough to acknowledge and perhaps even to defend his activities during the German occupation. His paranoia, his belief in society's rejection of him, his rage against his condition and that of the world about him, are manifestations of his feelings of *self*-rejection.

The self-pity of Céline's narrator is so vast, his fantasy is so immense, that by association he experiences an *imitatio Christi.* La Vigue, the narrator informs us, had acted the part of Christ in a film version of *The Passion.* Ever since then he has identified himself with that role and frequently thought himself to be Christ suffering on the cross. Upon request, so to speak, he will literally assume a similar position for everyone to see.

La Vigue may be looked upon as a projection of the narrator, who views himself as a latter-day Christ figure, a sacrificial agent, a man broken by those who are incapable of understanding his—His?—message of peace. The narrator, either overtly or covertly, believes that he, like Christ, has broken the shackles of tradition by not fighting the Germans, France's traditional enemy, and that he has preached against established religions and thus invited his own crucifixion. Christ commanded that each man should ruthlessly separate himself from parents and previous environment, so as to permit the growth of self and independence of spirit and soul. The narrator, after his curious fashion, attempts to follow this command.

Such an association is not only difficult to make but is perhaps valid only in terms of Céline's vision of himself. Is the narrator's belief in his martyrdom an objective assessment of his situation? He had practiced medicine, in a desultory fashion, at Bezons (Seine et Oise) until June 1944, and in 1942 he had taken a trip to Germany, ostensibly to visit hospitals there but actually in order to get out of France and to make his way to Denmark, where he could convert his francs into gold bullion and put them in a Copenhagen bank for safekeeping. Céline had been asked to join the French Maquis and to help the Resistance fighters (as so many other doctors, men of letters, and others did during World War II, at the risk of their lives); Céline had refused, claiming that he was a "pacifist." He had also been invited to go to England to contribute his services to General de Gaulle's forces; he and the "narrator" had rejected this offer, too. Whether Céline was a full-fledged collaborator or not is a moot question. It is fair to say that his behavior was not to be favorably compared to the sterling courage of such men as Camus, Malraux, Beckett, Vercors . . .

In sum, the narrator's "suffering" has been extraordinarily peripheral, considering all the circumstances, and obviously it has not succeeded in enlarging his vision, implementing his judgment, or fostering in him a rational evaluation of himself and his situation vis-à-vis others. He is like the Lotus Eaters that Odysseus came upon when returning to his homeland, who had fallen under the enchantment of ease and sloth, relinquishing the fight for life, succumbing to weariness by choosing the easy way out and not the righteous. It is not integrity that the narrator seeks; integrity never enters the picture. Sometimes, however, such an unabashed lack of values has a way of catching up with one. The narrator takes refuge not only in hatred, as we have seen, thus vindicating himself of any guilt, but also in extreme self-pity and feelings of martyrdom. Suffering, as Nietzsche knew, can have healthy results:

> . . . he shows us how necessary is the entire world of suffering, that by means of it the individual may be impelled to realize the redeeming vision, and then, sunk in contemplation of it, sit quietly in his tossing barque, amid the waves.[18]

Céline's "suffering" has no such positive effects.

Céline's vision is not always all that earthbound during his Berlin visit. The upper spheres also come into focus. When the narrator looks at his hotel and at the ruins all about him, he sees facades of buildings standing like skeletons; he sees columns, naked against a gray sky, with roofing, gutters, bricks of all types sagging and spilling over onto the street. The city, in sum, takes on an eerie cast, as if each building were suspended in space and each facade were devoid of insides. Céline's vision might be considered a type of spiritual accent into a realm that has no depth for him. His view of life, as mirrored in the hollow facades about him, his negation of the divine, as it appears in the empty, bombed-out buildings that hover around, seem to be symptomatic of his whole frame of reference. Just as there is no depth or substance to his vision, so his attitude might be considered as a series of vacuous attempts at self-justification.

It is from the toppling Hotel Steinbock, which he inhabits (from a precarious position *above* the city), that the narrator observes and takes notes of the destruction of Berlin. Just as he complained of dizziness when walking, indicating a malfunction in his relationship with the earth, so the lack of steadiness and equilibrium is now experienced, far more severely, from the heights of his hotel. The implication is that his attitude toward spiritual values is even more unbalanced than his rapport with the earthly dominion.

The third phase of the narrator's Berlin adventure takes his readers to the invisible city beneath the streets, to the bunkers.

Doctor Harras (Hauboldt in the original version), a super SS, president of the Order of Doctors of the Reich, and a wise man (according to the narrator), with a good sense of humor and complete forthrightness, helps Céline and his group. He is a Nazi; everyone knows it, and he makes no bones about it. In this respect, Céline writes, he is admirable.

> . . . he was a Nazi, granted! but when I think, so many years later, how many used him, the many that used him, those who became leftists who put aside thousands with the Jews and Nazis . . . I realize that we were just beginners in this game . . .[19]

Doctor Harras takes the narrator and his group to the darker regions of Berlin, to the bunkers. There the narrator views a microcosm of the city, a vast complex of rooms, offices with air conditioning, neon lights, restaurants, and enormous sofas. The narrator marvels at the order, the efficiency, the planning that the Nazis have put into this endeavor. They are, he remarks an industrious people, and "so clean." If one compares the German with the French in terms of neatness, the narrator goes on, the disorder and lack of cleanliness of the French will be readily apparent. Even in the streets above, the narrator tells us, the dirt and rubble have been gathered up in neat little piles. Imagine, he continues, if Paris were destroyed, what a mess everything would be in![20]

What does the narrator admire in those underground regions? The order, the efficiency, the comfort—three characteristics typical of the German way, three qualities that Céline lacks. He came from a land whose national characteristics are at the opposite pole from those manifested by the Reich. In Germany, where everything is in its proper place, where all is accounted for, where obedience is obligatory, where questions are never posed, where conflicts are forbidden, Céline's narrator has found his ideal at last. Germany stands for what he is not.

ZORNHOF-KRÄNZLIN

The third section of *North,* its apotheosis, is a most fascinating and terrifying expression of a psychological state as revealed through a modern reenactment of the ancient mystery practices in quasi-dream form.

Dreams, as we know, are essentially "message carriers" from the arcane world of the instincts to the land of consciousness. It is through them, in large measure, that the individual may come to understand the nearly forgotten or as yet undeciphered area of the instincts.[21] One may look upon the maniacal characters (prostitutes, gnomes, murderers, cripples, psychotics) in this third section of *North* as dream motifs. It is as if Céline were being constantly "shadowed" by certain mysterious unconscious entities living within him and demanding expression.

So universal are Céline's visions that they may be alluded to as archetypes. As such, they are manifestations not only of his own complexes but also of the anxieties of the times in which he lived. For this reason, Céline's modern reenactment of the mystery rituals performed in Egypt, Babylonia, Greece, and Rome takes on even more profound meaning.

It will be recalled that the Dionysian revelers of ancient times communed with the cosmos and experienced during their rituals the very meaning of creation. As the mystes danced, their physical and psychic energy flowed outward into nature, engulfing all in their embrace. Intoxication was the rule of the day; sensation led them back to their archaic regions. In *The Birth of Tragedy,* Nietzsche extolled this world of delight and savage pleasure:

> Under the charm of the Dionysian not only is the union between man and man reaffirmed, but Nature which has become estranged, hostile, or subjugated, celebrates once more her reconciliation with her prodigal son, man.[22]

For Nietzsche, these orgiastic revelers were beautiful beings, divinely inspired. Céline's creatures are the reverse: ugly in body and soul, the earth's excrescences, its dejecta—made "mad" not to arouse the god but rather the devil within them. Céline's cultists do not celebrate the raw substance of life, demonstrating thereby the ascension of all that is animal and natural within man to a higher plane, but rather man's utter subjugation by these forces.[23]

Let us compare the rituals of ancient times with those celebrated by Céline in terms of the Female Principle, Madness, Dancing, and Animals.

THE FEMALE PRINCIPLE

In ancient days, war was waged between Solar (Male) and the Lunar (Female) cults. This conflict arose out of the unwillingness of either sex to bow to the other. In Thrace, for example, a patriarchal society, the female element refused to cater to the male-dominated group; bloody battles ensued and dangerous passions were unleashed.[24] During the mystery rites at Eleusis, when women experienced themselves as the true source of life, as culture-creative principles, any male intruder would be put to death;[25] the intruder was considered an alien come to destroy and demean women's power and their rights as creative forces. When the female element dominated, they believed, Mother Earth was satisfied and would be fruitful. Women who served the Great Mother acted through her, gave themselves to men, prostituted themselves in order to fertilize the earth. As a result, the male became a fecundating phallus.

These women, alluded to as Bacchantes or Maenads, worshiped Dionysos. When they were struck by the "rage" ("mania," which means a "raging" love or anger), they donned a long robe, wreathed their heads in ivy, carried a thyrsus (phallic symbol), and danced lasciviously laughing and singing to the accompaniment of the flute, drums, or whatever instrument suited their fancy. Some girls, when undergoing "extreme rage," thought themselves to be cows and were overcome with a desire for men.

Most of the various rituals of the many ancient mystery cults followed a general pattern that included ritual prostitution, dismemberment (purification by fire), madness, dancing, animal participation. Céline follows this same pattern in *North*.

Céline's women are for the most part destructive, prostitute types, either overtly or covertly. Except for Lili, his wife, who appears usually as a passive, totally innocuous being (but when she dances, her female sexual side comes to life), there are no positive female figures in *North*. Céline's women do not possess feelings; indeed, they are excluded from this world. His women are "phallus bearers" who burn for men; they bear their womb and use the male merely as a fecundating agent. There is rarely any kind of rapport between male and female society in Céline's novels. The women belong to no man but rather to all men. They are anonymous, transpersonal beings, incarnations of the Great Mother. Like Yoni and Lingam, Céline's female and male principles unite on a collective level; their personal existences pass unnoticed.[26]

Inge von Leiden is a covert prostitute type. In the original version of *North* her name had been Isis, an obvious association with the Isis mystery cult in antiquity. She is married to a paraplegic, one of the owners of the immense Zornhof estate, and it was through this marriage that she obtained both a title and a fortune. Céline describes her as still attractive and charming but rather "difficult" at times because she is going through menopause. He also speaks of her as a nymphomaniac who enjoys SS men in particular.[27] Though her almond-shaped eyes are pleasing to him, the narrator adds, even the most beautiful women belong to a "museum of horrors." [28]

Céline seems to be revolted by this kind of female and perhaps by all women. Except for the utterly passive types he disdains them; he looks upon them as overbearing agents, as a threat to man's well-being. At best they are a necessary evil. When Inge greets him at her home, she is dressed in a rose and green negligee. She has donned this revealing garb, he assumes, and has lain down on her couch, stretching out her legs so that her thighs are plainly visible, and letting her unbrassiered breasts hang limp, to entice him.[29] It is not that she is attracted to him sexually. She needs him only to write a prescription for poison with which to do away with her paraplegic husband. Having acquired a title, money, and a child from this man, she has no further need of him. To win the narrator to her side, she takes him for a ride through the countryside. When she tries to seduce him, he considers her repulsive and objectionable. Furthermore, he confesses, he is terribly priapic.[30]

Inge (Isis), as we have seen, is a prostitute type, a female figure who tries to lure men to her fold and bend them to her will. Psychologically, one could consider her one of the Bacchantes, those intent upon castrating men, annihilating their power and using it for their own ends.

What kind of man would lend himself to such a fate? Inge von Leiden's husband is, as we have stated, a paraplegic.[31] In constant pain, he is always under sedation. He is also given to maniacal fits of anger during which he takes out his gun, loads it, and threatens his wife and daughter or anyone who enters his room.[32] He is a reincarnation of the cripple described in *Fairy-Play for Another Time I.* Emotionally, however, von Leiden's condition is far worse, because he cannot function on any level, either physically or mentally.

Céline's portrayal of the paraplegic is devoid of compassion. Indeed, it is hard, ruthless, even brutal, as if he himself were fed up with atrophied beings, in both the physical and moral sense, as the earth's waste products. One almost comes away with the feeling that Céline is in effect trying to destroy the weak, the feeble, and the sick. If we look upon von Leiden as a projection of the author, we can readily understand his desire to obliterate this kind of destructive individual, perhaps that very aspect of himself—his own sick, weak, irritable, and violent tendencies.

How is von Leiden destroyed? One day while his handyman, Nicolas, is carrying him to the courtyard he drops him, either by mistake or on purpose, into a cesspool. This cesspool has not been emptied in three years and is filled to the hilt with the excrement of four hundred cows. When he is fished out of the cesspool, dead, he is in a fetal position: "folded over on himself, a large trunk, with atrophied legs, covered over with yellow and black liquid manure . . ." [33] The fact that he has not died in a beatific manner, but rather in the most ignominious of ways (bathed in excrement), indicates that he represents waste material. Crippled, he had no longer been a source of nourishment.

Equally useless and unproductive is Otto von Simmer, the *Landrat* at Zornhof, a member of the Prussian aristocracy and a colonel during World War I (he was at Verdun), the son of the governor of the Grand Duchy of Schleswig.[34] This great warrior type is a pederast who not only wears powder but paints his nails bright red and wears lipstick and amethyst rings. As a homosexual, he is a member of a degenerate group unable to serve Inge's female cult. Though effeminate psychologically, he tries to be outwardly masculine—not in his dress but in his manner. He is terribly cruel, shoots prisoners at the slightest provocation, sometimes only because they might utter words such as *"sales boches"* ("dirty krauts").[35]

By identifying with what he considers to be "male" virtues, the *Landrat* feels all-powerful, strong, and courageous, and fortitude seems to flow into him. He tries to experience the patriarchal society of Nazi Germany, where force, vigor, and war are greatly admired. It must be noted here that many of the Nazis who believed in the "absolute" male virtues as an ideal to be established were compensating for their own weaknesses, both sexual and moral. One need only examine some of the Nazi groups: Ernst Röhm and his Brown Shirts, most of whom were homosexuals; Joseph Goebbels, who had a club foot; Hermann Göring, who was so obese that he could hardly walk with ease; not to speak of Hitler and his sexual difficulties. The list is long.

How does the *Landrat* Otto von Simmer meet his death? He is beaten to death with a pickax, after which he is strangled with a silk cord, thrown into a stagnant mud pool filled with algae "grass and sand . . ."[36] When he is withdrawn from the mud he is placed on his side and the vomit, mucus, the poisons that are in him ooze out—a fitting end for another of Mother Nature's waste products.

One of the most breathtaking and excoriating pictures that Céline ever drew is that of the hundred prostitutes celebrating their own mystery cult in a thickly forested region not far from Zornhof.

One day, as the narrator and his companions walk in the forest, they see a hundred prostitutes sitting around a huge wood fire in a muddy crevice. They are cooking enormous chunks of strong-smelling meat and eating them. When they spy the narrator and his group they scream, bellow like animals, insult them, call them traitors and thieves, and finally bedlam breaks loose. They are in such a frenzy that they begin beating each other with sticks, falling to the ground, howling like savages, heaving about in "the muddy bottom" of the abyss. Suddenly these furies, these modern incarnations of the Dionysian revelers, run toward the intruders, ready to tear them into a thousand pieces.[37]

Realizing that his life is in danger, the narrator decides to leave the area as quickly as possible. Just as he is about to depart he sees two forms lying in the slime before him: that of the *Rittmeister* and of the *Revizor*. Their bones have been fractured, their heads, limbs, and thoraxes twisted; blood is spurting from their noses and mouths. They are, nevertheless, still alive.[38]

Who was the Baron von Rittmeister von Leiden? A Prussian, eighty-four years old, who had been educated at the Sorbonne, who spoke French fluently, and who was a total degenerate. What was his pastime? Having himself whipped by little Polish servant girls until blood was drawn, then crawling about the floor, and finally lying down limp from exhaustion.[39] At the end of the orgy the senile codger would amuse himself by "urinating on them and they on him." [40]

The *Rittmeister* was never without his dog, Iago, who protected him against all unwanted violence. Iago may be looked upon in this instance as a representative of evil, inspiring malevolence, misery, and despair, or at least furthering it by his protection of such a degenerate force as the *Rittmeister*. During the course of the story Iago is found dead. Fearing for his life, the *Rittmeister* had decided that whenever he left the premises of the estate thenceforth, he would go by horse. Mounted on his white steed one day, in full military regalia, with saber, revolver, medals, epaulettes, he rode out into the countryside. He took the wrong path, came across the prostitutes. Fearing he would denounce them to the authorities, these Bacchantes armed themselves with sticks, shovels, pots, and pickaxes, and like a horde of screeching Maenads tore through the fields, seized the *Rittmeister* and his companion (the *Revizor,* whom he had met along the way), threw them in the mud, and beat them.[41]

The *Rittmeister's* fate is almost ironic. As one who sought his sexual fulfillment through being beaten, he is annihilated in this same manner by the prostitutes. As for the horses, the Dionysian worshippers beat in their stomachs with pickaxes, smashed their heads, cut their bodies to pieces, roasted them, and ate them.[42]

In ancient times such slaughtering and dismembering was not considered cruel. On the contrary, such acts were looked upon by the ancients as a guarantee of fertility. It was believed that the earth must drink of blood, either human blood or that of a wild or domesticated animal; such blood fertilized the earth, increasing its power and fecundity. In many tribes, even today, flesh (either animal or human) is eaten for religious purposes, the belief being that the celebrant is filled with the strength of the dead man or animal. The same message is of course intended in the ritual of Holy Communion when the participants drink and eat the blood and flesh of Christ in the form of wine and the Host.

The prostitutes in *North,* like witches, ate the horses, a ritual action that imbued them, symbolically at least, with the horse's spirit and vital power and helped them in their task of subduing the male, a threat to their well-being.

The horse, it will be recalled, had a particular significance in ancient mystery rituals. In the Kabeiroi mysteries, for example, it was said that the god Poseidon had assumed the form of a stallion and appeared to Demeter as a bridegroom, as a fertilizing agent, forcing himself upon her. In pre-Hellenic Arcadian cults, Demeter came to Thelpusa in the form of a mare and was mounted by the stallion Poseidon, the issue of this union being Persephone.[43]

It is understandable, then, that Céline's prostitutes should seek to eat the horses' flesh. It is their way of seeking revenge on the animal that had so angered Demeter by taking advantage of her, or, symbolically speaking, on the men who had tried to impose their superiority upon them by forcing them to play the degrading role of the prostitute in society.

The fire over which the prostitutes roast the horses' flesh may also be looked upon as part of the mystery cult rituals: purification by fire. It is the light that appears after the "night" has been experienced by the initiate, the light that, symbolically, is "engendered" from the night and terminates in the most radiant vision.[44]

The bludgeoning of the two men, the dismembering of the animals, and the feasting are indeed a terrifying display of the ultra-emotional and irrational side of women. Yet it is the irrational, the core of certain mysteries, that brings about the flow of new life.[46]

When the narrator is exposed to such a sight, it is no wonder that he recoils with horror. In modern times, particularly in patriarchal societies, this frenetic aspect of women has been suppressed and therefore minimized and misunderstood, making it that much more dangerous when it erupts. Certain writers—Claudel and Racine among them—have expressed this violence, this domineering, lascivious aspect of the female personality, in highly poetic form. In ancient times, the sexual and animal sides of women were revealed in mystery cults, in fresco paintings, in drawings on jars, in sculptures of all types, and in literary works.

Céline was, to be sure, fascinated by the elemental aspect of the Eternal Feminine, but he was also horrified and repelled by this powerful display of animalism. His attitude toward women, as we have seen, had always been ambivalent; he admired their physical beauty and hated their power over him. In *North,* the narrator intimates that he has become priapic, "a pathological condition characterized by persistent erection of the penis." [47] To suffer from such a condition is to experience extreme discomfort both physically and psychologically, physically because of the pain involved, and psychologically because of the drive toward more and more sexual experiences, each as unsatisfying as the one before. Such a person is in constant need of a woman (but only of the prostitute type) for he can experience only momentary release. This type of male nymphomaniac is never fulfilled. To be in constant need of the opposite sex is to be under its spell, to be victimized by it. The priapism of Céline's narrator may be a partial explanation for his ambivalent reaction toward women at this time: his rejection of them and his deep dependence upon them, and his deep resentment, all the while, of this need.

MADNESS

Another aspect of the ancient mystery cult ritual was madness, which may be defined as a "psychological dismemberment," that is, the dissolution of the personality. Ritual physical dismemberment (human or animal) was looked upon as a guarantee of earthly fertility. Madness was the psychological analogue of this concept.[48]

In all his works Céline portrays men and women who are mad in varying ways and degrees. Le Vigan, for example, is distinctly peculiar—not violently insane, but suffering from fantasies and delusions. In *North* he is given a cellar room, way down near the stairwell. It is totally black, sinister looking, dirty. He hasn't even a bed to lie on—only a heap of straw. Garbage of all sorts is dumped, if not actually in his living quarters then just outside them.[49] After the dog Iago's death, rats begin invading the room. On one occasion, Le Vigan screams outright: a rat has bitten his finger, has broken the skin on his leg, has torn his pants.[50] He is so frightened of these rats (and who wouldn't be) that he begins to see them everywhere, and not as mere animals but as personifications of "evil," ready to hunt him down.

Antonin Artaud and Albert Camus, each of whom depicted rats as plague-bringers (both literally and in a psychological sense), acknowledged them as positive forces in man's life. The shock of their visitation upon humanity could act, they supposed, as a catalyzing agency, enlarging man's consciousness, permitting him to see what had been dulled or taken for granted. Le Vigan, rather than seeing himself more clearly, groans with anguish, flees his doom, becomes incapable of any kind of objective reasoning. He is constantly beset by fear. He can relate to nothing and to no one. He expresses few if any ideas and is incapable of any activity other than following the narrator on his journey. The description accorded the mud pond outside of Le Vigan's room is a concrete manifestation of his inner world: ". . . a large puddle . . . a pool of yellow mud . . ." [51] Le Vigan, then, as a representative of turgid and stagnant forces, is certainly of no use to any Maenad in her fertility ritual! Obviously he has to be mentally dismembered.

Frau Kretzer's insanity is considerably more pronounced and considerably more poignant. The loss of her two sons in World War II has been too much for her to bear. Like Demeter, who experienced pain at the loss of her daughter Persephone, so Frau Kretzer experiences, in her madness, extreme anguish, mixed with feelings of anger and a desire for revenge. She is pictured as giving in to bouts of hysterical crying, screaming, groaning, after which she drapes the picture of her two sons in black cloth. Céline's descriptions of her frantic actions, her slobbering noises, her mangled screeches, her animal-like gestures, is reminiscent of certain horrendous incidents in William Burroughs' *Naked Lunch.* In both works one sees men and women reaching the depths of degradation.

At times, Frau Kretzer looks upon herself as "a mother martyr." [52] At other times, in the grip of feelings of aggressive hate, she will grab a mauser and wave it about, seemingly ready to kill anyone who dares oppose her will. In particularly poignant instances, she carries her sons' black tunics around with her, clutching them tightly about her head. The narrator writes that he has heard many cries in his life, "cries of orators, cries of prisoners, cries of the cancerous, cries of ministers, cries of generals, cries of mothers giving birth, and many others," [53] but never such sounds as those emanating from Frau Kretzer when she is kissing her sons' tunics. Her wails are like those of a hyena, her hysteria is all-encompassing; madness has so ravished her mind that she will urinate on her chair and bark like a dog.[54]

The *Rittmeister's* sister, Marie-Thérèse, sixty years old, is yet another mental aberrant. An accomplished pianist and fluent in French—a gifted woman—she refuses to see any member of her family, so convinced is she that they want to poison her.[55] As her paranoia worsens, her hatred of her family becomes the more pronounced.

Céline's description of paranoia is comparable in some respects to Allen Ginsberg's remarkable evocation of this mental disease in his poem *Kaddish.*[56] In these verses Ginsberg depicts, in the most sordid detail, his mother's fear of Hitler, the spies she believes are always present and trying to hunt her down, and her eventual confinement in a mental institution. Céline does likewise. The reader is spared nothing in the way of ignominious and perverse details.

Céline excels in the depiction of protoplasmic images. Man's "reason," generally considered his highest and most godlike aspect, lies dormant or withers as mixtures of all manner of organic and inorganic entities arise from his unconscious. Out of this mass, memories both concrete and amorphous come into being and whirl about in the conscious mess—fleeting, transfigured, distorted, grotesque.

Céline's embodiments remain clutched in a primal world. They participate in nature's embrace. In ancient times the Bacchantes expected to emerge refreshed from their contact with nature—and presumably they did so. Céline's pathetic creatures experience a breakdown in consciousness, but no rebirth.

DANCING

A major element in the Eleusinian mystery cults of ancient times was the dance. Among primitive peoples, it should be remembered, the dance came to have the same function as prayer. It became a means of communing with nature, of reaching one's metaphysical depths, of contacting the very roots of existence. Since dancing pays respect to the god, the dancer becomes infused with the god's power. As such, he becomes a creator (a fertilizing agent) in this most orgiastic, and aphrodisiac of spectacles—the dance. We recall in this connection that, in Hindu lore, it was when Shiva danced that he created the world.[57]

The dance is the most basic of all cultic expressions. The repetitive movements and the frantic contortions, and the extreme expenditure of energy involved in both, enable the participants to "open" up their depths and thereby experience direct contact with the cosmos. Pausanius wrote: "Only he who has been initiated may enter" [58] the sacred grove of Demeter and her Daughter. The dancer was an initiate.

The dancer, the Great Mother's votary, was looked upon as a type of sorceress capable of enticing men into her fold. The dance aroused the sexual appetite; the singing and the clashing of "sistrums," the rattling of necklaces, the beating of drums and other noisemakers, brought the participants to an orgiastic frenzy. "Music-sparks" were unleashed.

Frenetic music and dance belongs, as we have already noted in connection with Céline's ballets to the Dionysian cult of nature worshipers, not to the Apollonian cultivation of inward vision, moderation, and restraint. The Dionysian motto is abandon, not reserve. Euripides, Nietzsche wrote in *The Birth of Tragedy,*[59] included musical interludes in his play *The Bacchae,* arousing enormous emotions. A world of delight and destruction is born with dancing and music, for

> It is with them that nature for the first time attains her artistic jubilee; it is with them that the destruction of the *principium individuationis* for the first time becomes an artistic phenomenon.[60]

In the passage in *North* devoted to dancing, Céline's "mad" participants range from the ugly to the beautiful. All are incarnations of the Eternal Feminine. Their dances usually begin with rather delicate, limbering-up movements, then increase in wildness, madness, noise, and frenzy until voluptuousness reigns unrestrained.

According to the narrator, some of the female initiates are old, degenerate, filthy, and decrepit, "with rolls of fat . . . men's arms . . . a stomach which had at least three fibrome tumors . . . tits . . ." [61] When one such reveler raises her skirts and begins to dance, her entire body trembles as the masses of fat shake up and down in counterpoint to the rhythm of the music. When the homosexuals on the farm join this raging crowd, the women compel them to kiss them on their mouths. When they try to break away, they are slapped. The audience, convulsed with joy, screams its approval in frantic bravas and is itself caught up in the dance.[62]

The gypsies on the farm dance wearing heteroclitic costumes of green, rose, and yellow. The men dance fandangos, perform acrobatic stunts, read crystal balls. The women beat drums, shake castanets. As the gypsies dance, there seems to be something wildly inhuman about them: they glide, twirl, turn, bend, bump, seemingly defying all the laws of gravity, breaking out into bizarre spatial patterns. It was as if Nietzsche had been uttering his famous statement: "Lift up your heads, my brothers, high, higher! And neither forget the legs." [63]

Finally the narrator's wife, Lili, joins the festivities. She is a real artist, he declares. She can twirl, trill, and use her castanets superlatively well. The gypsies, on the other hand, are creating a plastic vision, relying almost exclusively on fulgurating activity. Theirs is a strange mixture of twirling circles, cubes, curves, squares, all etched in space. Because of the design, they look like fragmented human figures, floating about in an unusual continuum.[64] All individuality has vanished.

ANIMALS

The ancient mystery cults gave animals and symbols of animals a prominent role in their rites. The initiates, for example, would don animal skins symbolic of various theriomorphic deities (cows, storks, geese, horses, bulls, etc.) which, they believed, would imbue them with the power of the gods. Frequently, as we have already noted, the participants would dismember and devour sacred animals in the belief that so doing increased their own fertility and that of the earth.

Animals have a "universal" quality about them. Many people look upon them as emerging from the "bowels of the earth," that is, from the unconscious. They are thought to bring into consciousness the chthonic elements that they represent; they are message-bearers who may take on the form of hope, fear, pain, or joy.[65] The painter Franz Marc observed that for some people animals offer a refuge: "Very early in life I felt that man was ugly. The animals seemed to be more lovely and pure." [66]

Animals figure in all of Céline's books but most prominently in the later ones. They participate in his life. In *North,* for example, his cat, Bebert, is with him constantly. Bebert represents his most precious possessions, for the cat is probably the only entity (aside from his wife) with whom Céline ever related. Céline's cat is a devoted servant, obedient, more worthy of trust than a child.

The horses in *North*, as we have seen, are symbolically representative of instinctuality and energy. They are bludgeoned to death by the hundred prostitutes, roasted, consumed. Iago, the *Rittmeister's* dog, the protector of a depraved human being, is a negative creature since he protects the status quo. The rats that run rampant in *North* are a sign of evil taking over, of confusion, and of aggressivity.

Perhaps one of the most arresting animal incidents in this volume is played out by geese, an animal not known for its intelligence but one that is symbolically oriented both to the spirit and to the earth: as birds, they can fly, but they are also earthbound, since they swim. Historically, it is said, geese saved Rome from the barbarian invasions; they have, therefore, a premonitory capacity and make a great racket whenever something strange or frightening takes place.

In *North*, the narrator tells of the day on which, all of a sudden, there are thousands of geese all around him in the courtyard of the Leiden estate. They seem to have come from all over, like a veritable scourge. They are mad, even furious, fighting, screaming, acting as if they have been organized by some leader. It seems that nettles have been placed all over the courtyard and the geese don't like it. When a whole sea of geese gets angry, the narrator tells us, it is like the pouring out of an army. They push, huddle, repulse everyone who approaches the area. In this capacity, they signify powerful will, the perseverance of those having a goal to pursue.

On another occasion, when the narrator and his companions try to leave the courtyard, they are attacked by the geese. Hundreds seem to come from everywhere, charging, forcing their way toward the narrator and his companions and refusing to let them pass: ". . . avid gluttons . . ."[67] In this frame of reference, the geese may be understood as a microcosm of the world, or at least of the Nazi's world. They charge noisily, seeking everything for themselves, grabbing, mutilating. Once their task has been accomplished, they look upon their former enemy, the narrator and his friends, with indifference and contempt. There is no longer anything to fight about—nothing further to be gained.[68] We are reminded that once the Bacchantes had experienced rebirth, or had restored contact with the disparate forces of nature, they discarded their animal vestments.

One of the most imaginative of Céline's animal visions is the one in which he tells of the departure from Zornhof. All the travelers are placed in a cart drawn by twenty cows. Marie-Thérèse is so drunk she has to be carried to the cart. Frau Kretzer is given an injection of morphine to allay a fit of hysteria. Frau von Thorfels and the *Revizor* are also given morphine.

The departure from Zornhof is described as a "retreat from Russia, but backwards."[69] The fact that this chariot is drawn by cows is a fitting finale to the Zornhof sequence. Cows symbolize fertility and were worshiped in the Isis cults in Egypt. They are also associated with the earth and moon and are still sacred today in India. They are considered part of the primal principle—the possessor of "vital heat" and, as such, as the "Cow of Abundance."

As a symbol of fertility, the cows in this last image draw the degenerate, negative, and sickly people away from the stagnant atmosphere that Zornhof represents, perhaps bringing them to a more abundant and fruitful realm. Away from this "pool of urine and dung," a fitting description of Zornhof, renewal will be sought.

The power of Céline's imagination is expressed in *North* not only in terms of the images, the style, and the characterizations, but most spectacularly as the supreme manipulator of a giant mystery cult ritual. Céline has become a thaumaturge who has been given, and has used, the key to a closeted world. He has opened the door onto a domain of horror.

Céline's fascination with the mystery cult is a manifestation of his own inner rage and torment. All about him, in the disintegrating patriarchal society in which he found himself at this period (Nazi Germany), he saw Wotan worshipers whose exaggerated male identification was a compensation for their sexual confusion. The ambiguity manifest in the psyches of his characters and concretized in the form of cripples, prostitutes, and psychotics is a reflection of the trends of the time as well as of his own disquietude. In his early novels—*Journey to the End of the Night, Death on the Installment Plan, Guignol's Band,* etc.—he fancied himself a very male fellow indeed, one whose relationships with women with rare exceptions (Molly and his wife) were strictly on the phallic level. A change is discernible, however, in *From Castle to Castle* and *North.* The narrator has become an observer rather than a participant. He feels himself cut off from nature. The reenactment of the mysteries permits him to experience the animal within him vicariously, through projection, to extract this raw substance—man's instinct—from the earth and transform it into a viable and creative agent. Only through renewed contact with that fertile force can he pursue his existence.

13

RIGODON

> Heaven grant the reader the boldness to become ferocious, momentarily; like what he is reading, to find, without being disoriented, his abrupt and savage path through the desolate swamps of these somber and poison-filled pages.
>
> LAUTRÉAMONT, *Les Chants de Maldoror*

Rigodon, THE CONCLUDING VOLUME OF CÉLINE'S TRILOGY, RECOUNTS his odyssey through war-torn Germany, from the beginning through the end of March 1945, and his safe arrival in Copenhagen.

Like the two previous novels in this trilogy *(From Castle to Castle* and *North),* the work is episodic. It is likewise semi-autobiographical, interspersed with dream visions of the most macabre type, accounting in part for the extreme *malaise* radiating from this work.

After a brief plot summary, a discussion of Céline's political views as they emerge in *Rigodon* will be undertaken. The second section of this chapter will deal with Céline's style: his verbal collage and time-travel technique and the optical and retinal illusion he creates in *Rigodon.*

PLOT

After Céline and his party leave Zornhof (described in *North),* he takes the Berlin-Rostock train en route—it is hoped—to Copenhagen. *Rigodon* tells of the constant frustrations and hardships endured by Céline, his wife, and his cat as they make their way through Germany to Copenhagen. They are constantly climbing in and out of trains going in the direction opposite to their destination. They wander through cities (Warenmunde, Leipzig, Hamburg, Ulm, Oddort, Hanover, Kiel, Flensburg). They witness bombings and endure cold, hunger, and disease before being rescued, finally, by the Red Cross. The volume ends with their arrival in Copenhagen.

CÉLINE'S POLITICAL VIEWS AND THE POLITICAL SITUATION IN GERMANY

The title *Rigodon* is an indication of both a physical and political situation. By dictionary definition, the word can signify a lively dance for a single couple, with a peculiar jumping step and usually in duple time. It can also mean "bull's eye." In the novel, the lively two-step and duple beat may be associated with the enormous difficulties that Céline encounters as he hobbles his way, with the help of two canes; through Germany. The "bull's eye," of course, refers to the German cities of Duisburg, Essen, Cologne, Dresden, Würzburg, Darmstadt, etc.—all perfect targets for Allied bombers.

The political and military situations in Germany in 1945 posed moral problems. When fighting a war, how many enemy cities does one try to reduce to rubble? How many (presumed) innocents does one destroy? What of the Allies' bombing of Dresden (so brilliantly evoked in Kurt Vonnegut's *Slaughterhouse Five*)—a city thought at the time to be of no military significance whatever? Did the need, or the desire, to destroy the enemy's "will to fight" justify the slaughter there—or at Hiroshima, another nonmilitary city?

According to Céline, and without reference to the special case of Dresden, the Allies were utterly ruthless in all their bombings and killed tens of thousands of people for no reason. To this assertion, of course, one might respond with a platitude, yet one that has some relevance in this context: war, in general, is a cruelty. Yet who wages war, if not people?

Hitler's armies and air force, for example, were made up of individuals, each of whom, in his own way, helped perpetrate crime upon crime. Whether the individual acted out of fear or fevor, whether he had joined Hitler's armed forces because he was compelled to or because he wanted to, is beside the point. The fact remains that every individual was a party, in one degree or another, to the most excoriating crimes the world had ever known. The passivity of the great majority of the German people in the early days of Hitler's rise to power does not exonerate them. Passivity can be as criminal as direct action, and certainly amounted to the same horror in the end. A dictator can remain in power only so long as the people want him to do so or are not sufficiently interested in ridding themselves of him.

The Americans, British, French, and Russians pursued their destructive course in 1945 because Hitler, despite the fact that he knew that the war had to all intents and purposes been lost, refused to sign an armistice. By January 23 Soviet troops had already reached the Oder in Lower Silesia; by February 26 they had arrived at the Baltic Sea; by March 30 they had taken Danzig; by April 24 Berlin was encircled. British troops had crossed the Rhine on March 23. Fighting was still going on in the Ruhr. Troop movements, strafings and bombings, evacuation of people from east to west and from north to south, were being carried out. Germany was in a state of chaos.[1] Hitler knew all this.

The political, economic, and sociological situation within Germany during Céline's stay had worsened as a result of the indecisiveness of the leaders of the Reich. Albert Speer, the minister of armaments in charge of war production since 1942, was fully aware of the military defeat Germany had experienced. Indeed, he had sent several notes to Hitler asking him to negotiate peace terms with the enemy. Hitler's favorite general, Field Marshal Rommel, had advocated much the same thing—and had ceased to be Hitler's favorite general. Hitler would not countenance such defeatist talk. The "annihilation" of Germany would be more desirable, he felt (and said), than its conquest by foreign nations. To this end Hitler even sent young children into battle, knowing as he did so that all would be slaughtered almost immediately.

Some critics and political analysts say that Hitler sought to continue the fight because of his sense of identification with Germany: he "mistook the fate of the German people for his own fate." [2] Whatever the reasons, he was so adamant in his point of view that he would not even listen when Hermann Rauschning broached the subject of a possible German defeat. "Even though we cannot win," Hitler said, "we shall go down and pull half the world [down] with us to destruction." [3]

On March 19 during Céline's sojourn in Germany, Hitler gave his infamous "scorched earth order," calling for the destruction of Germany.

> All military transportation, communication, industrial, and distribution facilities, as well as all objects of value found within the Reich territory, as far as the enemy would be able to use them immediately or in the foreseeable future for military purposes, must be destroyed.[4]

Lieutenant Colonel von Posner, Speer's liaison officer to the general staff, issued contrary orders.[5] Many army units never received them, however, and began demolishing the various military installations in question.

Albert Speer says in his memoirs that he made several trips to see Hitler, attempting each time to persuade the Führer to alter his plans. Hitler refused to do so. "If we are going to lose the war," he hold Speer,

> the nation, too, will perish. The outcome is inevitable. It is not necessary to worry about the minimum needs of the people and how they are to live later at subsistence level. On the contrary, it [the German people] will have proved to be the weaker one. The future will belong exclusively to the stronger nations of the East. Those who survive the war are, in any event, the inferior ones, for the good ones have been killed.[6]

It has been claimed that Hitler's propaganda machine was still highly effective, even at this late date, and that the German people were unaware of the actual state of affairs. Thus, despite the constant bombings by Allied aircraft, the majority of the German people were unwilling to believe even as late as April, 1945, in the enemy's twenty-five-to-one air superiority. Indeed, some citizens were still convinced that their *Vaterland* would yet emerge victorious! They had been informed, seemingly, of Hitler's "secret weapon," which he had refrained from using, up to now, for "humanitarian reasons," since it was capable of reducing the enemy to rubble.[7]

By January, 1945, the situation had grown so precarious that Hitler moved to the bunker of the chancellery in Berlin. Speer describes this area as a "tomb" and calls the entire implacement "The Isle of the Departed." [8] In these underworld quarters Hitler lived essentially isolated in a megalomaniacal fantasy world until April 30, 1945, when he shot—or by another account, poisoned—himself to death. On May 1, Grand Admiral Karl Dönitz succeeded Hitler as leader of the Reich, and eight days later Germany surrendered.

The moral question posed at the outset of this chapter can only be answered in terms of the hard facts. Allied bombings had to continue until the Nazi government agreed to surrender. As for the millions of victims? This was the frightful price paid in all wars: the "slaughter of the innocents."

As the entire German social and political structure collapsed, Céline was caught in the midst of the dismantling of what had once seemed to be a powerful, orderly, and efficient machine. Hitler's dream of establishing an Aryan race that would rule Europe for two thousand or more years, giving the Germans sufficient *Lebensraum* to carry out his visions, had come to an end—in a nightmare.

Céline's political pronouncements in *Rigodon* pepper the entire volume. As one would expect, they are all extremely subjective and usually emerge in the form of irrational prognostications. Most frequently they are expressions of his hatred of the Allies and of the fearful situation in which he now found himself.

Céline predicts the end of Occidental civilization and the extinction of the white race. He is not, of course, the first to come forth with such a dire view of the West's rapid fragmentation. He is, however, one of the most outspoken and most powerful contemporary exponents of this attitude.

Céline further decrees that Europe died at Stalingrad. With the loss of this battle, Germany, which he considers a protective buffer zone against invasions from the east (that is, from Russia) becomes helpless. A comparison between German aggression and Russian conquest is then offered, in what seems to be an oversimplification of the entire picture.

> They're crazy here [in Germany]! as crazy as the Soviets, but the Soviets are far stronger, more enormous . . . they can permit themselves their fables here: race, land, blood only interests a small family . . . village snobbism . . . the Soviets don't need it . . . they want to take everything, they will take everything.[9]

It is difficult to understand how Céline could dismiss Germany's war machine, the holocaust to which it gave rise, the uncounted millions killed in concentration camps and elsewhere, as mere "snobbism." But then Céline was never known for his anti-Nazi beliefs or for his reasonable assessment and evaluation of situations—certainly not political ones. Indeed, his ideational content and his fictional world are always so interwoven as to be hardly distinguishable one from the other. Now that it is himself who is caught up in the melee and in real personal danger, his perception of life in general becomes even foggier.

Europe, according to Céline, is doomed to collapse. He feels that this continent is no longer worth saving, that the European "civilization" has no future, and yet, somewhat paradoxically, he views the possibility of invasion from the east and the extermination of the white race with horror. The implication here would indicate a deep attachment to European civilization and to the "white" race. "The white man is dead!," murmurs Céline;[10] "he no longer exists." "Colored" people (red, yellow, black), he goes on to say, pride themselves on their nonracial politics. Yet whenever yellow, red, or black people come to France, they always manage to seek out white girls! Since, according to the laws of heredity, white is not a predominant color, the children of "mixed" couples have little or no chance of being white.

As for religion as part of the European framework, this too is experiencing its last gasp. When the critic Robert Poulet questions him, he relates in *Rigodon,* concerning his personal spiritual beliefs, Céline answers vociferously. Religion, he concludes, has done more to "bestialize, to destroy the white race" than almost anything else. Religions, particularly those centering around "a little Jesus," have done absolutely nothing to alleviate man's plight. They have advocated the same "imposture, tittle-tattle, swindles" as all the others have.[11] As for the Bible, the most widely read volume in the world, it has done nothing to elevate man, either ethically or spiritually. On the contrary, it is "filthier, more racist, more sadistic than twenty centuries of arenas." [12]

Céline's wrath concerning religion, politics, and the racial situation,[13] as expressed in *Rigodon*, hardly comes as a surprise. It is merely a reiteration of what he has been saying right along. He has spent his whole life attacking what he considers to be old forms, worn-out attitudes and traditions, unproductive philosophies—man in general—in what Henry Miller has alluded to as those "Céline-like blasts." [14]

Céline's ethos had not changed.

STYLE

Verbal Collages and Time-travel Technique. In recounting his harrowing experiences as he makes his way through the charnel house that was Germany, Céline still has recourse to the ugliness and the hateful aspects of life (the lack of food in Germany, the intense cold, the bombardments, the killings, etc.). But the manner in which the horrors are revealed to the reader is different.[15] Stylistically, the entire volume may be looked upon as a series of verbal collages.

These collages consist of an almost continuous interchange of images and the superimposition of these images upon one another. Several striking examples of this technique come to mind. Thus: Céline rushing frantically for a train just as it pulls out of the station; his entering the dismal and dark railroad station; the crowds wearing expressions of despair as they watch trains, unwilling to take them, chug out of the station; the bombings; the lepers with their oozing pustules; a group of retarded children. In this instance, there are four parts to each image: the train in the railroad station, the people rushing toward it, the city in the background, the bombs as they burst. These four parts of a single vision are described almost simultaneously. Céline achieves this effect by superimposing one part of the image on another. In this manner he creates a whole complex of rapports between the four aspects of the image. As each segment of the image flashes into view, associations are built up, intensifying the magnitude, momentum, and depth of the picture.

This collage is also fascinating from the point of view of rhythm. The pull of the people rushing for the train, the speed of the train as it pulls out of the station, and the juxtaposition of the static quality of the city looming in the background and the dynamism of the falling bombs and flashing lights create a series of alternating motions. The vertigo experienced by the narrator (the dizziness he describes throughout *Rigodon*) is now felt by the reader. The protagonist and the reader alike feel themselves dragged and driven along, trying all the while to maintain some semblance of equilibrium, trying to grasp some steadying force in a world built upon quicksand.

Céline's visual memory is remarkable. His success at transliterating the image, both visually and sensorially, increases its emotional impact, creating a visceral rapport between the activities narrated in *Rigodon* and the reader.

The verbal collages in *Rigodon* are reminiscent of those created by the Dadaists and Surrealists and refined by William Burroughs in his novels

Naked Lunch (1959) and *Nova Express* (1964). Burroughs defines his understanding of the verbal collage and the association blocks to which they give rise in the following manner:

> I've recently done a lot of experiments with scrapbooks. I'll read in the newspaper something that reminds me or has relations to something I've written. I'll cut out the picture or article and paste it in a scrapbook beside the words from my book. I'll be walking down the street and I'll suddenly see a scene from my book and I'll photograph it and put it in a scrapbook. . . . I'll almost invariably dream that night something relating to this juxtaposition of word and image. In other words, I've been interested in precisely how word and image get around on very, very complex association lines.[16]

To the verbal collages and the association blocks to which they gave rise a "time-travel" technique may be added, extending Céline's extreme creativity in this domain.

The events described by Céline in *Rigodon,* though written about in 1960, had been experienced some fifteen years earlier. This lapse of time was not experienced by Céline as a void, nor was it "recaptured" via the Proustian involuntary-memory technique. The past lived within Céline as a viable and productive force that catapulted into view as a dynamic and energetic entity in its own right. Céline, therefore, projected himself back in time, recreating the past as he recalled it, but enriching it by means of his contact with the present. A new reality, then, came into being.

Céline's time-travel technique is virtually identical with a technique described by William Burroughs as follows:

> I call time travel, in taking coordinates, such as what I photographed on the train, what I was thinking about at the time, what I was reading and what I wrote: all of this to see how completely I can project myself back to that one point in time.[17]

The fusion of Céline's verbal collages, association blocks, and the time-travel technique increases the density, the power, and the scope of each of the descriptions in *Rigodon.* The visual stimuli, evoked by means of associations and nuances, lend extraordinary credibility to each of the sequences. The reader, reacting to the author's expanded perception, by means of the picture featured, responds forcibly to the shocking, clashing, dynamic phenomena imprinted upon the pages.

One of the most excoriating collages in *Rigodon* concerns the lepers that Céline meets in Germany. The extremely detailed description of these disease-filled beings, juxtaposed or superimposed upon the image of the Nazi doctor *Oberarzt* Haupt, who believes in the perfect physical specimen, the *Übermensch,* ushers in not guffaws but feelings of utter horror.

The group of lepers who came from Berlin are described in fluoroscopic manner. Every physical and psychological detail of their make-up is included: their eyes and noses are a mass of blood, the oozing pustules, the members eaten half away with rot—all evoke feelings of nausea in the onlooker (and in the reader). As the image grows more and more unbearable, a second image is added: a nun enters and begins bandaging the lepers.[18]

Céline's fluoroscopic vision sees beyond the world of appearances. In this instance he sees the bandages that the nun puts on the lepers as just one more of those deceits that society is wont to heap upon its members. To bandage a leper is to cover up a disease that not only corrodes the entire system of the individual but spreads throughout mankind. Society has always erected barricades to stem the spread of this virus, either consciously (leprosaria) or unconsciously (feelings of revulsion). The disease, however, knows no boundaries. It inflicts itself upon individuals of all types, gnawing right through their bones and into their vitals, forcing them to swim in the very venom of its bleeding sores.

Leprosy for Céline is concomitant with evil. Hidden under the bandages, the disease is allowed to fester, to grow unchecked and to become the more virulent because its destructive path goes unobserved. Were the bandages to be removed, were the disease to be examined openly, sincerely, a cure might be found—evil might die from exposure.[19]

The bombing sequences in *Rigodon*—Hanover, Hamburg, Berlin, etc.—also take the form of verbal collages.

Hanover, a commercial city known for its mining industry, its dense population, its sandy and damp climate, a city that had been Europe's battlefield in the eighteenth century, had again become the focus of destruction in 1945:

> . . . hotter, more flamboyant . . . and the flames . . . and the flames rising higher in eddies . . . higher . . . dancing about . . . greener . . . pink between the walls . . . I had never yet seen such flames . . . they must have been using some horrible incendiary devices . . . the funny part of it all was that on each crumbling house, each heap of wreckage, the green . . . pink . . . flames danced around . . . and another round . . . toward Heaven.[20]

As the reader is enveloped in this glazed horror, identifying unconsciously with the horrendous spectacle of the burning city, another image looms forth: Céline, his wife, and their cat enter the waiting room of a railroad station. The place is filled to capacity, with people sitting, standing, or lying all about in the station itself, on the platform, in shelters, some even on the railroad tracks. Céline feels there is something sinister, even ghostly, about the vision. He observes some of the people more closely. He touches one or two of them. They fall over dead. He has difficulty distinguishing the blank stare of the dead from the fixed and despairing eyes of the living.

Hamburg is another dangerous area visited by Céline. The commandant of the city is under orders to fight to the end. But the British have made it known that, if the city is not surrendered, the heaviest bombs possible will be dropped upon it. *Gauleiter* Kaufman issues "a proclamation to the people to defend themselves to the last"—and then clears out himself, leaving the city to be demolished by air raids. When Dönitz appraises the situation, he realizes that the citizens of Hamburg are ready to rebel and orders its immediate surrender.

Céline describes the bombs being dropped on Hamburg in terms of a series of flares and flames. He takes this one image, that of the city, and divides it up into a series of close-ups and distant shots, each imposed and superimposed upon the other in rapid succession. The rhythms set up by such visual dynamism catch the onlooker (and the reader) unawares in the turbulence of the entire sequence.

> Heaps of rubbish and parts of stores . . . right on the streets in mounds, in types of heaps . . . trolley cars one on top of another, upright, sideways . . . beyond recognition . . . particularly with the smoke . . . so thick, so greasy, black and yellow . . .[21]

Perhaps the strangest incident to be described in the collage technique concerns a group of children that Céline meets on the train going to Hamburg. An attractive young woman in his compartment, Odile Pomare, was teaching these children in Breslau until forced to flee that city by the war. She escaped with around twelve of her pupils. She cannot continue her journey and take the children to a safe place because she has become seriously ill. Céline takes her temperature; it is quite high. She grows increasingly weaker as the journey progresses. Her only desire is to see to the childrens' safety. She begs Céline to take them out of the war zone. Though he has always harbored a profound distaste for children—children are filthy, insidious, deceitful, snotty, and egotistical—he cannot abandon them, somehow. But he wants to: when he arrives in Hamburg with these "repulsive gnomes," his first impulse is to lose them someplace in the rubble and leave them to die. "They stink, they're oozing with filth," [22] he thinks, as he observes them falling about and playing in every torn-up gutter.

As Céline watches the children run about in the garbage pits of Hamburg, in rotting and tottering buildings and in stores with their decaying merchandise, the time-travel technique comes into focus. Linear time is abolished. Céline's vision invades the past, the Hamburg that used to be: the small fortress built by Charlemagne and subsequently devastated by a succession of invaders (the Saxons, the Danes, and so many more), the great commercial city destroyed by fire in 1842 and once again in 1945. The historical image is not detailed; it just seems to float into the atmosphere, impregnating the entire scene with depth and an eternal quality.

A second image hovers over the scene: a close-up of the filthy street urchins as they scurry about, like a group of bubonic-infested rats. As he observes the children, the image of the writer François Mauriac comes into Céline's mind, "that cancerous old man" wearing his long cape with its "new look" as he strides about in the French Academy, the man who writes pro-Pétain articles when the political climate calls for them and pro-de Gaulle statements as that general's star rises. Céline can even hear Mauriac's voice ringing in his ear, advising the children before him to work hard so that one day they may amount to something "under any regime." Hypocrisy, Céline concludes, is Mauriac's cardinal rule. Beware, he mutters under his breath, of the man who speaks sincerely against a government that is *in* power (beware, that is, of a Céline); this man will be denounced.

Céline's vision returns to the children scampering about the torn concrete, amusing themselves running in and out of destroyed ships, urinating when the spirit moves them, laughing, screeching, jumping over piles of debris. In their world, destruction has become something positive, a playground, a toy. What fun they have climbing through tunnel upon tunnel, playing hide and seek, exploring the dismal abysses, canals, bridges, craters—all the work of the bombings. In and out of the bunkers they run; the cadavers strewn about, the rats scurrying past, never once hinder their frantic joy.

As Céline observes the tunnels, cellars, and bunkers in which the children are playing, he thinks himself "to be in a giant boat . . .,"[24] off some remote isle of the dead. As the children emerge from these cadaver-stenched realms, making their way up to street level, they are greeted with waves of smoke pouring forth from the wreckage, soaking up the entire atmosphere. All about them are masses of giant red and blue flames, undulating platforms, steel structures crashing down in a series of deafening cacophonies.[25] It is like Pompeii, Céline writes, after the eruption of Vesuvius.[26] The bombings have left gaping holes; the tar of the streets has melted from the heat of the bombs. Each step Céline takes is like trying to steady himself on quicksand. He slides and slips, his shoes become stuck in the sticky substance, which seems to pull and tug at his feet. Any thought of escape is out of the question.

The association with sticky and nearly liquefied tar might indicate, symbolically, man's eternal attempt to rise above difficulties, to create a niche of his own in society—and his incapacity to do so.

The giant abysses or maws created by the bombs, the catacombs that Céline and the children enter, are a concrete transposition of man's powerlessness when confronted with cosmic forces. It also indicates man's inability to understand the scope of his own power. He has created a technological, industrial society and become the slave of his own creation. Nothing can save the world from utter ruin, Céline implies, neither the Mauriacs nor the Claudels, the bourgeoisie nor the communists, the man of God nor the child of the gutter.

Optical Illusion. There is one incident related in *Rigodon* that bothered Céline intensely. He had experienced what is called an optical, or retinal, illusion. He could not distinguish fiction from reality—or were they to be distinguished?

"Esse est percipi," wrote George Berkeley. That is, the "existence of the physical world consists solely in its perceptibility." Anything exists, therefore, that is conceived in the mind. Modern artists believe, similarly, that the eye is endowed with unusual sensibility. When it perceives an object that is bereft of its usual conceptual associations, references, and habits (a chair and table, for example), a whole new world is ushered in.

The eye, that most delicate of optical instruments, responds to all sorts of ideographs, signs, and symbols that can serve to alter the shapes of the objects before it. A motionless object can appear to be moving and so create tension and energy. An object in motion can elicit an impression of stillness or of inertia. In its normal habitat an object tends to draw natural responses and associations from the viewer. If it is placed in a new environment, or if it assumes strange proportions or contours, or if it is simply viewed upside down, perceptual alterations occur in the viewer: spatial radiation, asymmetry, lateral movements, sensations of advancement or recession (or both), kaleidoscopic colors. These alterations are frequently "optical" and if considered sensorially, according to the painter Joseph Albers, may lead to a "discrepancy between physical fact and psychic effect." This division, Albers declares, is the basis of his art.[27] If certain objects or scenes are viewed in real life in unnatural places or in odd positions, these may be considered a "hostile attack on the senses." [28]

The impression, or image, that Céline experienced troubled him greatly. It is described as follows. Céline, his wife, and their cat are waiting at the Hamburg railroad station. It begins to rain. Céline feels terribly uncomfortable. He is suffering from head pains because in Hanover, a while back, he was struck on the head by a falling brick.[29] He is bleeding, slightly from the mouth and the nose. After he gets on the train and it begins to move, he develops fever and chills, which he diagnoses as a recurrence of his malaria. After a while, he falls asleep. Suddenly the train stops in the middle of a field. Céline opens his eyes slightly. He can barely see—his head is throbbing, his body is shaking with fever and chills.

> . . . Our train had stopped and in front of us was a type of mountain of scrap metal about a hundred meters into the field . . . and above, a locomotive standing upside down . . . perched up there . . . and not a small one I tell you, one with twelve wheels . . . in the air, upside down with twelve wheels . . . I counted them, I counted them once again . . . there must have been an explosion . . .[30]

Later, he asks Lili and others on the train whether the vision was based on reality or whether he had been imagining things. They all affirm the reality of his vision. They do so, however, in a way that leads Céline to suspect that they are trying to relieve his apparent fear of being no longer able to differentiate between his fantasy world and the workaday world.[31] Céline remains unconvinced. He can't be sure of anything any more. As the hours pass, he experiences extreme giddiness, as if he were drunk.

> . . . I could not budge either . . . it's rare that I remain this way on my back . . . without any strength at all . . . not my type . . . but at this point I had had it . . . I can't say that I had fainted, but I was dead . . . rigid . . . the train . . . I wondered . . . whether if I opened my eyes I would know where I was . . . but I tried in vain, my eyes hurt me and that's all, they remain closed, glued, with eyelids made of lead . . . I touched them . . . enormous . . . I have oedema, not only in the eyes, but the mouth, the ears . . .[32]

Even if Céline's vision was a fantasy, even if the train he saw had not been overturned, with its twelve wheels thrust up in the air, the fact that he thought he saw it made it true *(esse est percipi).*

If Céline's vision is interpreted symbolically, it could signify both the topsy-turvy nature of Céline's inner world and the upheaval confronting Germany at this time. In both cases there was utter disorientation. The train, a vehicle intended for transportation, had been impeded in its journey. Upside down, it could no longer function in its habitual manner and had lost its usefulness. It had become a sterile force. It was time, therefore, for some kind of reappraisal, for a drastic reevaluation of the train's (of Céline's and of Germany's) capacities and its relationship to the world at large.

Céline refers to this vision over and over again in *Rigodon.* It had become traumatic for him. It frightened him. It seemed to activate his strong fears of a loss of identity, of a confused mental state—of death.

Some critics consider *Rigodon* to be more difficult and more illogical—and less interesting—than Céline's earlier works. They attribute these differences to the fact that Céline, perhaps having had some kind of intimation that he was near death, finished the work in considerable haste.

Céline completed *Rigodon* on June 30, 1961, and died the next day of a cerebral hemorrhage. Time had not been allotted him to revise the proofs.

CONCLUSION

We have followed the trajectory that hate took in Céline's writings—its manifestation, evolution, eruption, and final adaptation to the forces surrounding it.

Hate, for Céline, was a propulsive agent, a force capable of igniting his rage, a wand by which the amorphous, ephemeral, and individual entities buried within his subliminal world were transformed into the concrete, eternal, and collective work of art.

Many artists—Céline is a case in point—proceed in their creative endeavors more by means of their intuitive and feeling functions than by their intellect. They are gifted with sensitive antennae that lie deep within the fibers of their being but reach out into limitless space. Céline's creative works, like those of most great artists, may be considered not only as expressions of his personal chaos but as exteriorizations of feelings and situations that touch everyone.

Creative acts can, and often do, indicate that certain unconscious forces have taken temporary possession of the author. Autonomous complexes were surely at work in each of Céline's works. They bombarded and terrorized him until he could bear their pain no longer. They cut their way through the various layers of his psyche, thrashed about, wrought havoc until they reached the light of consciousness in the form of the *word.* Had these autonomous complexes, or unintegrated aspects of Céline's psyche, not caused such extreme hate, anger, and excoriating suffering, his desire to liberate himself from these integuments might not have been so compelling and his creative works, had he written them at all, would almost certainly have been of a quite different character.

Céline was not the "master" of his subject matter. He was mastered by it. His works, therefore, can be considered as upheavals, gasps, discharges of poisons that, had they not been released, would surely have smothered him. The extraordinary dynamism of his writings and the sharply delineated frescoes that the reader encounters on nearly every page are rhythmic and visual depictions of his own cataclysmic inner state.

The seeds of Céline's writings were implanted in his very first work, the doctoral dissertation on Ignaz Semmelweis. Hatred, fear, anger, despair, hero worship, suffering, identification with and compassion for the wronged of this earth—all were present in budding form in this treatise. In *Journey to the End of the Night,* Céline's hatred emerged as a flaming force, searing individuals, peoples, nations. Disease likewise took precedence. Treated in a clinical manner in his doctoral dissertation, disease was approached affectively and symbolically in *Journey to the End of the Night.* Deterioration of the organism by sickness became a tremendously disturbing force for Céline: it became a visible expression of man's evil nature. He went to great lengths to describe sores, pustules, fungi, in the most expressionistic of manners. He was paving the way for "body consciousness," for a physical rapport with his readers. In *Death on the Installment Plan* he exposed his enmity toward the family and bourgeois society in particular, and toward humanity in general, viscerally—through images of vomiting and excrement.

It was not until the middle and late 1930s and early 1940s—before and during World War II—that Céline's hatred was transformed into an enormously destructive instrument, a weapon that he could and did use to give vent to his personal rage. Not disguised by a veneer of novelistic structure, his polemical works *(Bagatelles for a Massacre, School for Cadavers, Some State of Affairs)* excoriated those upon whom his hatred had come to focus. Like grenades, these books ravaged, scourged, mutilated all who happened into his line of fire.

Following the war and Céline's imprisonment in Denmark, he went through a period of almost complete psychological disarray. Forces were at work within him—volleys of subliminal sparks—that he could neither understand nor control. Like battering rams, they catapulted, extirpated, demolished, crushing all semblance of rational thought. *Guignol's Band* and *Fairy-Play for Another Time I and II* are the literary extensions of his inner conflicts during this period. They seem to spring forth directly from the deep and onto the printed page. But slowly, out of the shambles, the chaos that was his inner world, a kind of order began to take shape. *London's Bridge* attests to an inchoate coalescing of disparate forces, a knotting together.

In the trilogy that followed *(From Castle to Castle, North,* and *Rigodon)* a kind of adaptation to himself and to the world becomes discernible. One can hardly call any of Céline's novels calm or collected, and yet the trilogy, by comparison with the polemical volumes and the novels written immediately after the war, gives the impression of a man who has gained in his understanding of life's forces. Archetypal figures, now plentiful, stalk the pages. Mythic beings span continents and centuries, examining, judging, evaluating the debris about them. Céline's vision had grown in depth and in magnitude. He was now capable of peering into the very essence of life.

What do Céline's writings mean to us today, so many years after his death? How can today's readers experience what is essentially destructive in Céline's work—his hatred—in a constructive manner?

To study the growth process of a tree, for example, or of a work of art, one must take into consideration the soil that nourishes it, the vegetation that surrounds it. So with Céline's creations.

We have referred to his novels as "eruptions." Eruptions, whether considered from an artistic, a political, or a merely physical point of view, seem to be the more violent in civilizations that are "based on stability" and "systematized consciousness" than they are in primitive cultures. "Modern" civilization, with its still rigid, unshakable cultural canon, has created a cleavage within man himself. Virtually no rapport exists between man's conscious activities and his unconscious leanings or desires. When extremes are the rule of the day—in the individual and in the social organism—the development of a fruitful rapport between the two worlds, conscious and unconscious, is thwarted, giving rise to an imbalance. Man's inherent tendency to seek to rectify such lack of equilibrium (to bring about a state of wholeness in the individual or in the society) leads either to a gradual transformation or to an unleashing of cataclysmic forces such as those evinced by mass murders or in violent revolutions.

The creative individual who suffers such a blockage between his conscious outlook (the culture in which he has been nurtured) and his unconscious realm (which seeks to unburden itself of what he considers to have become decadent and unproductive) may be able to release what has been imprisoned within him in the form of fantasies and images. These may explode or catapult forth, passing through the locked doors and bringing illumination into the darker regions of the psyche. The creative individual will have succeeded, thereby, in expelling what had become unbearable to him personally. More important, perhaps, is the fact that he will have put this *prima materia* to use in the fashioning of his works of art.

How do *we* experience Céline's novels and polemical works?

Some readers squirm in disgust and in horror before Céline's revelations. Others find themselves laughing. Some react cerebrally, analytically, pointing to the immense political, economic, philosophical frescoes that Céline painted of our vice-ridden, corrupt, and cruel world. Others are angered by Céline's bestiality, his violence, his terror-drenched pages, his sadism, his masochism. Still others become passionate devotees of his work, admiring his courage to express what they fear to say. Few people, if any, can read Céline's works passively. He has the power to destroy our complacency, to call into question our pat answers to life's problems, to compel us to reassess ourselves and the world about us. The basic questions are posed anew (if not consciously, then unconsciously in our dreams). Reading Céline, our equilibrium is profoundly disturbed, we are engulfed by feelings of malaise. We are deprived of our spiritual crutches (our political, religious, and economic convictions), deprived of our pseudo-idealism and all the "good deeds" we do to assuage our conscience, deprived of a sense of our own "righteousness." If that is so, we have read him on his own terms, honestly, with an eye to our own negative qualities, our own shadow.

Above all, Céline inspires fright at the prospect of the future—for us as individuals and for man in general. Solitude, fear, hatred, anger, chaos—any or all of these can overpower us as we peer, with Céline as our guide, into our own smouldering depths, our own void, and as we bring back from these terrifying regions the very material needed to create our own work of art, our life.

> And the earth was without form, and void; and darkness was upon the face of the deep. And the Spirit of God moved upon the face of the waters. And God said, Let there be light: and there was light.
>
> Genesis 1:2–3.

NOTES

INTRODUCTION (pages 1–8)

1. Eric Neumann, *Depth Psychology and a New Ethic,* p. 30.
2. Ibid., p. 107.
3. Ibid.
4. Johann Wolfgand von Goethe, *Faust I* (translation by Philip Wayne, p. 75, but modified by the editors of C. G. Jung, *Symbols of Transformation,* p. 125).
5. Anneliese Aumüller, "Jungian Psychology in Wartime Germany," *Spring,* 1950, pp. 17–19.
6. Goethe, *Faust* II (translation based on MacNeice, p. 177, quoted from *Symbols of Transformation,* p. 125.)

CHAPTER 1 (pages 11–21)

1. *Oeuvres de Louis-Ferdinand Céline,* p. 581.
2. Ibid., p. 584.
3. Ibid., p. 587.
4. Ibid.
5. Ibid., p. 591.
6. Ibid., p. 596.
7. Ibid., p. 606.
8. Ibid., p. 608.
9. Ibid., p. 618.
10. Helmuth Plessner, "On the Relation of Time to Death," *Eranos Yearbooks,* III, p. 233.
11. Ibid., pp. 239–40.
12. William Barrett, *Irrational Man,* p. 63.
13. Plessner, p. 253.
14. Ibid., p. 255.
15. Ibid., p. 248.
16. Edward Edinger, "An Outline of Analytical Psychology," *Quadrant,* No. I (1968) p. 11.
17. C. G. Jung, *Symbols of Transformation,* p. 112.
18. Bettina Knapp, *Georges Duhamel,* Chapters I-V.
19. *Oeuvres,* p. 18.
20. Eric Neumann, "Art and Time," *Eranos Yearbooks,* III, p. 16.

CHAPTER 2 (pages 22–51)

1. Céline dedicated the finished volume to Elisabeth Craig "l'Impératrice," as he called her, a dancer whom he had met in Geneva.

2. Robert Scholes, *The Fabulators,* p. 61.
3. Edgar Herzog, *Psyche and Death,* p. 18.
4. *Journey to the End of the Night* (translated by John H. P. Marks), p. 4.
5. Eric Neumann, *Depth Psychology and a New Ethic,* p. 75.
6. Céline/Marks, *Journey,* p. 13.
7. Ibid., p. 9.
8. Ibid., p. 13.
9. Ibid., p. 25.
10. Ibid., p. 9.
11. Ibid., p. 12.
12. Ibid., p. 53.
13. Ibid., p. 48.
14. *Oeuvres de Louis-Ferdinand Céline,* p. 16.
15. Céline/Marks, *Journey,* p. 5.
16. Ibid., p. 66.
17. Ibid., p. 51.
18. Ibid., p. 51.
19. Ibid., p. 48.
20. Ibid., p. 47.
21. Ibid., p. 61.
22. Ibid., p. 60.
23. Ibid., p. 87.
24. Ibid., p. 97.
25. Ibid., p. 108.
26. Ibid., p. 113.
27. Ibid., p. 109.
28. Ibid., p. 115.
29. C. G. Jung, *Structure and Dynamics of the Psyche,* p. 308.
30. Ibid.
31. Céline/Marks, *Journey,* p. 119.
32. Ibid., p. 121.
33. Edgar Herzog, p. 81.
34. Ibid., p. 19.
35. Earl Rovit, *Ernest Hemingway,* p. 36.
36. Frederick J. Hoffman, *William Faulkner,* p. 62.
37. Ibid., p. 64.
38. Herzog, pp. 27–33.
39. Walter Allen, *The Modern Novel,* p. 300.
40. Céline/Marks, *Journey,* p. 165.
41. Ibid., p. 178.
42. Ibid., p. 168.
43. Ibid.
44. Ibid.
45. Céline/Marks, *Journey,* p. 192.
46. Ibid., p. 202.
47. Ibid.
48. Ibid., p. 201.
49. Siegfried Kracauer, *Theory of Film,* p. 159.
50. Ibid., p. 159.
51. Ibid., p. 167.
52. Céline/Marks, *Journey,* p. 232.
53. Liliane Frey-Rohn, "Evil from the Psychological Point of View," *Evil,* p. 195.

54. Ibid., p. 157.
55. Ibid. (quoting Nietzsche but from Liliane Frey-Rohn's article "Evil from the Psychological Point of View.")
56. Ibid., p. 158.
57. Céline/Marks, *Journey*, pp. 225–32.
58. Ibid., p. 268.
59. Ibid., p. 325.
60. Ibid., p. 296.
61. Liliane Frey-Rohn, p. 198.
62. Céline/Marks, *Journey*, p. 426.
63. Ibid., p. 504.
64. Ibid.
65. Ibid.
66. *Oeuvres*, p. 781.
67. Ibid., p. 792.
68. Ibid., p. 798.
69. Ibid., p. 800.
70. Ibid., p. 810.
71. Ibid., p. 808.

CHAPTER 3 (pages 52–60)

1. *Oeuvres de Louis-Ferdinand Céline*, p. 390.
2. Ibid.
3. Ibid., p. 735.
4. In Act III, Yudenzweck says of Bardamu: "He's a lad without any collective importance, he's just about an individual." Sartre must have been impressed by this statement, since he quoted it in his novel *Nausea.*
5. Céline, p. 391.
6. Ibid., p. 412.
7. Ibid., p. 487.
8. Ibid., p. 488.
9. Rabi, "Un ennemi de l'homme," *Céline, les cahiers de l'herne en poche-club*, pp. 216–25.
10. Jeanine Parisier-Plottel, *Les Dialogues de Paul Valéry*, pp. 30–35.
11. Paul Valéry, *Oeuvres*, Gallimard, 2, p. 156.
12. Ibid., p. 161.
13. Ibid., p. 163.
14. Ibid., p. 1391.
15. *Oeuvres*, p. 475.
16. C. G. Jung, *Psychological Types*, p. 178.
17. Ibid., p. 180.

CHAPTER 4 (pages 61–85)

1. Céline, *Death on the Installment Plan*, (translated by Ralph Manheim), p. 15.
2. Jean-Paul Sartre, *What is Literature?* pp. 210–11.
3. C. G. Jung, *Psychological Types*, p. 43.
4. *Oeuvres de Louis-Ferdinand Céline*, p. 717.
5. Céline/Manheim, *Death*, p. 67.
6. Ibid., p. 455.
7. Ibid., p. 224.
8. Robert Champigny, *Le Genre dramatique*, p. 39.
9. Céline/Manheim, *Death*, p. 64.
10. Ibid., p. 106.
11. Ibid., p. 67.
12. Ibid., p. 123.

13. Ibid., p. 220.
14. Ibid., p. 122.
15. Ibid., p. 176.
16. *Oeuvres,* p. 38.
17. Henri Bergson, *Le Rire,* p. 3.
18. *Oeuvres,* p. 39.
19. Ibid., p. 58.
20. Bergson, p. 20.
21. Céline/Manheim, *Death,* p. 93.
22. Ibid., p. 200.
23. Ibid., p. 223.
24. Ibid., p. 212.
25. Ibid., p. 228.
26. Ibid., p. 403.
27. Robert G. Elliott, *The Power of Satire,* p. 264.
28. R.-M. Albérès, Sartre, p. 38.
29. Céline/Manheim, *Death,* p. 43.
30. Ibid., p. 57.
31. Ibid., p. 111.
32. Ibid., p. 319.
33. Ibid., p. 570.
34. Ibid., p. 89.
35. Robert Scholes, *The Fabulators,* pp. 137–39.
36. Eric Neumann, *The Origins and History of Consciousness,* p. 27.
37. C. G. Jung, *Symbols of Transformation,* p. 189.
38. Erik Erikson, *Martin Luther,* p. 247.
39. Ibid., p. 244.
40. Ibid., p. 206.
41. Léon Poliakov, *Histoire de l'antisémitisme de Voltaire à Wagner,* p. 110.
42. Robert Scholes, *The Fabulators,* p. 142.
43. Céline/Manheim, *Death,* p. 48.
44. Ibid., p. 69.
45. Ibid., p. 134.
46. Ibid., p. 275.
47. Ibid., p. 143.
48. Ibid., p. 136.
49. Ibid., p. 143.
50. Ibid., p. 241.
51. Ibid., p. 68.
52. Ibid., p. 314.
53. Ibid., p. 27.
54. Carl Kerenyi, "The Problem of Evil in Mythology," *Evil,* pp. 3–17.
55. *Oeuvres,* pp. 739–53.

CHAPTER 5 (pages 86–90)

1. *Oeuvres de Louis-Ferdinand Céline,* p. 459.
2. Ibid., p. 486.
3. Ibid., p. 494.

CHAPTER 6 (pages 93–130)

1. Malcolm Hay, *Europe and the Jews,* p. 33.
2. Salo W. Baron, *A Social and Religious History of the Jews,* ix,x,xi,xii,xiii,xiv.
3. Hay, p. 37.
4. Ibid.

5. Ibid., p. 43.
6. Ibid., p. 55.
7. Jacob R. Marcus, *The Jew in the Medieval World,* p. 65.
8. Ibid., p. 42.
9. Hay, p. 92.
10. Ibid., p. 142.
11. Ibid., p. 143.
12. Arthur Herzberg, *The French Enlightenment and the Jews,* p. 120.
13. Ibid., p. 14.
14. Hay, p. 173.
15. *Oeuvres de Louis-Ferdinand Céline,* p. 628.
16. Léon Poliakov, *Histoire de l'antisémitisme de Voltaire à Wagner,* p. 88.
17. Ibid., p. 89.
18. Ibid., p. 97.
19. Ibid., p. 103.
20. Ibid., p. 106.
21. Ibid.
22. Ibid., p. 107.
23. Ibid., p. 120.
24. Ibid., p. 121.
25. Ibid., p. 122.
26. Ibid., p. 129.
27. Ibid.
28. Ibid.
29. Herzberg, p. 1.
30. Hay, p. 171.
31. Poliakov, p. 161.
32. Ibid., p. 351.
33. Ibid., p. 369.
34. Ibid., p. 357.
35. Ibid., p. 371.
36. Ibid., p. 372.
37. Robert Byrnes, *Antisemitism in Modern France,* p. 48.
38. Hay, p. 179.
39. Poliakov, pp. 380–83.
40. Ibid., p. 282.
41. Byrnes, pp. 119–20.
42. Poliakov, p. 386–91.
43. Ibid., p. 387.
44. Byrnes, pp. 157–58.
45. Ibid.
46. Hay, p. 177.
47. Ibid., p. 178.
48. Ibid., p. 177.
49. Ibid., p. 178.
50. Ibid., p. 180.
51. Ibid., p. 187.
52. Ibid.
53. Georges Bernanos, *Les Grands cimetières sous la lune,* p. 126.
54. Hay, p. 196.
55. Ibid.
56. Ibid., p. 196.
57. *La Libre Parole,* Feb. 12, 1898.

58. Byrnes, p. 44.
59. Hay, p. 205.
60. William Shirer, *The Collapse of the Third Republic*, p. 285.
61. Ibid., p. 411.
62. Ibid., p. 441.
63. Ibid.
64. Ibid., p. 285.
65. Ibid., p. 292.
66. Ibid.
67. Ibid., p. 300.
68. William Shirer, *Berlin Diary*, 1941, p. 86.
69. *The Goebbels Diaries: 1941–1943*, p. 18.
70. Shirer, *The Collapse of the Third Republic*, p. 550.
71. Ibid., p. 336.
72. Ibid.
73. Ibid., p. 337.
74. Ibid., p. 339.
75. Ibid., p. 351.
76. Ibid., p. 384.
77. Ibid., p. 384.
78. Ibid., p. 515.
79. Shirer, *Berlin Diary*, p. 412.
80. Ibid., p. 417.
81. Nathan Ackerman and Marie Jahoda, *Anti-Semitism and Emotional Disorder*, p. 2.
82. James Parkes, *Anti-Semitism*, p. 9.
83. Richard Brickner, *Is Germany Curable?* p. 34.
84. Ackerman and Jahoda, p. 34.
85. Paul W. Massing, *Rehearsal for Destruction*, pp. 165–80.
86. Ackerman and Jahoda, p. 55.
87. *Essays on Anti-Semitism*, p. 87.
88. Ackerman and Jahoda, p. 4.
89. Parkes, p. 88.
90. *Essays on Anti-Semitism*, p. 197.
91. Parkes, p. 88.
92. Hay, p. 3.
93. Ibid., p. 7.
94. Massing, p. 167.
95. *Essays on Anti-Semitism*, pp. 187–98.
96. Hay, XXI.
97. "Anti-Semitism is Called Evasion of Self-Criticism," The *New York Times* (Jan. 10, 1971).
98. Jean-Paul Sartre, *Anti-Semite and Jew*, p. 13.
99. Ibid., p. 27.
100. Ibid., p. 40.
101. Ibid., p. 43.
102. *Céline, les cahiers de l'herne en poche-club*, pp. 32–33.
103. C. G. Jung, *The Psychogenesis of Mental Disease*, p. 55.
104. Edward Edinger, "An Outline of Analytical Psychology," pp. 8–9.
105. Eric Neumann, *Depth Psychology and a New Ethic*, p. 40.
106. Ibid., p. 50.
107. Parkes, p. 11.
108. Ibid.
109. Hay, p. 37.

110. Neumann, p. 52.
111. Ibid., p. 55.
112. Ibid., p. 57.
113. Richard Brickner, *Is Germany Curable?* p. 43.
114. Ibid., p. 93.
115. Ibid.
116. Neumann, p. 41–43.
117. Ibid.
118. Ibid., p. 71.
119. Ibid., p. 79.
120. Ibid., p. 98.
121. C. G. Jung, *The Psychogenesis of Mental Disease,* p. 40.
122. Ibid., p. 240.
123. Ibid., p. 56.
124. C. G. Jung, p. 45.
125. Ibid., p. 87.
126. Neumann, *History of the Origins of Consciousness,* p. 288.
127. Jung, *Psychogenesis,* p. 47.
128. Céline, *Bagatelles pour un massacre,* p. 305.
129. Jean-Paul Sartre, *Anti-Semite and Jew,* p. 41.
130. *Oeuvres de Louis-Ferdinand Céline,* pp. 415–16.
131. C. G. Jung, *Psychogenesis,* p. 53.
132. Ibid., p. 39.
133. Ibid., p. 41.
134. Ibid., p. 21.
135. Ibid., p. 113.
136. Ibid., p. 23.
137. Ibid., p. 25.
138. Ibid., p. 41.
139. Ibid., p. 77.
140. Ibid., p. 79.
141. Céline, *Bagatelles pour un massacre,* p. 56.
142. Ibid., p. 15.
143. Ibid., p. 76.
144. Ibid., p. 71.
145. Ibid., p. 219.
146. Ibid., p. 170.
147. Ibid.
148. Ibid., p. 172.
149. Ibid., p. 126.
150. Ibid., p. 181.
151. Ibid., p. 192.
152. Ibid., p. 188.
153. Ibid.
154. Ibid., p. 16.
155. Ibid., pp. 42–43.
156. *Céline, les cahiers de l'herne en poche-club,* p. 17.
157. Ibid., p. 336.
158. *Voyou Paul, Brave Virginie,* a ballet mime, was published in 1959. It is an interpretation of the well-known romantic novel *Paul and Virginia* by Bernardin de St. Pierre.

The ballet is marked by tremendous activity. The opening scene is one of festivity, beautiful trees, waterways, flowers, and a tropical countryside. The lovers, Paul and Virginia, dance in happiness. When Paul, however, begins paying attention to other young lasses, Virginia cannot help but become troubled. In desperation she takes a vial from a sorceress and drinks it. Removing her clothes in a state of utter frenzy, she dances like a flame; delirium takes hold of her. She is no longer the gentle Virginia but a burst of extraordinary cadences, leaps, and prances. Paul watches her, subjugated. He leaves the other girls. Furious at his departure, one of them grabs a pistol from a nearby sailor and shoots Virginia. Paul despairs. He suffers deeply from her death. Soon, however, the young girl is dancing about him and interests him in life again. He drinks and forgets her in merriment.

In this ballet Céline confronts his viewers with the pure virgin (as he had in his previous ballet, *The Birth of a Fairy,* discussed in chapter three), the perfect girl who cannot keep the affection of her beloved. Man, as represented by Paul, is faithless. He is dominated by the sensual and cannot settle down. To try to break his pattern, Virginia attempts to rise above her mortal stature, availing herself of the secret of the dance. Only as a "flame," as pure dance, as the Ideal will Paul adore her—not as a mortal. Virginia, no more than the fairy in *The Birth of a Fairy,* cannot take unto herself what does not properly belong to her dominion. She must, therefore, die, and die she does.

159. *Bagatelles pour un massacre,* p. 27.
160. Ibid., p. 28.
161. Ibid.
162. Ibid., p. 45.
163. Ibid., p. 47.
164. Ibid., p. 51.
165. Ibid., p. 50.
166. Ibid., p. 51.
167. Ibid., p. 53.
168. Ibid., p. 91.
169. Ibid., p. 83.
170. Ibid., p. 317.
171. Ibid., p. 318.
172. Ibid.
173. Ibid., p. 323.
174. Ibid., p. 78.
175. Ibid., p. 188.
176. Ibid., p. 191.
177. Ibid., p. 275.
178. Ibid., p. 250.
179. Ibid., p. 131.
180. Ibid., p. 192.
181. Ibid., p. 45.
182. Ibid., p. 67.
183. Ibid., p. 57.
185. Céline, *L'Ecole des cadavres,* pp. 62–100.
186. Ibid., p. 245.
187. Ibid., p. 258.
188. William E. Shirer, *Berlin Diary,* p. 52.
189. *L'École des cadavres,* p. 203.
190. Ibid., p. 98.
191. *Les Beaux draps,* p. 115.
192. *Céline, les cahiers de l'herne en poche-club,* p. 247.
193. Ibid.. p. 70.

194. *Bagatelles pour un massacre,* p. 96.
195. Ibid., p. 318.
196. All of Céline's quotations from the Talmud were distorted by him. For a full discussion of the subject of distortions see: R. Travers Herford, *Christianity in Talmud and Midrash* (reprinted), Clifton, New Jersey: Library of Religious and Philosophical Thought, 1966; Joseph S. Block, *Israel and the Nations,* Vienna-Berlin: Benjamin Harz, 1927; and Edward H. Flannery, *The Anguish of the Jews,* New York: Macmillan & Company 1965.
197. Ibid., p. 284.
198. *Céline les cahiers de l'herne en poche-club,* p. 43.
199. *Les Beaux draps,* p. 194.
200. Ibid., p. 115.
201. Ibid., p. 193.
202. Ibid., pp. 197–98.

CHAPTER 7 (pages 133–146)

1. Gerhard Adler, *The Living Symbol,* p. 72.
2. Helen Weinberg, *The New Novel in America,* pp. 11–14.
3. Will Durant, *The Story of Philosophy,* p. 399.
4. Ibid., p. 352.
5. C. G. Jung, *The Spirit in Man, Art, and Literature,* p. 137.
6. *Guignol's Band* (translated by Bernard Frechtman and Jack T. Nile), p. 7.
7. Joshua Taylor, *Futurism,* pp. 25–41.
8. Katherine Kuh, *Art Explained,* p. 45.
9. C. G. Jung, *Man and His Symbols,* pp. 264–65.
10. *Guignol's Band,* p. 79.
11. Ibid., p. 82.
12. Ibid., p. 83.
13. Ibid., p. 198.
14. *Oeuvres de Louis-Ferdinand Céline,* p. 523, 538, 550.
15. Ibid.
16. *Guignol's Band,* p. 55.
17. C. G. Jung, *Psychogenesis of Mental Disease,* pp. 94–95; 109–21; 78.
18. *Guignol's Band,* pp. 176, 178, 180.
19. Bettina Knapp, *Le Mirliton: A Novel Based on the Life of Aristide Bruant,* p. 218.
20. *Guignol's Band,* p. 38.
21. *Oeuvres,* p. 729.
22. Ibid., p. 730.

CHAPTER 8 (pages 147–156)

1. Marie-Louise von Franz, *Apuleius' Golden Ass,* VI, p. 12.
2. *Oeuvres de Louis-Ferdinand Céline,* p. 424.
3. Ibid., p. 426.
4. Ibid., p. 428.
5. Ibid., p. 430.
6. Ibid., p. 431.
7. Ibid., p. 445.
8. Ibid., p. 437.
9. Ibid., p. 441.
10. Ibid., p. 441.
11. C. G. Jung, *The Spirit in Man, Art, and Literature,* p. 138.
12. Ritchie Andre, C. *Masters of British Painting.*

13. *Oeuvres*, p. 431.
14. *Bref* (October, 1970), p. 3.
15. June Singer, *The Unholy Bible*, p. 244.
16. *Oeuvres*, p. 526.
17. J. E. Cirlot, *A Dictionary of Symbols*, p. 130.
18. Sandor Lorand and Michael Balint, *Perversions*, p. 243.
19. *Oeuvres*, p. 357.
20. Ibid., p. 359.
21. Walter Allen, *The Modern Novel*, p. 9.

CHAPTER 9 (pages 157–166)

1. Pierre-Henri Simon, *L'Homme en procés*, pp. 29–51.
2. Norman Mailer, *Advertisements for Myself*, "White Negro," p. 336.
3. Barry H. Leeds, *The Structured Vision of Norman Mailer*, pp. 227–29.
4. J. E. Circlot, *A Dictionary of Symbols*, p. 241.
5. *Oeuvres de Louis-Ferdinand Céline*, p. 10.
6. Ibid., p. 11.
7. Ibid., p. 6.
8. Ibid., p. 10.
9. Ibid., p. 15.
10. Ibid., p. 185.
11. Herbert Reed, *Art and Alienation*, pp. 40–56.
12. Ibid., p. 43.

CHAPTER 10 (pages 167–177)

1. *Oeuvres de Louis-Ferdinand Céline*, p. 17.
2. Molière, *Don Juan*, I, 11.
3. *Oeuvres*, p. 32.
4. Ibid., p. 53.
5. Ibid., p. 78.
6. Ibid.
7. Ibid.
8. Ibid., p. 80.
9. Ibid., p. 250.
10. Aaron Copland, *The New Music 1900–1960*, p. 178.
11. This passage is also reminiscent of Céline's ballet. Céline never lost his passion for his art form. In fact, he wrote several ballets during the war and afterward. Perhaps the most intriguing of these was *Scandal in the Depths*. This work, published in 1950 with drawings by Pierre-Marie Benet, was written, according to the author's letter to Milton Hindus, before 1947. It is a mythological ballet in which the old Neptune, the god of captain. Tragedy fills the air as Neptune suffers pain, for he sends a typhoon which destroys the murderous captain's ship: as Neptune's fury rages, so the ship is destroyed. At the end Neptune, still disconsolate, flees from Venus' sight to live in solitude.

    The visual images in Céline's novels stand out as one of the most potent forces in his literary style. They are equally important in *Scandal in the Depths*. It is the ballet's philosophical message, however, so expertly expressed, that makes for its import. Neptune and Venus are symbols of decadence, of sterility, of power lost and gone.

    The king, in a most general sense, usually represents universal man. As a ruler, he possesses supernatural powers, wisdom, supreme consciousness, the virtues of sound judgment and self-control. Such would be the characteristics of Jupiter, for example, who lives in the "upper regions" of the universe, referred to at times as the "Upper Ocean" (the clouds, rain, or fresh water). Neptune, on the other hand, lives in the ocean and personifies the depths of the unconscious in its most regressive form. Since Neptune is already old and feeble, his power has already waned. Such impotence indicates decadence, not merely physical decline but also an ineffectuality in his role in life and in his way of life. He is comparable to Dhritarashtra, the aged monarch of the Vedic epic, and to King Lear. It is Neptune who unleashes the storm that represents passion at the end of the ballet and who acts as the captain's destroyer, thus avenging the death of the beautiful maiden. But this outburst only serves to emphasize the prevailing atmosphere of weakness and decrepitude.

Venus, once beautiful, is now ugliness personified. Because she is unwilling to accept life's vicissitudes (that is, old age) she is a caricature of her former self, a creature distorted and bizarre in both body and soul.

Thus we are introduced to two decadent rulers who have refused to abdicate their predominant roles, refused to fulfill nature's decree that they pass on to another phase of existence, thereby completing life's circle. Having rejected what is natural, they have made a mockery of themselves, and no longer command respect, and they suffer intense anguish as a result.

What Céline indicates in this superb ballet is man's refusal to accept death as part of life, his refusal to recognize that there is a time to rule, to live, to procreate, to energize, to catalyze, to slumber, to retreat—to die. As was said in *Ecclesiastes* (3:1 and 2):

> To everything there is a season, and a time to every
> purpose under the heaven;
> A time to be born, and a time to die; a time to plant and
> a time to pluck up what is planted . . .

So with people, so with governments, civilizations . . .

Just as man is strong when young and weak when old, so do civilizations rise and fall. Edward Gibbon, in his *Decline and Fall of the Roman Empire,* observed that history, that record of "little more than the crimes, follies, and misfortunes of mankind," has its birth, development, and demise. Similarly, Oswald Spengler contended in *The Decline of the West* that history has a natural development, that every culture has a distinct organic form that grows, matures, and decays, that Western (European) culture is in its last stages and about ready to come to an end. Arnold Toynbee, less objectively and less scientifically, reached a similar conclusion in his twelve-volume *A Study of History,* in which he compared twenty-one "civilizations," tracing their cyclical patterns of growth, maturity, and decay. Societies, he claims, are at their best when responding to challenges. Religion is the most important aspect of social order in this respect, and although Western civilization is in its last phase, Toynbee thinks, a spiritually oriented society may yet be formed.

In *Scandal in the Depths* Céline delineates the decline of a form of government (that has become worn and impotent, the chaos that must of necessity ensue as it paves the way for a new era. He gives us no clue, however, as to what he imagines may be in store for us in future.

Thunder and Arrows, published in 1949, is also a mythological ballet featuring Jupiter and Juno, but in this work the King of Heaven is not only old but is also senile—a libertine who is forever pursuing beautiful maidens. Juno tries to capture his affection by dancing lasciviously before him in the nude. He remains impervious to her wiles. A storm ensues. Juno goes to sleep and Jupiter, first assuming the form of a merchant and then that of a miraculous bird, visits the earth. After enjoying himself with beautiful maidens he returns. Juno rages. War is declared between Jupiter and Achilles, Ajax and others. Jupiter wins the first battle, but the Greeks, resorting to ruse (as Greeks were wont to do), put on horrendous masks that terrify the enemy. Even the gods are frightened. Jupiter puts his hands in front of his eyes. Inhuman forms lunge about. Achilles wins. Juno, angered at Jupiter's infidelities, forces the maid whom Jupiter covets to marry a Cyclops. All is resolved at the end. Only Mars, the god of war, prepares for his next battle.

It is said that in this ballet Céline depicted real situations and made allusions to actual personalities.

In *Thunder and Arrows,* as the title suggests, fury, pain, and ugliness take precedence. War, not beauty, stands uppermost. It is not, however, a battle between the forces of good and evil; it is merely a struggle between one species of ugliness and another. Righteousness does not win out at the end. One has the distinct impression that something ominous is in the offing, that man is preparing for some new horrendous, deceitful, and destructive escapade.

12. Oeuvres, p. 86.
13. Joseph L. Henderson and Maud Oakes, *The Wisdom of the Serpent,* p. 13.
14. Ibid., p. 14.
15. Aaron Copland, p. 177.
16. *Oeuvres,* p. 110.
17. Ibid., p. 109.
18. Ibid., p. 334.

CHAPTER 11 (pages 181–200)

1. *Céline, les cahiers de l'herne en poche-club,* pp. 44–46.
2. Marie-Louise von Franz, *Apuleius' Golden Ass,* IV, p. 6.
3. *Oeuvres de Louis-Ferdinand Céline,* p. 318
4. Ibid., p. 312.
5. Dorsha Hayes, "Conrad's Heart of Darkness: An Aspect of the Shadow", *Spring,* 1956, p. 65.
6. *Oeuvres,* p. 318.
7. Ibid., p. 321.
8. "Collective Unconscious in Literature," *Spring* (1958), p. 65.
9. *Apuleius' Golden Ass,* VI.
10. Ibid., VI, p. 7.
11. C. G. Jung, "Interpretation of Visions," *Spring* (1963), p. 113.
12. William Burroughs, *Naked Lunch,* p. 243.
13. Celine *Oeuvres,* p. 318.
14. *Genesis,* p. 21.
15. *Oeuvres,* p. 317.
16. "Interpretation of Visions," *Spring* (1963), p. 133.
17. C. G. Jung, *Symbols of Transformation,* p. 110.
18. John Hawkes, *The Cannibal,* p. 3.
19. *Oeuvres,* p. 410.
20. Ibid., p. 348.
21. Ibid., p. 342.
22. Ibid.
23. Ibid., p. 338.
24. Ibid., p. 339.
25. Céline, *From Castle to Castle,* (translated by Ralph Manheim), p. 12.
26. Ibid.
27. Robert Donington, *Wagner's Ring,* p. 50.

28. *Oeuvres*, p. 267.
29. Albert Speer, *Inside the Third Reich*, p. 55.
30. Gerhard Adler, *The Living Symbol*, p. 146.
31. Marie-Louise von Franz, "Archetypal Patterns in Fairy Tales, 1951, (unpublished).
32. *Oeuvres*, p. 386.
33. *Time Magazine*, Jan. 11, 1971.
34. *Oeuvres*, p. 383.
35. Ibid., p. 461.
36. William Shirer, *The Collapse of the Third Republic*, p. 858.
37. *Oeuvres*, p. 356.
38. Ibid., p. 369.
39. Hannah Vogt, *The Burden of Guilt*, p. 129.
40. *Apuleius' Golden Ass*, IV, pp. 10–12.
41. *Oeuvres*, p. 376.
42. Albert Speer, *Inside the Third Reich*, pp. 125–27.
43. *Oeuvres*, p. 432.
44. Shirer, p. 441.
45. June Singer, *The Unholy Bible*, p. 115.
46. *Oeuvres*, p. 420.
47. Shirer, p. 892.
48. André Bazin, *What Is Cinema*, p. 35.
49. Speer, p. 272.
50. John Barth, *Lost in the Funhouse*, Xi.
51. Elliott Arnold, *A Night of Watching*, p. 413–41.
52. *Oeuvres*, p. 401.
53. Ibid., p. 340.
54. Ibid., p. 401.
55. Ibid., p. 305.
56. Ibid., p. 371.
57. "Archetypal Patterns in Fairy Tales."
58. *Oeuvres*, p. 540.
59. Ibid., p. 378.
60. Ibid., p. 413.
61. Ibid., p. 380.
62. Ibid., p. 363.

CHAPTER 12 (pages 201–221)

1. Eric Neumann, "Art and Time," *The Eranos Yearbooks*, III, pp. 11–12.
2. Bettina Knapp, *Jean Genet*, p. 141.
3. *Oeuvres de Louis-Ferdinand Céline*, pp. 21–25.
4. Norman MacKenzie, *Dreams and Dreaming*, p. 17.
5. Ibid., p. 19.
6. *Oeuvres*, p. 26.
7. Ibid.
8. C. G. Jung, *Man and His Symbols*, p. 141.
9. Marie-Louise von Franz, "Archetypal Patterns in Fairy Tales," (unpublished), p. 16.
10. *Oeuvres*, pp. 28–29.
11. *Man and His Symbols*, p. 148.
12. Eric Neumann, *The Origins and History of Consciousness*, p. 84.
13. C. Kerenyi, "The Mysteries of the Kabeiroi," *The Eranos Yearbooks*, II, p. 39.
14. Ibid.

15. *Oeuvres*, p. 187.
16. Ibid., p. 201.
17. *Jean Genet*, p. 19.
18. Friedrich Nietzsche, *The Birth of Tragedy*, p. 186.
19. *Oeuvres*, p. 66.
20. Ibid., p. 35–36.
21. *Man and His Symbols*, p. 52.
22. Nietzsche, p. 173.
23. Kerenyi, pp. 33–34.
24. Edouard Schure, *The Great Initiates*, p. 229.
25. *The Origins and History of Consciousness*, p. 305.
26. Ibid., pp. 252–3.
27. *Oeuvres*, p. 127.
28. Ibid., p. 150.
29. Ibid., p. 151.
30. Ibid., pp. 290–10.
31. Ibid., p. 152.
32. Ibid., p. 111.
33. Ibid.
34. Ibid., p. 383.
35. Ibid., p. 222.
36. Ibid., p. 279.
37. Ibid., p. 253.
38. Ibid.
39. Ibid., p. 101.
40. Ibid., p. 127.
41. Ibid., p. 229.
42. Ibid., p. 255.
43. Walter F. Otto, "The Meanings of the Eleusinian Mysteries," *The Eranos Yearbooks*, II, p. 15.
44. According to Cicero's description in *De Legibus*, II.
45. "The Mysteries of the Kabeiroi," *The Eranos Yearbooks*, II, pp. 32–64.
46. Walter Wili, "The Orphic Mysteries and the Greek Spirit," *The Eranos Yearbooks*, II, pp. 64–90.
47. *Webster's New World Dictionary*.
48. *Oeuvres*, p. 225.
49. Ibid.
50. Ibid., p. 161.
51. Ibid., p. 161.
52. Ibid., p. 106.
53. Ibid., p. 183.
54. Ibid., p. 233.
55. Ibid., pp. 77, 128.
56. Stephen Stepaneber, *American Poetry Since 1945*.
57. Gerard Adler, *The Living Symbol*, p. 120.
58. Kerenyi, p. 47.
59. Nietzsche, *The Birth of Tragedy*, pp. 192–93.
60. Ibid., p. 177.
61. *Oeuvres*, p. 276.
62. Ibid.
63. C. G. Jung, *Psychological Types*, p. 178.
64. "Art and Time," p. 28.
65. *Man and His Symbols*, p. 154.

66. Ibid., p. 265.
67. *Oeuvres,* p. 234.
68. Ibid., p. 266.
69. Ibid., p. 322.

CHAPTER 13 (pages 222–232)

1. Though Céline had not witnessed the Allied bombings of Germany's gasoline supply in the spring of 1944 (he had left France a month after the allies landed in Normandy on June 6, 1944), he did describe the intense conflagrations he had witnessed in both Berlin and Hamburg.
2. Hannah Vogt, *The Burden of Guilt,* p. 274.
3. Ibid.
4. Ibid.
5. Albert Speer, *Inside the Third Reich,* p. 555.
6. Vogt, p. 275.
7. Ibid., p. 277.
8. Speer, p. 561.
9. *Oeuvres de Louis-Ferdinand Céline,* p. 359.
10. Ibid., p. 336.
11. Ibid., p. 335.
12. Ibid., p. 343.
13. Ibid., p. 336.
14. Henry Miller, *A Private Correspondence,* p. 340.
15. Warren French, *John Steinbeck,* p. 85. Like Steinbeck, Céline most frequently uses periods in history, particularly repulsive ones, not as objects in their own right but as a means of revealing truth as he saw it—truth that might otherwise have remained hidden.
16. *Writers at Work,* p. 150.
17. Ibid., p. 149.
18. *Oeuvres,* p. 360.
19. Ibid., p. 417.
20. Ibid., p. 418.
21. Ibid., p. 452.
22. Ibid., p. 448.
23. Ibid.
24. Ibid., p. 455.
25. Ibid., p. 468.
26. Ibid., p. 468.
27. William C. Seitz, *The Responsive Eye,* pp. 5–20.
28. Ibid., p. 19.
29. *Oeuvres,* p. 425.
30. Ibid., p. 430.
31. Ibid., p. 431.
32. Ibid., p. 437.

BIBLIOGRAPHY

WORKS BY CÉLINE

Oeuvres de Louis-Ferdinand Céline, Paris: André Balland.

VOLUME 1 (1966)

Voyage au bout de la nuit [Paris: Denoël et Steele, 1932].
L'Eglise [Paris: Denoël et Steele, 1933].
Scandale aux Abysses [Paris: F. Chambriand, 1950].
La Naissance d'une fée [Paris: Gallimard, 1959].
Voyou Paul. Pauvre Virginie [Paris: Gallimard, 1959].
Van Bagaden [Paris: Denoël, 1937].
Foudres et flèches [Paris: C. de Jonquières, 1949].
Secrets dans l'île [Paris: Gallimard, 1936].
La Vie et l'oeuvre de Philippe-Ignace Semmelweis, 1818–1865 [Paris: Imprimerie Francis Simon, 1924].
La Quinine en thérapeutique [Paris: Doin, 1925].
La Médecine chez Ford [Paris: Lectures 40, 1941].
Les Assurances sociales et une politique économique de la santé publique [*La Presse médicale,* November 24, 1928].
Pour tuer le chômage, tueront-ils les chômeurs? [*République,* March 19, 1933].

VOLUME 2 (1967)

Mort à credit [Paris: Denoël et Steele, 1936].
Casse-pipe [Paris: F. Chambriand, 1949].
Hommage à Zola [Paris: Denoël et Steele, 1936].
Préface pour Bezons à travers les ages [Paris: Denoël, 1944].
Guignol's Band, I [Paris: Denoël, 1944].

VOLUME 3 (1967)

Guignol s Band, II (Le Pont de Londres) [Paris: Gallimard, 1964].
Mea Culpa [Paris: Denoël et Steele, 1936].
Entretiens avec le Professeur Y [Paris: Gallimard, 1955].
A l'agité du bocal [Paris: P. L. de Tartas, 1948].
Féerie pour une autre fois, I [Paris: Gallimard, 1952].

VOLUME 4 (1967)

Féerie pour une autre fois, II (Normance) [Paris: Gallimard, 1954].
D'un Château l'autre [Paris: Gallimard, 1959].

VOLUME 5 (1969)

Nord [Paris: Gallimard, 1960].
Rigodon [Paris: Gallimard, 1969].

Bagatelles pour un massacre, Paris: Denoël, 1937.
L'École des cadavres. Paris: Denoël, 1938.
Les Beaux draps. Paris: Nouvelles éditions françaises, 1941.

English Translations

Journey to the End of the Night. Translated by J. P. Marks. New York: Little, Brown & Co., 1934; New York: Grossett & Dunlap, 1934; New York: New Directions, 1961.
Death on the Installment Plan. Translated by Ralph Manheim. New York: New Directions, 1966.
Mea Culpa and the Life and Work of Semmelweis. Translated by Robert Allerton Parker. Boston: Little, Brown & Company, 1937.
Guignol's Band. Translated by B. Frechtman and J. T. Nile. New York: New Directions, 1954.
From Castle to Castle. Translated by Ralph Manheim. New York: Delacorte Press, 1968.
North. Translated by Ralph Manheim. New York: Delacorte Press, 1972.

Secondary Sources

Ackerman, Nathan and Jahoda, Marie. *Anti-Semitism and Emotional Disorder.* New York: Harper & Brothers, 1950.
Adler, Gerard. *The Living Symbol.* New York: Pantheon Books, 1961.
Albérès, R.-M. *Sartre.* Paris: Editions universitaires, 1960.
Allen, Walter. *The Modern Novel.* New York: E. P. Dutton & Co., 1965.
Alméras, Philippe. "Quatre Lettres de Louis Ferdinand Céline (sic) Céline aux journaux de l'Occupation," *French Review,* 44 (1971), 831–38.
______. "L'Onomastique caricaturale de Louis-Ferdinand Céline," *Revue Internationale d'onomastique,* (July 1971).
Arnold, Elliott. *A Night of Watching.* New York: Charles Scribner's Sons, 1967.

Baron, Salo W. *A Social and Religious History of the Jews,* IX–XIV. New York: Columbia University Press, 1965–1969.
Barrett, William. *Irrational Man.* New York: A Doubleday Anchor Book, 1962.
Barth, John. *Lost in the Funhouse.* New York: Bantam Books, 1969.
Barthes, Roland, *Le Degré Zéro de la littérature.* Paris: Editions du Seuil, 1953.
Bazin, André. *What is Cinema?* Berkeley: University of California Press, 1970.
Bergson, Henri. *Le Rire.* Paris: Presses Universitaires, 1969.
Bracher, Karl Dietrich. *The Origins, Structure, and Effects of National Socialism.* New York: Praeger Publishers, 1971.
Brée, Germaine. *Twentieth Century French Literature.* New York: The Macmillan Co. 1962.
Brodin, Pierre. *Présences contemporaines,* III. Paris: Debresse, 1957.
Brickner, Richard. *Is Germany Curable.* Philadelphia: J. B. Lippincott Co., 1943.
Burroughs, William. *Naked Lunch.* New York: Grove Press, 1959.
______. *Nova Express.* New York: Grove Press, 1964.
Byrnes, Robert. *Antisemitism in Modern France.* New Brunswick: Rutgers University Press, 1950.

Cahiers de L'Herne. Nos. 3 and 5. Paris: L'Herne, 1963.
Céline Les Cahiers de L'Herne en Poche-Club. Paris: Pierre Belfond, 1968.
Champigny, Robert. *Le Genre dramatique.* Monte-Carlo: Regain, 1965.
Cirlot, J. E. *A Dictionary of Symbols.* New York: Philosophical Library, 1962.
Clouard, Henri. *Histoire de la Littérature française du symbolisme à nos jours, 1915–1960,* II. Paris: Albin Michel, 1962.
Cox, David. *Modern Psychology.* New York: Barnes & Noble, 1968.

Diesendruck, Z. "Anti-Semitism and Ourselves," *Essays on Anti-Semitism.* New York: Conference on Jewish Relations, 1942.

Dennington, Robert. *Wagner's Ring.* London: Faber & Faber, 1963.
Durant, Will. *The Story of Philosophy.* New York: Simon & Schuster, 1926.

Edinger, Edward. "An Outline of Analytical Psychology." Unpublished.
Elliott, Robert G. *The Power of Satire.* Princeton: Princeton University Press, 1966.
Epting, Karl. *Frankreich im Widerspruch.* Hamburg: Hanseatische Verlagsanstalt, 1943.
Erikson, Erik. *Young Man Luther.* New York: W. W. Norton & Co., 1962.

Feingold, Henry L. *The Politics of Rescue.* New Brunswick: Rutgers University Press, 1967.
Franz, Marie-Louise von. "Archetypal Patterns in Fairy Tales." Unpublished, 1951.
———. "Creation Myths." Unpublished. 1961.
———. *Puer Aeternus.* New York: Spring, 1970.
———. *Apuleius' Golden Ass.* New York: Spring, 1970.
French, Warren. *John Steinbeck.* New York: Twayne Publishers, 1961.
Frey-Rohn, Liliane. "Evil from the Psychological Point of View," *Evil.* Evanston: Northwestern University Press, 1967.

Gerber, Philip. *Theodore Dreiser,* New York: Twayne Publishers, 1964.
Goebbels Diaries: 1941–1943, The. New York: Doubleday & Co., 1948.

Hanrez, Marc. *Céline.* Paris: Gallimard, 1961.
Hawkes, John. *The Cannibal.* New York: New Directions, 1962.
———. *The Beetle Leg.* New York: A New Directions Book, 1951.
Hay, Malcolm. *Europe and the Jews.* Boston: Beacon Press, 1961.
Hayman, David. *Louis-Ferdinand Céline.* New York: Columbia University Press, 1965.
Henderson, Joseph L., and Oakes, Maud. *The Wisdom of the Serpent.* New York: George Braziller, 1963.
Herzberg, Arthur. *The French Enlightenment and the Jews.* New York: Schocken Books, 1968.
Herzberg, Max J. *Classical Myths.* New York: Allyn & Bacon, 1935.
Herzog, Edgar. *Psyche and Death.* New York: G. P. Putnam's Sons, 1967.
Hindus, Milton. *The Crippled Giant.* New York: Boar's Head Books, 1950.
Hoffman, Frederick. *William Faulkner.* New York: Twayne Publishers, 1966.
Hytier, Adrienne. *Two Years of French Foreign Policy.* Geneva: Droz, 1958.

Jaffe, Aniela. *The Myth of Meaning.* New York: G. P. Putnam's Sons, 1971.
Jung, C. G. *Aion.* Princeton: Princeton University Press, 1959.
———. *Interpretation of Visions.* New York: Spring, 1963.
———. *Man and His Symbols.* New York: Doubleday & Co., 1964.
———. *Psychology and Religion: West and East.* New York: Pantheon Books, 1963.
———. *Psychological Types.* New York: Pantheon Books, 1964.
———. *Psychogenesis of Mental Disease.* New York: Pantheon Books, 1960.
———. *Structures and Dynamics of the Psyche.* Princeton: Princeton University Press, 1969.
———. *Symbols of Transformation.* New York: Pantheon Books, 1956.
———. *The Development of Personality.* New York: Pantheon Books, 1964.
———. *The Practice of Psychotherapy.* New York: Pantheon Books, 1966.
———. *The Spirit in Man, Art, and Literature.* New York: Pantheon Books, 1966.

Kalsched, Donald. "Hesse's Demian as an Exemplar of the Individuation Process." Unpublished.

Kerenyi, Carl. "The Mysteries of the Kabeiroi," *The Eranos Yearbooks*, II. New York: Pantheon Books, 1955.

______. *The Gods of the Greeks.* New York: Grove Press, 1960.

______. "The Problem of Evil in Mythology," *Evil.* Evanston: Northwestern University Press, 1967.

Kerouac, Jack. *On the Road.* New York: A Signet Book, 1957.

______. *The Subterraneans.* New York: Grove Press, 1957.

Knapp, Bettina. *Jean Genet.* New York: Twayne Publishers, 1968.

______. *Le Mirliton: A Novel Based on the Life of Aristide Bruant.* Paris: Nouvelles Editions Debresse, 1968.

Kracauer, Siegfried. *Theory of Film.* New York: Oxford University Press, 1970.

Kramer, Jane. *Allen Ginsberg in America.* New York: A Vintage Book, 1970.

Kuh, Katherine. *Art Explained.* London: Cory, Adame & MacKay, 1965.

Leeds, Barry H. *The Structured Vision of Norman Mailer.* New York: New York University Press, 1969.

Loewenstein, R. M. *A Psychoanalytical Study.* New York: International Universities Press, 1951.

Lorand, Sandor, and Balint, Michael. *Perversions.* New York: Gramercy Publishing Co., 1956.

MacKenzie, Norman. *Dreams and Dreaming.* New York: Vanguard Press, 1965.

Marcus, Jacob R. *The Jew in the Medieval World.* New York: Harper Torchbooks, 1965.

Massing, Paul. *Rehearsals for Destruction.* New York: Harper & Brothers, 1949.

Miller, Henry. *A Private Correspondence. Lawrence Durrell and Henry Miller.* New York: E. P. Dutton & Co., 1963.

Neumann, Erich. *Art and the Creative Unconscious.* New Yorl: Pantheon Books, 1959.

______. "Art and Time," *The Eranos Yearbooks*, III. New York: Pantheon Books, 1957.

______. *Depth Psychology and a New Ethic.* New York: G. P. Putnam's Sons, 1969.

______. The Origins and History of Consciousness. New York: Pantheon Books, 1954.

Nietzsche, Friedrich. *The Birth of Tragedy.* New York: The Modern Library, 1934.

Nimier, Roger. "Céline au catéchisme," *La Nouvelle Revue Française,* (5:54).

______. *Le Nouveau Céline: D'un Château l'autre.* Paris: Gallimard, 1957.

Ostrovsky, Erika. *Céline and his Vision.* New York: New York University Press, 1967.

______. *Voyeur, Voyant. A Potrait of Louis-Ferdinand Céline.* New York: Random House, 1971.

Otto, Walter. "The Meaning of the Eleusinian Mysteries. *The Eranos Yearbooks,* II. New York: Pantheon Books, 1955.

Paraz, Albert. *Le Gala des vaches.* Paris: Editions de l'Elan, 1948.

______. *Le Menuet du haricot.* Genève: Connaître, 1958.

Parinaud, Andre. "L.-F. Céline," *Arts* (July, 1961).

Parisier-Plottel, Jeanine. *Les Dialogues de Paul Valéry.* Paris: Presses Universitaire, 1960.

Parkes, James. *Anti-Semitism.* Chicago: A Quadrangle Paperback, 1963.

Peyre, Henri. *The Contemporary French Novel.* New York: Oxford University Press, 1955.

Pia, Pascal. "Céline au bout de la nuit," *Carrefour* (February 13, 1963).

Picon, Gaëtan. *Panorama de la Nouvelle littérature française.* Paris: Gallimard, 1951.

Pierrard, Pierre. *Juifs et Catholiques Français.* Paris: Fayard, 1970.

Plessner, Helmuth. "On the Relation of Time to Death." *Eranos Yearbooks,* III. New York: Pantheon Books, 1957.

Poliakov, Léon. *Histoire de l'Antisémitisme de Voltaire à Wagner.* Paris: Calmann-Lévy, 1968.

Poulet, Robert. *Entretiens familiers avec Louis-Ferdinand Céline.* Paris: Plon, 1958.
———. "Céline et son château." *La Table ronde,* no. 121, 1958.
Pynchon, Thomas. *The Crying of Lot 49.* New York: Bantam Books, 1967.

Reed, Herbert. *Art and Alienation.* New York: Viking Compass Book, 1970.
Rheingold, Joseph. *The Mother Anxiety and Death.* Boston: Little, Brown & Co., 1967.
Richard, Jean-Pierre. "La Nausée de Céline." *La Nouvelle Revue Française,* no. 115, pp. 33–47 and no. 116, pp. 235–252.
Ritchie, Andrew, C. *Masters of British Painting 1800–1950.* New York: The Museum of Modern Art, 1957.
Rosenthal, M. L. *The New Poets.* New York: Oxford University Press, 1968.
Roux, Dominique de. *La Mort de Louis-Ferdinand Céline.* Paris: Christian Bourgois, 1966.
Rovit, Earl. *Ernest Hemingway.* New York: Twayne Publishers, 1963.

Sartre, Jean-Paul. *Anti-Semite and Jew.* New York: Schocken Books, 1948.
What Is Literature?
Scholes, Robert. *The Fabulators.* New York: Oxford University Press, 1967.
Schuré, Edouard. *The Great Initiates.* West Nyack: St. George Books, 1961.
Seitz, William. *The Responsive Eye.* New York: The Museum of Modern Art, 1965.
Serant, Paul. *Le Romantisme fasciste.* Paris: Fasquelle, 1959.
Shirer, William E. *Berlin Diary.* New York: Alfred A. Knopf, 1941.
The Collapse of the Third Republic. New York: Simon & Schuster, 1969.
Simon, Pierre-Henri. *L'Homme en procès.* Neuchâtel: A la Baconnière, 1950.
Singer, June. *The Unholy Bible.* New York: G. P. Putnam's Sons, 1970.
Speer, Albert. *Inside the Third Reich.* New York: The Macmillan Co., 1969.
Stepaneber, Stephen. *American Poetry Since 1945.* New York: Harper & Row, 1965.

Taylor, Joshua. *Futurism.* New York: The Museum of Modern Art, 1961.
Tenebaum, S. *Why Men Hate.* New York: Jewish Book Guild of America, 1947.
Thiher, Allen. *Céline: The Novel as Delirium.* New Brunswick: Rutgers University Press, 1972.

Valéry, Paul. *Oeuvres.* Paris: Pleiade, 1 (1957), 2 (1960).
Vandrome, Pol. *Céline.* Paris: Classique de XXeme siècle, 1963.
Vanino, Maurice. *L'Affaire Céline. La Résistance ouvre ses dossiers.* Paris: Editions Créator, 1952.
Vogt, Hannah. *The Burden of Guilt.* New York: Oxford University Press, 1964.
Vonnegut, Kurt, Jr. *Slaughterhouse Five.* New York: Delta Books, 1969.
Godbless You, Mr. Rosewater. New York: Dell Publishing Co., 1970.
Mother Night. New York: Bard Books, 1970.

Wechsler, W.I.S. "Some Remarks on the Psychology of Antisemitism," *Essays on Antisemitism.* New York: Conference on Jewish Relations, 1942.
Weinberg, Helen. *The New Novel in America.* Ithaca: Cornell University Press, 1970.
Wili, Walter. "The Orphic Mysteries and the Greek Spirit," *The Eranos Yearbooks,* II. New York: Pantheon Books, 1955.
Wren, John H. *John Dos Passos.* New York: Twayne Publishers, 1961.
Writers at Work. New York: The Viking Press, 1963, 1967.
Wylder, Delbert. *Hemingway's Heroes.* Albuquerque: University of New Mexico Press, 1969.

Zuckerkandl, Victor. *Sound and Symbol.* New York: Pantheon Books, 1956.

INDEX

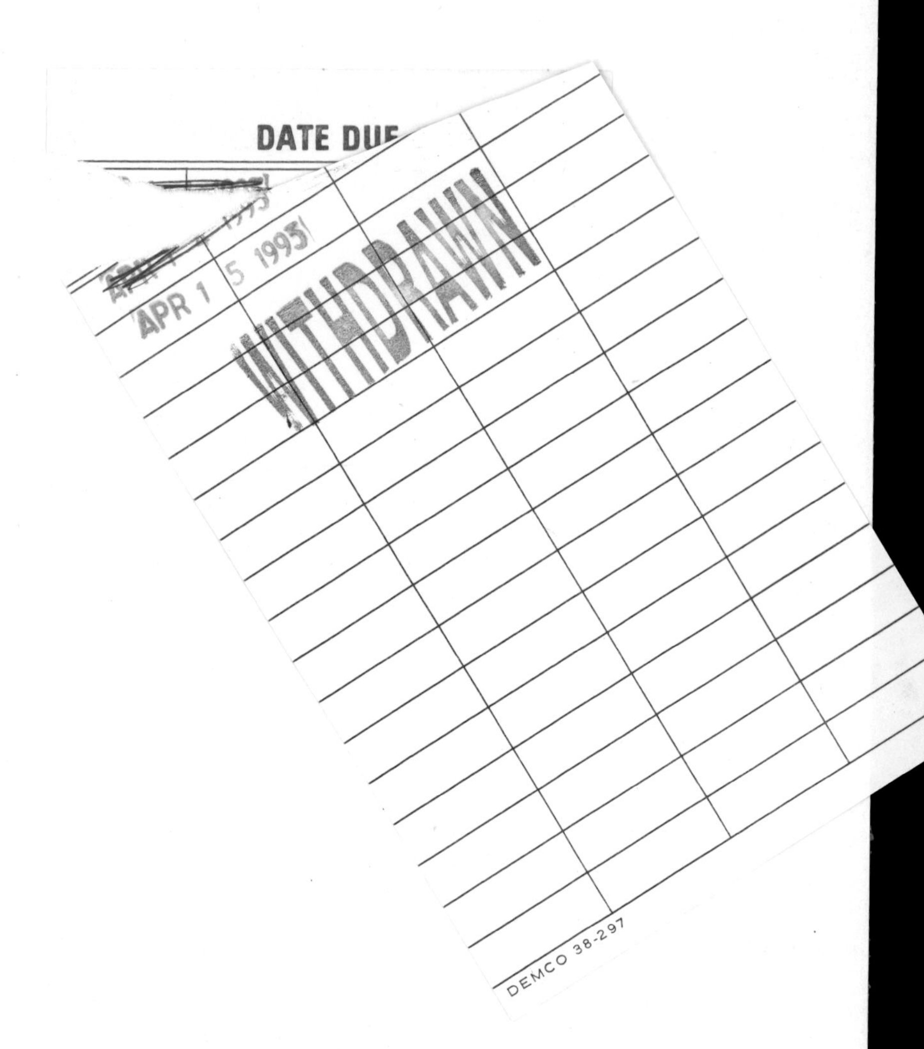
DATE DUE
APR 1 5 1993
WITHDRAWN
DEMCO 38-297